BICYCLE TOURING IN THE WESTERN UNITED STATES

Also by Karen and Gary Hawkins

BICYCLE TOURING IN EUROPE

By Gary Hawkins

U.S.A. BY BUS AND TRAIN

Pantheon Books
New York

BICYCLE TOURING IN THE WESTERN UNITED STATES

Karen and Gary Hawkins

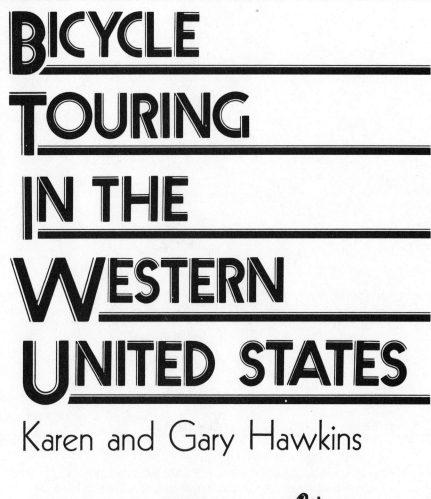

Copyright © 1982 by Karen and Gary Hawkins

All rights reserved under International and Pan-American
Copyright Conventions. Published in the United States by
Pantheon Books, a division of Random House, Inc., New York,
and simultaneously in Canada by Random House of Canada
Limited, Toronto.

LIBRARY OF CONGRESS CATALOGING IN PUBLICATION DATA

Hawkins, Karen.
  Bicycle touring in the western United States.

  Includes index.
  1. Bicycle touring—West (U.S.)—Guide-books.
  2. West (U.S.)—Description and travel—Guide-books.
  I. Hawkins, Gary. II. Title.
  GV1045.5.W3H38   917.8   81-48223
  ISBN 0-394-74807-7   AACR2

Manufactured in the United States of America

9876543

Contents

PREFACE

An old man woke us one morning when we were camping on a ridge high above the little Mormon town of Loa, Utah. It was so cold that during the night, water from the sprinklers had frozen on the fields below us. A swatch of white ice alternated with the green of the alfalfa.

The place in which we were camping was less than salubrious. It had been used for years as a depository for various kinds of rubble, though for that matter, most of it had reached an age where it could be regarded as benign. It hadn't mattered much to us anyway, as we had come in late the night before and had eaten, fallen down, and slept.

We crawled out of the tent when we heard the old man's car drive up. His old skin was stretched thin across his cheekbones. His clothes looked like something he had grabbed at random out of a discard box. He had a tropical pith helmet on his head, white cotton garden gloves on his hands, and floppy rubber Wellingtons on his feet. He did a jitterbugging kind of dance in the cold.

He said he had come to tend a grave. We were astonished, but sure enough, down the ridge line not a quarter of a mile off, we saw a grill of iron pickets marking the site. It was a child's grave, he said, the first white child to die in this valley. The child was no more than a toddler when it wandered into a millrace. In an instant it was gone.

We talked for a while longer, then the man left, his pith helmet bobbing among the rocks and low brush as he made his way down the slant of the ridge toward the grave.

Later, we were working up a long path that rises above Loa. All the incongruities of the little encounter occupied each of us, although we didn't speak. The odd collection of his clothes, the grave we hadn't seen, the rubble, the great caring of an old man for a child who had died more than a century ago. There were so many contrasts there that they seemed to whipsaw our emotions back and forth as we made our way higher. Also contributing was the presence of our own son, whom we pull in a trailer. He is four. More than once we contemplated the fragility of his position behind us. Even as we thought these things his little voice was singing. A child's song.

We were never able to pin down exactly what it was about the little incident that so exemplified the West to us. Certainly many of the contrasts were there, the casual attitude about dumping aside that which is no longer useful, the elaborate care to preserve history. Old people. Young. Ice on alfalfa.

We think, perhaps, that there is no way to align all the contrasts. That all the things that make up the West are simply held there, as if the territory were a box indifferent to its own contents.

But one thing is certain. The contrasts strike you. Whether they are ones as big as the Grand Canyon, where you look down and see an airplane flying below your feet, or small ones like an old man tending a gravesite in a dump on a hill above Loa.

You don't have to be on a bicycle to be struck by the contrasts. But it helps.

ONE

Bicycling in the West:

An overview

No area of the United States has more variety for the bicyclist than the region stretching from the Pacific Ocean to the high ridges of the Rocky Mountains. You may find other places richer in tradition, blessed with a more intricate road network, or perhaps less demanding on you physically. But the West stands alone as a place where you are struck again and again with the incredible variety of the land, its soaring grandeur, its generous expanse of scenery. It is difficult to imagine another place with such variety of touring possibilities.

The highest point within the contiguous forty-eight states is found there, reached at 14,495 feet on Mount Whitney, in California. So is the lowest, some 282 feet below sea level in Death Valley, also in California. The highest national daytime temperatures are consistently recorded in the West. So are the lowest. The world's oldest vegetation, the gnarled bristlecone pine, is found in the West. The oldest exposed rock formations in this country are found there, at the base of the Grand Canyon, where even now the Colorado is cutting still deeper. In another part of the West the newest geologic formations are under way, the very latest seen in the tortured destruction of Mount Saint Helens, in Washington. The world's greatest collection of geysers is found in the West. The world's largest tree grows there.

Reflecting this great variety is the list of national parks, national monuments, national recreation areas, national forests, and state equivalents which lay vast swatches of green across any map of the West. Within the eleven Western states treated in this book—California, Oregon, Washington, Idaho, Montana, Wyoming, Utah, New Mexico, Colorado, Arizona, and Nevada—there are twenty-two major national parks. There are six major national recreation areas. There is one national seashore. And there are some sixty-nine other national monuments, historic sites, and memorials. It would take many pages to detail equivalent facilities under the jurisdiction of the various states, ranging in size from parcels a few hundred square feet to the giant Anza-Borrego Desert Park in California, with its two hundred camping and picnic sites scattered over some 488,000 acres.

The case for the West's uniqueness could be made on these physical features alone. But beyond the variety of its geography, the West possesses a culture and tradition unlike any other place in the world. It has spawned its own dress, its own customs, its own holidays, its own manner of speaking—and, some would say, even its own way of thinking. Its history, which began as fact, quickly moved into a myth that has been carefully nursed and perpetuated. It is full of quirks and contrasts.

It developed recklessly. You don't find towns in the West where you expect to find them. They hide up canyons. They cling to the side of a hill that has been half washed away by gigantic nozzles spouting water, with men below scrambling in the rubble looking for gold. A major Western city lies on the edge of a vast salt lake, its brackish water useless. There are towns in the Rockies where summer never comes, where the air is so thin even the sun can't warm it.

In the physical barriers to its own development were found gold mines. Into the deserts that once swallowed up horses, oxen, and the cattle of pioneers, men and women have brought water, then homes, then gardens and fields, then vast tracts where cotton grows as far as the eye can see, where sorghum and alfalfa pulse in response to water and sun, where orchards flower in places which once grew only spiny grasses.

The culture that developed out of this rush for land, for timber, minerals, even for religious and social freedom, has the reputation for being a little odd. It is a place where fads originate, where pretty girls ride on flowered floats, to be viewed somewhat askance by the Midwesterner, sitting in the forced-air heat of a January living room, staring at his television screen. Where in the rest of the country do men ride wild horses for pay, climb on the backs of mad bulls, legs flopping like a distorted set of second ears?

In the West.

What does it mean to bicycle in the West? It's an experience as unique as the land itself. The bicyclist moves through great expanses of unique geography, past cultural peculiarities and remnants of events found nowhere else. It is as different from cycling in any other part of the country as it would be to cycle in France, or England, or Greece.

To begin with, distances are vaster. There is no other part of the country where the next town—the place you can get water, get bread, even find a place where someone else lives—can be 120 miles down the road. In no other area of the United States can you go nowhere but up for 30 or 35 miles—all over a single mountain range.

Even the great natural attractions of the West—the rim of the Grand Canyon, Yellowstone, Rocky Mountain National Park, Mesa Verde, Bryce Canyon, to name just a few—put physical demands on the bicyclist that simply don't exist elsewhere in the United States. All of these lie at elevations higher than the tallest peak found anywhere in the country, if one excludes Alaska and Hawaii.

The climate of the West—the relatively dry summers, the crystalline air of its mountains, the mildness of its winters in some areas—can also produce gross extremes of heat and cold, wet and dry, within a single day, or even an hour. In some regions, temperature variations between day and night will span 50 or even 60 degrees with great regularity.

Even the "lore" of the West—the romanticized history of gold, of cattle barons, of railroad kings—has another side for the bicyclist. Inherent in this "lore" is the fact that the West developed very rapidly, most of its basic settlement taking place within the span of a hundred years. Much of this development centered around mineral exploitation and large-scale cattle ranching in mountainous or semi-arid regions. Towns are few and far between. Even in the most populous states of California, Oregon, and Washington, some 85 percent of the population lives within 30 miles of the coast.

Because of this great variety, the extremes of climate and geography, the word that creeps most often into our thinking and into our speech when dealing with bicycling in the West is challenge. It is a place where, for all its rewards of culture, history, and scenery, bicycle tours must be thought out more carefully, where the day-to-day life of touring takes place within the context of often rugged terrain.

This does not make the West uncyclable. We, and many others, have bicycled through every part of it at one time or another. Nor is it all mountainous. There are many easy tours. But for people venturing very far in the West, the key to a successful bicycle tour is planning.

You begin this planning with some understanding of the West's geography, its road network, and its climate. More than anything else, these three factors affect the day-to-day life of the bicycle tourist. We will make some preliminary remarks about each by way of introduction here, and we will refer more or less constantly to them throughout the rest of this book.

WESTERN GEOGRAPHY

More than anything else, the West is distinguished by its mountains. We have found it helpful in our own thinking to regard the West as something of a giant washboard, the "ribs" running north to south in an area stretching from the Pacific Ocean to just east of the Rocky Mountains. An airplane flying from San Francisco to Denver would pass over one mountain range after another, most following the general north-south pattern. Between ranges would be relatively flat or rolling areas, very often quite dry or semi-arid.

Of course any such generalization about geography is subject to modification, and this is no exception. But the pattern is more consistent than not. Moreover, it points up a very relevant fact for the bicyclist: Pick any relatively flat area of the West—the high plateau of Wyoming, the Sacramento Valley in California, the Willamette Valley in Oregon, the Great Basin in Utah—then bicycle for four days in any single direction, and you very likely will be climbing a significant mountain range.

Thus, a bicyclist who wishes to do more than make just a circular tour in a valley or high plateau must confront the fact that it is a mountainous region, with all the demands that can make. It means that you should look over your equipment very thoroughly in advance. You must have a bicycle equipped for climbing long hills, of course; but also be aware that higher elevations usually mean extremes in temperatures which require certain types of clothing choices, as well as food and water.

The physical demands that mountains or hilly terrain can make on you and your equipment also can affect tours in other ways. For one, difficult terrain such as is found in some of the West can drastically reduce the distances you can cover in a day. It is not uncommon to spend an afternoon negotiating a 14- or 15-mile mountain pass. This can be enjoyable if you are in good condition, are well equipped, and have planned ahead so that you are either carrying food or know where you can get it. It becomes another matter if you are still on the pass, sundown is approaching, and you're not sure you'll find a place to eat in the town 5 miles away, or whether it will be 30 miles to a grocery store or restaurant. Planning itineraries, finding out where the next grocery store or restaurant is, and assessing your own abilities to handle the kind of terrain you meet—all are crucially important. While we can't make any of the hills flatter, most of this book is devoted to showing you how to handle such contingencies, and to giving you route guides that cover 9,000 miles of Western geography. These guides will give you, from a cyclist's viewpoint, the details you need to know about the length of hills or where the next food stop is.

WESTERN ROADS

While geography has certainly played a part in determining the sort of road network that exists in the West, economic development has played at least an equal, if not greater, role. People built roads to get them to places where other people lived, or where they could earn money.

In comparison to the Midwest and East, as well as much of the South, the West does not have an intricate network of secondary roads. In the former regions, roads were built to connect small farming communities to one another, and later, to connect individual farms, resulting in an interlacing of roads. Moreover, these places were settled slowly in comparison to the West, having three or in some cases even four hundred years to gradually improve the road network and extend it as necessary.

In the West, nearly everything was the opposite. Much of its development centered around exploitation of minerals, timber, or in establishing vast grazing areas. As a result, towns often grew up in the unlikeliest places—from thin perches in the Rockies 10,000 feet above sea level to places on high, arid plateaus that served as collection stations for cattle drives. Other towns grew up in the middle of a desert because oil was discovered there, or because water could be found. And all this happened essentially within a hundred years, even over this vast territory. Towns leap-frogged over one another, often leaving 50 or 100 miles undeveloped in the process. Because water was not always available in these nether regions, or because climate or soil made it impossible to do anything much with them, these gaps remained undeveloped.

Today, this uneven development is reflected in a road network that, by and large, lacks secondary roads. Only in the agricultural valleys of central and northern California, in Oregon, and to a lesser extent in Washington, is there anything resembling the small farm-originated road networks typical of the East and Midwest.

Nor are there many major population centers in the West, given its size. Outside the three coastal states, there are only two cities in the West with populations greater than 500,000—Phoenix and Denver. What this means for the bicyclist is that often there is only one way to get from point A to point B. This can be either good or bad—good if the places are relatively unimportant or not located on a major tourist track, bad if the two places have sizable populations jamming the same two-lane road to get from one to the other.

The lack of a highly developed road network can also affect the bicyclist in other ways. A rider in Wyoming, for instance, who is dissatisfied with a given route because of westerly headwinds may have to travel half a day or more before encountering a road running north and south. The same could be true for parts of nearly any other Western state, including the most populous one, California. Thus in many parts of the West, you need to know ahead of your tour about road conditions, traffic, terrain, and availability of services. Later on, we go into considerable detail about road networks within various regions of the West, and in the tours we've developed and included in Chapters 6, 7, and 8, we have taken considerable pains to alert the cyclist as to exactly what lies ahead. We also tell you how you can go about finding out these details for yourself if you need to.

WESTERN WEATHER

There is probably no area of the country with better bicycling weather than the West. In some areas, you can tour both winter and summer. But for most bicycle tourists, it is the consistency of good summertime weather that makes the West such an attractive bicycle area.

Most of the West can be classified as arid or semi-arid. Even areas that are not so classified—much of California and southern Oregon —often receive their precipitation only in the winter months. What this means for the bicyclist in a great deal of the West is summer days when the chances of rain are low. Even in a region subject to summer rain, those storms are often predictable, coming primarily in the afternoon. The thundershowers in many mountainous regions of the West and those of the plateau regions of Wyoming, southern Colorado, and New Mexico are the best examples of this.

Of course you can't throw away your raingear and head for the Rocky Mountains in a T shirt. There are regions of the West where summers are wet, or even drenching. The Olympic rain forest on the Washington coast is the best known example, but good portions of Idaho, Colorado, and Montana also get their fair share of rain. Taken as a whole, however, the West is more dry than it is wet, and the bicyclist can usually plan a two- or three-week tour in nearly any of its regions and be comfortable that there will be no rain, or at the worst, that the riding days will far outnumber the rainy ones.

There is another side to this matter of bright, sunny weather, however, as we indicated briefly already. The same sun that means pleasant cycling weather in the Logan Canyon of central Utah absolutely bakes the Salt Lake Basin just 100 miles to the west of it, where temperatures can soar into the low 100s every afternoon. Any bicyclist trying to forge across that area at two in the afternoon with only the typical half-liter of water will be in for some very interesting times, to say the least.

The point is that for all the blessings of the West's good weather, anyone bicycling there must be prepared for extremes not found elsewhere in the United States. We discuss specific weather patterns later on and tell you how to deal with some of the extremes you may encounter on your own trips.

MAKING CHOICES

Throughout the rest of this book we return often to these matters of geography, road conditions, and weather. For above all other, they constitute the stuff of bicycle touring. In the next chapter we give an overview of Western geography, dividing it into three regions. We also discuss some choices you need to make as to touring style, whether you will camp out or stay in motels, or take an organized tour where such matters are decided for you. In Chapter 3 we cover some of the particular things you need to do in plotting a tour—where to get specific information such as bicycle-route guides, and how to plan your own route. Chapter 4 covers the equipment you'll need for both you and your bicycle on a Western tour, depending on the touring style you choose and where you go. In Chapter 5 we give details of the everyday conditions you'll meet once on the road, and explain how to handle extremes of heat and cold, rain, distance, hills, and such matters as replenishing your stock in small rural stores.

Each of the last three chapters of the book is devoted to a particular region—the Far West, the Mountain States, and the Southwest. Here we talk specifically about each state's terrain, climate, and road network, and tell you some of the best places to tour. In addition, we offer for each region a number of long-range tours, including complete details of road conditions, probable weather patterns, camping and hotel facilities, and sights you can expect to see —as well as the crucial information on how hard the hills will be and the exact point you'll stop climbing and start going down. Besides our own twenty-three tours, we also summarize a number of compatible route guides developed by other people which allow you to extend your exploration of a region, or make a circular route. These summaries are meant to be suggestive, not comprehensive, and we advise you to secure the original guides before setting out. Details for doing so are included.

Our tour routes reflect of course our own feelings about what constitutes good bicycling country. When possible, we choose back roads, but at some points there was a conflict between finding quiet roads and providing routes that are easy to follow. If we point you to a more heavily trafficked road, it's usually because in our experience, most long-range tourists don't want to spend inordinate amounts of time slipping through fences, searching for intersections on unposted roads, or following other paths that seem perfectly acceptable on a Sunday-afternoon spin but become exasperating if you're trying to get to a destination some miles off.

For most riders, even the shortest of the tours will take at least two days to cover, and most require more time than that. We have not indicated minimum or maximum time periods, just total mileage, leaving the pace up to the individual riders. In instances where there are long gaps between services, we've indicated this in the summaries presented at the beginning of each tour and noted those spots specifically on the route guide itself. There are some tours that inexperienced riders should not try, at least not alone or without the company of someone versed in long-range touring. These are also indicated.

We have made two important limitations in the scope of this book.

Because of their relative inaccessibility to most bicyclists, we have not included Alaska or Hawaii, although each offers some excellent cycling opportunities. In the Bibliography at the end of the book, though, we indicate the literature available to help the bicyclist explore those states.

The other limitation is that most of what we discuss is meant for the bicycle tourist planning trips of more than just a day's length. Obviously the needs of a tourist out for a day's jaunt differ from those of one who must deal with eating and sleeping on the road. There is a growing body of literature aimed at the day tourist, describing short excursions that most often radiate out from major population areas. We list these volumes also in our Bibliography.

TWO

Choosing your touring area

and style

Trail Ridge is the name of the highest paved pass road in the United States. It threads its way far above timberline in Colorado's Rocky Mountain National Park, cresting at 12,183 feet above sea level.

It isn't just the elevation gain that makes Trail Ridge hard, or the fact that you must pull an unforgiving pass road that winds constantly upward for some 25 miles. Weather is an even more significant factor. Rain or sleet can pummel you any day of the year, particularly in the afternoon when clouds pile up behind the peaks. It can—and will—snow here on any given summer day.

For us, Trail Ridge was a most significant challenge. It marked the highest we had ever climbed. Moreover, each of us was pedaling a fully packed bicycle, one equipped both with front and rear panniers, oversize handlebar pack, and an oversize tent loaded on the rear carrier. The other pulled a trailer with child and gear, the total weight of which pushed 100 pounds.

Because of this, we planned our ride over Trail Ridge with all the care of a major expedition. We had plotted every detail of the climb, from clothing to gear to emergency rations, and even had a clearly established timetable for crossing major points along the route. We had planned everything, that is, except where we would camp once we were over. This omission turned into something of a personal disaster.

To meet our schedule for Trail Ridge, we started the seven-hour climb just at dawn. The thermometer at the campground at Lake Granby on the west side of the park registered 27 degrees. We skirted a pretty alpine lake just above Granby, then turned north into a long, narrow valley. Feet numbed quickly in the metal toe clips. Even in gloves, our hands grew rigid, and we had difficulty manipulating gear levers. The ride itself warmed us a little, but we still wore everything we owned—long pants over cycling shorts, turtlenecks, shirts, sweaters, windbreakers, stocking hats.

Benjamin, our four-year-old son, travels with us in a specially built bicycle trailer. Although a veteran of many miles, he too was bundled to meet the elements, looking more like a miniature Santa Claus than anything else, with shirts and sweaters topped by a red pullover anorak, its hood revealing only eyes and nose. He sat uncomplaining, silently regarding the meadow we skirted as we edged gradually toward a series of switchbacks that marked the first critical stages of the climb. We were already above 8,000 feet elevation.

We fell into a familiar rhythm of breathing and pedaling as we gained altitude, rising off the floor of the valley, laboring slowly up one switchback after another. Tourists in cars stopped to take pictures, both of us and of the valleys below. Some watched us wordlessly as we went by. We could see over the edge of the road, but we didn't break our pace to stop or take pictures. Pace was everything to us at the moment. Push just hard enough; allow just so much elastic in the legs in case we had to use them harder higher up.

A hard wind caught us as we rounded a sixth switchback and commenced the last long pull to Milner Pass. Unlike other passes, you don't go down after you hit Milner. It is 10,759 feet in the air, and once you pass it you just begin climbing again.

Mostly, the wind pushed us away from the road edge. At times it maliciously swung around and hit us face-on, driving us back down the mountain.

But after some buffeting, we could tell by the way the road leveled off that we were getting close to the first pass, as if the mountain were giving us a breather, knowing it would turn it all around within a few hundred feet higher up.

Finally we rolled into the parking area next to the sign that marked the pass. We lolled over the handlebars and waited for a moment, then got off and wheeled the bicycles toward the sign. We paused in a howling wind, our nylon windbreakers rattling noisily. Someone volunteered to take a picture of us.

Before our legs cooled off, we started up again, and after a few brief stretches of relatively gradual rise, we saw the road switching back high above us. The sight was surreal. We were already well over 11,000 feet, gulping thin air; yet high above us, twisting left and right, the road rose and disappeared behind a distant ridge.

The wind picked up force, one time slamming us 5 feet out into a lane of passing traffic. People stared, some incredulous—particularly those who had already crossed and were on their way down. Many shouted encouragement. Our heads bent down so we could pull harder on the handlebars to counter the force of the wind. The next day our shoulders were sore from the effort it took to keep the pedals moving.

We switchbacked and passed a tourist center. We glanced at each other and both shook our heads no. There would be no stopping. Keep the pace.

Another stretch of road showed itself above us. Finally we too were there, battling the wind. Benjamin huddled over in his trailer, his head almost touching his knees. Perhaps because he had traveled this way since he was two years old, he sensed the difficulty we were having, and made no demands on us. Perhaps it was something in his genes. In any case, he never complained, seemingly lost in his own struggle to keep as little of himself as possible exposed to the biting edge of the wind.

Burnt-orange and yellow tundra was the only vegetation for miles around. We looked down on half a dozen peaks of lower stature. At one point we swung close to the shoulder of the road and glanced down at the valley from where we had begun that morning. We calculated the drop to be in the neighborhood of 4,000 feet. At that moment, a chilling sense of exhilaration swept over us. We were on the highest paved pass road in the United States. Plunging our torsos harder into the wind, we spurted just a bit faster upward. We were going to beat Trail Ridge.

Anticlimactically, the crest at High Point—12,183 feet—is unmarked. So many tourists had been stopping there to take pictures that the Park Service took down the sign. But gravity told us we had arrived. We took a long sweep deeper into the flank of the mountain, passed a ghostly stand of dead lodgepole, so many white arms stretching into the thin sky, then started downward, twisting through switchbacks so rapidly that we lost track of the count.

Fingers and wrists ached—not from the cold now, but from the fatigue of constant braking. We alternated from front to rear brakes, slid them on in spurts, turned our legs to keep them from stiffening, but we never really worked hard enough to put any bite into the pedals. As far as we were concerned, we were through for the day. We had challenged Trail Ridge, and we had beaten it.

Finally, we coasted into Estes Park, a somewhat overused resort nestling below 8,000 feet on the eastern side of the Rockies. We celebrated our victory with a good bit of self-congratulation—and if memory serves us correctly, probably some liquid elixir of uncertain vintage.

Toward evening, we wheeled our bicycles out off the lawn behind the town library. We started southward on a predetermined route. All the time we were celebrating in Estes Park, we had assured one another that within a mile or so of town we would find a convenient tree to nestle under. We had loaded up with water, food, and additional elixir, looking forward to getting Benjamin to bed and having time to calmly assess all we had done that day.

Within a few miles of town, a slow, stunning realization began to anger us. We had hoped to find open spaces, a tuft of grass, where no one cared if we camped. After all, we were still within eyesight of one of the highest mountain ranges in the United States. What we found instead were series of subdevelopments, private houses, barbed-wire fences, and so many NO TRESPASSING signs that they could have been dropped from an airplane.

Worse, darkness was falling around us like a shroud.

But the most insulting, the most unjust, trick was played by the road itself. Weary from a long climb, emotionally and psychically done in, we had every reason to believe that we would be continuing downward. Yet even in the half-gloom, there was no denying the reality: we were climbing again. And after nearly two months of bicycling in high mountains, we could not fool ourselves into thinking we were on an intermediate hill. We were mounting another major climb, perhaps over another pass. We couldn't be certain from the details given on our map.

At the base of a steepening hill, a front derailleur refused to slip the chain over on the small chainwheel, giving us the lower gear we needed. We tried to nudge the derailleur over with a heel while still coasting, but it wouldn't budge.

All the injustice of our fate seemed embodied for the moment in the recalcitrant bicycle part. Swearing filled the air. Nothing happened, and, much kicked, the bicycle wobbled gracelessly to a stop.

In the process of dismounting, a curtain of restraint tore silently apart. Holding the bicycle firmly in two hands, we began kicking the derailleur, delivering one satisfying blow after another into its shiny cage. Nearly gleefully, we shouted a stream of curses into the night.

The irrationality probably would have worn itself out eventually, anyway. But somewhere after the third kick (which missed the derailleur and bent the large sprocket instead), out of the corner of an eye we caught a glimpse of someone coming through the gloom. It was a lone bicyclist, ambling down a dirt road just off to our right, gingerly dodging potholes as she came. As she pulled somewhat hesitantly to a stop near us, we saw it was a woman, riding a bicycle with upright handlebars, a white bicycle helmet glimmering in the dusk.

Our own shame brought the kicking to a stop. We swallowed and started the sort of conversation that always arises when bicyclists meet, hoping she hadn't seen us. No doubt she had, but nothing was mentioned. Then, after a moment or two of remarks, she said, probably not realizing how welcome her words were, "My husband and I are building a house just up the road. Would you like to come up and spend the night with us?"

At last, Trail Ridge finally seemed ours.

Such little surprises—pleasant and unpleasant—are part of bicycle touring. We were victims, of course, of our own folly. For all the planning we had done in crossing Trail Ridge, we had not paid any attention to what was to come after. Moreover, we had fallen into the trap that besets nearly every longe-range cyclist at some point or another—we had relied on a state highway map for details of terrain.

Trip planning will not eliminate all surprises or spontaneity from bicycle touring. Nor perhaps should it. Our night spent outside Estes Park with the Haineses, talking long into the night under a canopy of brilliant western stars, was one of that trip's high points. We have others that came from the unexpected, and no doubt you will discover your own.

But surprises should be occasional, not common. Moreover, they need to be minor, not major. Lest they become major, you need to plan. It can mean just the difference between convenience and annoyance. Knowing where campgrounds are can mean a restful day's end instead of one last hurdle. But other kinds of planning are more essential. What do you do if you arrive at a spot on the map where you hoped to find a source to replenish your water, and discover only a nameless crossroads instead? It is one thing if you are fresh, and it is morning. It is more serious if it is late in the day, you are already suffering from a headache and out of water, and the next town is 30 miles away.

These kinds of situations are not lurking, ready to ensnare you every day, and certainly not in every section of the West. But the fact that they can happen (and have) points to the need for doing something in advance to avoid them.

PRELIMINARY THINKING

Tour planning really involves a number of interrelated processes. The first is a more general one of acquainting yourself with conditions of terrain and climate you will encounter, and adjusting your thinking accordingly. You also need to make some basic decisions about touring style in this stage of your thinking—will you camp out, or stay in motels, cook for yourself or eat out? Or will you opt for a guided tour where most of these details are decided beforehand? These decisions will obviously have a great effect on the rest of your tour planning.

A second part of tour planning involves more specific matters—where are the better areas to tour by bicycle? Which roads should you take? How can you find quiet roads? What information is available that will tell you how hard the climbs will be, or where you will find campgrounds? These and related questions involve a process called route-finding. It is the crux of tour planning, and there is a growing body of information now available to the touring cyclist to help him or her find answers to these questions.

Next, you must anticipate and prepare to deal with conditions you meet on the road—how to handle things when it rains, for instance, or what to do when temperatures get very high.

Finally, tour planning involves thinking about equipment. Having decided upon a touring style and laid out a route, what sort of clothing do you need to take along? How must your bicycle be equipped? If you are camping, what kind of tent do you need?

All the foregoing elements of tour planning are dealt with in this and the following three chapters. In the present chapter we will discuss the general aspects of planning a tour in the West, which involves coming to grips with the basics of the West's geography and the sort of touring style options open to you.

WHERE TO GO TOURING

Even with people who live in the West, there often is a fundamental haziness about Western geography and weather; people also tend to think of touring only in certain areas, overlooking less obvious choices that offer equal beauty and often much quieter riding conditions. For

Summary of tour routes

instance, one of the most heavily toured regions of the West is the Pacific coastline, stretching from the Canadian to the Mexican border. Its reputation for scenic beauty is justly deserved, and many stretches of it make superb bicycling. But bicyclists who follow the route mind-lessly are often subject to roads with incredibly heavy traffic, huge masses of sprawling metropolitan excess, and howling, consistent northwesterly winds and summer fog that can make bicycling one un-ending purgatory. All this could be avoided by more inventive route planning—using some of the very scenic interior valleys with quiet roads and quaint small towns, and getting into regions not inundated by other cyclists, so that your reception will be altogether different.

For these and other reasons, we offer a brief summary of Western geography and weather and point out some excellent yet relatively unknown touring areas that we hope will open up new horizons for you. The three regions of the West are united primarily by geo-graphic and climatic similarities, but we have also made the division with an eye to the convenience of grouping certain states together, since most of us think more in terms of state boundaries than we do geographic divisions.

THE FAR WEST:
CALIFORNIA, OREGON, WASHINGTON, NEVADA

Terrain. The three coastal states of California, Oregon, and Wash-ington, and the state of Nevada make up the Far West. Three of the states share a common coastline. The fourth, Nevada, lies primarily in the Great Basin, a large area from which there is no drainage; some of eastern California also lies within the Great Basin.

It is in the Far West that the "washboard" effect spoken of in the first chapter begins. California, Oregon, and Washington all have ranges of mountains lying near the coast. Just to the east of these ranges there is the characteristic valley or series of valleys; the great agricultural valleys of California, the Willamette Valley in Oregon, and the valley formed by the Cowlitz River in Washington are typical. In Nevada, which lies east of the Sierra, are a number of broad basin-lands broken by periodic ranges that rise up to 6,000 feet from the basin floor.

For the most part, mountain ranges run north-south throughout the Far West. In California, Oregon, and Washington, the Cascades and Sierra Nevada form something of a single north-south line stretching from the Canadian border almost to Mexico. Both the Cascades and the Sierra have numerous peaks reaching above 12,000 feet.

To the east of this long line of mountains are lesser ranges, which, although nearly as high as the Sierra or Cascades, are not as long. The Blue Mountains of eastern Washington and Oregon and the Ruby Mountains of Nevada are two examples among many. Because the Cascades and Sierra collect most of the moisture from Pacific storms, these interior ranges of Washington, Oregon, and Nevada are much drier. Their western sides normally catch most of what moisture is left, and their eastern slopes are much more arid.

Given this pattern of mountains and valleys, accompanied by increasing distance from the influential coastal waters of the Pacific, you can imagine the great variety of bicycling conditions found in the Far West. Precipitation ranges are extreme: in the rain forest of western Washington more than 12 feet of rain fall in a year; parts of Nevada and eastern California receive far less than 12 inches a year.

There are level rides of several hundred miles in some of the longer valleys, and mountain tours where you may pass two weeks or more amidst high peaks and mountain greenery.

The mountains themselves exhibit great variety. The bicyclist in the Cascades of Oregon and Washington will find the mountains softer, more gentle, than the drier and rockier Sierra. Cascade pass roads are lower, between about 3,000 feet and just over 5,000 feet high. Obviously, there is less climbing involved in crossing them; for the most part the passage is made without breaking the treeline. Dense forests of fir, cedar, and western hemlock, spurred on by abundant rainfall, cover most of the mountains, with an occasional volcanic peak rising far into the sky, snow clad the year round.

The Sierra, on the other hand, is dramatic. Walls and rock peaks break the uniformity of the forests. The forests themselves are different, comprised mostly of ponderosa pine and red fir, with relatively little underbrush. For this reason, it is a bit easier to get off into the forest in the Sierra, whereas parts of the Cascades are nearly impenetrable. Even the streams of the two ranges seem to be of different colors, the Cascades typified by a dark, lush green, the Sierra by a sparkling blue purity.

In any case, bicycling in either range is exciting riding. Snow clothes the higher peaks the year round. Streams and rivers tumble alongside the road. There is an abundance of campgrounds in national forests or national parks, as well as ample opportunity for camping off on your own.

Some of the great parks of the West are here also, with Rainier, Crater Lake, Lassen, Yosemite, and Kings Canyon–Sequoia topping the list. But perhaps the most spectacular for the cyclist is one of the lesser known, which is the North Cascades National Park in Washington. The beauty of the alpine scenery equals anything found in the rest of the country. An excellent road winds up through the park, culminating in two lovely passes within a few miles of each other. Our Tour 12, p. 207, explores this land of peaks, hanging glaciers, and clear, cold streams and lakes.

If the mountains of the coastal states form their most important attraction, then the valleys offer a distinct and pleasant counterpoint. In fact, bicyclists who judge an area on the criteria of a good network of quiet roads, numerous towns and villages, and a quantity of "undiscovered" places might prefer the valleys of Oregon, California, and Washington over any other area in the region.

Before the lure of gold brought crushing waves of population, these valleys were being quietly settled, and the villages and towns established during this time still maintain much of their rural character. Main streets are quiet. There is an openness about people, which seems in character with the hardware stores with wooden floors worn smooth by a century or more of patronage, false-fronted buildings, coffee shops where the owner cooks for you while you wait in an honest wooden booth. These and a hundred other images typify the region.

Still unmentioned in all this are the roads which hug the intricate and impressive coastline of the Pacific. Here again, variety is the keynote. The bicyclist venturing southward on California's fabled Route 1 through Big Sur will be treated to swirling displays of blue and white water immediately below, of a thousand hidden beaches behind wet rock cliffs. In Oregon, you can leave your bicycle and trudge over sand dunes, the barest of vegetation clinging tenaciously to the shifting soil. In Washington, huge waves beat weathered logs together as if they were so many matchsticks.

Of course these and other attractions are not exclusive to the bicyclist, and this poses the greatest problem to a tour in any of the coastal regions. Roads in many areas are crowded, including, of course, the best-known areas. We deal with this problem later on in our discussion of each region, and also offer general information about route-finding and map-reading that will help you avoid some of the more congested areas along the coast.

If crowds are sometimes a problem in Washington, Oregon, or California, just the opposite is true in Nevada. It is the most sparsely settled state in the nation, with only two important urban areas, Reno in the north and Las Vegas in the south. The high basinland of most of the state offers mile after mile of houseless terrain. Since it is also the driest state in the nation, its mountains have been broken down less by water erosion. Rock seems a bit harsher, the effect accentuated by many of the slopes being treeless or only sparsely covered with juniper and other heat-resistant vegetation.

But it is a mistake to write off Nevada as one endless expanse of high desert. The northern part is watered, well enough, particularly during the winter, to support good forest growth on the higher slopes, and although streams do not bubble and tumble downward with great frequency, the generally sparse rainfall makes it an excellent place for off-season riding, with spring and fall tours in the north, and good winter rides in the south. Obviously, because of the lack of population, you need to ascertain ahead of time exactly what lies down the road, and be prepared to handle unexpected contingencies.

Climate.   Climate in the Far West varies as much as the terrain. Weather is strongly affected by two factors: latitude and distance from the Pacific Ocean. The mountain ranges also have important local effects; they tend to drain off water on the western slopes and leave what is called a rain shadow to the east.

The great latitude range, running from the Canadian border to the Mexican, results in a relatively short riding season in some parts of Washington to year-round riding conditions in southern California. Perhaps this range is best seen by comparing the temperatures you will experience on the Washington coast in July—in the mid-60s most days—to the temperatures of 105 and 110 degrees you would experience in El Centro, California, on the same day. This range is even greater in winter; on a typical January day in Palm Springs, California, the daily maximum would be in the low 70s, while in sections of eastern Washington it could well be 15 degrees below zero.

But more important than latitude is the effect of mountain ranges and distance from the ocean. Storms move in off the Pacific. Each succeeding range rakes off more water. Thus in the Washington Cascades, rainfall totals 60 inches a year or more. But in the eastern part of the state, many weather stations report 10 inches or less of rain a year. The same pattern exists for California and Oregon—and to a much lesser extent in Nevada, where the west winds have already lost most of their moisture to California.

Mountain ranges also cause temperatures to vary between coastal areas and interior valleys. A typical example are temperatures in Eureka, along the northern California coast, as opposed to those in Red Bluff, about 100 miles inland in the upper Sacramento Valley. If you could cover this distance in one day (many bicyclists can), you might typically ride on the coast in foggy weather with temperatures in the mid-50s and end up in afternoon heat of 110 degrees near Red Bluff. Although this may represent something of an extreme, the same pattern is repeated throughout the coast and interior valleys of Oregon, Washington, and California.

The states of the Far West are also affected greatly by more or less permanent high-pressure systems out in the Pacific. In summer, this high-pressure system keeps rain from reaching most of California and much of Oregon. It also causes a two-month season of relatively little rainfall in western Washington (July and August). This means typically dry summertime riding for all of California, Nevada, and most of Oregon, and only occasional rain in western Washington. The area east of the Cascades and Sierra, of course, is even drier, with the mountains serving as an additional barrier to any rain that might get in past the predominant high-pressure center.

THE MOUNTAIN STATES:
IDAHO, MONTANA, WYOMING, COLORADO, NORTHERN UTAH

Terrain. Idaho, Montana, Wyoming, Colorado, and northern Utah make up the region we call the Mountain States. It is here that massive layers of rock have been thrust skyward and the cyclist encounters peak after peak topping 13,000 and 14,000 feet. The Continental Divide snakes through the region in enormous sweeps, at some points nearly doubling back on itself. Some of our great national parks preserve this outstanding scenery. In addition to these, there are countless lesser-known areas, less visited, more pristine, and in certain respects more lovely because of it. Glaciers carve away at granite and sandstone high above you. Small roads hug the edges of delicate meadows. Heavy timber suddenly gives way to scarred, treeless rock. Crusted snow lies in shady depressions just off the pavement even in midsummer.

While much of the area is mountains, not all of it is so, but what isn't mountainous is usually high. Idaho has an average elevation of 5,000 feet. Wyoming and Utah are even higher. Colorado tops them all with an average elevation of 6,800 feet, and many of its valleys lie at 7,000 and 8,000 feet. Much of the high plateau area of Wyoming likewise lies above 6,000 feet. The alternating high plateaus and mountain ranges reintroduce the washboard effect found in the coastal states, but at much greater elevations. A typical pattern on any linear tour in this region is to ride along rolling, semi-arid sagebrush plateau, then cross passes at 8,000 or 9,000 feet. Once off the mountains, you hit another piece of rolling terrain that may go on for a day or more's riding.

Most of these plateaus are dry. Towns are spaced out, and tiny general stores become veritable oases for replenishing water and supplies. The long stretches of arid region are popularly called jackrabbit-and-sagebrush desert, after the two most common forms of life found there (although unless you scare them up, jackrabbits tend to roam more often at night). You'll find about as much jackrabbit-and-sagebrush desert in the Mountain States as you will mountains. Much of Wyoming, areas of southern and eastern Montana, southern Idaho, western Colorado, and northern Utah all fit this description.

If these arid lands are less spectacular than the high peaks, they usually are easier riding. Your body becomes accustomed to the altitude, and touring places no more demands on you physically than it would in any similar but lower topographical formation. Wind can be a problem, because of the fairly open nature of the land and lack of tree cover. Because of the altitude, it can also be cold, particularly in the mornings. We cover details of how to deal with these two elements in Chapter 4.

For the Midwesterner, Easterner, or resident of the lusher portions of the coastal states, long stretches of sagebrush take some getting used to, and some effort not to let the eyes glaze over and see nothing but sameness. In fact, there is a great deal of life and variety, but you have to be attuned to looking for it. Just stop your bike, walk off the road, and listen for a moment. The air is filled with noise, a subtle, unobtrusive humming of quiet life. Looking carefully at a 10-yard-square section of earth, you will begin to notice a great variety of plants, small insects, and if you are lucky, charming oddities such as the kangaroo rat or cottontail, both of which seem quite willing to go about all their business whether you are there or not.

Standing in contrast to these regions, of course, are the great mountains. Organized campgrounds abound, and there are vast spaces under the jurisdiction of the National Forest Service or Bureau of Land Management where you can camp off on your own, with trees as your backrests, and softly fallen pine needles or juniper leaves for seats and tables.

Then there are the great national parks. If you think you know these well already, you will find in them a new magnificence when explored on a bicycle—Yellowstone, which, along with its geysers, has some of the best high-peak scenery in the West; Glacier, with its deep U-shaped valleys; the beautiful symmetry of the Grand Tetons;

and the soaring roads high above timberline in Rocky Mountain National Park. These form a chain of sights that would be very difficult to duplicate anywhere in the world.

Largely because of these parks, the Mountain States receive rather heavy concentrations of bicycle tourists, and the visitor from the East, Midwest, or South may be surprised to see streams of bicyclists going down the roads that connect these parks, or gather with them in special 50¢-per-night campgrounds reserved for bicyclists and hikers, swapping routes over flickering campfires, all at elevations consistently over 7,000 and 8,000 feet! In Chapter 7 we give a number of tours that allow you to visit the great mountain parks of the West.

Climate. Climate in the Mountain States is still largely under the influence of the Pacific Ocean, although to a much lesser extent than the Far West. Since the Cascades and Sierra Nevada steal much of the moisture that is part of the Pacific storms, it is typically only the higher ranges in the Mountain States that get what is left—this is what is responsible for the sagebrush-and-jackrabbit deserts.

For the bicyclist, how much rain you see in most of the Mountain States thus depends on your position relative to the mountains themselves. Weather east of the Rockies in Montana and Colorado will be drier than to the west. The Bitterroots in Wyoming will create the same pattern, as will the lesser ranges of Idaho or Utah.

Temperatures, of course, vary with altitude, and this is the most noticeable weather pattern in this region. But there is also an effect of latitude, with Idaho and Montana having moderate daytime temperatures and areas of southern Colorado and much of Utah experiencing daily maximums 10 or even 20 degrees higher.

THE SOUTHWEST:
ARIZONA, NEW MEXICO, SOUTHERN UTAH

Terrain. Any bicyclist venturing into the great Southwest will probably remember most vividly its remarkable colors. Blazing oranges, vermilion, burnt yellows, rust, and chocolate browns cover the entire horizon. Winding through the deep gorges of Zion National Park, for instance, the bicyclist has the feeling of being immersed in color. Just to the north, Bryce National Park is a riot of elaborate spires of intricately carved layer cakes in orange, yellow, and brown. Less known are the blood-red of the earth in New Mexico and the orange monuments of Capitol Reef in Utah—the list goes on.

To bicycle in this region may be one of the least discovered joys in the United States. Probably because many people equate the Southwest with blazing heat and hours of monotonous desert travel (generally made so because people stay cooped up in their cars the entire time), fewer people venture here. In fact, because most or much of the region is high, between 4,000 and 6,000 feet, it has reasonable summer bicycling weather. A fair percentage of the Southwest is covered with high coniferous forests, ranging from the fragrant junipers that dot the lower mountain slopes to great stands of ponderosa pine growing at 7,000 and 8,000 feet. The region to the north of the Grand Canyon in Arizona and the Sangre de Cristo mountains of New Mexico are just two examples. There are numerous others.

If it sounds like we are enthusiastic about the Southwest—we are. The openness of the terrain, the fact that the cycling is generally easier than in many parts of the Mountain States, the relative lack of traffic in most areas—even the logistical problems of covering considerable distances where there are no towns—all please us. In addition, there is the desert. We love the solitude of it, we love to ride in it, to camp in it. It's sort of like olives and anchovies. You are never born liking them, but once the taste is acquired, you can't give them up.

To begin with, the desert is not empty. It abounds in game. Jackrabbits and cottontails dart from one sagebrush to another as you cycle by. Herds of antelope and mule deer lift their heads to solemnly gaze at your passing. You'll meet porcupines, badgers, skunks, prairie dogs, and even beavers in some desert regions. Then, there is the great comic of the desert, the coyote. We defy anyone to listen to the hilarious yapping of this creature in the middle of the night and not break up in sympathetic cackles.

We might also pause to mention some of the traditional bugaboos of the desert, the myth of a land crawling with tarantulas and rattlesnakes. In fact, tarantula bites are harmless in and of themselves, with the exception of a bacterial infection caused by the opening of the skin. As for rattlesnakes, in all of our Western camping, spanning some twenty years, we have yet to see our first live rattlesnake in the desert. This does not mean they are not perhaps present, but you simply don't stumble onto them every other step. Most of these fantasies of the desert were made in Hollywood, not Arizona.

Climate. The most common errors strangers to the Southwest make about its weather is to consider it a uniformly hot climate with little or no rainfall. Although this picture is true enough of the lower desert regions, most of the area of Arizona, New Mexico, and southern Utah does not in fact fit this description. The Southwest has considerable variety both in terms of rainfall and temperature.

Rainfall may be the biggest surprise. July and August are rainy months through much of the region, with regular afternoon thundershowers. Flagstaff, Arizona, for example, gets more than 2 inches of rain per month in July and August—more than Seattle (in the rainy Pacific Northwest). Tucson, Albuquerque, and Santa Fe have similar summer rainfall patterns. Both before and after this rainy period, though, weather gets much drier, with rain in many cases dropping to negligible levels, to match the stereotypes.

A second surprising aspect of the Southwest's weather is the range of temperatures you can experience. True enough, the low desert region of southern Arizona and New Mexico, and to a lesser extent southern Utah, can have daily maximums in the high 90s or low 100s throughout much of the summer. Even in winter, many areas have high temperatures in the low 70s or high 60s. But most of the Southwest lies at elevations above 4,000 feet, and there is considerable modification of low desert heat the higher you climb. Flagstaff, Santa Fe, and even Albuquerque have summer weather with daily maximum in the high 70s and 80s, not the 100s. This, in combination with the naturally cooling afternoon rains, makes most of the Southwest suitable for summer riding—as long as you take the normal arid-region precautions regarding water: carry extra supplies, and make sure more is available down the road.

In Chapter 8 we outline several tours of the Southwest, discuss the best times of year to take them, and describe more of the specific rewards in store for you.

CHOOSING TOURING STYLES

As you accumulate information about the terrain and climate in the West, you can begin to assess what style or mode of travel best suits your needs and the regions you will be traversing. This business of touring style deals with the mode of travel you choose to follow—decisions such as where you will sleep and how you will eat. It can also refer to whether you are traveling on your own or as part of a guided tour where matters of route, accommodations, and cost are determined for you beforehand.

Touring style thus is a combination of economics, personal needs, and demands of terrain. It as much as anything will affect your day-to-day experiences in the West. It will determine how much equipment and clothing you have to carry. It will affect how far you can go in a day, or at least how easy it is to cover that distance. It will also determine how carefully you must plan your trip in advance, as some touring styles offer more flexibility than others. Finally, touring style will determine how much you spend on your trip.

We will treat three aspects of touring style in the rest of this chapter: where you will sleep, how you will eat, and information on guided tours.

SLEEPING

Camping. Most people who bicycle tour in the West camp out at night. This choice is only natural, given the considerable scenic beauty and the great number of private and public campgrounds available. There are also vast areas of the West where it is possible to camp outside organized campgrounds, and this too offers experiences of independence and peace unique to the camping cyclist.

There are a number of advantages to camping out. First is flexibility. In rural, mountainous, and sparsely populated regions of the West, campgrounds outnumber other kinds of accommodations by a large margin. You have a great deal of freedom as to stopping points, allowing the day's ride to be tailored to its own needs. Strong headwinds can be countered with early afternoon stops. In case of rain, you have an immediate shelter you can erect—something of an advantage in regions where trees are sparse and afternoon rains common.

Camping life also has its own rhythm, putting you in contact with other travelers, offering a sense of independence, often granting you solitude that seems to combine well with the pace of bicycling.

Beyond all these advantages, there is the matter of cost. Inflation has had a way of making a mockery of any cost projections more than six months old, so it is difficult to predict what will happen to camping costs in the future. But based on 1980–81 figures, you can camp in most public campgrounds from $2 to $5 per night; federal campgrounds usually cost less than state ones. Private campgrounds cost more, generally around $5 to $12 per night, the higher figure only in cases where the campground has unusual amenities or is located in a prime resort area. In California, and in some of the national parks, special spaces are reserved for the use of bicyclists and backpackers. Current prices for these spots is 50¢ per night. Usually you get a space and little else, but the ambience is good and the price can't be beaten. This is also one way of beating the problems of campgrounds where no regular spaces are left. The bicycle-camping areas are usually flexible as to their capacity, at least to some extent.

Most private campgrounds will accept reservations, many requiring advance deposit. State parks in California and Oregon will take reservations. It is not possible to reserve spaces in National Forest Service campgrounds nor in the National Parks system. Our common procedure for handling campgrounds listed as full is to circle through looking for someone with extra space they're not using, and ask to share the spot with them. We share the costs.

A good campground directory (see the Bibliography) will give you specific detail about costs and reservation requirements.

For all the advantages of camping, there are some drawbacks. Even the most minimally equipped camper will carry 5 to 10 pounds of additional weight in form of sleeping bag and shelter. This will increase if you are carrying cooking equipment, as most camping cyclists do. As a result of the extra weight, hills and mountains are harder to climb. Headwinds become more oppressive. Handling characteristics of the bicycle suffer.

There are some other inconveniences, mostly minor, but which can add up over a period of time. There is no soft easychair awaiting you at the end of the day—or even the sturdy one your back cries out for when you sit. You may have to clean up with only a sponge bath, not a tub. Most private campgrounds do have showers, though, and more and more public campgrounds, particularly in state and national parks, are installing shower facilities. But National Forest campgrounds, which comprise the largest single category, are without showers, and frequently have only pit toilets. When you are camping on your own, even these necessities must be improvised.

Motels. The main alternative to camping is to use motels. In some places there are youth hostels, although not enough for you to use throughout a long tour.

In addition to the advantages in comfort which motel accommodations offer, they relieve you of a good bit of paraphernalia. Your bicycle stays responsive. A lighter load means fewer spoke problems, particularly on the rear wheel, which takes a tough beating when a bicycle is fully laden with clothing and camping gear. And given the West's mountainous geography, the advantage of traveling with a lighter bicycle will be felt from the first moments of a tour to the last.

There are the psychological advantages—a clean bed, all the hot water you want, even a sense of being pampered at the end of a day. Often you are staying in motels not on a well-beaten tourist track, and your status as a touring bicyclist will make welcomes warmer, services a bit more gracious. For many, these advantages far outweigh the extra costs motel travel entails.

The only problem with staying in motels, other than their cost, is their scarcity in certain areas. If you are eating in restaurants as well, the problem can be compounded.

In certain parts of every region we have discussed, motels are spaced out at distances which are farther than you may wish to travel in a day. In practical terms, what this usually means is a few days when your distance stretches out to 60 or 70 miles. There will be other times when you may not be able to find a motel exactly where you want one, and you may have to pull up short, then take a longer stretch the following day.

This points up the need for careful trip planning in certain areas, and determining in advance if the destination you are aiming for actually has a motel—and preferably more than one. There are some auto club guides and other privately published guides that are of some use, but most of them do not list the small, out-of-the-way motels you are likely to be looking for. You can use them making reservations in larger towns, and usually for better motels in popular resort or park areas. But the best place to locate small motels is the Yellow Pages. When you are fairly certain of your day's stopping point, check in the Yellow Pages about availability; you can also telephone a reservation if you wish. Bicycle route guides of the kind we present in the last three chapters also normally note the availability of motels along the tour route.

In heavily populated areas you usually have plenty of motels to choose from. In more remote areas, the best way to secure space is either to telephone ahead or to stop early in the afternoon.

Youth Hostels. The youth-hostel network that is being developed in this country, modeled after the hostel system in Europe and other parts of the world, strikes a reasonable compromise between the convenience of motels and the lower costs of camping. Youth hostels offer dormitory accommodation, or in some cases hotel rooms with several beds, at a minimal cost. Fees can range from about $2 to up to $10 per night, although most of them cluster toward the lower end of the scale. Often, users are asked to perform a small chore dealing with the operation of the hostel, such as general clean-up or supervising a laundering.

Hostels are located both within the major cities of the West and in some more out-of-the-way places. You should join the American Youth Hostel Association if you intend to use hostels. Details about joining and securing publications that indicate locations of hostels are found in Appendix 2.

EATING

To a great extent, the kind of accommodations you choose will determine where you're going to eat when touring. Camping and cooking your own food seem to be a natural combination, both because of their economic affinity and because campgrounds tend to be isolated, in many cases giving you little choice. Conversely, staying in motels and eating out tend to go together, especially because of the obvious difficulties of cooking in a motel room.

But there are many exceptions. Camping cyclists often vary their camp-cooked meals with a splurge in a restaurant. Also, in some areas of the West, cyclists can combine camping and restaurant meals by staying in private campgrounds in towns where other amenities are available. Conversely, motel users, by judicious use of city parks or similar facilities, can consistently avoid restaurant eating if they choose to do so.

Whatever the case, where you eat will have implications beyond economics, as it will affect both your flexibility and the amount of equipment you carry.

If you are planning to eat most of your meals in restaurants, you have some of the same problems in tour flexibility that you have when using motels. Although restaurants are far better distributed than motels, you still can't always find one exactly where you want it, and this calls for some adjusting on your part. We try to solve as many of these problems as possible with the information on tours presented in Chapters 6, 7, and 8. The only other problem is the frequency with which a drive-in hamburger stand turns out to be your only choice in a small town.

Cooking for yourself largely eliminates these problems, as the grocery store is the most common sort of service in the West; you are almost always able to count on finding food when you need it. Naturally, there is another side of the coin: the equipment you need to carry in order to cook your own meals.

First is a stove. If you are counting on doing much real cooking, as opposed to just eating cold foods, a stove is a must. Even though you will find a liberal sprinkling of campgrounds in most areas that provide fire pits and have wood available, there are many important exceptions—and the trend toward the exceptions is growing every year.

In heavily used campgrounds, for instance, such as certain state parks and nearly all popular national parks, it is prohibited to gather firewood. Often you can buy it, but it is expensive, and unless you are staying more than a day, the minimum quantity you can buy is more than you need. You face the choice of either leaving it, or stoking up a rip-roaring—and wasteful—bonfire. Most private campgrounds, particularly those located within small towns or cities, prohibit open fires entirely.

Finally—and we will make a stronger case for this in Chapter 4—if you are camping off on your own, it is often inadvisable to build a fire. Sometimes you just don't want to be noticed. More often than not when you are using *ad hoc* campsites, you are on someone else's land. Even if your intentions are good, you often can't ask permission, because the owner is miles away, or even in another state. Landowners may not object should they discover you on their land, but they are much more likely to if you have a fire. Fire presents a real hazard in much of the West, and it is never taken lightly.

For all these reasons, and in some instances for reasons of ecology, most camping cyclists carry a small stove. We go into this and other equipment in more detail in Chapter 5. For now, suffice it to say that the weight of the stove, the fuel, and cooking apparatus will add significantly to the weight and bulk of what you'll have to carry.

GUIDED TOURS

The distinguishing marks of a guided tour are the presence of an experienced bicycle tourist who has covered the route before and the fact that nearly all the uncertainties of the trip (with the exception of bad weather) are taken care of for you. The planners of the trip will have solved such unknowns as where to stop for the night, which maps you'll need, where you must stop, and where you're going to eat. Guided tours vary enormously—from the kind that feature camping and camp-cooked meals to ones that offer all the indoor amenities of restaurants and motels. In many instances, even if you're doing your own camp cooking, menu planning and shopping are done for you, and you usually get some relief from KP duty, as these tasks are shared by the group. Your trip costs are also calculated before you go, so you can know ahead of time what your vacation will cost instead of discovering it piecemeal while on the road.

An important advantage of a guided tour—especially for a novice tourist—is an accurate assessment of the tour's difficulty. You can read the literature provided by the tour's leader or sponsor, and talk to the planners as well as to others who've traveled with the same organization. That way you'll get a much better sense of what to expect en route than you can from a highway map.

Besides this advantage of advance information, various tours will offer other kinds of benefits. Some will make all motel or campground reservations in advance. Others will include a sag wagon—a support vehicle that carries luggage and, if need be, tired bicyclists.

What are the costs? You're paying for the services of a leader, sometimes for amenities such as a sag wagon, not to mention a profit if the tour is run by a private concern—so a guided tour will usually cost more than if you were to travel in the same manner on your own. But there are savings, too. Campground and food costs go down proportionally when traveling with a group. Sometimes, too, the inexperienced solo cyclist might pay more than need be as a result of that inexperience. You might buy equipment you don't need, might not find the cheapest motel or restaurant available, or might make mistakes in route-planning that end up costing more money.

Because no two tour organizers are exactly alike in what they provide, it is impossible to give accurate per-day costs. If the group is a nonprofit organization—the American Youth Hostel Association, Bikecentennial, and the International Bicycle Touring Society are the three largest organizations of this kind—then you can expect your per day costs to be only slightly *above* what an experienced bicycle tourist would pay for similar accommodations. This additional cost reflects things such as sag wagons, or the costs of the tour leader. Private groups that must provide all or some of these things, and still make a profit, will charge you proportionally more. Appendix 2 gives further details of bicycle touring organizations, many of which offer tours; and Appendix 3 lists the names, addresses, and range of tours for both nonprofit and private organizations.

THREE

Planning your route

Once you have a general idea of where you want to tour and a concept of your touring style, you need to start specific planning. Drawing up a complete route usually doesn't work out to be a step-by-step process. Each decision affects other areas of tour planning. You decide to take a tour of a relatively flat region, such as the Willamette Valley in Oregon, and this in turn means that you'll have to work harder to avoid busy roads, as the valley is far more populous than the mountain regions of Oregon. It also might mean that you will have to rely more on private campgrounds, rather than state, county, or federal ones, which will increase your daily cost somewhat. It may also mean that you'll be able to go farther each day, since the terrain is relatively flat, and this will affect overall tour distance. Thus, although we spell out in this chapter something of a step-by-step process you can follow, in reality your own experiences will likely involve some jumping back and forth between sequences as your final plans round into shape.

INITIAL PLANNING WITH MAPS

So with this in mind, how do you go about planning a tour? Assuming you have settled on a general region to tour, or perhaps decided on a starting and stopping point, you need to get a good state highway map that will allow you to answer some preliminary questions. You can get such maps from service stations or from the department of transportation of each state, entities we will discuss later in this chapter. We need to emphasize here that you should use these maps primarily for general orientation, for they are full of treachery if you rely on them totally. Our experience outside Estes Park is only one such example. With this note of caution, look at your map and try to answer some preliminary questions.

First, calculate roughly the distance your tour will take. Don't worry about the fact that you may end up taking some roads that aren't shown on the map, or may alter your tour route somewhat. Just get at least a general idea of how much distance is involved and whether you have time to cover it.

To determine the latter, divide the total trip distance by the number of days you plan to spend touring. You will then have an average of how much you must cover a day. If you're an experienced bicycle tourist, you will know what sort of distances are within your range (although beware of obstacles such as mountains, wind, or urban centers—any of which will slow you up considerably). If you aren't experienced, then you'll need to make some decisions as to how far you want to travel in a day, or perhaps more accurately, how far you're able to travel in a day. The latter is such an important question that we need to spend a moment considering it.

It is a rare tour that ends up being too short. Experienced and inexperienced alike, we tend to extend ourselves too far. And unless you are traveling alone, there is no issue more vexing than trying to reach agreement with others on how much distance you must cover each day to complete a tour. (The nettlesome subject of how fast you cover the distance is close on its heels.)

Most touring cyclists in the West average 50 to 100 miles a day. There's nothing magic about these figures; they just represent a norm. Throughout much of the West, you can plan tours with daily distances shorter than 50 miles and still find the facilities you need at each night's stopping points. We took a tour of the Idaho Panhandle with a spunky, but inexperienced and out-of-condition fifty-year-old sister and brother-in-law. The tour we planned for them averaged somewhere near 30 miles a day. It was a delightful change of pace for us (who had traveled up to 85 miles per day), with long afternoons spent in the crystalline waters of the Panhandle's many lakes, easy evenings, long lunch breaks, and even movies at night when we happened to camp in town near a theater. Our experience was so pleasurable that we formalized it into a tour of the Panhandle, found in Chapter 7.

But your decision as to how far you can go in the time you have must be geared to your own wishes. Under no conditions should you plan a tour, or go on a tour someone else has planned, that exceeds what you are comfortable with physically or psychologically. This does not mean that you won't have to push on certain days. You will. But taking a tour where you are constantly overtaxed, exhausted, and unhappy is an experience you'd be better off without. In Chapter 4 we give some hints for those traveling with other people as to how variations in personal tastes and riding capabilities may be adjusted to insure better human relationships. But for the moment, you need to make some assessment of what you are capable of, day-in, day-out, in order to determine how much of a piece of real estate you can comfortably cover in the time you have.

While we don't prescribe how far you should go or what your average should be, we do need to make one point. In some areas of the West you must be capable of putting in a 60-mile day, particularly when cycling away from the Pacific coast or the relatively well-populated valleys of the coastal states. In much of the rest of the West there are many areas where you'll need to travel 60 miles in order to reach the specific kinds of services you require—a motel close to a restaurant, say, or a National Forest Service campground. You won't have to *average* 60 miles a day—but there are some days you'll be required to go that far. After that, you can usually drop back down to a significantly lower mileage.

Once you have used your highway map to assess the sort of distances involved in your prospective tour and determined that it is feasible from this standpoint, you can cull it for other pieces of information.

One very important consideration is the extent of the secondary-road network in the chosen area. By secondary roads we mean two-lane highways with relatively light traffic. Sometimes they are state or national highways; often they are local roads.

Look at your map to see what alternatives exist to the freeways and major roads between large cities. If all you see in your tour area are interstate highways and obviously important roads, you should move with caution. You can legally ride on freeways in most states, at least when there are no secondary roads lying close enough to give you an alternative; but travel on them can be fatiguing because of constant noise and a constant line of debris cluttering the shoulder. And getting onto a major highway that has no ridable shoulder can be just plain suicidal. Now there are some areas of the West where all you have is a major roadway, but in many instances, traffic on them becomes relatively light away from the cities. Thus we advise you only to use caution, not to give up your plans entirely. We'll show you presently how to find out just how much traffic a road is carrying, as well as whether it has a ridable shoulder.

Look also at your map to see how far apart the towns are. You'll notice that in the eastern parts of Oregon, California, and Washington, towns are few and far between. They get downright scarce in states such as Wyoming or Nevada. Usually this means you'll have to exercise more care in the logistics of supply in these areas. Do you notice a heavy clustering of towns and cities? Areas such as southern California between Los Angeles and San Diego are little more than one dreary metropolis. Riding through this means heavy traffic, daily distances that will be shorter than usual because of stoplights and other impediments, difficulty in finding campgrounds, and general fatigue caused by the constant tension which heavy traffic induces.

You should also look for some of the general features of the terrain. Most highway maps are not very specific, but with careful looking you'll be able to detect mountain passes and roads around lakes or along rivers. The latter are often crowded with vacation traffic, and the passes, of course, mean slow going.

Your highway map may also indicate which areas of the state are part of national forest lands—generally ideal cycling locations because of their beauty and their camping grounds, but also generally mountainous. Often you'll also have difficulty finding motels and even restaurants in or near much national forest land. This should be noted as it may make some difference in your route planning.

What this process of preliminary map-gazing will do for you is to give you a general idea of cycling conditions. We need to emphasize the word *general*. Most highway maps are woefully deficient in the specifics you need to know in order to assure the best possible cycling conditions. So before you set plans in concrete based on what you find in a service-station highway map, you need to know some of these limitations.

WHY MOST MAPS DON'T WORK

Someday, we hope, someone will produce a series of maps covering the United States that will be as useful to the bicycle tourist as to the motorist, or as detailed as the ones European mapmakers have published for their tourists. Briefly, the highway maps readily available to an American bicycle tourist are not drawn on a scale that offers enough detail for good touring. A map made for an oil company or a state department of transportation must fit on a relatively small piece of paper. For the motorist concerned only with state or national roads connecting cities and towns, the resulting maps are excellent. But because they are drawn on so small a scale, they cannot show (or the mapmakers don't choose to put in) the details you need to know about. The first of these omissions are secondary-road networks.

Among all the elements of a successful bicycle tour, the discovery and use of back roads that are not overburdened with traffic is most critical. This not only affects safety, it ultimately determines whether you'll be able to look around and enjoy where you are, or whether your eyes will be glued to the road shoulder with panicked glances backward to see when the next stream of traffic will roar by.

Very often the state and federal routes shown on a general highway map will be quiet roads. Sometimes even a busy road will have a wide, well-paved shoulder that will reduce the fatiguing effects of cars and trucks passing at high speeds. But general highway maps don't show the difference.

Most highway maps also fail to note specifics about geography. They usually do show major passes, but what about other conditions that may call for nearly as strenuous cycling? Short hills 2 or 3 miles long can produce about the same cycling conditions as the latter part of a major mountain pass; the only real differences are the elevation and the difficulty of the riding leading up to that point. What about a road that runs alongside a river? These can be very gradual inclines or they can be extremely steep, depending on the fall of the river itself. There is nothing in most maps to help you distinguish.

Highway maps will usually give you no information on the services you will need when you're on tour. This becomes critical in regions where towns are often very far apart. Not all crossroads towns have grocery stores, or even a place to get water. Many are without cafés or restaurants. Motels are even more scarce. Some road maps indicate state, national, or county campgrounds, but most are incomplete in this respect, and none notes information on private campgrounds. When you need a bicycle shop, you want to know whether it will be an hour or a week before you find one. A road map won't tell you.

Finally, you can tell nothing about a region's weather from looking at a road map. You can make some intelligent guesses about general rainfall patterns by noting which areas lie on the leeward side of mountain ranges, or by taking into account the elevations of towns, a detail some maps give. This can tell you, for instance, that Albuquerque, at 5,000 feet, will be warmer than Santa Fe, at 7,000 feet. But the information of this kind you can draw from a general map is limited.

So if you are going to plan adequately for a tour, you will have to get your information elsewhere. Fortunately, there has recently been a rapid growth of literature to supply that information. A few bicycling organizations are also active in developing tour information. Finally, a number of other information sources, while not aimed specifically at bicyclists, can nonetheless help them greatly in tour planning. We'll spend most of the rest of this chapter discussing these other sources.

BICYCLE ROUTE GUIDES AND TOUR INFORMATION

The growing popularity of bicycle touring within the past decade has prompted the publication of route guides planned just for bicyclists. These guides give all the details that regular road maps omit. The better ones give information about distances, road conditions, traffic patterns, shoulder widths, length and difficulty of hills, and where to find necessary services including bicycle-repair shops. They usually also offer something about the culture, geology, history, or general geography of the region through which the tours pass. Most offer an annotated map that can be carried in the front handlebar map pocket, or used as a supplement to a general highway map.

In addition to this book, there are a number of other sources for route guides or for maps and literature that detail bicycling conditions within specific regions of the West.

STATE AGENCIES

Primary among these are state departments of transportation, some of which actually have bicycling sections under their aegis. These departments or their agencies have recently become active in developing and supplying information to touring bicyclists. The quantity and quality of this information varies greatly, ranging from specific details on traffic flows, hills, passes, and available services, to rather cryptic maps that point out possible bicycle touring routes in a state or region. Some states have gone so far as to produce handsome packets which include strip maps and detailed written cue sheets to accompany them. The state of Washington actually will assemble for you a tour packet complete with strip maps and written route information, all based on the starting and end points of your own tour.

Below is a state-by-state breakdown of information available to you. Addresses for organizations and agencies mentioned are given in the appendices.

ARIZONA

At this time, Arizona has not developed any material designed specifically for the bicycle tourist, but it has long been active in promoting tourism, and produces a considerable body of literature useful to the long-distance rider. Most notable is the monthly magazine *Arizona Highways*, dedicated to exploring various areas within the state. You can subscribe to this magazine (see Appendix 4), and you can find copies of it in most large libraries. Also available is a good free road map that shows paved roads and general features of the terrain.

Beyond this, the Arizona Office of Tourism offers a variety of free descriptive brochures that indicate the more popular sights in the state and give some helpful information on temperatures and precipitation patterns. A separate Calendar of Events will inform you of festivals and other events throughout the state. With Arizona's heavy concentration of Indian populations, many of these events are very colorful, and many, of course, are centuries old. For all of the above information, write the *Arizona Highways* magazine.

CALIFORNIA

California has put together an excellent body of information for the touring cyclist. The department of transportation (Caltrans) has a bicycle coordinator whose duty it is to oversee all bicycling activities as they relate to the state's transportation system. Centralizing these functions has had a great effect on the amount of literature, maps, and route guides available to the bicyclist.

The most important Caltrans publications are bicycle maps covering the eleven transportation districts of the state. Since each district has developed its own bicycle map, they vary in format and quality. But generally speaking, they detail routes on which bicycling is prohibited, and usually suggest routes that avoid the most congested roads. Some district maps are much more elaborate, noting traffic counts (the average number of vehicles passing a given point in twenty-four hours), width of shoulders, locations of hills, and most importantly, the mileage marker number at which the hill crests. The best maps are those covering the northern counties. Besides all the information just described, they note where critical services are located—campgrounds, motels, grocery stores, restaurants, and bicycle shops.

The district maps are distributed free out of each district office. The office addresses and the area covered by each map are given in Appendix 1.

In addition to its regional maps, the bicycling division of Caltrans has developed or reproduced a number of bicycle route guides. The most important is a guide to the Pacific coastline. This exceptionally well-designed flip-map book gives details for a linear tour along the coast from Oregon to the Mexican border. It notes all details of the tour route, including traffic counts, campground locations, and general information as to difficulty. A route profile is also included. It does not note locations of restaurants, grocery stores, or motels. In some instances, the guide is better than the route it describes—particularly in southern California, where it puts the bicyclist on some inevitably crowded urban routes from Santa Barbara to San Diego. You can buy it for $1 from Caltrans at the address given, along with a complete listing of Caltrans offerings, in Appendix 1.

COLORADO

For so mountainous a state, Colorado has a surprisingly extensive list of bicycle touring aids produced by the state government—surprisingly, that is, to anyone not familiar with the inhabitants. Cyclists there rightly regard the high mountains as distinct bicycling advantages rather than as detriments. The Bicycle Program of the Colorado Department of Highways (address in Appendix 4) has prepared four special bicycle itineraries that cross the state in various directions. These bicycle route guides are well-designed packets that include written descriptions of the route and two-color route maps depicting elevation profiles, noting distances between points, and indicating locations of restaurants, grocery stores, motels, and campgrounds. The guides even point out occasional hazards such as narrow bridges.

The backs of these strip maps are full of important data, including summaries of elevation changes and information about difficult parts of the routes. The guides follow major Interstate highway corridors, using adjoining roads where possible, but following the freeways when not. This is probably their greatest disadvantage. Many areas of the state provide routes equally scenic, yet do not thread the rider on and off an Interstate with the frequency of these routes. Fortunately, the quality of the maps is excellent, and the notations are quite complete. Of great help are the routes through and around cities such as Denver or Colorado Springs.

These four routes are summarized in Chapter 7. You can order the free route guides from the Colorado Department of Highways at the address in Appendix 1. The state and various local governments have also produced bicycle route maps for a number of cities, including Denver, Colorado Springs, and Pueblo. Addresses for securing these are also in Appendix 1.

IDAHO _____

The Idaho Department of Parks and Recreation puts out a one-sheet state map detailing a number of suggested bicycling routes. The map also indicates locations of state campgrounds (but not national forest or other public campgrounds). The information is minimal, but the map does at least indicate areas throughout the state where bicycle tours are possible. The department also gives away a brochure on the state park system, which is useful in planning routes. (Address is given in Appendix 4.)

MONTANA _____

The Montana Travel Promotion Unit can supply you with a reasonably detailed state road map that denotes topographical features quite well. In addition, there is a state publication that lists four routes connecting the two great national parks found in the state, Glacier and (marginally) Yellowstone. These four routes are for motorists, but bicyclists can also use them as a basis for constructing their own routes. All of the above information is free from the Montana Travel Promotion Unit, whose address is in Appendix 4.

NEVADA _____

Nevada at this time has no specific information for bicycle tourists, although the department of transportation will furnish a usable state map, which notes topographic features and includes most paved roadways in the state. Address is in Appendix 4.

NEW MEXICO _____

You can secure a free highway map from the state transportation department (address in Appendix 4). The map is adequate for general planning, as it denotes topographic features and is drawn on a large scale. The state also offers descriptive brochures that give general information about history, climate, and recreational opportunities.

OREGON _____

The Travel Information Section of the Oregon Department of Transportation produces a bicycle route map that details four major tour routes through the state—a Pacific coast route, a route through the

Willamette Valley, a circular route from Portland to the Pacific and back, and an west–east route from Astoria (with a branch from Reedsport) to the Idaho state line. (The latter is essentially a copy of the Trans America Trail developed by the bicycling organization, Bikecentennial; see below.) In addition, there are elevation profiles and route details for other portions of the state, particularly route information for persons traversing the larger cities and towns. Details of campgrounds and bicycle-repair facilities are noted. All this excellent data is crammed onto a large, single foldout sheet available free from the Oregon Department of Transportation (address in Appendix 1). If you cross into the state on Interstate 5 from either the north or south, you can get a copy from the tourist-information offices located just inside the border.

UTAH

In addition to a free highway map, the Utah Department of Transportation provides cyclists with a written summary of state laws relative to bicycling, and two pages of useful advice for persons cycling in the state's remote regions. The department also has been responsive to individual cyclists' requests for detailed information of specific routes. Such requests should be sent to the Transportation Planning Division of the Utah Department of Transportation (address in Appendix 4).

In addition, there are a number of well-designed publications meant primarily for motorists, but useful to bicyclists as well. The Utah Recreation Guide lists information on tours, campsites, and other service facilities for all of the popular tourist regions of the state. It also details tour routes, some suitable for bicycle travel.

Of special use to a bicyclist is an eight-map set published by the Utah Travel Council. These maps show more detail than a regular road map, noting hiking trails, scenic areas, elevations, and the like. The set may be purchased from the Utah Travel Council for $4. See Appendix 4 for address.

WASHINGTON

The Washington State Department of Transportation has developed the most extensive set of route maps for the bicyclist of any Western state. These are in the form of eighty-nine "Bike Trip" maps, which are made up into flip-map packets designed to go in the map compartment of your handlebar pack. Each map covers a relatively short distance; several may be added together to form a linear route. They are then bound into one set of covers to form a complete tour guide.

The great flexibility offered by this system, and the fact that the individual strips cover most of the important roads within the state, make them the most useful and informative guides offered by any state government.

The maps themselves and the accompanying route descriptions are excellent. They show the route clearly, note details such as paving conditions, width of shoulder, potential hazards, locations of hills and passes, and scenic or descriptive information. A general introduction in each map packet gives highly useful information, such as addresses of state agencies, information on ferry travel, and a summary of laws relating to bicycle travel in the state.

A list of the routes covered by each map packet is given in Appendix 1 under Washington, or you may write the State Department of Transportation (address in Appendix 4) and request the covering guide, *Bicycling through the Evergreen State: Bicycle Strip Maps,* which gives details about the maps.

If you have a specific idea of where you wish to go, including of course your starting and end points, you may give this information to the transportation office and they will assemble the relevant strip maps for you. The cost for each packet when assembled is minimal— a donation of $1.50 per packet to cover handling and mailing expenses (a stamped envelope is included with your packets for your donation). Given the complexities of assembling individual packets, their response time is good. Leave at least three weeks, however, and more during the spring and summer cycling seasons.

WYOMING _____

While Wyoming has not developed literature specifically for the bicycle tourist, the state does try to promote tourism, and some of its publications contain excellent details.

Chief among these are four free pamphlets outlining self-guided tours; each covering roughly a quarter of the state. These large fold-out sheets give a great deal of written information on tourist attractions, details of geology, national parks and recreation areas, and major touristic events and their dates. Each sheet also has a map, which while not noting details of topography, does give an enlarged view of the portion of the state being dealt with.

A highly useful free state highway map does an excellent job of noting details of terrain, streams, and railroad tracks, and indicates a plethora of historical sites and their significance.

You can also request a small free booklet in magazine format that

depicts various sites of scenic or historic significance throughout the
state, and another pamphlet that lists locations of campgrounds, motels, hotels, dude ranches, lodges, and resorts. Address of the Wyoming Travel Commission is in Appendix 4.

BIKECENTENNIAL

Probably the most significant development for bicycle touring in the
United States within the last ten years has been the formation of an
organization called Bikecentennial. Bikecentennial was founded with
the intention of developing a coast-to-coast bicycle route in honor of
the United States Bicentennial celebration. The resulting five-volume
set of route maps with accompanying descriptive volumes has
been used by thousands of cyclists since the Bicentennial summer
of 1976.

The success of this initial effort gave the organization the impetus
to continue in existence and expand its services to the touring cyclist.
As a result, Bikecentennial has become the foremost bicycle touring
organization in the United States, and one of the best ones in the
world. The variety of services provided to the touring cyclist expands
each year, as does the quality of the publications issued.

Foremost among these publications are its route guides. The oldest
of these are the original Trans America guides. Three of them deal
with the region of the West covered in this volume, *Cost–Cascades,
The Rockies,* and to a much more limited extent, *Plains–Ozarks.* The
route begins on the Oregon coast, with two possible starting points,
one in Astoria, the other in Reedsport. The two alternatives join in
Eugene, and then a single route leads eastward through the Cascades,
across eastern Oregon to Idaho, then northeasterly through Idaho
along the Lochsa River to Missoula, Montana. From Missoula the
route goes south to Yellowstone National Park, through Wyoming
and into the Rockies of Colorado to Pueblo, then across the plains
and into Kansas. Other volumes detail the remainder of the route to
the Atlantic near Washington, D.C.

Included in the route books are complete maps, with topography
indicated (actually, the route is overlaid on a United States Geological Survey topographical map). The accompanying booklet gives
details of geography, botany, and history; route description; and locations of hotels, motels, campgrounds, and bicycle shops.

Two more recent publications from Bikecentennial are a two-
volume set describing a Great Parks Bicycle Route. One volume cov-

ers a route from Jasper National Park in Canada to Colorado, passing through Yellowstone and Grand Tetons National Parks en route. The second volume goes from Steamboat Springs to Durango, Colorado, crossing Rocky Mountain National Park and touching Mesa Verde National Park. Details of topography and locations of basic services are clearly noted.

A third route guide describes a large circle around the northwestern tip of Oregon.

In addition to its own route guides, Bikecentennial serves as collector, collator, and clearinghouse for a great deal of information on bicycle touring. Much of this is described in an extremely useful publication, *Cyclists' Yellow Pages*. In addition to listing all its own publications, the *Yellow Pages* lists books, state transportation guides, and route guides developed by other organizations such as the American Youth Hostel Association and YMCA. Also included are listings of routes developed by members of Bikecentennial. These latter routes, although sometimes uneven in quality, fill gaps in the organization's own program of tour-guide development.

Most of the material listed in the *Yellow Pages* can be ordered from Bikecentennial. This makes it very convenient to purchase, from one source, most of the material you need to plan a trip. In cases where Bikecentennial does not handle the map or guide itself, addresses and ordering information are given.

You save money on publications if you join Bikecentennial, as members pay discount prices on all publications the organization handles. By joining you also contribute needed funds for the continuing development of other publications useful to the touring bicyclist.

SUPPLEMENTAL INFORMATION

If you cannot find information about specific routes from publications supplied by state agencies or bicycling organizations, or if you wish to supplement this information, there are a number of other sources. Some of these are specialized maps, others are books and periodicals from which you can extract information, even though the publication may not be aimed specifically at the bicycle tourist. We'll review first some specialized maps, then turn to some more general publications.

SPECIALIZED MAPS

County Maps.   Often county maps are available from a state department of transportation, or are sold privately in local stores. They are most helpful in giving you specific route information within a fairly tight region. They often are excellent in detailing alternatives to crowded highways in urban areas or in popular tourist areas. If your tour is going to be within a relatively small region, then county maps are undoubtedly the best thing you can use, inasmuch as they supplement most of the critical route details left out by larger highway maps.

But they have some limitations. They won't detail significant services, and often don't indicate anything about terrain. Yet we find their greatest disadvantage is really a result of their being so detailed. If you are on a very long tour, you may well cross fifteen or twenty counties in two or three weeks. Carrying this many maps becomes a great burden, not to mention the cost of buying them. Trying to find them while on the road is difficult also. Many stores that specialize in hunting or fishing equipment carry them, but not all. Moreover, commercially prepared maps are expensive—most about $3.

For these reasons, we'd recommend using county maps only in specific situations where the amount of road detail they provide is important. At other times, rely on the sources discussed above.

USGS Topographical Maps.   The United States Geological Survey produces a number of topographical map series, with details of terrain indicated by contour lines. The chief advantage of the topos, as they are called, is that they give you a very accurate idea of elevation change, and once you learn to read them, they will enable you to predict with great accuracy how difficult or easy your cycling will be. They also point out features such as small streams, which can make campsite selection more accurate and agreeable.

The most useful maps for the bicycle tourist are the 1:250,000 scale topos. In these, one inch equals roughly four miles. The extent of how useful these will be to you depends upon how tight a tour you plan (i.e., an intensive exploration of a relatively small area) and how much detail you want to know ahead of time. If you are rambling over a large area, you may want to use topographic maps only for difficult segments, as their cost (about $2) may be prohibitive, not to mention the bulk of carrying many of them on a tour. They also are more concerned with showing topography rather than roads, and are particularly difficult to read when moving on a bicycle.

Traffic-Flow Maps.   Traffic-flow maps are publications developed by state departments of transportation that indicate how much traffic passes a particular point on the road in a given period. They are exceptionally useful in plotting tours on quiet roads. If you are doing intensive touring within one state or area of a state, it may be worth your while to have these. For extensive touring across several states, ordering traffic-flow maps may be something of an overkill, as you will end up with a good bit of information (and a sizable bill) that you may not need. But for the dedicated cycle tourist or for navigation around particularly tricky metropolitan areas, flow maps are very helpful. Addresses of state departments of transportation from which you may secure price lists are found in Appendix 4.

BICYCLING BOOKS AND PERIODICALS

You will find a number of books dealing with bicycling in the West in the Bibliography. Almost all of these deal with a specific region of the West, and most of the tours given are of fairly short duration, usually one day. But these sources are exceptionally valuable in exploring a small region in depth, and a bicyclist using them can often string several together to make a route through an area, or invent a larger circle composed of several tours. Many of the books dealing with bicycling around metropolitan areas such as Los Angeles, San Francisco, and Seattle can also be used by cyclists who must traverse these cities.

There are also a number of books that deal with bicycle touring in general. Books such as Tim and Glenda Wilheim's *The Bicycle Touring Book* and Gail Heilman's *Complete Outfitting and Sourcebook for Bicycle Touring* cover such matters as equipment, touring styles, map-reading, and the like, and are useful for the beginning tourist especially as sources of information developed by experienced bicyclists.

A number of periodicals dealing with bicycling have come and gone. Of those able to endure in a competitive market, the one with the greatest longevity and of most use to the tourist is *Bicycling.* You can, by leafing through its back issues, often come upon excellent information about touring a specific region, or find actual tour routes that others have developed.

GENERAL PUBLICATIONS

Beyond publications intended especially for bicyclists, there are a number of other books which the cyclist will find useful in tour planning. We list many of these specifically in the Bibliography, but the kinds of books you will find useful are these:

Campground Guides. Campground guides are essential not only for pinpointing the locations of public and private campgrounds on your tour route, but are also helpful in a number of other respects. By scanning the maps usually found in such books, you can get a good idea of regions where campgrounds are plentiful. Usually, although not always, these clusters are excellent bicycling areas, at least from a standpoint of scenery.

Some of these guides, such as the *Sunset Guide to Western Campgrounds*, also give the elevation of the campground and the distance to the nearest grocery store and to other amenities such as restaurants. The grocery-store information is helpful in pinpointing your last shopping possibility for the day. The elevation figures will help you in choosing appropriate equipment in plotting elevation changes in your routes.

Almanacs. Often you can use information provided in almanacs, such as the population of towns on your route. Dense population means bad cycling unless bicycle routes are available. Often you can get information of elevations and temperatures for regions, also helpful in trip planning.

Atlases. A general atlas is a useful aid in planning a bicycle tour, inasmuch as it can give you a good idea of overall terrain. From that, you can draw a general conclusion regarding a tour's difficulty. It is particularly useful if you have such an atlas at home where you can match it up with a general highway map. You can, if you wish, even sketch in significant details of geography on your highway map to make it more useful.

But the limitations of most atlases are the same as those of a normal highway map. Most atlases squeeze too much territory on too small a piece of paper to give you an accurate day-by-day idea of what you'll encounter. Moreover, they omit most details of road systems and locations of small towns to be of consistent use in tour planning.

Weather guides. One book specifically is an excellent source of information for the tourist—*Weatherwise, USA*. It gives temperature, rainfall, and sunshine data for several points in each state. With it, you'll know whether you need to bring an overcoat or not.

Motorists' Touring Books. Many motorists' touring books, often produced by major petroleum companies, are helpful to bicyclists in giving information about lesser-known touring areas, lists and prices of motels, and the like. Their chief limitation, of course, is that they often route the reader down the Interstate, and although many miles of Interstate are now accessible to the bicyclist, they usually are used only when nothing else is available.

State histories. State histories are numerous, and are most helpful in detailing how a region was settled, pointing out some of the history, and giving you a much deeper appreciation of the region through which you are traveling. Usually the more you know about an area, the more enjoyable your tour will be.

PLOTTING YOUR OWN TOUR ROUTE

How much of the foregoing information you use in plotting a tour route is somewhat a matter of personal preference. Some people do little more than get hold of a state highway map, pack their bicycles, remember their wallets, and set off. Others very meticulously research every aspect of the tour, using many sources just discussed. Oftentimes, tours are plotted down to the last detail, including each day's travel distance, sometimes even to the point of noting where lunch stops and breaks will occur.

Our experience has been that both extremes can be enjoyed by certain kinds of people, so we are reluctant to give specific advice. But in the balance, there are a good many arguments for making fairly comprehensive tour planning before you leave home. This need grows more acute if you do not have a great deal of touring experience, or if touring in the West is a new venture for you.

Whichever your own temperament is, or your level of experience, you should at least consider these points in mapping out your route.

Leave some flexibility for unexpected contingencies. Even the best-planned tour cannot account for unexpected weather. One of our wettest rides ever was in northern New Mexico in late summer, when things should have been dry. In late October, when the Arizona desert should have been cooling off, daytime temperatures were still blazing at 105 and 110 degrees. In sections of southern Montana when one normally would expect westerly winds, we had several days of hard easterlies, slowing our progress. Other bicyclists could extend this list of the unexpected nearly to infinity. It should serve as a caution that even in an area where weather is normally predictable, there are enough exceptions so that you should make allowances for them. Depending on how wet the area of the West is where you intend to tour, you should schedule in at least one contingency day for every two weeks on the road, more in obviously wet areas such as the Pacific Northwest, or areas of consistent summer fog, such as the California coast.

Flexibility is also important in meeting other contingencies beyond unpleasant weather. You might not like the scenery, and want to go elsewhere. Perhaps through conversations with other cyclists you discover a route much more suitable than the one you planned. Our own routes have sometimes resembled the pathways of the demented because passing cyclists suggested alternatives to the route we had decided upon.

Avoid plotting your tour through large cities and towns.   For most bicyclists, nothing but grief awaits them in crowded cities. Navigation becomes difficult, if not dangerous. All the services you normally find in a large city can usually be found in smaller towns (perhaps with the exception of bicycle shops in certain areas). Once out of town, you often have endless suburban stretches with narrow road shoulders and heavy commuter traffic. Even cities with bicycle paths and marked bicycle routes are not havens for out-of-town bicyclists. Usually you need a map to use such routes properly, and a good knowledge of the city in question is something of a prerequisite too. We once spent three hours getting out of Eugene, Oregon—not your most elaborate metropolis—because we were trying to follow bicycle routes meant primarily for people who knew ahead of time where the routes led. After several fruitless forays along the Willamette River, portages over strange bridges, and sallies down streets lined with factories and warehouses, we finally abandoned the effort and got onto a major highway leading out of town. Riding was more precarious, but at least it allowed us meaningful passage outward. At another point in a tour we became so frustrated trying to navigate into Phoenix that we finally pulled off the road and hitchhiked ourselves and bicycles to the center of town, then got up before dawn on a Sunday morning (the best light-traffic period) and made it out before things got impossible again.

When possible avoid roads that lead from cities to nearby bodies of water. We are little better than lemmings in controlling our impulses with regard to lakes, rivers, ponds, or oceans. Nearly any of these will attract enough of us to make roads crowded, particularly on weekends. If necessary, cover these stretches midweek. Otherwise, try to avoid them altogether.

Plan your day's distances with mountains, wind, and heat in mind. All three will slow your pace. Both wind and heat can make riding during parts of the day, particularly afternoons, all but impossible. You can usually predict when you'll encounter mountains and heat, but wind is more difficult to fix a definite pattern to. Even in areas with prevailing winds, there are day-to-day variations in direction and force. The regional descriptions offered in the last three chapters of this book will help, as well as the weather data given in Appendix 6. Route guides sometimes are helpful in allowing you to predict wind, as better ones will note directions of prevailing winds and times of day or year when winds are strongest.

If possible, leave yourself an alternative to your nightly stopping point. Sometimes you will arrive at a campground to find it closed. At other times you'll find a town has no motel, or only a full one. There have been instances when we found grocery stores closed on Sunday (more common than you want it to be in rural areas—just when you need them the most). Because of this, if possible plot your stopping point so that you could conceivably get to another revitalization stop if you need to. Obviously, there will be times when this is impossible. Nonetheless, keep it in mind when planning. It's also a good idea to make consistent inquiries while on the road about what lies ahead, a matter we discuss more fully in Chapter 4.

FOUR

Collecting your equipment

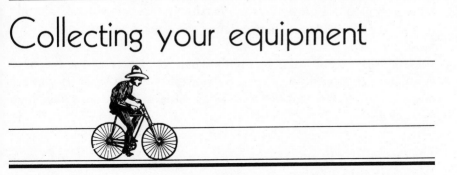

We are still learning about ways people equip themselves for a bicycle tour.

We met a man in France once who was on his way to India. He had found his bicycle frame in a ditch, outfitted it from junkyards, and fashioned his cooking gear out of old tin cans. He was doing quite well, living on about 20¢ a day. We once met a German man on the rim of the Grand Canyon who had bought a used discount-store ten-speed bicycle, fashioned a long piece of aluminum tubing that ran from its axles up to near his head, and onto this had strapped a backpack. He was walking a good many hills, and the contraption wobbled dangerously at any speed, but he was in high spirits and certain he'd reach Mexico on it. In southern Montana we met a Dutch couple on their way to Peru. They were on traditional Dutch three-speeds, enormously heavy, high-geared machines that we would be afraid to take beyond the flattest valley. They, too, were doing fine, thank you.

We have seen other bicycle tourists wrap up in a plastic sheet when it rained, and sleep the night in it. Others told us of nights spent under picnic tables, in barns, or under the eaves of public rest rooms. We have observed bicyclists eating dinner out of soup cans, cooking with twigs in campgrounds we thought totally bereft of wood, riding in bib overalls during the day, wearing leather dress shoes on their feet.

What this has taught us over the years is to be a bit less sure about what equipment you need in order to go bicycle touring. Rarely does a week go by on a tour without some preconception being shattered.

All the same, the fact that it is possible to tour on any bicycle that rolls, and to sleep in or on anything—provided one is tired enough—

does not answer the question of what sort of equipment works best for a long bicycle tour. Junk bicycles, charred tin cans, and cold spaghetti obviously have a place in the quickly developing history of bicycle tourism. But to tour at maximum efficiency in something resembling comfort and convenience, you need to go beyond this level.

With this qualification in mind, what follows is a discussion of equipment that works well for most bicyclists in the West. If you are new to touring, you can use it as a guideline as you secure your own equipment.

OUTFITTING YOUR BODY

HEAD

We'll talk in the next chapter about why it's so important to wear a well-designed (and adequately ventilated) bicycle helmet. If you do not wear a helmet, then you still need some equipment for your head. We consider a stocking hat essential for tours in all but the hottest weather, as we have already discussed. For very hot weather, a billed cap, preferably made of mesh material through which air can pass, is very useful in keeping the sun off your face and head. A visor is also useful this way. Give them a trial run, though, or you'll lose them on the first windy day! On very hot days you may also wish to tie a bandanna around your forehead or wear a sweat band, as perspiration will otherwise run into your eyes if you sweat much.

Sunglasses will save you much grief, cutting direct glare and also affording protection from sunburning your eyes. They also prevent you from squinting and tightening facial muscles, activity that makes you more susceptible to headaches. The sunglasses should fit snugly so they stay in place when your head is tilted downward in normal riding posture.

The skin on your face, as well as the rest of your body, needs protection when you are exposed to sun all day long, day after day, regardless of temperature. A sun block of some kind is especially important if you have fair skin or are traveling at high altitudes. Burned noses seem to be a particular mark of touring cyclists, and you must apply the sunblock repeatedly during the day, as it gets washed away by perspiration. You'll notice that the tops of your legs also tend to burn, as does the southern side of your calves. Sometimes you need to switch out of riding shorts into long pants for a day or two to give your skin time to recuperate.

HANDS

Your hands absorb more road vibration than any other area of your body. This can lead to serious and painful problems if you don't take precautions against it. What happens is that the nerve pathways in the hands and wrists become deadened by the vibration. Numbness and pain result. Women seem more disposed to this than men, although the latter are by no means immune.

Riding gloves are a helpful deterrent. Those with slightly padded palms are especially useful. They also give you a good grip on the handlebars, and aid you in performing the important functions of shifting and braking. They are of some help in insulating you from the cold conducted from your handlebars on chilly mornings.

You can purchase foam sleeves that go on your handlebars, which do even more to deaden road shock. These slip on above and below the brakes. Because they are made of foam, they absorb water in a rain, and also tend to wear out rather quickly under consistent touring conditions. Wrapping a layer of handlebar tape over them will help eliminate both problems.

For extensive mountain riding, or for spring and fall tours in some areas, a lightweight pair of wool mittens will save you much grief with cold hands. On extremely cold mornings, we have put hands and feet in plastic bags to cut the chilling effects of wind. Just save your grocery-store produce bags for this purpose.

SEATS

Your hands may absorb the most vibration and are the most sensitive to cold, but your seat gets the most wear on a bicycle tour. Until that part of you becomes accustomed to a day in the saddle, you will experience a certain degree of misery. It is much better to get yourself broken in before you leave home. If not, be prepared for several days of hurting, or even serious chafing.

To counteract these tendencies, we recommend riding in regular cyclist's riding shorts with a chamois crotch. The chamois gives you a firmer purchase on the seat, and lessens sideways sliding as you pedal. This in turn leads to less chafing. In addition, the chamois absorbs moisture, which also helps prevent chafing.

If you don't ride in riding shorts, then any garment which does not have exclusively heavy seams in the crotch will do. This becomes less important once you are broken in, but until that time, heavy seams can be especially irritating.

Other than your clothing, you can reduce problems of saddle soreness and chafing by thoroughly washing the salt off your skin each evening. Baby powder will soothe the skin and help prevent chafing during the day's ride. If nothing else works, try putting some additional padding under your crotch. One of us once used a disposable baby diaper to get over the first few days of road break-in. It was an inelegant, but effective, remedy.

FEET

The main requirement for footwear is that your foot be protected from the serrated edges of the pedals. Soles that are too thin will eventually transfer this pressure up into the balls of your feet and bring about soreness and discomfort.

Bicycle racers use shoes with thin, perforated leather uppers, and a thin leather sole reinforced by a metal shank. The shoe is light, aiding cycling efficiency, and the reinforced sole prevents soreness. The thin profile of these shoes also allows them to fit easily into toe clips.

Their only real disadvantage is that they do not work well off the bicycle. Walking in them very much will drive the metal shank right through the leather sole. If they have cleats (which fit down into the pedal and greatly increase your pedaling efficiency), they are awkward to walk in when shopping or sightseeing.

These limitations of the racer's shoe gave rise to a modified touring shoe. These look like jogging shoes, but usually have reinforced soles to prevent soreness. They also can be used for walking, and are thus an excellent compromise. Several companies make them, and they can be ordered by mail if a bicycle shop near you doesn't have them (see Appendix 5 for mail-order equipment suppliers).

Recently, we have toured in ordinary running shoes. They are readily available, and the soles are thick enough so that pedal pressure hasn't been a problem. Their versatility for other uses also makes them desirable, so that we need carry only one pair of shoes on a tour. We wash them about every other time we do a laundry. While they're not as efficient as our old racing shoes, they've more than made up for it in convenience and versatility.

Some touring cyclists ride without socks, or in peds, which works well in most conditions. We do recommend, however, that you at least carry with you one pair of heavy wool socks for wearing in the tent at night, or for riding in on cold days. Otherwise, the metal from the pedals and toe clips conducts the cold into your feet, leaving them feeling like globs of ice. For extensive cold-weather riding, you might consider a pair of insulated foot warmers, which cover your shoe but leave the sole exposed where it comes in contact with the pedal. These are available in well-equipped bicycle stores and from some mail-order houses.

BODY

We'll talk in Chapter 5 about why you need to have along some special items in order to keep your body warm and dry. In addition to windbreaker and wool sweater for cold and wet weather, we carry three T shirts of cotton or a cotton-acrylic blend. Cotton does a better job of breathing, but the blends dry faster. In any case, make certain that you choose bright, light colors. This helps automobiles see you, and is especially important in hot days in helping reflect the sun's rays away from your body. We have also found a cotton turtleneck helpful for cold-weather riding or for wearing in camp on chilly evenings. A long-sleeved blouse or shirt is useful as an extra insulating layer, and can be used for dress-up occasions if you wish.

For your legs, we suggest you carry slacks or pants made of synthetics, rather than all-cotton jeans or corduroys—cotton fabrics take too long to dry out, and jeans are heavy to carry.

Clothing Checklist

1 pair riding shorts
3 pairs of riding socks
1 nylon windbreaker or parka
1 wool sweater
3 cotton T shirts
1 pair riding shoes
1 pair riding gloves
1 hat or scarf
3 changes of cotton or cotton-blend underwear
1 pair casual shoes
1 pair of slacks
1 bathing suit
1 pair of sunglasses
1 wool cap
1 large bandanna

EQUIPPING YOUR BICYCLE

If you don't own a bicycle and must buy one for touring, then you need to spend as much time as possible talking with people who ride, and with dealers, and doing some reading in sources specializing in the subject. Tim and Glenda Wilhelm's *The Bicycle Touring Book, Delong's Guide to Bicycles,* by Fred Delong, and *Bike Touring: The Sierra Club Guide to Outing on Wheels,* by Raymond Bridge, are three recent publications that cover the subject of touring bicycles more extensively than we are able to do here.

If possible, try to ride the bicycle before you buy it. You will find that most bicycle dealers are glad to let you do this, at least for short rides. If you're fortunate enough to have a friend who will let you ride his or her bicycle for long periods, do it.

The problem with selecting a bicycle for touring—unless you are used to riding a lot—is that many of the important qualities become apparent only slowly. The stiffness of the frame, the quickness of response in turns, the effectiveness of the brake, the positiveness of the derailleur, are all difficult to assess with complete confidence in just a short ride. It is impossible to assess, of course, if you don't ride the bicycle at all now, and just rely on the advice of others.

Given the complexity of choice that you must make between frame models and components, we suggest the following, if you are buying your first bicycle:

1. Read, and talk to experienced riders, as much as possible before starting out on your shopping trip. Bicycle terminology can be bewildering if you must absorb it all within a half-hour spent talking to a bicycle dealer.

2. Don't buy the most expensive model available. This does not mean that you won't get your money's worth, but only that some high-cost components may not be what you need on a touring bicycle. Moreover, you will find in reviewing literature on the subject that some low-cost bicycle components work better for touring than ones costing much more. Derailleurs are an important example of this point.

3. Buy your bicycle from a bicycle dealer, not off the floor of a discount house. An inexpensive bicycle may be fine for casual Sunday rides, but starting out on a tour on one usually means a sorry history of derailleurs impossible to adjust, brakes that don't work well, spokes

that break, rims that bend easily, and long hunts for elusive replacement parts when you are thoroughly fed up with the original equipment.

Beyond this general advice, there are a number of specific things you need to consider when buying a bicycle for touring in the West, or when equipping your present bicycle. Some of the things we suggest are relevant for touring anywhere, of course, but most are especially significant for Western touring, because of the great variety you can encounter in terrain and climate. We will begin with the most important factor, your bicycle's gears.

GEARS

For handling the West's terrain, you need a wide gear range on your bicycle. This need increases in proportion to the amount of equipment you carry. Low gears allow you to climb mountains at a fairly high cadence (revolutions of the pedals per minute), and thus to avoid excessive fatigue and knee strain. High gears are necessary for the long descents, and for valley riding.

You need a bicycle with at least ten gears, as only this can give you the high and low ends you need, with enough steps in between to make cycling efficient. Of these ten gears, your low gears are the most critical. You can always coast down a mountain if your highest gear won't allow you to put pressure on the pedals as you go along. But lacking a sufficiently low gear is torture on a mountain tour, or one in which you are crossing many hills. You just work much harder than you have to.

Exactly how low a gear you need depends on your strength, the terrain you are covering, and the amount of weight you are carrying. Gearing is usually measured in inches, which refers to the number of linear inches you will move forward with one complete revolution of the pedals. But unless you are familiar with this system, and have a gear chart available, it may be easier to think of gears in terms of the number of teeth on your bicycle sprockets. The two critical sprockets are the smaller front sprocket and the largest rear sprocket. These in combination give you your lowest gear.

If you are going to do any significant climbing, and if your bicycle is well packed with clothing and camping equipment, our general rule of thumb is to bring the tooth count of these two sprockets as close as possible. Thus if your large rear sprocket has thirty teeth, you need to think of getting your small front sprocket down near that number, preferably within about six teeth. Your gear thus would be 36×30. We have used this combination for several years in all kinds of terrain. But some touring cyclists want the two tooth counts the same. In some cases they do this by mounting a triple front sprocket (chainwheel), the smallest of which has only 26 or 28 teeth. They then mount a large rear sprocket with the same number.

For your largest gear, a large front sprocket of 50 teeth and a small freewheel sprocket of 14 teeth is fairly standard. This can vary also; some people want just a bit higher gear for pedaling the down side of the mountain.

If your present bicycle doesn't have these gears, incidentally, you don't have to run out and buy a new one. Gear changes, particularly on the rear sprocket, can be made fairly easily and inexpensively by your dealer. It is a bit more expensive to change front sprockets.

In any case, when you change any of your rear, or freewheel, gears, you normally should change all of them, and mount a new chain. Otherwise, the combination of new gears and old chain can bring on a chattering, and will lead to difficulty in shifting. Once you select your high and low gears, your dealer can help you in selecting the others to maximize your gear choice within these extremes.

HANDLEBARS

Almost all bicycles sold for touring have what are called dropped handlebars. These curve downward like rams' horns. Novices, or people getting back on bicycles after years of absence, invariably find them uncomfortable. In fact, they do put your body in a position where there is more strain on the arms and shoulders, and where vision forward and to the side is impaired, because your head is thrust naturally downward. But the advantages they offer in terms of bicycling efficiency makes it worthwhile for you to try getting used to them, if possible.

First, dropped handlebars put your body in the best possible position to deliver maximum power to your pedals. They allow you to use your arms when cycling, which is important in that it disperses energy expenditure over a larger portion of your body. In addition, the old upright handlebars place all your weight on your seat, which will fatigue you in other ways. Finally, dropped handlebars allow you to adapt to varying conditions, particularly wind.

If you were to tour only at 4 or 5 miles an hour, and if all the days were still, then you could probably get away with nearly any kind of handlebar. But with the wind conditions in certain parts of the

West, or on a windy day in any region, you soon will bless your low-handlebar riding position. For most tours, then, equipping your bicycle with dropped handlebars, then practicing on them until you feel comfortable, should be a top priority.

If for some reason you can't ride with dropped handlebars, then of course use the upright variety. You'll improve your vision somewhat, but your seat may become a bit more tired and you'll lose a little efficiency—but you still can tour with them. On windy days, you'll just have to do the best you can.

Whatever you do, don't take a set of dropped handlebars and turn them upward so the ends point right at you. This may look more comfortable, but it's highly inefficient. The danger of having these projections sticking out is obvious. Even more dangerous is the position of your brake levers under such an arrangement. The levers point right at you. Any sudden stop immediately throws all your weight on them, with great risk of locking your brakes and tossing you right over the front handlebars.

SADDLES

For years the grin-and-bear-it philosophy dominated the manufacture of the saddles available for serious bicyclists. These narrow, hard things were designed for racers, particularly males, who need maximum efficiency, and who will do nearly anything to cut weight. Happily, some companies now make saddles for the tourist. They are wider, offer a little padding, and yet are stiff enough to still be efficient. Women will be especially happy with these changes. The wider female pelvis just wasn't suited for racing saddles, but men also suffered from soreness and numbing.

Although the newer touring saddles take much of this away, they still take getting used to. Since your saddle acts as the fulcrum in a lever (your arms and legs are the ends of the lever), you lose efficiency if the saddle has springs in it and "gives" as you pedal. This is the major reason why touring saddles are unsprung. You'll appreciate this efficiency eventually, but the breaking-in period can be trying. Keep at it, and after a week or so of touring the problem will go away. Most modern saddles, incidentally, unless they are all leather, do not break in. It is up to your body to adapt.

ADJUSTING SADDLES AND HANDLEBARS

A knowledgeable bicycle dealer is the best one to help you adjust saddle and handlebar height. Getting the saddle too low (most common) makes cycling harder and less efficient. Too high saddle leads to overextension of the leg, and can lead to knee problems.

There are a number of methods for determining optimum saddle height, and if there is no one around to advise you, we suggest the following procedure: Have someone hold the bicycle by the handlebars, facing you. Align one of the pedal shafts so that its downward angle is the same as that of the tube running from the saddle to the sprocket assembly. While sitting lightly on the saddle, rest your heel on the pedal. Your leg should be slightly bent. Raise or lower the saddle until this leg position is reached.

The upward or downward tilt of the saddle is a matter for some experimentation. Try first of all to adjust it so the saddle top is parallel with the ground. Tilting the saddle backward will take some weight off the arms, but can make the crotch uncomfortable. Tilting it forward reverses this relationship. Try to ride long enough with each adjustment so that you're thoroughly familiar with its merits before changing things.

The distance of the seat from the handlebars is another matter for adjusting. A good rule of thumb is to slide the saddle forward or backward on its carriage so that you can place your elbow on the saddle's nose and just touch the top bar of your handlebars. You can experiment with this adjustment to suit yourself.

The handlebars themselves should be raised or lowered so that the place where your hands normally rest is about the same height as the saddle.

TIRES AND TUBES

Most bicycles sold in this country come equipped with 27-inch wheels. Some bicycles coming from Europe or Japan, and some built for racing or high-speed road work, will come equipped with a slightly smaller wheel, normally referred to as a 700-c tire.

Either size works well for touring. The advantage to having 27-inch tires is that finding replacements on the road is easier, as 70-centimeter tires are often hard to come by. It is rare to ruin a tire, and simple foresight will prevent you from wearing one out unexpectedly—but emergencies can happen. Often you must rely on stores such as Western Auto or Coast-to-Coast for replacements. This is particularly true in small towns. It is very, very rare for these establishments to handle 700-c tires.

The same argument can be made for tubes, and the valve system used. Two valve types are common, one similar to the valve used on car tires, the other used on French and Italian tubes and bicycle-racing tires. The first type is called a Schrader, and is the most common in this country. Again, there is no great advantage of one valve over the other for touring, but when you look for replacement tubes, Presta valves will be hard to find, even in bicycle shops. Fortunately, most 27-inch tires have Schrader valves, so both problems are solved at once.

You'll also have a choice of using a tube-type tire known as a clincher, or one most often referred to as a sew-up. The latter were designed for racing, and have a very thin tube encased in a thin-walled tire, the lips of which have been sewn together. If you already have such tires, you are familiar with their merits, as well as the difficulty in patching punctures. We don't recommend them for touring. Nearly anyone who has used them for such, including ourselves, can provide an unhappy litany of evenings spent fixing punctures, a tedious job, exceptionally hard on the fingers and palms.

Fortunately, with the development of high-pressure rim and tire systems, you can get tube-type tires that inflate to very high pressures —from 85 to 110 pounds—giving you nearly as fast a ride as a sew-up. We recommend that you convert to these tires, or buy a bicycle which has them on it. The high pressure reduces road friction, making cycling easier and faster. Special touring models are now available which have a slightly raised rib in the center, which gives the tire a bit softer ride and adds to its longevity.

Such high-pressure tires come in varying widths, or thicknesses, usually running from 25 to 32 millimeters. The heavier ones are more resilient and better for most touring conditions, although not quite as quick as the more slender tires.

How long will such a tire last? That is difficult to say. Some people claim to have received 4,000, even 5,000 miles of use out of a modern high-pressure tire. This may be true for the front wheel, but we've never come close to that on rear tires, which carry most of the weight and receive the most friction. Depending upon load, road system, and how scrupulous we are in keeping them properly inflated, we get about 2,000 miles on a rear wheel, and about double that on a front. You can equalize this and extend wear by rotating tires.

Many cyclists tour with a spare tire twisted first into a figure eight, then with the two resulting loops tied together to form a smaller package. A dealer can show you how to do this. We don't carry a spare tire because of the extra bulk, and instead use a blowout repair kit suggested to us by a bicycle dealer in Spokane, Washington. It consists of a piece of old sew-up tire with the rubber tread peeled off, and a tube of Contact glue. In cases where the tire fabric is ruptured either by a blowout or a bad cut, we glue the piece of fabric on the inside of the tire, wait about fifteen minutes for it to dry, then put in a new tube (we do carry two tubes on long trips).

We've only had two instances in all our tours where a tire actually blew out. More common is to have it badly sliced. But in all cases our repair kit stood us in good stead, allowing us in one instance to travel over 250 miles on a badly cut tire until we got to a town with a bicycle shop that had a replacement.

WHEELS

Probably as important as anything on a touring bicycle is the wheel itself. Most critical are the spoke gauge and the strength of the rim. Bicycle wheels are "laced," or built, with varying spoke patterns. A dealer can detail the relative merits of these various patterns. What we would suggest is that if you have any money to spare, get your rear wheel built to the strongest possible specifications by the best dealer in town. This means a heavy-duty lacing pattern and heavy-gauge spokes made of the strongest possible alloy.

While you can change a flat tire relatively easily, changing broken spokes is difficult, and unless you are better than most touring bicyclists, you will pull your hair out trying to bring the wheel back in true after installing the new spoke. The best way to avoid this is to start with a strong, well-built wheel.

You aren't likely to break front-wheel spokes unless you hit something very hard or have an accident. The problem is almost always restricted to the rear wheel. Moreover, once spokes start to break, there seems to be a domino effect that causes others to follow suit. For our last tour, we had both our rear wheels completely rebuilt with new rims and 14-gauge spokes by an excellent dealer in town. In something close to 8,000 miles, carrying exceptionally heavy loads on sometimes badly paved roads, we broke about four spokes between the two of us. The initial cost was worth every cent to us.

You will need to carry extra spokes with you, as well as a freewheel remover for replacing rear wheel spokes that break on the freewheel side. They can't be replaced with the freewheel on. We cover these items in our list of repair and spare parts, below.

SELECTING BICYCLE ACCESSORIES

The well-equipped touring bicycle will have a number of accessories on it. What they are will depend to some extent on where you are touring, how much you are carrying, and your personal tastes. Some of these, such as a tire pump, you can't leave home without. Others are optional. Here are the accessories you should consider.

MAINTENANCE AND REPAIR EQUIPMENT

The most important maintenance-and-repair accessory is your tire pump. You can't tour without one. Buy the best you can afford; cheap pumps nearly always lead to poor performance, particularly when you need them the most.

Another helpful item to have along is a small piece of rag for wiping rims or your hands after changing a tire. An old toothbrush and a small plastic vial of alcohol are useful in cleaning chains and other moving parts, such as derailleur cogs. Keeping your tire rims clean with the cloth and alcohol will make your brakes more efficient. For lubricating chains, freeing sticky cables, and the like, we carry a small can of W-D 40. It has been invaluable.

As for tools, we favor carrying a minimal supply, and stick pretty much to nonspecialized items such as pliers and wrenches, since neither of us is a mechanic. The only specialized tools we think everyone should have are a freewheel remover and a spoke wrench. It is not difficult to change spokes, but you do need the tools, and bicycle shops are often 200 or 300 miles away. The remover weighs little, and the spoke wrench is even smaller. Ask your dealer to make certain your remover fits your freewheel, as there are several designs and sizes.

As for more specialized tools, whether you carry them is a matter of choice. Most of the things that go wrong on a bicycle are minor, and can be fixed with a bit of patience and common sense. But if you are a skilled bicycle mechanic, you may want to carry some specialized tools. At various times in our touring, we have found cone wrenches, a crank tool, and a suitable run of quality open-end wrenches to be extremely useful for more serious repair work. In the few instances when we had serious problems that we were not able to fix ourselves, such as badly worn crank bearings, we were always able to hobble to a bicycle shop for repairs.

Here is a basic kit we carry. You may add to it if you wish:

Tools

1 4-inch crescent wrench
1 pair small pliers
1 set of good wire snips for clipping brake and derailleur cables (A combination needle-nose pliers and snips is especially useful.)
1 medium screwdriver
1 freewheel remover
1 spoke wrench
1 tire repair kit, with extra patches and two tubes of glue
1 set tire irons
1 piece of old sew-up tire and a tube of contact cement for repairing blown-out or slashed tires

Spare Parts

2 brake cables
1 long derailleur cable (to fit either front or rear derailleur)
4 spokes
1 tube per person
1 tire, or the blowout repair kit listed under tools. An assortment of small nuts and bolts that will fit luggage racks, water-bottle holders, etc.
1 12-inch piece of wire (for holding things together when you don't have the proper bolt)
1 roll of handlebar tape (handy for all sorts of things)

TOE CLIPS

Toe clips, or traps, are devices attached to the pedals to hold your foot in place. Originally they were designed for racing, but most tourists have adopted them also. The traps can aid in cycling efficiency, and we find them helpful on long bumpy descents in keeping our feet firmly on the pedals.

Some cyclists worry that their feet will not slide out in an emergency. It's possible, but not nearly to the extent that the uninitiated fear. Since traps are fairly inexpensive, we suggest you mount them on your bicycle and give them a good trial before deciding you can't live with them. It'll help if you ride with them at first on uncrowded roads, with the straps loose. With some use, you'll become accustomed to them. When using them on tour, snug them up for regular use, but loosen the strap for riding in towns or heavy traffic.

FENDERS

Most touring bicycles, particularly in the West, are not equipped with fenders. This is because most cyclists don't ride in the rain, and if they do, they figure that they're getting so soaked on top that a little more on the legs or up the back won't matter much. In our own experience, we have bounced back and forth from having them to not having them. Currently we are in the not-having-them stage. When we had them, they were particularly helpful in riding just after the rain, or when fog had made the pavement unusually wet. In hard rains, they give the lower legs and feet some protection against road splash. Given our own ambivalence, we suggest you look carefully at the climates in which you will be touring, and make up your mind based on that.

LIGHTS

There is really no perfect solution to the problem of finding a decent bicycle light. Those run by a generator put drag on your wheel. Those run by batteries are often poorly made, and even when they're good, they won't hold up for many nights of extensive riding.

We have handled the entire problem by trying never to ride at night. On the few occasions we have been forced to do so, we rigged some sort of flashlight with a red bandanna, and strapped it onto a pannier. This gave a little assurance against being rear-ended, but did nothing to bring us to the attention of oncoming traffic or helping us see anything. Thus we can recommend it only as an emergency solution, and never for distances that are very great. If you do intend to do much night riding, then the best choice is to go to a generator-powered system, and live with the decrease in your pedaling efficiency.

WATER BOTTLES

Most bicycle water bottles are fairly similar. We recommend that you mount two of them for touring, one just below the other (but leave enough room to get the bottom one out!). Another possibility is to mount a quart water bottle, which is about double the normal half-liter capacity. These quart bottles are rectangular in shape, and we have seen bicyclists mount two of these for long-distance riding. If you can't find them elsewhere, you can order them from Hartley Alley's Bicycle Touring Shop, one of the equipment suppliers we list in Appendix 5.

For camping in places where water is not available, it is very difficult to carry enough of it in just your bicycle water bottles. There are a number of options. Most useful are liter bottles made of pliable plastic that have a stopper, plus a screw-on cap. Usually any backpacking store will have a variety of sizes. These can be stuck away in a pannier pocket, or attached to your bicycle.

We also carry a collapsible water container. After years of trying various kinds, we have found the best to be one comprised of a thin plastic membrane with an outer shell of tough nylon. These fold up to a size smaller than your fist, yet will hold up to 2 gallons of water. A number of companies make them. Ones with two carrying straps are the most convenient for attaching to a bicycle. See Appendix 5 for addresses of mail-order sources if you can't find these close to home.

PANNIERS

Panniers are packs, usually made of waterproof nylon, that straddle the front or rear wheels of a bicycle; they are your primary means of carrying gear. Unless you are touring with a support vehicle, you will undoubtedly mount some sort of pannier, usually on your rear carrier.

Because panniers carry most of your clothing and equipment, their choice is important. You must make an accurate assessment of how much gear you will be carrying, as panniers come in a variety of sizes, with capacities ranging from little more than 1,000 cubic inches to nearly 3,000. Panniers normally fasten over the rear wheel, but smaller sets are made for the front wheel. A second set allows for better distribution of weight, an important factor in preventing excessive tire wear and problems with broken spokes.

But don't run out and buy the largest set of panniers you can find. You will be amazed at how easily you fill them, often with things you don't really need. If you haven't toured before, lay out all the things you're thinking of carrying, put them in a sack, and go to the nearest bicycle store to see how large a set of panniers you will need. Such an expedition can bring a sobering awareness of how much you can—or cannot—carry.

Try to compare a number of pannier brands before buying, since weight of material used will vary, along with quality of workmanship. In general, look for heavy-gauge nylon—8-ounce is the best—as well as for heavy-gauge zippers. Look to see how easily the panniers come on and off the bicycle, and the strength of the devices which attach them. We list a number of equipment suppliers in Appendix 5, in case you can't find what you need near you.

HANDLEBAR PACKS

Handlebar packs are so useful that nearly every touring cyclist you see will have one mounted. They carry a myriad of things that you need to get at during the day—camera, snacks, windbreaker, maps, tools, sunglasses, diaries, books. Most also have a map pocket on top, absolutely crucial for navigating. Like panniers, handlebar packs are made in a variety of sizes, and usually of waterproof nylon. The better ones usually fasten onto some sort of auxiliary rack, so that you have full use of the handlebars when you ride. It is important to mount the handlebar pack on your bicycle before buying it, to make certain that the bottom doesn't ride on your wheel or front fender. This problem is common on very short bicycle frames. Some packs have a bottom support built in; some use a rack to keep it up off the wheel.

We find that packs with a number of pockets allow easier access to small items such as snacks, money, pocket knife, Chapstick, and allow us to get many of these items out while still riding, which is convenient.

TRAILERS

Since our son was two years old, he has accompanied us on our bicycle tours. He has traveled some 15,000 miles so far in his trailer, including considerable around-town riding. A number of companies now make trailers built specifically for carrying children, or trailers with adapter seats for that purpose. All of these are much safer and more humane for long tours than a child's seat fitted on your rear carrier.

Whoever is pulling the trailer will notice additional drag, caused by the extra wheels and weight. On level ground, with a moderate load, this usually will mean dropping one or two gears lower than normal. In pulling mountains, you need a no-nonsense mountain gear, preferably approaching a one-to-one ratio between small chainwheel and large freewheel sprockets. It will still be hard, and you need to be in good condition to do it. Since most trailers are quite spacious, you need to resist the temptation to overload them with things you don't need.

The trailer should have a seat belt, and should give the child some protection if you and the trailer tip. Although there is some risk with the latter, it is not nearly so hazardous as carrying a child in a seat attached to your rear carrier, which gives no protection to the child in case of a spill. In our experiences with the trailer, we have upset three times. There was no damage to the child on any of these occasions.

While on tour, one of us rides behind the trailer most of the time. When Benjamin was young, he would throw stuff out if we didn't. But the main reason was that with our Cannondale Bugger, the child faces backwards, and riding behind allows for talking, games, and even some preliminary kindergarten instruction on the road.

We mount two flags on the trailer, in addition to a variety of reflectors and reflecting tape. The width of the trailer forces you out a bit farther into the traffic lane, and you must compensate for this with extra defensiveness. If you have to go into the gravel part of the shoulder, incidentally, the trailer actually gives you stability.

We carry a waterproof nylon anorak with hood for rainy or cold weather, and wrap Benjamin's legs and feet in plastic. We don't ride in heavy rain. Since the child rides facing backwards, he actually is less susceptible to rain and cold wind than we.

In practice, a child traveling in a trailer is usually less of a problem than a child traveling in a car. Opportunities to sightsee and play games are great, and the fact that bicyclists usually stop and rest more often than automobile drivers allows for plenty of variation. In our case, and in the case of other families we know who tour with children, most of the adapting has to be done by the parents. You must be willing to give a little at day's end when you are tired and the child is full of energy. You also need to exercise some inventiveness in thinking up games or things to talk about. Over the years, Benjamin has adapted very well to touring life, and knows there are limits to how much attention we can pay him when climbing (or going down) hills, when riding in traffic, or in windy or rainy weather.

It is impossible to say what effect such extensive traveling has had on our own child, as we lack any basis for comparison. But it certainly has enriched our lives, kept us close as a family, and exposed him to a rich background of places and people he otherwise wouldn't have known. For all the evenings we were tired and he was rambunctious, the times we had to invent games and stories to amuse him, and the extra effort we had to put out to pull him and his equipment up mountains, we have been rewarded many times over.

CHOOSING CAMPING GEAR

SHELTER

Some cyclists carry no shelter at all, and alternate between sleeping under the stars and finding someplace to hide when it rains. While you gain a certain weight advantage with such a system, it hardly seems worthwhile if you are in an area where you risk getting rained on. One night spent dodging raindrops is usually one too many, at least for most of us.

If you don't want to just wing it, but also don't want a real tent, try a simple nylon tarp or plastic sheet which you can form with a string and rocks into some sort of A-frame or lean-to. You pick up a pound or two of weight that must be carried, but you can camp nearly anyplace you can find to string it, and the protection you get is well worth it. Initial cost is low also.

The disadvantages of such an arrangement is that it won't keep out a heavy, blowing storm. None will keep out mosquitoes. Also, any place your sleeping bag touches the tarp, it is likely to "sweat." That is, the fly or tarp will trap the water vapor passing out of your bag and condense it back onto the shell of the bag. This wetting can sometimes be significant.

An improvement on this situation which does not add much weight is a single-shell waterproof-nylon tent. The cost is a bit more, but it will keep the bugs out and will provide more protection in a real downpour. It has the same sweating problems as a simple tarp, if not greater, as there is usually less opportunity for air to circulate through it and carry evaporated sweat out into the night. This can be overcome to some extent by not allowing your bag to touch the sides.

In the past several years, shelter manufacturers have developed something called a bivouac (or "bivy") sack, or sleep sack, usually made of Gore-Tex fabrics (see Chapter 5 for a discussion of Gore-Tex). You put your sleeping bag into the bivy sack, which is only a bit larger than the bag. Simple curved wands are used to keep the bivy sack off your head, shoulders, and feet, and a panel of mosquito netting is sewn in right above your face for use on rainless nights. A flap comes down for bad weather. The sacks are exceptionally lightweight, and work reasonably well, although in a heavy downpour you may still get some condensation on the inside, as your body vapors have trouble getting out. Their greatest limitation is that they are not anything you'd want to spend thirty-six hours in, waiting out a rain. They are meant for sleeping only, and unless you are one of the rare souls without a scintilla of claustrophobia, and have a high boredom threshold to boot, you'll need to get out of them once you wake up. Bivy sacks come in both single and double sizes.

This brings us to the optimum sort of shelter, and the one we recommend if you can afford it, which is a nylon tent of breathable (uncoated) fabric with a separate, coated nylon rainfly. They weigh more than other shelters, and initial cost jumps significantly, but a well-constructed tent of this kind is bugproof, won't sweat, and is essentially stormproof. Tents can be set up anywhere, particularly the freestanding types that don't need to be staked out.

Look carefully at the sewing job done on these tents—or on bivy sacks—as quality varies widely. All seams should be sewn double, and all stress points reinforced. Floors particularly bear looking at. Rarely will you get leakage from the roof or sides, but water is likely to pool around the edges of the tent or underneath the floor, then seep in through floor seams. Insidiously, it will soak your bag without your realizing anything is happening, as you feel nothing splashing down on your face. Ideally, there should be no seams at the edge of the tent where floor meets wall. There should also be as few seams as possible running across the floor, as these are potential leak spots. You can buy a commercial nylon seam sealer that will help.

The weight of such tents varies from around 5 to 9 pounds. All sleep two people, so the weight can be shared if you're traveling with someone else.

SLEEPING BAGS

The most important thing about a sleeping bag is its filling. You'll find bags filled with either an artificial fiber or with natural goose or duck down. A few manufacturers try to combine the merits of both kinds of fill, and make the bottom of artificial fill and the top of down. The reason for this is that the artificial fill condenses less under your weight, and thus provides more thickness for insulation from the ground.

A sleeping bag insulates you from the cold because the fill creates thousands of tiny air pockets, which retard loss of body heat. Pound for pound, down is the most efficient at doing this. It also packs tighter, and in general it will have a longer life than a bag with artificial fill. Its disadvantages are its cost and, to a lesser extent, its limitations when wet. Artificial fibers are easier to dry, and most will continue to insulate you fairly well even if they get sopping wet. Artificial-fill bags are easier to wash than down, which requires either careful handwashing or a dry-cleaning by an establishment that keeps its solvent clean and knows how to handle down.

How much of either filling—down or artificial fibers—you need to keep you warm in the West depends upon where you'll be touring and how cold or warm you sleep. It also will vary depending upon whether you are in a tent or not, and what you have between you and the ground. But generally speaking, we recommend buying a bag from a reputable manufacturer who indicates the bag should keep you warm to 25 degrees Fahrenheit. In most instances you won't need this much insulation, but manufacturers vary as to how they assign thermal ratings, and within reason, it is better to err on the side of conservatism than risk a tour with cold nights. For tours entirely in the coastal valleys, or the Southwest, you can get away with a lighter bag. But even here nights can occasionally get cold, particularly at higher elevations.

A well-constructed down bag that meets these requirements can weigh as little as 2½ pounds. An equivalent fiber-filled bag, equally well constructed, will weigh from 3 to 5 pounds and will take more space when packed. While a down bag costs at least half again as much as the other kind, and often more, our experience has been that if you can afford it, and if you use it long enough, your investment will be more than repaid. Our own down bags are in their tenth season, and still maintain most of their initial insulating qualities. One of them has been stuffed in and out of its sack over a thousand times.

Whichever kind of bag you choose, consider these guidelines:

1. The shell should be of nylon. Anything else usually means inferior quality, and will be bulkier and heavier to carry.

2. The side zipper should be at least 72 inches long. It should be a double zipper that will open from either end. These features will allow you to ventilate the bag easily on warm nights.

3. The inside and outside of the bag should not be stitched together quilt-fashion. This reduces the loft, or thickness, and will produce cold spots at the stitching.

4. The bag should be tapered toward the feet ("mummy" or "modified mummy"). This saves on weight and is more efficient since your feet are your body's poorest heat-producers.

5. If you are traveling with someone, you can zip two bags together, if their zippers match. We now carry only one semi-rectangular down bag, which unzips so it lies flat. We sleep on foam pads and throw the bag over us. This saves enormously on weight and bulk we have to carry, and the arrangement keeps us warm down into the low 20s if we add extra clothing. Our foam pads are covered with washable nylon fabric, which we launder the same way and as often as one launders sheets.

6. Make certain your bag's stuff sack is waterproof. If there is any doubt (most leak at the seams in hard rain), wrap all of it in plastic when rain threatens.

SLEEPING PADS

We recommend you carry either an open-cell foam pad, or a thinner, closed-cell pad, rather than an air mattress. Besides going flat in the night, air mattresses conduct heat away from your body when the ground is cold. This heat loss can be significant, particularly with a down bag, since it compresses under your body. If you use an open-cell foam (generally the more comfortable), it helps if it is covered with nylon. You can then use it as a sitting pad outside the tent. If the pad is a closed cell material such as Ensolite, it is a bit less comfortable, but usually is a better insulator. It also can be rolled up into a smaller space.

Within the past several years, some manufacturers have tried to combine the comfort of an air mattress with the insulating qualities of foam. The result is a self-inflating mattress whose interior is composed of open-cell foam. The exterior is of nylon that is snag- and puncture-resistant, and the mat insulates you as well as anything. The complexity drives up the cost, but those who have used them swear by them.

STOVES

If you carry a stove, most likely it will be a single-burner model. Fuel will be either propane, butane, white gas, or kerosene. Each fuel type has its merits.

Propane or butane stoves are easy to light, their fuel cartridges don't leak, and they can be used safely inside a tent, providing you are careful with them and leave a flap open for ventilation. On the other hand, the fuel cartridges are expensive, sometimes hard to find, and not refillable. Butane stoves take longer to heat things than do white-gas or kerosene stoves, and do not function at peak efficiency when the cartridges get very cold, reducing the interior gas pressure.

Liquid-fuel stoves, either with white gas or kerosene, are better at heating, use less fuel, function better in extremely cold weather, and use less expensive fuel. Their disadvantages are that they cost more to buy, are more difficult to light, and are sometimes hard to regulate at low burn levels. Some of them also must be primed with a separate fuel before they will catch. With most, too, you usually must carry an extra fuel bottle. Finally, it is not recommended that you use them inside a tent, as they give off noxious gases.

In spite of their disadvantages, liquid-fuel stoves are probably the better choice for most touring in the West. The main problem with butane stoves is finding cartridges. In order to be certain that you don't run out, you have to carry at least one extra, and in some of the more sparsely populated regions, we have carried up to three extra cartridges. Current costs run well above $2.50 a cartridge, which makes cooking more and more expensive.

Liquid-fuel stoves, on the other hand, particularly those that use white gas, are more efficient, and fuel can usually be found anywhere. Most cyclists carry a 1-liter fuel bottle, and when in a campground just ask a car camper if he or she will sell that amount. Often the fuel is simply given away.

Some excellent books now on the market deal with single-burner cooking and allow you to extend your culinary scope. A recent one, John Rakowski's *Cooking on the Road,* gives an excellent review of one-burner stoves. We list this and some of the others in the Bibliography.

COOK SETS

The most convenient cook set is one whose pots nest inside one another. Those designed for a single person are usually flimsy, and make frying difficult because of the thinness of the aluminum. For this reason, we prefer a two-person set, even if one of us is traveling alone. Some newer cook sets are coated with Teflon or similar material, which is a great help. We supplement our regular set with a separate Teflon frying pan with folding handle.

You can buy interlocking flatware sets that come in plastic cases. These are convenient and easy to store. A Swiss Army knife is a great convenience, particularly one with can opener and an assortment of knife and screwdriver blades. If you are so inclined, get one with a corkscrew also.

We carry biodegradable liquid soap in a small plastic container. For cleanup, we prefer disposable paper rags, which we pack between the nesting pots to keep them from scraping one another or rattling in the panniers. The disposable rags actually last a very long time, and they dry out much more quickly than cotton.

Cooking Equipment Checklist

Nesting cooking pots with frying pan and pot gripper
Stove, fuel
Collapsible water container (minimum 1 gallon)
Cup
Flatware
Salt, pepper, and other condiments in spillproof containers
Pocket knife with can opener
Pot cleaner, disposable dishcloths
Dish soap (biodegradable)
Extra plastic bags
Nylon food bag that can be suspended from trees to keep animals out

Basic First Aid Kit
(Supplement according to individual needs)

Adhesive bandages
Gauze
Adhesive tape
Liquid antiseptic
Antibacterial cream
Aspirin
Vitamin C
Elastic bandage
Scissors
Insect repellant
Cotton-tipped applicators
Safety pins
Flashlight

While you're on the road

No matter how carefully you've planned a tour, how enjoyable it is depends largely on how you handle day-to-day situations on the road. In this chapter we will discuss some of these situations, especially those that crop up most often in the West—mountain riding, extremes of heat and cold, general safety, the logistics of food and water supply, and camping away from organized campgrounds. We end with some observations on traveling alone and with others, and some important information about transporting your bicycle to and from your tour.

RIDING ON MOUNTAIN ROADS

The fact that mountain riding is more strenuous than most other kinds is obvious. Anyone venturing out on a mountain tour should be physically and mentally ready to handle the contingencies it imposes. But in addition to being in condition to handle mountain travel, there are a number of demands made on you when traveling in Western ranges that are not typical of other regions.

UPHILL

For one thing, you'll find that roads through mountain passes are longer and peak at higher elevations than elsewhere in the United States. It is not at all unusual to have climbs of 15, 20, and even 30 miles to passes in the Rockies, Cascades, or the Sierra Nevada. The sheer distance calls for some special considerations. Rarely can you rush such a climb. You have to be willing to relax a bit and plug along. Sometimes you will have to camp on the way up such a pass road, continuing on to the summit the next day. There are some climbs that cyclists spend three days getting over.

To many cyclists, this may seem more like an ordeal than it is a vacation. But in fact, for a cyclist in good condition, mountains present a demanding but not exhausting experience. Depending upon your physical condition, the gearing on your bicycle, and the steepness of the ascent, most mountain pass roads are fairly gradual climbs for much of their length. The very difficult part usually comes near the end, particularly in the last 4 miles or so. Up until then it is a slow, laborious process, but not one that leaves you dead if you can pace yourself properly.

Thus for most conditioned cyclists—either people who have ridden long distances frequently before leaving home or tourists who have been on the road for three weeks or more—handling long passes as much a matter of mental and psychological adjustments as it is physical strain. But the adjustments must be made if you are not going to end up hating the mountain or bicycle touring in general.

Probably the first of these adjustments is actually liking mountains. If you don't, there is no reason in the world you should expect to enjoy a mountain tour, or one in which you must cross a good many passes. But even those of us who are thrilled by mountain scenery still must make adjustments in order to cope with the extra physical and mental discipline it takes to climb passes.

Different people use different means. Some see passes as challenges, pitting themselves essentially against the contour of the land. The summit becomes an exhilarating moment of personal victory. Others revel in the spectacular scenery mountain travel usually provides, indulging in pleasures of the senses, which soften the strain on muscles and lungs. Still others study the upward ascent as a series of microcosms, noting changes in bands of plant and tree life the higher they climb, watching changes in the nature of a river or stream bed, or looking for wildlife in the forest or rock above them. Still others liken high mountain cycling to soaring, catching vistas outward and downward normally reserved for birds or planes. In the end, most mountain travelers indulge in a bit of each of these.

We use these techniques as well. But we have found that the most important factor in climbing almost any hill is knowing where it ends. Not only is this critical for pacing, it avoids the desperation of looking around each bend and hoping you have reached the top, only to find the road rising further above you. Each turn then becomes a link in a chain of disappointments. In the end, you find yourself frustrated and angry.

Unless you have an odometer mounted on the front wheel of your bicycle to give you a mileage reading, the key to determining your position on a mountain or pass road is to become familiar with something called mileposts, or post markers. These small signs along the edge of the highway mark the distance that point on the road is from another point. Most highway departments start the mileage count for a highway at some obvious point—where the route begins, or where it crosses a state or county line.

The best way of finding out where a hill ends is to find out the number of the milepost closest to the summit. Our route guides in Chapters 6, 7, and 8, and some others you will find, give the number of the milepost (e.g., MP 82) nearest the point at which you'll cross a pass or hill, making it easy to chart your progress.

If you aren't using a route guide, then you have to find out the summit milepost by some other means. This is usually difficult, but if you can ask state patrol officers or highway maintenance workers who cover that particular road, they usually can tell you. If not, they can tell you about how many miles of climb you have—but be wary of such estimates, as motorists and cyclists have entirely different perspectives as to what constitutes a hill.

Lacking anyone to ask, you can use your highway map to try to estimate the distance to the summit. Unfortunately, some mapmakers are rather casual about putting a pass marking exactly where it belongs; and even if it's accurate, the nature of the marking itself makes it difficult to spot the summit. Nonetheless, using the map scale, you can make a fairly good guess as to the distance to the summit from some other point shown on the map, such as a crossroad, county line, or bridge. When you reach this point, make a note of the milepost, or get a reading from your odometer, and calculate from there.

Using mileposts is the most critical factor, in our opinion, in handling passes. By noting distance we can pace ourselves, schedule rest stops, or decide how much of the climb we'll leave for another day. We also use them in coming off a summit, particularly if we are looking for a campground on the way down, or want to avoid going too far down and running into private, fenced-in areas. Their use in other kinds of terrain, in fixing distances to the next town, water source, or evening's stopping point, is obvious. But the psychological boost they give in tackling passes is their most crucial function, eliminating the uncertainty over distance yet to be traveled, and how much longer you'll have to exert yourself before crossing over.

Beyond the mental preparation involved in such devices, there are some physical aspects of climbing that need to be dealt with. Of most importance is the pace you set going up the hill. Keep your cadence —the speed with which your pedals rotate—fairly high. Taking hills in too high a gear—one in which your legs turn slowly—is hard on your knees, calves, and bicycle power train. Don't push the hill so hard that climbing becomes erratic, where you are alternating between a fast rush and a labored reprieve while you get your breath.

You can also alternate standing and sitting. Each method of pedaling employs somewhat different muscles, and you'll give each group a bit of a rest while you employ the other.

DOWNHILL

As much attention as there is given to going up hills, there probably should be more given to going down—at least as far as safety is concerned. The high speeds you reach on long descents gravely lengthen your reaction distance and makes incidents that normally are not too serious potentially very dangerous.

Most are problems you might not worry about at first glance, such as brake failure or snapping brake cables. Although brakes suffer somewhat on a long downhill run, particularly if the bicycle is heavily weighted, a good set of brakes will lose only part of its effectiveness. If you alternate front and rear brakes, cut your speed down initially so there is not so much strain on them, and have performed simple maintenance tasks such as keeping your wheel rims clean, you'll have no trouble. Likewise, simply checking your brake cables regularly for wear will prevent any problems here.

Much more hazardous are errors in handling the bicycle. Because your available reaction time is so short, even a simple glance to the side can allow your bicycle to drift off the paved part of the roadway. Hitting gravel at a high speed carries a high risk of spilling, and of course the speed compounds all the effects of falling. Another hazard is drifting too far out to the left, either by trying to cut corners or from inattention. If you're in the path of an oncoming car, the combination of your speed and his spells disaster. One of us still bears scars from a descent in the French Pyrenees on a Sunday morning when the road should have been quiet and wasn't. We had half a second to choose between a head-on collision with a Citroën and a large swatch of gravel. Hitting the gravel at over 30 miles per hour put a damper on the rest of the day.

You will also notice that the handling characteristics of your bicycle when packed do not allow you to take bends at as high a speed as normal. You can bank less, and you must allow for this in taking turns. Even wind can be a problem. This is particularly true if you happened to use a freeway to climb a pass. Each car, and particularly each truck passing you on the down side pulls a very forceful wave of air in its wake. This air wave can push you to one side or the other quite unexpectedly.

To conclude, we suggest that when beginning a long descent, slow down right at the top, rather than waiting for your speed to build up first. This is much easier on brakes, and under normal conditions will eliminate all or most problems with brake fade. Then, because an accident suffered on the downhill can have such serious consequences, we suggest you keep your speed about 5 miles per hour slower than you really think it needs to be.

If this takes the thrill out of the long, fast run, try to get the thrill some other time—preferably when you are riding on an unpacked bicycle, near home, on familiar roads.

COPING WITH WEATHER

COLD

It is very natural to consider cold weather riding with mountain riding, as the two often occur together. Of course cold can strike anywhere, but most of your cold riding will be at high elevations, and most of it will occur in the mornings, just as you start out.

Remember that because you are moving through the air, it doesn't have to be excessively cold outside for you to get chilled—even though your body is producing heat as you cycle. A chilly 40-degree morning when there is a good bit of night moisture left in the air can leave you shivering with cold. And of course there are high mountain areas of the West when morning rides all through the summer often start in subfreezing temperatures.

We will not deal here with the cold you experience at night, once you have stopped. Having adequate shelter and a proper sleeping bag (discussed in the last chapter) will handle that. Here we discuss only riding in the cold.

You need to think about two things when riding in the cold. The first is staying warm, and the second is what to do if you do become chilled. Staying warm is largely a matter of proper clothing. Treating a cold body—particularly in instances where internal body temperature drops below normal—requires some special knowledge of diagnosis and treatment.

You lose heat most readily from your head, neck, face, armpits, and groin. Although you often feel cold at first in your hands or feet, more often than not this kind of chilling is more a discomfort than anything else. Basically, you need to dress in such a way that in cold weather your head and torso are well protected.

Given this, it won't take too long to realize that typical cycling clothing of shorts and T shirt won't do much for you if it gets cold. The additional clothing you need to have along with you on a tour is fairly simple. It is based on a system of layering, which allows you to adapt to a variety of conditions.

Begin with a wool sweater, preferably a pullover, with a coarse weave. Wool has special properties in keeping you warm, something we will get to in a bit. Add to this some sort of windbreaker, which keeps the chill wind out, and traps warm air and keeps it next to your body. A cotton or light wool turtleneck shirt is excellent for keeping the neck warm. Also include in your wardrobe a large scarf or bandanna for tying around your neck; you'll be amazed at how much heat loss you can prevent by using it. Finally, take along a wool stocking hat. You lose an incredible amount of heat from your head, and the old adage that says If your feet are cold, put on a hat, is absolute verity.

This should be basic for nearly any tourist in the West, whether heading high into the mountains or not. You can wear these clothes at night when it gets chilly, and they also serve as good rainy-weather gear, which we cover shortly. If your hands are sensitive to cold, a light pair of wool gloves or mittens will save you much grief on particularly cold mornings. A pair of heavy socks may be carried for your feet for both on and off the bicycle.

Most of these precautions against cold are matters of comfort. But there is another kind of cold that you need to be aware of, and that is an internal chilling, of becoming so cold that your vital internal temperature begins to drop below normal. This can lead to serious physical problems, and cyclists, because of increased exposure to chill winds, are particularly susceptible to it.

Consider this typical, and true, story. On a pleasant mountain morning a group of some thirty cyclists started westward from Estes Park in Colorado to cycle through neighboring Rocky Mountain National Park. (We described our own ride over this route earlier in this book.) The cyclists in the group were all in good physical condition. The sky that summer morning was cloudless, and it was comfortable to ride in shorts and short-sleeved shirts.

Sometime while the group was still climbing the eastern slopes, a few clouds began sliding in from the west. While their presence was scarcely noticeable from the drier eastern side, the clouds presaged a weather front moving in. Air temperatures began to drop, but the exertion of the climb kept most of the cyclists comfortable.

As the group broke timberline and began weaving along the road known as Trail Ridge, temperatures dropped more sharply. Clouds thickened and the wind picked up. Rain spattered the riders from time to time, wetting clothing already damp from perspiration.

The group did not stop to discuss it, but chose to go on, hoping to get off the high elevations before things got much worse. Cyclists hunched their shoulders. Some gobbled up candy or snacks carried to provide temporary energy and a bit of warmth. All kept going. Surprisingly, very few stopped to put on the extra clothing they had in their packs, most likely hoping that they could outrun the storm before they got any colder.

But high up on Trail Ridge, some members of the group were getting cold. Some were having trouble shifting gear levers with accuracy. Hands seemed a little clumsy, but the change was so subtle that neither they nor other members of the group noticed or thought much of it. Unknown to them, internal body temperatures were already dropping. In some it slid down only a fraction of a degree, but in a few cases much more.

Wind picked up, gusting to 35 miles per hour. Clouds had crept into the valleys below, and now boiled upward over the road. The moisture in the air drove the wind-chill factor even lower. More and more members of the group began to feel a bit awkward, some bodies stiffening, hands and arms moving mechanically. In others, shivering started, and they could not stop shivering.

Finally, the train of cyclists came to a disjointed halt. No one called the stop, but some consensus seemed to have been reached. People stood about in small clusters, some shivering excessively, but others apparently calm, not feeling the effects of the cold at all. Many still didn't bother to put on their sweaters.

When a park ranger arrived on the scene, he recognized the symptoms immediately. Some twenty-five out of the thirty-odd people in the group were suffering from some stage of hypothermia—an excessive drop in internal body temperature. If a ranger with twenty years' experience with winter rescues had not arrived, some of the cyclists would have become seriously ill, or might even have died. And the temperature that day never got below 32 degrees.

Hypothermia is sometimes called the killer of the unprepared. Its insidious nature is that it strikes through wind-chill factors, wetting through of garments, and loss of energy and strength due to exertion or poor conditioning as often as through subfreezing temperatures and blizzards. Worse, it impairs your judgment without you having any idea that it is happening. The cyclists on Trail Ridge never thought they should put on the extra clothing they had with them.

Because we bicyclists often dress so skimpily, we are susceptible to hypothermia if we don't take necessary precautions. Fortunately, riders use public roadways and help is usually available, so it is unlikely that hypothermia will ever end in tragedy. But becoming excessively cold can lower your resistance, and more importantly, it can disorient you, even in its early stages. This disorientation is excellent preparation for mistakes in judgment. If these mistakes occur on a steep downgrade when your speed has built up, then the side effects of hypothermia can be very grave indeed.

To prevent hypothermia, remember there are two broad stages through which the body passes. The first involves internal chilling, which necessitates getting the sufferer out of the elements and allowing the body to recuperate internal heat. The second stage is the more dangerous one, and that is when internal body temperatures drop so low that only an exterior source of heat can prevent the victim from sliding further and further into stupor, and ultimately death.

Briefly, this is the sequence of symptoms in hypothermia:

1. Slurred or stumbling speech
2. Numbness, clumsiness, shivering
3. Stumbling when moving
4. Unclear thinking or disorientation
5. Muscular rigidity
6. Unconsciousness, irregular heartbeat. If unattended and exposure continues, heart failure and death.

If you feel it happening to you—or, more likely, if you observe it happening to someone else—here is what to do:

1. Get out of the wind (and rain). In Wyoming one afternoon, we felt a significant threat of hypothermia. We pitched our tent right

over clumps of low sagebrush and got inside it until we could dry off and warm up.

2. Once you get sheltered, get out of wet clothing. Put on a dry T shirt, add your wool sweater, stocking hat, scarf, and windbreaker. Except for wool, don't put anything wet next to the skin.

3. Take in some high-energy food if you have it. Sweets or honey, crackers, bread, and cookies are all fine. Rubbing your sides or doing isometric exercise will help produce body heat. If you still feel chilled, crawl into a sleeping bag.

4. If a person gets to a point of severe disorientation, mumbling, or unresponsiveness, he or she must have an external heat source. One of the most effective methods is to strip both yourself and the victim and slip into a sleeping bag together. Hot water bottles are also helpful, but not as effective as your own body heat. Hailing a car and getting the victim to warm shelter or a medical aid center should be an immediate priority.

HEAT

You may encounter hot weather in any part of the West, even in coastal areas or high mountains where you might not normally expect it. But because certain areas of the West—the Southwest, the Great Basin, southeastern Washington, eastern Oregon, and the agricultural valleys of southern and central California—regularly have daytime temperatures in the 90s and 100s, most of our remarks will be directed at helping you meet the conditions in these areas. Of course the same advice can be modified to meet your needs anytime it becomes excessively hot.

There is a pattern to heat buildup during the day that the bicyclist ought to be aware of. Even in the hottest regions, mornings are reasonably cool, or at least not blistering. As the day wears on, it becomes increasingly hot until the warmest part comes in the afternoon, usually around two to four o'clock. Temperatures gradually taper off as sundown approaches; after sunset, they drop more rapidly.

Your typical bicycling progress interacts with this pattern. Most bicyclists start reasonably early in the morning, and are on the road by 9:00 A.M. As heat builds up, your body, which has been rehydrated by the fluids you drank the previous evening and this morning, begins to lose liquid in the form of sweat, which evaporates and cools you.

So far so good. The problem starts when, on very hot days, you start to lose fluids faster than you take them in. Unfortunately, your thirst mechanism doesn't work very well at this point. You normally will lose a significant amount of fluids before you feel thirsty. Because you don't feel particularly thirsty, you don't drink. By the time you do start feeling thirsty, you may have lost so much fluid that you have difficulty drinking enough to replace it, or you simply don't have enough with you to replace it.

By then it may be into the afternoon, air temperatures are at their maximum, and if you can't sweat enough, core temperatures of the body will begin to rise, producing heat illness.

All of this is a fairly technical explanation of something simple. You must drink enough to maintain fluid levels, and in hot weather you must drink *before* you feel thirsty. Finally—and this is most important—there are times of the day when air temperatures reach such levels that you shouldn't be bicycling. You simply cannot carry enough water to replace fluid loss, and even if you could, bodily evaporation isn't sufficient to cool you off.

It is difficult to give an exact temperature figure in which it is dangerous to ride. People adapt differently to heat. Some can't ride in temperatures in the high 70s without risking heat illness. Others do quite well right up through the high 90s or low 100s. It also depends on how hard you are cycling and on other weather conditions. Although most of the West has relatively low humidity, it does vary from region to region and even from hour to hour. Heavily irrigated fields can have high humidity levels. The higher the humidity, the less your body can cool itself through evaporation, and the hotter you'll become.

Finally, your ability to resist heat depends on how acclimatized you are to it. If you have lived and ridden in it for a long time, you will probably have fewer problems. This acclimatization can take place even over two or three weeks you are on tour.

Given all this, you must find your own level of heat tolerance, and be aware that it will vary from time to time. With this in mind, we offer the following guidelines and steps you can take to deal with heat.

1. Carry enough water on the bicycle so you can replace fluids as you lose them. In much of the West, the single half-liter water bottle fitted to most bicycles is not enough. In very hot weather you can lose up to 6 liters of water in a few hours. It is usually impossible to stop and fill up your little bottle often enough to compensate.

For our own hot-weather riding, in addition to our bicycle water bottles, we carry 1 liter per person in reserve. In desert riding, or for afternoon riding on very hot days, we carry a collapsible water container filled to about 6 to 8 liters. This gives us about 4 liters per person reserve. We have rarely used this much, but sometimes hot weather forces us to pull up short for a day, and we need that extra capacity for cooking that night and for minimal body clean-up, details we discuss presently.

2. Drink before you feel thirsty, and drink more fluids than your body seems to be asking for.

3. Slow down your pace. The amount of heat you produce is directly related to the amount of energy you expend.

4. Wear white or light-colored clothing to reflect heat away from your body. A white helmet or hat that allows air to pass through is also very useful. Some protection for your head is necessary; good air flow is needed if it is to function as an important part of your cooling mechanism; and you should keep the sun off it.

5. Acclimatize yourself to heat before your trip begins. If this is impossible, schedule a tour that gets all your riding in during the mornings for the first several days. Then gradually extend yourself into early afternoon, and finally to an all-day ride if this you wish.

6. If you can, stop in the shade for rests, or even in an air-conditioned café (but not a bar, unless you order Shirley Temples— alcohol and heat don't mix). Cold liquids stay in your stomach longer, and therefore are lost more slowly than hot drinks.

7. Add a small amount of glucose, or one of the electrolytic replacement products such as E.R.G., to your water bottle, particularly in the latter parts of the day. Some experts recommend about a 2 percent proportion of glucose to water. Too much, though, keeps the water from emptying out of your stomach. If possible, include in your diet foods such as bananas, peanuts, pears, almonds, spinach, and melons, which replace electrolytes.

8. A bandanna soaked in water and worn so it covers the nape of your neck is very helpful in cooling the blood flowing close to the surface of the skin in that area. Water sprayed into your hair is also excellent in cooling you.

9. If you begin to feel heat sickness, stop immediately. Get in the shade, start a gradual but regular intake of fluids, and if you have any extra water at all, soak your shirt with it. If you are not too nauseous, you may stand up to speed evaporation. But if you don't feel

well, try to lie or sit in a position that allows maximum evaporation from your head and torso.

RAIN

Unlike much of the country, where storms move in and out rather unpredictably, rainfall in the West follows patterns that are fairly steady.

On the Olympic peninsula in western Washington, for instance, it rains on and off all summer long. If you tour there, you must simply expect to ride in the rain.

In other parts of the West, rainfall patterns are predictable in another way. Much of the Southwest, the state of Wyoming, and mountain areas such as the Sierra, the southern Cascades, and the Rockies get afternoon rains, often in the form of thundershowers.

Still a third portion of the West gets virtually no summer rainfall at all. The southern desert regions of Arizona and New Mexico, Nevada, western Utah, most of California, and southern Oregon fall into this category. While you can get rained on during the summer in any of these regions, the chances are better than fifty-fifty that you will not.

Only the small portions of the West have unpredictable patterns— western Washington, central and northern Idaho, and western Montana, mainly. These regions are subject to cyclonic storms that move through in two or three days, and are difficult to forecast much in advance.

We make these observations because among cyclists who have not toured before, worries about what to do if it rains sometimes get blown out of proportion. In much of the West you won't be riding in the rain anyway. In another portion, rainfall patterns are fairly predictable, coming more often than not in the afternoon. Finally, in the rainier areas, storms usually last two or three days, not weeks, allowing you to last them out. In most cases in the West, you can ride around the rain, rather than in it, particularly if you know its patterns. This allows you to plan tours without undue concern about rain and also to adjust your foul-weather clothing requirements accordingly.

Clothing. You have a number of options regarding clothing. The first is to take along some sort of completely waterproof raingear. Most of this is made of polyurethane-coated nylon. The problem with coated nylon is that it does not breathe, and your body moisture has no way of escaping. Under the strenuous activity of bicycling, your own sweat starts to soak your clothing. You don't get as wet as if you were riding in the rain without protection, but you still get plenty wet. Moreover, waterproof raingear really can't be worn to ride in very cold weather either, because of the same problems of moisture buildup—and wet clothes conduct heat away from the body. Because of this, most cyclists don't use plain coated nylon.

Another option is waterproof raingear that is also breathable—that is, it will allow body vapor to pass out, but not let rainwater in. A number of manufacturers market such fabrics, the most commonly known being Gore-Tex. Gore-Tex is a tissuelike fabric made of synthetic materials, whose pores are large enough to permit sweat vapor to pass through, but too small to allow liquid rain to penetrate. It thus combines nearly perfectly the needs of your body to keep dry in a rain without getting soaked through "from the inside out."

But even these fabrics, in practice, permit a certain amount of moisture to build up on the inside, particularly when cycling hard. Moreover, Gore-Tex itself must be laminated to at least one other layer of fabric, usually two. This laminate is expensive to manufacture, drives up the cost of clothing, and is bulky to carry and pack. Because it's expensive and it takes too much luggage space for a fairly specialized use, most cyclists have not adopted it.

The third solution is to carry gear that is breathable, will keep you reasonably dry in a light rain, and also has other uses, thus eliminating a luggage problem. We wear single-ply nylon windbreakers with wool sweaters underneath. The nylon breathes, allowing perspiration to evaporate, yet it fends off a sprinkle fairly well. The wool sweater, even when damp, continues to insulate, thus preventing chilling. Although the nylon soaks through in a hard rain, it also dries quickly. What we do with this combination is to use a "ride-and-hide" method —riding during a light rain or sprinkle, and hiding out under trees, in barns, under bridges, or even under a tent fly when the rain gets too heavy.

The reason we have used this particular gear for so long, through many, many storms, is that each of the items has other uses. The windbreaker and sweater are also used for cold and wind. One dries quickly, the other insulates you even when wet. Of all the systems for dealing with rain, we have found it the most useful and convenient, and can recommend it highly.

Beyond this, you need to do a number of other things to meet rainy weather.

Strategy.   First of all, remember that your brakes lose much of their effectiveness when your rims are wet. You can travel 10 or 20 feet before a real braking action occurs. Also keep in mind that certain road surfaces, such as leaves, oily pavement, and railroad tracks, become hazardous in the rain. Your vision also suffers, as does your visibility to motorists. When it starts to rain hard enough so that you are blinking constantly, it is time to stop and seek shelter.

Unless your nylon panniers are sealed at the seams, they will probably leak in a heavy rain. For this reason, we suggest you wrap your clothing in plastic bags. Be certain that you have among your dry clothing one dry T shirt, and if possible, a dry long-sleeved shirt. When you get to permanent shelter, strip off the wet clothing from your torso, dry off, and put dry things next to your skin. You can put on a damp wool sweater over these dry things, and your body heat will soon begin to dry it too. If you are still cold, put on your wool stocking hat and socks and your windbreaker. Hot liquids will help warm you up and give your morale a boost.

Once you're into these dry things, you pretty much have to commit yourself to staying where you are, at least until the rain stops and you can move on. This may involve putting up your tent or shelter wherever you find yourself, or asking the indulgence of someone to camp on their land or sleep in their barn. If you have saved any money for a rainy day, this is an excellent time to use it to treat yourself to a hotel or motel room.

If you are able to reach a town, head for the nearest laundromat. Within the bounds of decency, strip off what you have been wearing, throw it in the dryer, and put on dry things. Laundromats also have the advantage of being invariably hot, a welcome relief from the clammy outdoors.

Unless it is very cold, we suggest you ride in shorts in a rain shower, not slacks. Save these for when you are dry. It even helps to strip off your socks—they'll get soaked from the road splash otherwise, and they'll do your feet a lot more good when they're dry and you're someplace out of the storm.

Safety during storms.   One important factor you should keep in mind is to seek appropriate shelter during summer thunderstorms. Lightning annually kills more people in the United States than all the floods, hurricanes, and tornadoes combined. You do not want to add numbers to this statistic. Seek indoor shelter if possible during lightning storms, and if you are not able to do so, get under a low-lying bush and cover yourself with a tent fly or some other protective covering. Forget about your bicycle—in fact, get away from it, as metal attracts lightning. If it looks particularly hazardous, take off your panniers and sit on them.

Be careful also of crossing any stream where water is running or likely to run. Flash floods are a very real event in the West, and people are drowned every year by them. Even if the water looks shallow, there may be potholes or other depressions hidden by the running water. Obviously, when camping out in the desert, stay out of dry washes. Heavy thunderstorms can start walls of water downward to areas where not a drop has fallen, quickly filling narrow canyons.

WIND

If rain worries inexperienced cyclists unduly, then wind is a factor that may surprise them in the toll it takes on strength and morale. Wind has rightly been described as "the hill that never stops." Even fairly light winds, when hitting you anywhere along your forward 180-degree radius, will slow you down, leave you bewildered as to why things are so hard, and before very long, begin to annoy and demoralize you. Heavier winds, even when coming from the side or slightly from the rear, will still slow you up.

The worst thing about wind is that you can do little about it. Most cyclists are not content to sit idle for a day waiting for winds to subside. Moreover, in some areas of the West—particularly along the Pacific and on the high plateaus of Wyoming, Utah, and Colorado—the winds can blow hard for days on end, and you simply can't wait them out. Thus you find yourself riding, and the wind blowing, and if you are typical, you find yourself muttering under your breath and cursing your fate.

Yet in spite of the persistence of wind in certain areas, you can do something to avoid it. To begin with, you can try to arrange tours so you travel with the wind and not against it. On the Pacific coast, this means moving from north to south. In high plateau areas, it usually means moving from west to east, and in some cases from south to north. We cover these consistent wind patterns in Chapters 6 through 8.

But don't expect that your calculations will work perfectly. Wind directions vary, even when they are called consistent. They change from day to day, and they will change from mile to mile on the road, depending upon topographic features such as mountains and valleys. And although it's possible to plan a trip that probably will minimize wind interference, we find it more helpful to employ some riding techniques and daily riding schedules that we can control, rather than waiting or hoping for favorable winds. Here are the adjustments we suggest:

The first adjustment is psychological. Try to think of a windy day as a day when you won't go as far as you usually do. The frustrating thing about wind is that even when the terrain is level or slightly downhill, you are still working in order to ride. But if you can alter your perceptions to realize that no matter how easy the terrain looks, there is a significant factor slowing you down—a factor just as concrete in its effects as a high mountain pass—then you ought to expect less of yourself in terms of distance made that day. Drop into a lower gear, work to keep your mind off the wind, or even pretend you are climbing a pass.

Windy days are also days when you should stop more often, just as you would if you were climbing hard. Pamper yourself a bit, eat lunch in a restaurant, visit a museum, do a little shopping. Whenever possible, plan your stops so you are out of the wind.

Beyond adjusting expectations, you need to alter your riding habits. Most important is to ride on the dropped part of your handlebars, which we discuss in the next chapter. Part of your tour preparation should be to spend at least an hour down on the low bars on each training ride, so that you grow used to this posture and the added strain it puts on your arms, shoulders, and neck. By riding down, you reduce your exposed surface area and consequently reduce wind resistance.

If you are traveling with someone, if you are an experienced rider, and if the road is quiet, then you can employ drafting. This is a technique of riding very close to the person in front of you, either following directly behind the rear wheel, or riding just off to the leeward side. Your leader serves as a windbreaker for you, actually creating something of a vacuum in which you ride. Usually you switch roles to give the lead rider a break.

Because you are so close to the other cyclist, usually within 6 to 18 inches, you must be very cautious in employing drafting. The danger is that the follower may run up on the bicycle in front. This can occur when the leader changes pace or swerves or brakes, or when either cyclist loses concentration—very easy to do after a while. The result usually is not so disastrous for the leader as for the one who is trailing. Normally you bump the lead cyclist's rear wheel, which might jar him but usually doesn't throw him off balance. But since you strike with your front wheel, almost invariably your bicycle is thrown to one side or the other. A hard jolt will throw you immediately to the ground with little you can do about it. This is why we caution you not to draft on a busy road. We also suggest that you use drafting for only short segments of time until you get used to it, and when drafting switch the lead often so you get a break from having to concentrate and not being able to look around.

The final technique we suggest for wind is actually the easiest of all to employ: ride early in the morning. Winds almost invariably diminish or die down at night. If you can start shortly after dawn, you will have the best chance of riding while the air is quiet or relatively so. If possible, plan your day's itinerary about the same as you would for very hot combinations, getting all or most of your ride out of the way by noon. Wind will have almost no effect on you if you are snug in a tent or motel room.

RIDING SAFELY

Most bicycling accidents do not involve cars or trucks. Typically, an inattentive bicyclist will drift off the shoulder, get caught in the gravel, and spill. Inattention to road surfaces, slipping on gravel, taking bends too fast, drifting to one side when looking back over your shoulder, and bumping into or being bumped by another cyclist are all common causes of such accidents, and must be on your mind more or less constantly as you ride.

Of course car-related accidents are much more serious, and most of our attention is rightly devoted to avoiding them. And the beginning to safety in this respect is to ride where there is little traffic. If you can't, then find roads with wide, paved shoulders to ride on, where you are out of the traffic flow.

VISIBILITY

In situations where you must ride in or close to traffic, you need to concentrate first on two things: seeing and being seen. Wearing white or light-colored clothing is essential. White helmets, white or orange bicycle flags, and reflecting triangles worn on your backside all aid this. If you ride at night or in fog, a full selection of front and rear lights and reflectors are usually required by law, and common sense dictates their use even more forcefully.

DEFENSIVE RIDING

Your second precaution should be a total commitment to defensive riding. Assume that cars do not see you. Always be aware of your options. Can you stop in time if the car from the side road pulls out in front of you? Can you drop into the dirt or gravel shoulder if the car approaching from the rear doesn't give you enough leeway? Can you avoid the gravel on the roadway ahead without veering into traffic? Will you and an oncoming car both meet on the same narrow bridge?

This list could be extended. Your common sense should forewarn you of these and other situations. The key to having a safe ride is to make that common sense part of your everyday bicycling habits, so it is as automatic as shifting gears or braking.

Your legal rights on a bicycle are now fairly consistent from state to state. As a bicyclist, you have a right to use a portion of the roadway. In some states you are required to ride as far to the right as is safe or possible, but in other states there is no such restrictions. In either case, you have all the rights and obligations of any slow-moving vehicle.

But such rights are rather hypothetical when an automobile or truck is bearing down on you at high speed. Most motorists don't know the specifics of the law, and often they don't see you. Because you always ride with traffic, your most vulnerable area is to the rear. You must train yourself to hear traffic coming, and to be prepared to react should you have to. A small bicycling mirror attached to your helmet or glasses is invaluable. But training your ears to hear traffic is just as essential. With practice, you will be able to distinguish cars from trucks, estimate distance, and even tell whether it is a single vehicle or several in a line.

Once you have been passed, assume that another car is following right behind, and never drift back out onto the main part of the roadway without assuring yourself that it is clear. Wait for the noise of the passing car to die down, listen, then glance back. Glancing back itself requires practice, and you should be aware that you tend to drift in the direction opposite from your glance.

Because of your vulnerability to oncoming traffic from the rear, we suggest you ride single file, and keep sufficient space between bicyclists to allow for emergency maneuvering. Even on quiet roads, you must use great caution when riding side by side; an absorbing conversation can diminish your ability to hear and watch out for approaching traffic.

HELMETS

The battle of convincing cyclists of the effectiveness of wearing a helmet is nearly won. You will find particularly ardent helmet advocates among those who have had bicycling accidents. There is no question that a well-designed helmet can protect you from serious head injury in many accidents. Bright-colored ones also make you more visible.

Some people have argued, however, that most bicycling accidents do not involve head injuries, but rather injuries to collarbones, arms, shoulders, and legs. Our own cycling injuries—all unrelated to cars—bear this out.

Nonetheless, erring on the side of caution is always wisest, and we recommend the use of a well-designed bicycle helmet. Articles in bicycling and consumer magazines will help you in choosing the one that offers the best protection.

SPECIAL PRECAUTIONS

There are a few factors when riding in the West which call for special attention. We have already discussed the problems of long descents and the attendant dangers of road drift, some lessening of braking effectiveness, and the loss of certain handling characteristics of the bicycle. There is also a tendency for the wind whistling past your ears to obscure your hearing, making it difficult for you to pick up the sound of cars approaching from your rear. Beware, too, of the tendency of nearly all cyclists to drift out into the traffic lane on a long downhill. Combined with a loss of hearing acuity, this can be disastrous. Sidewinds coming in from canyons are another hazard of the fast descent. They can knock you sideways.

The other particular hazard rather peculiar to the West is the logging truck. Most truck traffic everywhere else is confined to the major highways. Logging trucks, as often as not, are found on the narrow, otherwise quiet, mountain roads. They are wide and, when fully loaded, are difficult to stop. Moreover, drivers are often paid by the load, and drive hard.

You will always be able to hear a logging truck coming long before you see it. Prepare yourself. Scout the road ahead for possible places to pull off. If you hear one approaching from the rear, slow down or stop. If there ever is any doubt that there's room for clearance, get off the road.

Because the drivers of logging rigs drive under the most difficult circumstances, we believe they are among the best drivers in the world. We give them a wide berth, stop when necessary to allow them to pass, and usually get a cheery blare of a horn and a wave for our efforts. With a little caution, you can do likewise and achieve the same results.

EATING ON THE ROAD

FOOD AND DRINK

No matter how you have chosen to tour—alone or in groups, camping or in motels—you are going to have to eat. Cycle touring places a considerable energy demand on your body, and therefore food—the right kind in the proper amounts—is of paramount importance. If you are eating properly, you will have a consistent, reliable supply of energy available, and this makes cycling easier and more enjoyable.

No set food formulas can take into consideration all the radical differences between individuals. You have to develop your own formula for paying close attention to how you function and then manipulate the essential food groups to suit your needs. In our case one of us has to take in 5,000 or even 6,000 calories a day, while still losing weight. The other eats only a little more than normal, and maintains about the same weight throughout a four- or five-month tour.

Our advice is to use common sense, pay some attention to getting fresh fruits and vegetables, and avoid a tendency to stave off hunger with only empty sweets such as candy bars and soda pop. Nuts, fruit, trail mixes, peanut butter, and the like are much better in terms of the whole health picture, because they give you a sustained lift rather than just a sugar rush.

Your own eating schedule will also be highly personalized. We eat substantial, but uncooked, breakfasts. We normally have a fairly large lunch, and spend at least an hour resting and eating, often more. We try to cook a balanced dinner, with concentration on protein and carbohydrate sources.

Some cyclists do nothing more than stop at a grocery store, and eat what they have purchased while milling around their bicycles. They seem to do all right, too. Still others never stop for anything like lunch, but eat trail mixes more or less continually as they ride, eating a dinner in a restaurant or cooking an elaborate supper in a camp. For yourself, do what tastes good and seems to work for you.

During very hot weather we suggest you avoid drinking alcohol at night, as it raises your body temperature and causes increased loss of body fluid. This can have an effect on you the next day if you travel some time before finding an abundant water supply. Drinking alcohol when you are severely chilled—Saint Bernard dogs and myths of brandy casks to the contrary—is dangerous. Although it produces a momentary warming, drinking opens your pores and results in even faster heat loss in the long run.

No matter how you eat, sooner or later on your tour you will have to make use of the small rural grocery store, and this calls for some special comment.

Most of these stores are small mom-and-pop operations, filling a very vital need in isolated areas. Prices are invariably higher than what you would pay in an urban super market. This is not an effort at price gouging—these small stores have to pay more for their food supplies to begin with. Shipping costs more. Turnover, and thus profit, is much lower. Few, if any, of the owners become wealthy.

We make these comments because of the tendency on the part of a few bicyclists and other travelers to behave rather rudely when they see a 10- or 15-percent markup over what they normally pay. Such markups are usually what is necessary for the store to stay in business.

Because of low turnover and small size, these stores do not have a wide selection of food. Often they have no fresh meat. Sometimes they freeze a limited quantity, so look in the freezer case before giving up. Fresh fruits and vegetables are also somewhat scarce; you may have to substitute canned or frozen produce. By using some ingenuity and remaining flexible, you usually can fashion decent meals from what you find. We discuss cooking and eating equipment in Chapter 4.

We use these guidelines in our own shopping and food consumption:

1. Try to buy your food as near to the time you eat it as possible. This saves you from carrying extra weight over long distances.

2. In sparsely populated areas, find out ahead of time where the next grocery store is. The best source of information is the grocer where you are now. He or she is most aware of competition down the road.

3. If you must shop for two or more meals ahead of time, pick items

with less bulk and little or no need for refrigeration. This often means switching to canned fish or meats, powdered or condensed milk, and low-volume starches such as instant mashed potatoes or crackers.

4. Keep altitude in mind when selecting food. Some things just won't get done at elevations above 6,000 feet. Rice is always a little crunchy, dried soups never seem to totally reconstitute, string beans never seem to lose their stringiness. On the other hand, omelettes and pancakes are even lighter.

5. When you buy frozen foods, pack them together in a plastic bag to avoid making everything else wet. If you have room, pack other items that need to be kept cool, such as milk or butter, around your frozen foods. Keep the entire package insulated from the sun by packing clothing on top.

6. You can carry some condiments in small plastic bottles, and they will add considerable spice to your cuisine. "Luxuries" such as soy sauce, bouillon cubes, and garlic and onion powder can cheer up a rather bland meal.

7. If you are in a large group, delegate one or two to do the shopping, with decision-making powers. Nothing is worse than five or ten cyclists hanging over the meat counter haggling about what they'll eat for dinner that night. The problem is compounded when everyone is hungry. Afterwards, don't gripe about what they've chosen.

8. Keep a low-volume, spoilproof meal somewhere in reserve in your luggage. A small can of fish, a dried soup mix, a packaged spaghetti mix, or the like, can be a lifesaver when you thought you'd find a grocery store and didn't. This can happen more often than you want it to in the West.

CAMPING OUT

You have two choices of where you stop for the night when camping. Either you will stay in some kind of organized campground, or you will camp off on your own. In an organized campground, most of the unknowns are handled for you. You select (or are assigned) a site, pitch your tent or shelter, and go about the business of eating. Occasionally, you may end up in a campground without a fresh-water supply, and you need to pinpoint these in advance by using a good guide to campgrounds. Most of these dry campgrounds will be National Forest camps, although an occasional county or municipal camp will also be dry. In these instances, you will be thrown back to using some of the same techniques and approaches to touring life employed when camping off on your own. This is relatively common in Western bicycle touring.

SITE SELECTION

When looking for a camping spot, you should leave yourself time to look, time to set up, time to cook, and time to eat and clean up. Rushing to do everything at the last minute is hard on the weary under the best of circumstances, even when you aren't roughing it.

Look for a site in which you feel comfortable. Try to get away from the road and into a spot that doesn't allow easy access to cars or other people. Wheel your bicycle through the forest or up on a small ridge where access is difficult for others.

Sometimes you will see a good site with a fence around it, or sometimes both sides of the road are fenced. What to do? If there is a house nearby, it is safe to assume that the land is private. In this case, just ask if you can camp. If there aren't any buildings around, then what?

We assume that where people post NO TRESPASSING signs, they mean it, and we try not to camp in such places. Often you can find a gap where there are no signs, and enter there. In any case, we consider these rules absolute when you are camping on someone else's land:

1. Get out of direct sight of the road.
2. Don't start a campfire.
3. Close any gates you open. If you cross a fence, be particularly careful not to damage it. Fencing is expensive, and repairing fences is hard work. A landowner might forgive you for being on his land, but will have a hard time doing so if you've damaged fences or allowed livestock to escape.

In much of the West, vast stretches of land are owned by the federal government, administered by the Bureau of Land Management. Usually this land is posted as such, and if you close gates, you can use it without harassment. But you still need to observe the iron-clad rules noted above.

In selecting a site, do so with an eye to getting protection from unexpected weather. Try to set up on ground just a bit higher than normal drainage channels, in case of rain. In the desert, don't camp in dry washes. It can spell disaster from a flash flood originating some distance from you. In the mountains, camping in a gully or ravine will mean a colder, damper night than camping on a ridge. Gullies collect cold air and channel it downward in the same way that water is channeled. Also, these places are more likely to have insects.

If possible, particularly in the mountains, try to select a site with an eye to catching the morning sun as early as possible. This will warm you, help wake you up, and dry any moisture that has collected on equipment during the night.

WATER NEEDS OUTSIDE ORGANIZED CAMPGROUNDS

The critical element when camping outside organized campgrounds is water. With few exceptions, you must be able to carry your own drinking and cooking water to makeshift sites. Even if you camp near a stream or river, the chances are not good that the water is perfectly safe to drink. This holds true even in some high mountain areas where steam water normally has been considered drinkable. In the summer of 1980, there were pervasive outbreaks of a bacterial organism that is carried by both humans and lower animals, and is sometimes referred to as "backpacker's sickness." Warnings of it were posted even in relatively controlled areas such as Glacier National Park, and many parts of Utah, Colorado, and Wyoming. Given these and other problems, we recommend that you carry drinking water to most sites. If you do not, the best method of purifying water is to bring it to a rapid boil and keep it boiling for five minutes. This consumes considerable fuel and time.

You will need a container, or several of them, to carry your water. We discuss these in the next chapter. You can use stream water to wash yourself in, and assuming you dry your dishes thoroughly, it is generally permissible to wash them in clear stream water, although become wary if you think the water might be contaminated. If in doubt, assume that it is. Do not use suspect water to brush your teeth, as harmful bacteria will still enter your system even if you spit out the water. When using stream or lake water to wash in, take the water *away* from the stream and do your washing there. It helps to use a biodegradable soap. When finished, splatter the water around well away from river or lake bank, so you don't add to an already growing pollution problem.

Since carrying water is an additional burden, you need to do some planning during the day as to where you are likely to stop for the night. We always favor getting water at the surest possible point and carrying it farther than was perhaps necessary, rather than running into the end of the day with no water available. Check ahead. Ask at a service station if there is another station down the road where water is available. When asking for specifics such as this, you are better off asking someone in the same business (as we observed before), rather than relying on general advice. A local resident who has never needed these services is not as likely to have accurate information.

For cooking supper and breakfast, drinking, and toothbrushing, you need about a liter or two per person. If there is no water to wash in—very likely in ad hoc sites in the West—then you must figure on carrying additional water, unless you want to sleep with a pretty salty, gritty body. We've learned to cleanse ourselves adequately in a liter of water each, and we've done it on less when we needed to. We might not pass a mother's behind-the-ears test, but the worst is off.

You can reduce the amount of water you need to carry by planning meals that don't require much water. Fried foods, instant mashed potatoes, frozen vegetables, and the like are good examples. Noodles, spaghetti, and dried soups are items that need more water, and you should consider this. You can reduce your own water needs by buying a quart of cold milk or other beverage at the last grocery store. Remember, when cooking supper, that you will need water for breakfast the next morning.

"DANGEROUS" PLANTS AND ANIMALS

For us, camping and bicycling are so inextricably tied, that it would be hard to imagine one without the other. The two different but compatible activities form an extremely pleasant unity. Part of that pleasure is the restfulness of camp life itself. The routine of chores, the quiet and often remote sites, all very quickly soothe away the effects of a rigorous day.

At the same time, there is always a bit of an edge about it for those of us who still live most of our lives in cities. Noises we're not used to, the fact that most animals roam at night (or at least *seem* to when you're lying in a tent listening), all can contribute to a certain uneasiness.

Most of it is unwarranted. Wilderness creatures are in almost every instance terrified of us. No matter what our fears lead us to believe, most of our encounters with them involve nothing more than a match of wits as to who is going to enjoy our food—us or them.

Even the most timid creatures such as raccoons or possums can become uncannily insistent at night about getting into your food. Skunks are about as bad. For comfort and peace of mind, keep your food out of your tent. The chances are about one in a million that any animal will take an interest in you if it can't smell food nearby.

In bear country, this prohibition against food in the tent becomes especially important. In camps where bears have been a problem, ask to store your food in a neighbor's car or motor home. If that isn't convenient, string it from a tree, at least 10 feet above the ground, and at least 4 feet from anything a bear can climb up to get to it, like the treetrunk itself. You should also be sure that you are free from food odors before going to bed, including your hands and face. If possible, change the clothes you wore when cooking. It goes without saying that you never eat in your sleeping bag in bear country. The real chance of ever having trouble with a bear is very small indeed. However, you must prepare as if the chance were great.

Don't forget your garbage. You may not still be interested in it, but animals love to root through it. Put it in plastic bags and string it somewhere where animals can't get into it. When leaving, take it with you. Don't bury it. Animals will just dig it up anyway and start a dependency cycle that they have been quite able to do without. Easily available food attracts and nourishes animals, which become even greater nuisances.

The West also has its share of poisonous bugs and snakes. In all the time we have cycled or hiked there, we have never had a serious encounter with a poisonous reptile or bug. However, we are also careful and aware of their habits. Black widow spiders and scorpions are numerous in the Southwest. They like dark, still places. Never put your hand down under a picnic table, lift a rock, or search under bushes without looking first.

You also may see tarantulas in the Southwest. These are enormous, hairy spiders about the size of your fist. Contrary to popular belief, their bite is harmless. You can, however, get a bacterial infection from the bite if you do not put antiseptic on it. The chances of getting bitten by one of these interesting creatures is very low, but if you do, treat it the same as you would a cut or abrasion.

Now about snakes. Snakes don't want to be bothered with people. When walking always make enough noise to give a snake a chance to leave before you get there. Never put your foot or hand down where you can't see. If you follow these two rules, the chances are very small that you will even see a snake when camping. You are much more likely to see them sunning themselves along the edge of the roadway, and the vast majority of those you do see will be nonpoisonous. They'll scurry away from you quickly enough.

Most people spend an undue amount of time worrying about snake-bite. Within all of the United States, only about ten to twenty deaths a year are caused by snakebites. Most of these occur around homes—in woodpiles or rocks—and involve children, who are the most susceptible to the toxin. Your chances of being bitten are thus rather slim. In the unlikely event it does happen, about 20 or 30 percent of the time, the bite will not envenomate. That is, no significant amount of venom will be injected into your body.

But should you come out on the short side of these odds, stay calm. If someone else is bitten, try to keep them calm. Anxiety and effort increase the pulse and move the toxin into the system; you want it to stay where it is. Second, get to a road, a farmhouse, or other habitation and arrange for transportation to the nearest hospital. Hospitals in snake country have antitoxins available, and can treat you properly. Most experts now agree that the old cut-and-suction treatment for snakebite should be used only as a last resort. Under no circumstances should you apply a tourniquet that cuts off blood circulation. If anything, apply two firm, but not tight, tourniquets above and below the bite. If hospital treatment is far away or out of the question, then you can follow the directions in one of the snakebite kits currently on the market. But even after doing this, still make every effort to get yourself or the victim to a hospital.

Most of what you need for bites, or the more likely scratches and scrapes you will get some way or another, is a decent first-aid kit (see page 74).

One final note about animals and the wilds. Salt is a rare commodity in nature, and animals crave it. Headbands, gloves, and helmet straps are loaded with salt from your perspiration. Our own wild-animal experiences have centered around these objects more than any other. These include deer chewing the straps from a backpack, an unknown animal eating the handle of a favorite wooden spoon, and a herd of steers who kept trying to chew our water bottles where the plastic had absorbed the salt from our hands. Your own experiences will most likely reflect these kinds of surprises.

One of the peculiar problems of camping out in the West—particularly when you're off on your own—is thorns. The West is full of them. Cactus is the most obvious source, but there seems to be an infinite variety of others. When wheeling your bicycle off the road, always scout ahead. If in doubt about a particular plant, reach down and pat it gently. If it pricks, beware—you might be pulling it out of a deflated tire in the morning. We often carry our bicycles in to a camping spot, rather than rolling them; and just to be sure, we check our tires in the morning once we get back to the road. Most thorns are fairly harmless to tires if you pull them before riding on them. But once the tire has revolved and pressed it in, the thorn will snap off, and if it doesn't puncture the tire immediately, it will eventually. We have had thorns work into the tire for more than a week before finally puncturing the tube. The so-called thorn-proof or puncture-proof tubes help immeasurably.

CHOOSING YOUR COMPANY

RIDING WITH OTHERS

One of the greatest joys of touring is to share it with others. It can also be one of life's greatest trials. Few people are so perfectly matched in physical abilities and personal tastes that their needs will match. We know of marriages that have fallen apart and friendships that have been severed because of differing needs when bicycling. Fortunately, some adjustments can usually be made before things go that far.

The most important adjustments are usually not physical. They lie in the areas of how people wish to use their bodies. Some people thrive on exertion, others accept it only with resignation. Some are early risers, others sleep late. Some wish to ride quickly, others to stop often. The list goes on.

The most important step in adjusting to these differences is an understanding of others and a basic sympathy to their needs. This, and honest—but not recriminatory—communication, will go far toward mitigating individual differences. Beyond that, we have found these techniques helpful in touring with others:

1. Try to ride with your touring partners before you tour. As much as possible, ride to simulate touring conditions. Then, work out an overall plan together in advance. In doing so, try to make the plan match your individual tastes. Plan some leisurely days, if certain members like that pace, along with longer, harder days if they're pleasing to others.

2. Guard against thinking that there is something wrong with a slow rider. Too often we equate distance and speed with pleasure. There is no rational basis for this. If you are a faster rider, remember that someone going slowly is usually putting out as much energy as

you to maintain that pace. It simply is harder for them. Remember that no matter how much you want to go fast or far, an exhausted traveling companion makes poor company.

3. Slower riders, particularly inexperienced ones, must understand that strain and discomfort are an inherent part of physical exertion. There are times when you simply must push yourself beyond what is comfortable.

4. If you are in a group of four or more, riders with similar paces may wish to team up and travel together. We recommend that two cyclists always ride together in case of accident or other need. In addition, each member of the group should have a clear idea of the rendezvous point, and a map. In case of confusion, the rule of thumb is to go back to the point where you all last saw each other, and wait there. It is amazing how easy it is for bicyclists to become separated when such understandings are not clear. We have known some cases where such separation lasted through several weeks of a planned tour.

TRAVELING ALONE

About a third of the bicyclists you meet in the West are touring alone. Being able to set your own pace and make all your own decisions, and even the spiritual joy of time spent with yourself, are the obvious rewards.

Not surprisingly, nearly all the people you see touring alone are men. This brings us to a crucial question. Is it safe for a woman to bicycle alone?

There is no easy answer to the question. Almost certainly, a woman traveling alone very far will receive some sort of verbal harassment. This is usually worthy of nothing more than the contempt it has earned for itself. Much more difficult to assess is the danger of physical abuse or violence. Certainly it is present, as the threat is present to any woman in this country. How much more so because you are on a bicycle by yourself, often away from houses or other forms of civilization, is really impossible to say. Of the women we have met who bicycle alone, none had had serious problems. One knocked on the door of a home each evening, explained she was bicycling out from the East, and asked if there was a place she could spend the night. She invariably was asked inside. Another averaged over a hundred miles a day, carried no tent, and slept under picnic tables or rolled up in a sheet of plastic off in a field at night. Both had psyches like iron.

Most humans don't. And while the chances of serious threat to a solitary woman cyclist may not be great, there is a gnawing uneasiness within us when we see her.

If you are going to bicycle alone, then perhaps the most important thing is to understand the limitations and hazards of doing so. You should be competent with basic bicycle repairs. You need to have a well-thought-out series of options for situations that might arise, and you must feel confident you can bring off any of the options if you need to. This feeling of confidence is not only good for your own sense of well-being, it tends to show in your behavior to others, and it is important that they sense this also.

We would also recommend the following: Stay in organized facilities, if possible. If you are camping, camp next to someone. Introduce yourself. Make friends along the way—in cafés, among the highway patrol, with road-maintenance personnel, campground managers, rangers, fellow campers, and bicyclists. Exercise your "no, thank you" freely, and with firmness, any time you feel uneasy in a situation. Never put social niceties above your personal safety. If a situation appears threatening, do not inform people that you are alone.

All this advice may err on the side of caution, and could reflect our own feelings more than those of women who actually do solo touring. We hope we will all arrive at a point when no such feelings—reflecting reality or not—need be of concern.

TRANSPORTING YOUR BICYCLE

Not all tours need to be planned to start and finish from your own driveway. Some bicyclists transport bicycles to the starting point of a tour themselves, or rely on friends. But you can extend your touring horizons immeasurably if you rely on some form of public transportation to get both you and your bicycle to and from your tour route. All major air, bus and train lines will carry your bicycle, either as part of your regular luggage, or as freight.

CARRIERS

Airlines. All airlines charge a fee to transport your bicycle along domestic routes (now $14). Once you have paid this, your bicycle will be shipped with your luggage, provided it meets the company's packaging requirements (see next section). They all require that the pedals be removed and the handlebars turned sideways and secured. After this, some require you to box or bag your bike. The companies with packaging requirements may have a box available, but usually you have to get one from a bicycle dealer. If you travel on an airline that doesn't require boxing, be sure to check their liability—unboxed or unprotected bicycles are usually exempt from liability claims. Always check your bicycle upon arrival, as liability coverage ends when you leave the airport. It also is wise to check the total amount of liability the company will assume. Often your bicycle will count in your total luggage coverage, even though you've paid an additional fee for it.

Buses.   The two major bus lines, Greyhound and Trailways, will carry your bicycle as part of your luggage allotment, and at no extra fee, provided it is boxed with handlebars turned parallel and pedals removed. They do not have boxes available at their stations, but will provide you with tape or twine, if necessary. To insure that the bicycle gets on the bus with you, Greyhound advises you to check it at bus side yourself. Trailways wants all luggage checked beforehand, but you should watch just to make sure it is loaded on your bus. As a passenger, you have the right to request (or insist) that your luggage travel with you. Bus carriers won't assume more than $250 worth of liability. If you need more insurance, you will have to buy it from an independent agency. Always check your bicycle before you leave the stations, as it is very difficult to make a claim afterward.

Trains.   Amtrak is the only carrier with transcontinental routes. Its policies are, therefore, supposed to be uniform throughout the United States. In practice, they may vary from place to place, so check ahead. Its stated policy is to carry your bicycle at no extra cost if it is boxed and counted as one of your three pieces of luggage. If you have additional luggage you may count your bicycle as one piece and have the lightest one counted as excess. The fee is then computed on a poundage-distance scale, with a minimum $8.50 fee. You can be sure your bicycle will arrive with you if you don't have to change trains. If they don't have enough time to change baggage, your bicycle will be marked "subject to delay," and you will have to wait for it at your destination. Amtrak is obligated to tell you this in advance, but you would be prudent to inquire, anyway. Also, make certain that your destination has a baggage room, otherwise Amtrak won't carry it because it requires that all baggage be handled by certified personnel. If your destination doesn't have such facilities, you will have to pick one nearby that can provide this service and start your trip from there. If you are planning a round trip, you will have to make provision for storing your carton or getting another one for the return trip, as the station won't store the carton for you. Be certain to inspect your bicycle before leaving the station, as Amtrak doesn't honor claims made afterward.

BOXING YOUR BICYCLE

If a carrier requires that you box your bicycle, ask a local dealer to set aside a used carton for you. It's better to let him know several weeks in advance, to be sure of getting one.

Although baggage handlers are becoming more familiar with bicycles as luggage, you still need to exercise some overkill in protecting your bicycle. Assume that the carton will be thrown around some, and that heavy items will be stacked on top of it.

To get your bicycle into a bicycle carton, you'll need to take it apart to some extent. How much depends on the size of your bicycle and the size of the carton. Usually, it involves these steps:

1. Remove the pedals. Note that most left-hand pedals have reverse threads.
2. Remove the front wheel.
3. Loosen the handlebars and turn them sideways and downward, or if necessary, remove them. If you remove the handlebars, you need to disconnect the brake cables, loosen the cone nut, tap down on the handlebars with a wooden or rubber mallet, and slide them out of the headset. The best place to stow them is with the curved part wrapped around the front forks.
4. If your bicycle is very tall, you may have to remove the saddle and the seat post.
5. Deflate the tires—particularly crucial to allow for pressure drops in airplane baggage compartments.

Now that the bicycle is disassembled, get ready to put it into the carton. The important thing to remember here is that cardboard will only give your bicycle cosmetic protection. Think of things that stick out, or are in some way vulnerable to shock. The critical projections are the front forks (exposed, because you have removed the wheel), the axles, the rear derailleur, and the bottom of your large chainwheel (front sprocket).

1. Tape an appropriate-sized piece of wood between the front forks.

2. Wrap a generous amount of old cloth or towel around the rear derailleur and at the bottom of your chainwheel.

3. Build up small pieces of cardboard around your axles by cutting holes in the cardboard and slipping them over the axle ends. Tape in place.

4. Since the carton is most vulnerable to shock from the side, it is desirable to cut some pieces of cardboard the width of the carton, roll them into tubes, and fasten them inside. Thread two or three through the spokes of the wheel near the axles. The most secure way of fixing these is to cut holes in the sides of the box and thread rope through the tubes, passing the ropes around the exterior of the box.

5. Label the carton clearly with name and address, and if it is to be held for you, write HOLD, WILL CALL on the outside. Somewhere inside the carton, put a slip of paper with your name and address on it.

The regulations of individual carriers vary, and some carriers have had a habit of changing regulations often, or not sticking to the ones they make. The best procedure is to call the carrier several weeks ahead of time, and get the regulations from it, not from a travel agent. Then, before you put your bicycle in a carton, phone and check again, stating the date you will be traveling.

If you are using the bus, get to the station early enough so that you can get your carton checked in with the baggage handler. In smaller stations, you can usually load the bicycle yourself, or oversee it personally (a good idea in any case). Trailways buses, by the way, have luggage compartments tall enough to accommodate the carton in an upright position. On Greyhound, it will have to lie flat, or be angled in. Remember that buses on major intercity runs are usually crowded, and get to the station as early as possible.

SIX

The Far West:

California, Nevada, Oregon,

and  Washington

CALIFORNIA

At one time, residents and promoters of California were unabashed in proclaiming its virtues. Its climate, range of topography, the mystique of Hollywood, the urbanity of San Francisco—all were the subjects of a boosterism that seemed unquenchable.

In many respects, the campaign was the source of its own demise. One day in 1965, California threw itself an enormous party to celebrate becoming the most populous state in the Union. It seemed to wake up the next day with a huge hangover.

Largely without control, city had grown to meet city, one village had expanded to the limits of the next, and in some instances entire towns had been created, as if to fill in the few gaps left. Many parts of the state had become so crowded that there were problems handling the side effects of overpopulation, the most notable one being air pollution.

This isn't meant to be unduly negative, just a preamble to the thesis that California, of all the states in the West, requires the most care in terms of your route-finding. Many parts of the state, including the entire megalopolis stretching from Santa Barbara to the Mexican border and all the area surrounding San Francisco Bay, should be left to the day tourist. Congestion is such that you cannot plan a long tour without encountering, sooner or later, large stretches that are uncomfortable or dangerous to ride. Also to be avoided are the coastal areas near these megalopolises, and the major roads leading from them into the mountains.

With this word of forewarning, let's look at what is left of California. There is a great deal. To begin with, the things that originally lured people to the state still remain. Its physical aspects, viewed from a quantitative basis alone, are sparkling with superlatives. The highest mountain in the continental United States is in California, as is the lowest point. The longest coastline contained in any one state is there (1,300 miles). Yosemite Falls is the second highest waterfall in the world. Lake Tahoe, which straddles the California-Nevada border, is the highest large body of water in the world. The largest living thing, a Giant Sequoia, is found along the northern coast. To top everything off are five great national parks, eight national monuments, a national seashore, a national recreation area, and a host of state parks and preserves that include every imaginable kind of topography and cultural attraction. All of this is ample lure for the bicyclist, and justifiably so. With care, almost all of it can be enjoyed fully by the bicycling tourist.

MOUNTAINS

There are two major mountain chains in California, both running north-south almost the entire length of the state.

The first of these is the Coast Range, which stretches from the Oregon border to the Los Angeles basin. A spur of the Coast Range circles behind the Los Angeles area and runs on south to the Mexican border.

The Coast Range varies in both elevation and overall character. In the south, summits are relatively low, peaking at about 3,000 to 4,000 feet. In spite of this, the mountains are often rugged and even inaccessible except by trail. The earth is stony, and ridges are steep. A relatively arid climate has not produced enough rainfall and snow runoff to break down and soften the harsh contours of the uplifted rock. Lower slopes are covered with chaparral and scrub oak; only the higher elevations supporting stands of conifers.

From San Francisco northward, the nature of the Coast Range changes. Heavier rainfall produces dense stands of pine, fir, redwood, and cedar. The forest floor is softened with a dense mat of needles.

The peaks are higher, rising as far as 8,000 feet above the neighboring ocean. More rainfall is trapped, and there are numerous streams and rivers, particularly on the westward slopes.

Since the coastal mountains plunge directly into the Pacific, this has a great effect on the roads running along the ocean. With few exceptions, riding the coast is a constant up-and-down roller coaster, although there is a large payoff in terms of your proximity to beautifully sculptured rock formations, the sea wearing away at the land and making minute changes in it even as you ride by. On some parts of the coast, particularly the stretch below Monterey known as Big Sur, you can experience some of the most striking ocean scenery found anywhere in the West. Tours 3, 6, and 7 allow you to explore this region of California.

Lying 50 to 100 miles inland from the Coast Range and separated from them by a long, flat valley is another line of mountains that run north-south almost the length of the state. Although this line of mountains is really composed of two ranges—the Cascades in the far north and the Sierra Nevada forming the central and southern part—for all practical purposes they form a single barrier. But the geological underpinnings of the two ranges do make them different for the bicyclist. In the north, the Cascades are dominated by two important volcanic peaks, Mount Lassen and Mount Shasta. Much of the area surrounding these mountains is gently rolling highlands, and there are numerous wide valleys that are nearly level. The entire region is covered in nearly uniform stands of ponderosa pine. Thus the north offers numerous rides that are high—from 4,000 to 6,000 feet—but are much easier than you will find in the more rugged Sierra Nevada to the south. Tour 5 takes you through some of this terrain.

The Sierra Nevada is higher than the Cascades. Pass roads through the Sierra run at 7,000 feet or more. Tioga Pass in Yosemite National Park is nearly 10,000 feet. By contrast, the loop road that actually climbs the flank of Mount Lassen in the Cascades crests just over 8,500 feet. Nor will you find in the Sierra the level or rolling terrain characteristic of the California Cascades. In the Sierra you climb sharply upward, then descend. There are few opportunities for staying high.

The Coast Range and the range formed by the Cascades and Sierra Nevada are pinched off at the north and south by still other mountains, forming a long, almost completely enclosed valley. In the north, the Coast Range and the Cascades merge into a swath of mountains some 200 miles wide, oriented generally in an east-west direction. Some of California's most beautiful mountain scenery is found here, including the Trinity Alps and the Marble Mountain Wilderness Areas. The Marble Mountains are accessible only by trail, but a number of roads bring you quite close to the Trinity Alps, and we use some of these roads in our northern California tours described later in the chapter.

The southern wall of the long Central Valley is formed by the Tehachapi and Peninsular ranges. These are low mountains, mostly 3,000 to 4,000 feet in elevation. They get relatively little rain or snow, and are characterized by rugged canyons and sharp-backed ridges. An extension of these mountains forms a semicircle behind the long coastal basin stretching from San Diego to Los Angeles. Some of these small ranges are quite pretty, but touring here is frequently complicated by the enormous megalopolis lying just to the west.

VALLEYS, BASINS, AND DESERTS

The Central Valley, formed by the two lines of mountains running the length of California, is a trough nearly 500 miles long, about 50 miles wide, and almost perfectly level. Red Bluff, near its northern end, has an altitude of about 300 feet. Bakersfield, in the south, is at about 400 feet. The land slopes gently downward from both these places and reaches a low point just east of San Francisco Bay. This valley is one of the most intensively cultivated in the world, and the cyclist touring there will see crops of almost infinite variety. Cotton, rice, nuts, table and wine grapes, tomatoes, lemons, oranges, grapefruit, melons, celery, potatoes, sugar beets, wheat, oats, corn, and hops, as well as more exotic foods such as avocados, olives, and persimmons, are all cultivated there with great success. Riding in the Central Valley, needless to say, is almost always easy, although summer heat can complicate itineraries for some cyclists.

The extreme northeastern part of California is part of the Great Basin, a large plateau stretching into Utah, and from which there is no outward drainage. It is semi-arid land, generally level, although broken intermittently by sharp ridges and hills.

In southeastern California are found two great deserts, the Mojave and the Colorado. The Colorado Desert extends down into Mexico, and the Mojave stretches eastward from Barstow into Arizona. Although at first glance somewhat forbidding to the bicyclist, some of these desert regions make excellent off-season riding. Our Tour 1, which heads eastward out of San Diego and goes through Anza-Borrego, is one such possibility. There are a number of others, including winter rides in Death Valley, where you are actually well below sea level.

CLIMATE

Because of the great variety of topography within California, climate patterns are very complicated. The primary generator of weather systems for most of the state is the Pacific Ocean. Low-pressure centers bring currents of moist air in off the ocean. As these currents cross the land, they lose much of their water. Rainfall and temperature both vary in relationship to an area's elevation and distance from the Pacific.

Temperatures.   First-time visitors to California who are tempted to rush down for a swim in this vast body of water won't stay in long if they do so anywhere north of San Francisco. It's cold. Even in late summer, water temperatures rarely rise above 55 degrees along the northern coast. Swimming is for the hardy, or for the judicious who clothe themselves in wet suits. The reason for the cold water, in spite of abundant California sunshine, is the California Current. This stream of water flows southward 50 miles or more off the coast. Although not excessively cold itself, the California Current draws much colder water from lower ocean depths upward in its wake. It is this cold water into which the expectant swimmer plunges. In fact, the water just along the coast is colder by several degrees than the water 25 or 50 miles offshore.

Given the origin of the water fringing California's coast, sea temperature varies little from winter to summer, ranging from 49 to 55 degrees in northern California, and from 51 to 65 degrees in the south. In addition to being a deterrent to bathing, it is responsible for the more or less permanent fog bank that hovers off the northern coastal areas. Relatively warm air masses move in off the Pacific, pass over the cold water, a dew point is reached, and fog is created. This fog is driven inland by the prevailing winds. As the day moves on and the sun heats up the air, the fog is usually dissipated. But there are many days, particularly in northern California, when it never disappears. Visibility is limited to a few hundred feet, and air temperatures are cool.

The farther you go inland from the ocean, particularly in summer, the warmer the temperatures become. Near San Francisco, the average high temperature along the coast in July is about 64 degrees. But at the little town of Walnut Creek, 25 miles inland, the average high reaches 87 degrees in July. Go a bit farther, to Tracy, which is 50 miles inland, and daytime highs in July average 95 degrees. A similar pattern exists in the south. Los Angeles has a normal July maximum of 75 degrees. But the average at Canoga Park in the San Fernando Valley just 15 miles inland goes up to 95 degrees in the same month.

The shielding effect of the Coast Range is primarily responsible for these changes, and the entire Central Valley experiences warm or hot weather from late spring to midautumn. Red Bluff, in the northern valley, has daily maximums of from 90 to 98 degrees from June through September. Highs in May and October are near 80 degrees. Sacramento has daily maximums of 70 degrees or more from April through October, with July and August the warmest months, daily highs hovering near 92 degrees. Bakersfield, in the southern end of the valley, is considerably warmer, with many days during the summer months where temperatures reach 100.

As you leave the valley floor and climb up into the mountains, temperatures drop about 3 degrees for each 1,000 feet gained. This makes most of the high mountains of California pleasant riding during summer months; you can expect relief from the intense valley heat once you climb above 2,000 feet.

Low temperatures during the summer follow a similar pattern. Evening lows along the north coast are in the high 50s or low 60s. In the south, low temperatures are in the low to mid-60s. For all the daytime heat in the interior valley, the clear air usually brings cool evening temperatures. Minimums during the summer months range from the high 50s to the mid-60s.

In the mountains, nighttime lows are cool, but generally not below freezing—except sometimes on exceptionally high pass roads such as Yosemite's Tioga Pass. The town of Shasta City (3,500 feet) in northern California has nighttime lows in the summer of about 50 degrees. Truckee, in the central part of the state at 6,000 feet, has minimum temperatures in the low 40s on most summer nights.

Precipitation.   Rainfall in California is controlled largely by the Pacific high, a permanent high-pressure center which hovers out in the Pacific, moving north or south depending upon the season. In summer, the Pacific high pressure center intensifies and moves northward. The effect of this movement is to form a barrier through which Pacific storms cannot pass. There is a natural lessening of storms during summer anyway, and what storm centers there are normally slide north of the Pacific high and strike Washington or northern Oregon. During winter, the Pacific high weakens and moves southward, allowing clear passage for storms.

Thus rainfall patterns throughout all of California are the reverse of what is experienced in many other parts of the country. Winters are wet and green, summers are dry and brown. Eureka, one of the rainiest spots in the state, gets only half an inch of rain or less per month from June through September. Red Bluff gets 0.47 inch in June, and less through the remaining months of summer. San Francisco has almost no rain from June to September. Sacramento gets 0.10 inch in June, and minuscule amounts until the rainy season starts in late October. San Diego and Los Angeles are even drier.

In the mountains, summer thundershowers are likely, but these are scattered and do not bring heavy precipitation. Truckee gets only half an inch of rain or less during June, July, and August. Weather stations south of Lake Tahoe report even less precipitation.

Wind.   Wind patterns in California are largely generated by the weather systems moving in off the coast. There are important exceptions, such as the forceful Santa Ana winds of southern California, which actually come from the Great Basin of California and Nevada. But these exceptions aside, most of the state is subject to westerly or northwesterly winds. Once these winds strike the coast they are subject to considerable modification by topographical features. Winds entering the gap in the Coast Range near San Francisco, for instance, swing northward through the upper Central Valley. Thus Sacramento and Red Bluff experience southeasterly winds much of the year, while San Francisco has consistent westerly or northwesterly winds.

Wind velocities attenuate the farther south you go in the state. San Francisco has average velocities of 13 and 14 miles per hour throughout the summer. Wind velocities in both Los Angeles and San Diego are about half that. In the interior valley, winds are moderate most of the summer, averaging about 7 or 8 miles per hour. Winds in the mountains are generally light and westerly.

More detailed data for wind, precipitation, and temperatures for each state in this volume are given in Appendix 6.

WINTER RIDING

Almost all of California's southern coastal regions (below Monterey), the Central Valley south of Fresno, and its southeastern desert regions lend themselves well to off-season riding. Some of these areas are more suited to spring or autumn trips, others actually being ideal for winter rides.

Although you cannot be guaranteed consistent good weather either on the southern coast or southern Central Valley, temperature and precipitation levels there make for good weather during spring and fall. San Francisco receives 1.59 inches of rain in April, and daily maximum temperatures are in the low 60s. At the southern end of the coast, San Diego's rainiest month is January, with 1.88 inches and daily high temperatures near 65 degrees. Other months on either side of January are drier and warmer.

In the Central Valley, spring is an excellent time to tour, as fruit and nut trees are in bloom and temperatures are moderate. Sacramento begins to dry up in spring; only about six days in April have measurable precipitation. Farther south, Fresno is drier. Both places have average highs in the low 70s. A similar pattern exists in autumn, and cyclists can count on good riding weather until the first part of November in the southern Central Valley.

The southern desert regions can be cycled all year long, but one of the best times is winter. The Imperial Valley at the southernmost part of the state gets only 0.49 inches of rain in December—its rainiest month. Temperatures average around 55 degrees. Palm Springs is a bit wetter, with a bit more than an inch of rain in both December and January, and average temperatures (taking into account nighttime lows and daytime highs) are in the mid-50s. Death Valley gets almost no rain anytime during the year, and has good daytime temperatures in the 50s or 60s throughout winter. Tours of Anza-Borrego Desert State Park or of Joshua Tree National Monument present excellent winter riding opportunities.

ROAD NETWORKS AND ROUTE GUIDES

The heavy concentrations of people in certain parts of California create serious route-finding problems for the cyclist. There are a number of aspects to the problem.

Of first importance are the sprawling urban areas of the south. Squeezed between the mountains and the ocean of southern California live millions and millions of bodies. There seem to be about as many who have come to look. The effect of this on the bicyclist out for more than just a day's tour is very chilling indeed. It is nearly impossible to find a connecting route that will thread you through the maze in any sort of tranquillity. Only by going inland as far as the desert regions behind the San Gabriel and Santa Ana mountains can you find relatively quiet riding, and even there you must still choose your roads carefully.

Although not as serious, a comparable situation exists in the San Francisco Bay area. There are some excellent commuter routes, and a number of pleasing day tours, but long tours in the area are neither relaxing nor particularly safe.

Our advice to the long-distance tourist is to avoid both urban areas. You can still explore them by bicycle of course, but there is a world of difference between the day tourist on an empty bicycle who can return to a fixed place each night and the long-distance tourist, laden with heavy baggage, trying to navigate either Los Angeles or the Bay Area.

A second factor that complicates riding in some parts of the state is the lack of small secondary roads. Much of the state developed in relatively isolated pockets, with little opportunity or need to develop more than one route between points. Only in the Central Valley is there anything approaching the sort of rural demographics and road systems you will find in states such as Pennsylvania, Ohio, New York, or Virginia.

This relative lack of quiet secondary roads is reflected also in mountain travel. The Sierra is particularly difficult to cross, as early settlers found on their way west. Today, because of the heavy population along the coast and the relatively few east-west roads through the Sierra, a great deal of traffic is squeezed onto what roads there are.

If this sounds unduly gloomy, remember that California is a large state, and although crowded in some regions, it is sparsely populated and relatively little visited in others. Let's look at some of these prime touring regions next.

The best touring region in California, both in terms of scenery and availability of quiet roads, is in the north part of the state, which includes most of the area north of San Francisco and Sacramento. Although you can't get on just any road here and expect it to be quiet, the area's sparser population makes your chances much better. Our own tours concentrate rather heavily in northern California for this reason.

Of great help to the cyclist developing a tour route in any part of California, but particularly in the north, are the bicycling route guides published by the state's department of transportation, Caltrans. Districts 1, 2, 3, and 4 cover the area from San Francisco on north, and the guides for these regions are generally excellent. They give important details such as average daily traffic counts for state routes, indicate shoulder widths, and note sharp grades. The best guides also tell what sort of services you will find in the various towns. (For more details, see Appendix 1.)

The second area where riding is quiet is the Central Valley. Although by no means as picturesque as either the mountains or the coastline of California, the Central Valley has the advantages of being lightly populated and possessing a decent network of secondary roads. For summer riding, the main detriment is the heat, with highs in the 80s and 90s nearly every day, and hot spells of a week or more with highs above 100 degrees. But with a combination of morning riding and some acclimatization to the heat, you can do much to overcome the problem. Once attuned to the agrarian nature of the landscape, you can find much that is interesting, if not spectacular. Many of the valley towns are among California's oldest and are the least touched by modernization. Early founders were careful to plant trees, and almost all towns have quiet parks where you can while away time in the shade. Finally, the Central Valley offers more miles of level riding than you will find in nearly any other part of the West. Only the eastern parts of Montana and Colorado, the plateau area of Wyoming, and the low desert of Arizona offer such a large area with comparably easy riding conditions, and California's Central Valley compares favorably in scenic interest to all of these places.

A third region of California that offers good, if not absolutely quiet, riding conditions, are most sections of the coastal road. Caltrans has developed an excellent route guide for the entire coastline, and some of our own tours take advantage of the more interesting parts of the coast, including the redwood forests in the north and the picturesque Big Sur. Riding on the coast, you often must share the roadway with a good bit of other tourist traffic, but the winding roads slow that traffic down considerably. To be avoided, in our opinion, are the stretches from San Francisco to Santa Cruz, and the entire strip from Santa Barbara to Mexico. There is simply too much traffic for safe or comfortable riding.

Whichever part of the coast you intend to explore, try to do it from north to south. Strong, consistent northwesterly winds blow year round. Riders trying the coast road from San Francisco north often report dismal days of only 30 or 35 miles gained against fierce headwinds.

In addition to the route information furnished by Caltrans, which covers most of the state and national highways within California, a number of other books and guides describe tour routes. Almost all of these are for day tours in either the San Francisco Bay Area or in southern California, but some are oriented to the long-distance cyclist. Of particular note is the little volume by Bill Paul, *Cycling California's Spine*, which details his own route from Lassen National

Park to Kern County, at the south end of the Sierra Nevada. (This and other books offering tours of lesser scope are detailed in Appendix 1 and are noted in the Bibliography.)

NEVADA

Nevada is the driest state in the nation, as the Coast Range and Sierra Nevada of California rake off almost all available water from the storms coming in off the Pacific. Given these conditions, most of the state wears a brown, brittle appearance, which at first exposure (or for many, after every exposure) is forbidding.

We first discovered the possibilities of riding in Nevada when we went there to escape a rainy California winter. Although it was still mid-March, daytime temperatures were warm enough for sunbathing, and we happened to camp near a bubbling spring that supplied enough water for limited forms of splashing. This, and watching a full moon rise over the scarred sides of a neighboring mountain, the cool beams scintillating in the pure air, were enough to endear the state to us. Spring and autumn are particularly good times for touring there, when the combination of mild temperatures and clear air provides excellent riding conditions. As with any sparsely populated state, your major concern must be to make inquiries ahead about the availability of water and services you will need. Many towns marked on maps turn out to be nothing more than a scattering of outbuildings, marking either a place that knew better days or one whose promise never materialized at all.

TERRAIN

Most of Nevada is high, with elevations of about 5,000 to 6,000 feet in the eastern portion and between 3,800 and 5,000 feet in the west. The southern regions generally run about 2,000 to 3,000 feet. Almost the entire state lies within the Great Basin, a sunken plateau from which there is no outward drainage of water. Jutting off the floor of this basin are many mountain ranges, most of them 50 to 100 miles long, running north to south. Because rainfall is so light, relatively little erosion has taken place to soften the brittle upthrust of rock. Only one range runs east to west, and that is in the northeast, forming the southern limit to the Columbia River basin.

About the only part of the state where water has a chance to go someplace is in the southeast, where some intermittent streams drain into the Colorado. Other than this, streams simply disappear in the desert in places known as "sinks," or are trapped to form lakes. This characteristic caused much chagrin to early pioneers crossing the vast arid regions on their way to California.

In spite of the overall aridity of Nevada, its tallest mountain ranges trap enough winter rainfall to support good tree cover, and the mountains in the north half of the state have a good distribution of national forest lands. Roads tend to go around these mountains rather than over them, but the broken terrain still leaves a good many pass climbs at about 6,000 to 7,000 feet. These may appear more strenuous than they actually are, inasmuch as base elevations run just a thousand feet or so longer than the passes.

The southern part of the state is much more level, composed primarily of rolling hills and broad, open valleys.

CLIMATE

With its varied topography, running from low valleys and basins at 2,000-foot elevations to mountain peaks well over 11,000 and 12,000 feet, there are wide temperature ranges within the state. Its considerable length, nearly as long as California, also creates wide differences in temperatures between north and south. Finally, the dryness of the air creates a great disparity between daytime highs and nighttime lows. Balmy daytime weather in the spring or fall can be accompanied by water freezing solid in water bottles every night.

In summer, temperatures above 100 degrees are very common all through the south. Las Vegas has average maximum daily temperatures of 97 in June, 104 in July, 101 in August, and 99 in September. In the northern part of the state these extremes are moderated somewhat. Reno has daily maximums in the high 80s or low 90s from July through September. Elko, in the northeastern part of the state, has highs ranging from 78 to 90 degrees in those months.

Nights in Nevada's desert air get cool. Average minimum temperatures in Reno, for example, stay well below 32 degrees through May. The average minimum in Elko is 35 in May, and below freezing earlier in the year. By October, nights are again very cold in the north, averaging below freezing from mid-October onward. Nighttime lows in the south are more moderate. Las Vegas approaches freezing only during December and January.

Temperatures during the spring and autumn are excellent for bicycling in the northern part of the state, and in the south only December and January are somewhat chilly, daily maximums ranging in the low to mid-50s. In northern Nevada, Reno records a daily maximum of 64 in April, 72 in May, and 80 in June. During autumn there, October has a 70-degree average maximum. After that, the weather cools rapidly. November has an average maximum of 56 degrees.

Of rain, there is little to say in Nevada, as there is so little of the substance. Although the upper slopes no doubt get more rain than is recorded in the lower elevations, it is not a significant factor through the state except in the winter months. Reno, which manages to scavenge some moisture from the nearby Sierra, gets a little rain all through the spring and summer, most months averaging from a quarter to half an inch. Elko is a bit wetter, getting over an inch of rain in May and June, but the rest of the summer is quite dry; only a few days a month have measurable rainfall. Las Vegas never has more than three days during any month of the year when it gets rain.

ROAD NETWORKS AND ROUTE GUIDES

Roads are about as sparse in Nevada as people. Two Interstates cross it, one near Las Vegas in the south, the other cutting across the northern part of the state between Reno and Wells. There are only two other east-west routes, U.S. 50, which runs east from Lake Tahoe, and U.S. 6, which runs through the lower third of the state. U.S. 93 in the east and U.S. 95 in the west are the only continuous north-south routes through Nevada, although other routes may be devised, using a variety of state roads.

Traffic on Nevada's roads is concentrated around its two major population centers, Reno–Lake Tahoe and Las Vegas, and on the major throughways through the state. But even here, traffic tends to be sparser as you move away from the cities. Most of the state routes have light to moderate traffic.

Other than the tour presented in this book (Number 13), there are no route guides for Nevada, nor does the state department of transportation have information designed specifically for the cyclist. For the most part, the rider needs to use a good highway map that shows camping areas in the national forests, and to be independent enough to make it over stretches of 50 to 70 miles where there may be no services, or even houses. You must also check carefully to determine if you can get water and food on down the road. Our rule of thumb is to check until at least two sources give an affirmative answer before we count on it.

OREGON

No state in the West has done more to accommodate the bicyclist than Oregon. It was the first state in the West to open up its entire freeway system to bicyclists. Numerous cities, particularly those in the Willamette Valley, have taken great effort to develop bicycle lanes. Many of the state's two-lane highways have ample riding shoulders, kept in good repair. Efforts made by lawmakers, bicycle advocates, and environmentalists have been directed specifically to improving bicycling.

A number of more general factors contribute to excellent bicycling conditions in Oregon. To begin with, its population, although growing, is not as crushing as that of California's. Even in the heavily populated Willamette Valley, the agrarian countryside offers plentiful secondary roads. Unlike California, Oregon was settled primarily by people coming to till the land, not to mine gold. Early settlers arrived well-equipped to make their livelihood at farming. They immediately began to establish permanent settlements, rather than the tent cities and shantytowns that sprang up in gold country. These little farming towns, which liberally dot much of Oregon west of the Cascades, still bear the subdued—yet substantial—air they wore a century ago. Although by no means giving the feeling of being "preserved" places, they wear an atmosphere that is less than completely modern. For many of us, this opportunity to step rather effortlessly back through time is one of the primary attractions to bicycling in this part of the West.

Also, the geography and climate of Oregon lend themselves well to bicycling. There is a great variety of riding conditions, with a long coastline, numerous agricultural valleys, a high interior plateau, and two important mountain ranges in the western part of the state. A number of small ranges rise in the east. We'll look at some of the aspects of this topography first, then turn to some rather surprising facts about Oregon's summer climate.

MOUNTAINS

There are two important mountain groups in Oregon, the Coast Range and the Cascades. An important small range, the Blue Mountains, is located in the northeastern corner of the state.

The Coast Range continues up from California. Peaks are from 2,000 to 3,000 feet in elevation, making east-west passage relatively easy. Considerable winter rainfall creates a number of well-fed streams, and roads tend to thread their way up the gradual valleys, then cross summits at elevations under 1,000 feet.

Because the Coast Range gets the first wave of all Pacific storms, precipitation is heavy and the resultant forest growth dense. Here and there, particularly along the drier eastern slopes, valleys have been cleared for lush pasturelands where dairy cattle and other stock are grazed. Logging is also important here.

The second major mountain range in Oregon is the Cascades, extending unbroken from California to the gorge cut by the Columbia River on the Oregon-Washington border. They lie about 75 miles inland, and are much higher than the Coast Range. The highest Cascade peak is 11,245-foot Mount Hood, east of Portland. The other peaks in the Cascades do not approach this height, although many reach 8,000 to 9,000 feet.

The Coast Range in Oregon offers less rigorous riding than the Coast Range in California; so also the Oregon Cascades are easier than the Sierra. Ascents, particularly from the western slopes, are gradual, aided by roads that follow rivers flowing from the well-watered upper slopes. Almost all of the Cascade range in Oregon is part of the National Forest System. Tree cover is almost uniformly dense, with the exception of the higher mountains where heavy winter snowfall and thin soil limit timber growth. The heavy winter rain and snow in the Cascades insure a plentiful water supply in the streams during the summer. There are a number of small to medium lakes, many of which are accessible by paved road. The most spectacular is Crater Lake, at about 6,000 feet. Our own tour of southern Oregon takes you up and around the western rim of this unique and exceptionally beautiful body of water.

The third important range in Oregon is the Blue Mountains. These extend from the John Day and Deschutes Rivers in the north-central part of the state northeasterly into neighboring Washington. A number of branches of the Blue Mountains reach southward and southeastward over into the Snake River basin on the Oregon-Idaho border. The elevation of the peaks—between 5,000 and 6,000 feet for the most part—serves to catch what water is left from Pacific storms after they have passed over the Coast Range and the Cascades. National forests are amply distributed throughout the region, and although the road network is not extensive, this part of eastern Oregon is excellent cycling country. The Trans America Bicycle Trail, whose route we summarize later in the chapter, cuts across the Blue Mountains at Blue Mountain Summit.

A number of other small mountain chains rise from the broad plateau region of eastern Oregon. The Stevens Mountains, the Jackass Mountains, the Grassy Mountains, and the Steens Mountain are some of these small ranges. They're not very high, nor do they have extensive road systems, but they do break up the rolling terrain of the eastern plateau.

VALLEYS AND PLATEAUS

Between Oregon's mountain ranges are a number of important valleys and basins. Of most interest to the cyclist, probably, is the Willamette Valley, sandwiched between the Coast Range and the Cascades in the northwestern part of the state. It is a rich agricultural region, and was the primary attraction for Oregon's first white settlers. It is easy riding, towns are plentiful, and it has many excellent small roads, offering the bicyclist more choice than any comparable region in the entire West. Unlike the great Central Valley of California, the Willamette has kept much of the small-farm character of its earlier history. The cyclist can pass many days riding by small family-run farms, where excellent crops of apples, pears, sweet cherries, strawberries, hops, nuts, flax, wheat, and rye grass are grown.

Oregon's eastern plateau, part of the Great Basin, lies east of the Cascades and stretches to the Idaho border, covering about a third of the state's total area. Elevations run from about 4,000 to 6,000 feet above sea level. The two ranges lying west of the plateau drain off most of the water, so rainfall is light. But stock is raised here, and irrigation is permitting agricultural development of some sections. Riding here is mostly a matter of crossing rolling, rather than flat terrain, and the cyclist going very far will sooner or later encounter one of the ranges that thrust upward from the basin floor. Much of the land is dotted with juniper, which gives its own character—including a distinctive, fragrant smell—to the land.

CLIMATE

Among outsiders, the predominant image of Oregon is that of a beautiful land of green forests constantly enshrouded in rainclouds. For part of the year—the winter months—the image is correct, at least in the western part. Astoria, at the mouth of the Columbia, gets 9 or

10 inches of rain per month through most of the winter. Portland is not quite so soggy, but still averages 4 to 6 inches of rain per month all winter. On days when it isn't raining, it is often slate gray, a continual, unbroken layer of low clouds that nestle in valleys or cling to evergreens on the slopes. Lewis and Clark, who had to winter near the mouth of the Columbia, complained in their journals often and bitterly of Oregon's climate.

But Oregon's winter image is remarkably different from its summertime reality. Summer, particularly July and August (but also including June and September in much of this state), is actually arid. Ashland, Medford, Salem, and Portland usually have less rainfall during July and August than places one normally thinks of as much drier—including Coeur d'Alene, Denver, Yellowstone Park, Casper, and Salt Lake City. Portland receives an average of 0.41 inch of rain in July and 0.65 in August; about 25 days a month have no measurable precipitation. Even Astoria, in the direct path of Pacific storms, averages only 0.96 inch in July and 1.46 in August, with from 20 to 25 rainless days a month. Weather stations in the lower Willamette and Rogue River valleys report even less summer rain.

Eastern Oregon, as you might expect, is even drier, as most rainfall is drawn off by the Coast Range and the Cascades. Bend gets far less than an inch of rain per month from July through October. The Dalles, in the Columbia gorge in the north-central part of the state, gets less than an inch of rain per month from spring through Christmastime. Burns, in east-central Oregon, is officially classified as semiarid, with less than 12 inches of rain a year. Much of the eastern plateau shares the same weather pattern. Some stations there report less than 8 inches of rain a year.

What this means for the cyclist in Oregon, particularly in the summer or early autumn, is day after day of dry-weather riding, with only a few days per month in most of the state when rain is a possibility.

In addition to the nearly rainless summer, temperatures are moderate through much of the state. The coastal region has generally cool weather, with relatively little variation from day to night. Astoria has an average daily maximum of 64 degrees in June, 68 in July and August, and 67 in September. Nighttime minimums hover in the low 50s throughout the summer. Temperatures in the Willamette Valley and in the Rogue River valley to the south are warmer, but still moderate. Portland has daytime highs in the 70s during the summer. Medford, in the Rogue River valley, has daytime highs in the high

80s from July through August. June and September are pleasantly moderate, with maximums near 80 degrees.

In eastern Oregon, the overall elevation tempers the effects of an arid climate, and heat is not excessive. Burns reports average maximums of 86 and 83 degrees in July and August, and average highs in the mid-70s for the rest of summer.

Mountain temperatures in the state vary depending upon distance from the coast and elevation. In the coastal range, if fog is a factor, high temperatures will be in the low 60s. On sunny days, rides through the coastal range are pleasant, highs running in the 70s in the north, a bit warmer in the south. In the Cascades, you can normally expect to lose about 3 degrees of temperature for each 1,000 feet of elevation gained. Nights in the Cascades are cool, but freezes during the night are rare in most places where bicyclists will find themselves—although as with any mountain travel, you must be prepared for freezing temperatures any night of the year. We sat at the edge of Diamond Lake (5,200 feet) in June and watched snow collect on the slopes just a few hundred feet above.

Winds generally come from the west or northwest—but this generalization is subject to great variation, depending upon local topography. Astoria, for example, relatively exposed to the sea, has northwest winds at average velocities of about 8 miles per hour all through the summer. Portland's winds are similar, but its inland position means reduced wind speeds—around 6 or 7 miles per hour. The Willamette and Rogue River valleys have mainly northwesterly winds of very moderate velocity, averaging under 6 miles per hour. We have, however, experienced some long afternoon rides in the Willamette Valley when consistent northwesterly winds got a little tiresome by four or five o'clock. In the mountains, winds get funneled up canyons, particularly those with a westerly exposure, and velocities can get fairly strong.

ROAD NETWORKS AND ROUTE GUIDES

The road network west of the Cascades in Oregon is generally excellent. As we have already mentioned, the agricultural character of the Willamette Valley, and to a lesser extent the Rogue, have been instrumental in creating a good system of two-lane roads that carry light traffic. The cyclist must exercise some care in the Medford–Grants Pass area in southwestern Oregon, as there is a population and building boom going on there—fueled largely by escapees from California

—and the roads are becoming more and more crowded. There is also a tendency for many paved roads to turn to dirt when the going gets tough, so check ahead.

The Willamette Valley itself has excellent roads, although you will find that many of them do not appear on typical state maps, and you must either use county maps or navigate on inspiration. Generally speaking, the state does a good job of signposting routes, so it is not difficult to navigate from town to town over county roads that do not appear on your map.

The Portland area is another place you must cycle with care. You can get a well-drawn city map of Portland that shows bicycle routes, and the state department of transportation also provides a map showing routes through the crowded parts of the upper Willamette Valley, including Portland (see Appendix 1). But our advice is that unless you have a special reason for visiting Portland, you're better off avoiding it. There are a number of suitable routes to the west of it.

Routes through both the Coast Range and the Cascades of Oregon are well distributed, although you must use caution in the mountains on roads leading away from major population centers, particularly on weekends. The Cascades are also gentle enough so that you can fashion a north-south route through them, although this involves slipping from one side to the other. We suggest avoiding U.S. 97, which runs north-south on the east flank of the Cascades, as it is a popular truck route and much of it is two-lane.

North-south routes through the Rogue and Willamette Valleys are also possible. Old U.S. 99 has been bypassed by Interstate 5 through much of the state, and stretches of it are quiet enough for good riding. Of course you may also use the Interstate in Oregon, although there's nothing at all relaxing about riding on it. But for short stretches, particularly over passes, we are unabashed about employing the Interstate routes as an alternative to much harder and usually much longer rides in specific areas—especially if the alternative is a dirt or gravel road.

The coast road through Oregon, U.S. 101, is generally good riding. There are no major population centers on the coast, so there is little through traffic. But most of U.S. 101 is two-lane, and you must use caution at all times, particularly in summer fog.

In addition to the tours presented here, there are a number of route guides for Oregon.

First and foremost is the Bikecentennial Trans America Trail, which runs through the state. It starts at either of two towns on the

Oregon coast, Astoria and Reedsport, and these spurs join in the Willamette Valley. From there the trail crosses the Cascades, continues eastward along the Mitchell and John Day Rivers, then through the Blue Mountains and into Idaho. We summarize this route later in the chapter.

Bikecentennial also has developed a circular tour out of Portland which follows the Columbia River valley to the Pacific, goes down the coast to the village of Otis, heads inland on Oregon 18 to the Willamette Valley, then returns to Portland. We summarize this route later, and the complete guide is available from Bikecentennial (see Appendix 2 for address).

The Travel Information Section of the Oregon Department of Transportation publishes a large-scale map that summarizes route details for both the Bikecentennial tours just described. It also gives details of the coastal route using U.S. 101, and details an excellent Willamette Valley route from Portland to Eugene. All these, plus route guides for some of the more populous towns in the Willamette Valley, are on one large sheet, with details of campgrounds and bicycle repair shops noted. The guide is available from the Oregon Department of Transportation or from Bikecentennial (for addresses see Appendix 1).

WASHINGTON

Divided by the Cascade Mountains into eastern and western segments, Washington wears two faces. On the west, it's a varied land of timber-covered mountains, green pastoral valleys, with salty arms of Puget Sound reaching from the north deep down into the bottom third of the state. In the east, there are arid lands with black lava formations, rolling sagebrush plateaus, deep gorges cut by the Snake and Columbia Rivers, and undulating hills of dry-farmed wheat.

Although this picture is basically accurate, there are some exceptions. Much of eastern Washington is arid only in comparison to the west, which has some of the rainiest weather found within the continental United States. The northern part of Washington east of the Cascades has a series of north-south-oriented mountains and hills, all of which receive abundant rainfall during the year and wear extensive forests of yellow pine on their slopes. In the southeast, the Blue Mountains swing through a corner of the state, with peaks of 5,000 and 6,000 feet.

A look at the topography of mountains, plains and valleys, and seacoast will help refine the basic east-west dichotomy.

MOUNTAINS

Of all the mountains in the state, the Cascades are by far the most important, both in total area and in their effect upon climate and riding conditions. The Cascades form an unbroken volcanic chain from the Canadian border to the Columbia River. Some of the peaks are among the highest found in the country, topped by 14,408-foot Mount Rainier, but including also Mount Adams (12,307 feet) and Mount Baker (10,730 feet). Mount Saint Helens, which used to top out at 9,667 feet, was the highest peak in the southern part of this chain until it erupted in 1980, blowing about a third of its height to smithereens. What is left at this writing resembles a gigantic cigar butt stuck into a mound of gray mashed potatoes.

The north-south orientation of the Cascades puts them in direct line of the storms sweeping in off the Pacific. Beneficiaries are the forests of fir and hemlock along the western slopes; they are particularly dense and produce a great deal of commercially valuable lumber. The heavy snowfall also leaves many of the peaks snow-clad year round, and the highest mountains, such as Rainier, support extensive glacial fields. In fact, about one-third of all the glacial area in the lower forty-eight states is found on Mount Rainier.

The heavy rainfall on the western slopes also has had an effect upon the terrain and feel of the Cascades. Consistent water erosion has softened the contours considerably. Road systems follow river valleys upstream, then cross relatively low passes, most of which are between 3,000 and 5,000 feet. Climbs on the eastern side tend to be a bit stiffer. A rider following our tour through northern Washington will experience this change, with a long sloping climb from the west through North Cascade National Park, then a very quick descent down the eastern side to the valley floor.

The second important mountain range in Washington are the Olympics, in northwestern Washington's Olympic Peninsula. Although not as high as the Cascades—most peaks range from 6,000 to just under 8,000 feet—the position of the Olympics, lying as they do just off the coast and in the pathway of the continual Pacific winter storms, causes them to rake off a great deal of moisture. The result is the only true rain forest found in the contiguous 48 states. Here, fallen logs of gargantuan dimensions support foot-thick growths of moss. Sugary sitka spruce trunks as wide as a small house sit ponderously on the forest floor. Vine maple and thick undergrowth close off passage to areas except where trails are hacked out and maintained. A number of spur roads go up into the rain forest, but its density and the perpetual snow and glacial fields on the upper slopes have been safeguarded as part of Olympic National Park, and there are no through roads.

The third mountain group of importance in Washington is a series of lesser ranges that seem to hang like icicles down from the Canadian border southward to the latitude of Seattle or Spokane. Between these ranges is a series of rivers, including the Methow, the Okanogan, the Columbia, and the Pend Oreille. Riders crossing on an east-west route will climb over these ranges then fall into the intervening valleys. Our tour of northern Washington (Number 12), which takes the rider from near Seattle to Sandpoint, Idaho, crosses five passes as it traverses the state. This line of the rivers, most of which flow generally south, also allows for relatively easy rides through the valleys.

VALLEYS AND BASINS

There are a number of large areas within Washington that are level, or nearly so, with excellent riding possibilities. With slight exceptions, the entire southeastern quarter of the state is level or rolling basinland, extending from the area around Ellenburg almost to the Idaho border, where it gives way to rolling hills. North to south it extends from the south of Spokane and Grand Coulee Dam to the southern border of the state. Elevation within the plateau range from about 400 feet near the confluence of the Snake and Columbia Rivers to just under 2,000 feet in the northeast. It is hot, arid land, marked by sagebrush and undulating hills. An enormous lava flow once covered the area, and traces of it are still visible as lava beds. In some areas the topsoil that once covered the lava has been eroded away, leaving the earlier formations exposed to view. A number of small ranges of hills rise from the floor of the eastern basin, including the Frenchman Hills east of Ellenburg and the Palous Hills south of Spokane near the Oregon border. The Blue Mountains extend up from Oregon just east of Walla Walla. In other areas, sand dunes and shallow lakes speckle the land.

In western Washington, the area south of Puget Sound is rolling country and easy riding. The corridor created by the Cowlitz River makes an excellent pathway between the Oregon border and Puget Sound. As you move northward through this valley, you pass pasture-lands and clusters of dense hemlock and fir forests. Near the Sound itself you encounter an extensive urban buildup not well suited to the tourist seeking a through route. The best route is actually to swing slightly westward and use the islands and peninsulas of the Sound to go northward. An excellent network of ferries connects major points all along the Sound, and bicycles get first-class treatment, first on and first off, with fares significantly lower than for automobiles. North of Seattle another long stretch of level and rolling terrain runs clear to the Canadian border. This is excellent cycling country, with a num-ber of back roads that carry little traffic (discussed below).

Finally, the western and southern edges of the Olympic Peninsula offer gentle grades and relatively easy riding, although the northern part of the peninsula is hilly and there are major traffic problems for the bicyclist.

CLIMATE

It's evident by now that Washington is only partly "The Evergreen State." Much of the southeast is arid enough to be classified as desert. The rolling wheat-covered hills around Spokane are golden-brown, not green, and there is little vegetation at all along the Columbia where it forms a border between Washington and Oregon.

But during the dry summer months the green parts offer striking vistas for the tourist, particularly with the counterpoint of an island-dotted sound in the west and snow-covered Mount Rainier shoulder-ing its way into the sky to the southeast of the Seattle-Tacoma area. But one question remains: How rainy is it really?

Looked at on the basis of an entire year, it is definitely rainy—in some places, enormously so, with over 12 feet of rain a year. But it is not consistently rainy the year round, and much of the state is arid. There are instances where "rainy" Washington is actually drier in the summer months than places we normally think of as arid. Let's make a few comparisons.

Aberdeen, which lies in the west-central part of the state on an inlet of the Pacific Ocean called Grays Harbor, is one of Washing-ton's wettest towns. Between late fall and early spring Aberdeen seems as if it might float away, and between October and December, it sees almost 34 inches of rain on the average. Spring is almost as rainy, and only with the coming of May does average monthly rainfall decline to what would seem normal most other places in the country (3.43 inches).

But by summer, the Pacific high-pressure center, which shields California and much of Oregon from Pacific storms, gravitates northward and offers some of its protection to the western coast of Washington as well. At the same time, a more or less permanent low-pressure center located in the Pacific north of the state, which is responsible for much of the rain during the winter, weakens considerably, and the skies almost miraculously dry up. July in Aberdeen has an average rainfall of 1.51 inches, and August is only a little wetter with 1.79 inches. Compare these figures to some other weather stations in the West: Denver is wetter than Aberdeen in July (1.8 inches) and only a little drier in August (1.3 inches). Great Falls, Montana, is drier than Aberdeen, but only slightly (1.27 and 1.09 inches). Tucson and Flagstaff, Arizona, aren't even close—Tucson averages 2.06 inches in July and 2.88 in August, and Flagstaff gets 2.28 and 2.84 inches. The fact is, you have a much greater chance of getting rained on in parts of Arizona, New Mexico, and Montana, in the summer than you have of getting wet in one of the wettest areas of Washington.

Other spots in the western part of the state receive even less rain than Aberdeen. Seattle is relatively dry all through the summer, with only 0.71 inches in July and 1.08 in August. June and September bring 1.53 inches and 1.99 inches respectively. On the average, this means about six to nine days out of most summer months when measurable precipitation falls. Anacortes, on Whidbey Island in Puget Sound, averages 1.57 inches in June, 0.78 in July, and 0.87 inches in August; September is still relatively dry with 1.45 inches.

Thus in general, the cyclist venturing into western Washington during the dry season—namely July and August—can count on one day or so a week when it will rain. Chances of getting rained on are greater in June, and by mid-September, chances of rain increase significantly.

Eastern Washington is much drier than the west, of course, as the Cascades rake off much of the rain, and once winds have passed over the mountains and flow down the eastern slopes, compression raises air temperatures away from the dew point. Yakima, in south-central Washington, gets only 0.73 inches of rain in June, and a quarter-inch or less through the rest of the summer. This minimal precipitation falls on two or three days a month. Walla Walla, in southeastern Washington, has a fairly rainy June (1.18 inches) but July through

September have only three to five days a month when measurable precipitation falls, adding up to less than an inch a month. Spokane in the northeast follows a similar pattern. In general, the rainiest month of summer all through the state is June, with only minimal precipitation falling thereafter.

The influence of the sea and the latitude of the state keep summer temperatures moderate through most of Washington. Along the edge of Puget Sound or on the Pacific, daytime maximums run from about 65 degrees near the water to 70 or 75 inland. In the low-lying corridor that stretches from the Columbia River northward to Tacoma-Seattle, then on up into Canada, average summer maximum temperatures range from 73 to 78 degrees. Although temperatures have reached 100 degrees or more in this area, this is exceptionally rare, and during most summers only three to five days go above 90 degrees.

Eastern Washington presents quite a different picture. The mountain chains in the north of the state have temperatures in midsummer in the mid-80s. There is considerable difference, of course, between temperatures recorded in the northeastern river valleys and those in the mountains surrounding them. The Okanogan Valley, for instance, usually records summer highs well into the 90s. Temperatures in the surrounding mountains drop about 3 degrees for each 1,000 feet of elevation gain. Spokane records maximum temperatures in the low 80s for July and August, and moderate temperatures in the low 70s for June and September. Walla Walla is hotter, as are the towns lying close to the Columbia Gorge. Walla Walla has maximum temperatures in the high 80s during July and August, and records maximums in the high 70s during June and September.

Nights are moderate in summer throughout the state, but there is a greater variation in temperatures in the more arid eastern part of the state. Summer evenings around Spokane are in the low 50s at their coolest. Walla Walla has minimums about 5 degrees higher. Seattle, which is representative of much of western Washington, has nighttime minimum temperatures in the low to mid-50s all summer long.

Wind velocities are moderate throughout the state, speeds averaging 8 or 9 miles per hour around Puget Sound, and generally less inland. Winds are primarily westerly, but the complex topography of mountains and the Sound create variations. Wind blows primarily from the southwest in the Seattle area, but east of the Cascades varies from predominantly northwest at Yakima to southerly in Spokane and Walla Walla.

ROAD NETWORKS AND ROUTE GUIDES

Population density on the western side of the Cascades has led to the development of a more extensive road network than in eastern Washington. The best secondary road system is in the low valleys bordering Puget Sound north of the town of Everett. Upper Snohomish, Skagit, and Whatcom counties are agrarian, and there are many small, quiet roads you can use. To a lesser extent the region south of the town of Olympia to the Columbia River has good roads, and there is an excellent north-south corridor paralleling Interstate 5. Some of this is old Route 99, which still has its original concrete surface in places. The joints between the slabs remind you that you are on an old highway, but otherwise the riding is good, and quiet.

You will also find good riding on many of the islands and peninsulas in Puget Sound. Part of our tour of western Washington (Tour 11) takes advantage of some of these roads, along with the pleasant hiatus in riding offered by Washington's excellent ferry system.

Other than Interstate 90, on which bicyclists are prohibited, there are only four roads through the Cascades. Of these four, the best crossing is in the northern part of the state on Washington 20. We use this route in our North Cascades tour (Tour 12). Both U.S. 12 and U.S. 2 through the Cascades carry heavy traffic. There is no north-south route in the mountains, although there is an interesting loop around Mount Rainier using routes Washington 410 and 123, and U.S. 12.

Eastern Washington has a fair network of roads. Some of these routes, such as the corridor from Yakima to the Richland-Kennewick area, are crowded. But others that serve the arid regions of the eastern basin offer good riding possibilities. You do need to make inquiries ahead of time to determine availability of services and water. The roads north of the Columbia River in northeastern Washington make a bit more interesting riding, as the area is greener and terrain nicely varied from mountains to valley riding.

One of the great advantages to touring in Washington are the route guides offered by the Washington Department of Transportation, discussed in Chapter 3, with strip maps that can be joined to make a superb long-distance guide. Road conditions, amount of shoulder, services found in towns, and scenic points are all described. See Appendix 1 for more on these maps, which along with a generally good free state map, will allow you to tour nearly anywhere in Washington and know ahead of time the conditions you will face.

A number of books detail short to medium tours in western Washington. Best of these are two volumes by Erin and Bill Woods, *Bicycling the Backroads of Northwest Washington* and *Bicycling the Backroads of Southwest Washington*. A third volume, *Bicycling the Backroads of Puget Sound*, is out of print but may be available in libraries. The Woodses have written their guides with great care, and tours may be strung together to form long-distance routes. A helpful index tells you where tours intersect.

There are also several books and pamphlets dealing with smaller regions. Most notable of these is *A Whatcom County Bike Book* by Patrick Vala, which describes tours in the Bellingham area. (For details of this and other volumes see the Bibliography and Appendix 1.)

ROUTE GUIDES

TOUR #1: SAN DIEGO—ANZA-BORREGO DESERT STATE PARK—OCEANSIDE

Distance: 212 miles.

Terrain: Steep climbs into the Laguna Mountains behind San Diego, gradual uphill along desert floor, hilly return to Oceanside.

Roads and Traffic: Busy urban traffic getting out of San Diego, then quiet riding on old Highway 80, quiet two-lane roads through Anza-Borrego Desert State Park, moderate traffic through the hills behind Oceanside.

Season: All year, but it may be rainy and cold in the mountains (high points above 3,000 feet) in the winter.

Weather: Moderate coastal weather near San Diego and immediate foothills year round, hot riding through Anza-Borrego in summer, mild and usually dry in winter. Hot on the eastern sides of the Laguna Mountains in summer.

Special Features: By using old Highway 80 you pass many quiet miles making your way through old towns in the Laguna Mountains. Excellent desert terrain in Anza-Borrego Park. Good riding conditions in the nonsummer months.

Connecting Transportation:

San Diego: Greyhound, Trailways, Amtrak, air service.

Oceanside: Greyhound, Trailways, Amtrak.

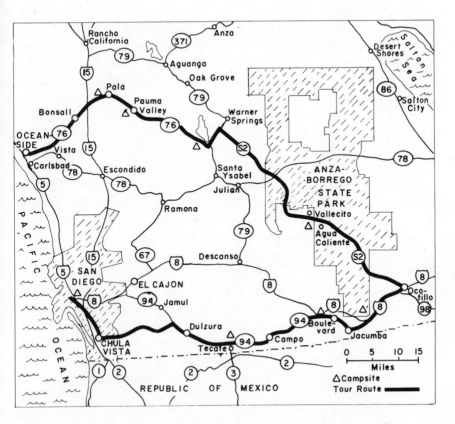

Tour #1   San Diego—Anza-Borrego Desert State Park—Oceanside

If you love dry weather and desert riding, you would be hard pressed to find in the West an area more accommodating to your riding than the mountains behind San Diego and the desert preserve of Anza-Borrego Desert State Park. Although you soon leave the heaviest trappings of civilization, you are never very far away from some small settlement or other, even in the giant park. Many of the small towns behind San Diego date from the Spanish period. The desert route through Anza-Borrego was actually pioneered by the Butterfield and Overland Stages over a century ago, and a scattering of settlements remain to remind you of the times when stage stops had to be 20 miles apart. Thus you have all the joys of remote country riding combined with all the advantages of frequent stops for food, and even a hot spring or two to plunge into if you wish.

You can take the tour year round, although you should use caution in the winter months, when temperatures in the Laguna Mountains will be low. You pass several points above 3,000 feet. In early springtime you can take advantage of the blooming of desert cactus. Autumn brings mild temperatures and a lessening of tourist traffic. Summer tours through Anza-Borrego should be taken with caution, and then only by persons used to very hot-weather rides. Carry extra water, wear light-colored clothing, and plan your rides for morning or late afternoon.

San Diego (grocery, motels, restaurants, camping, youth hostel, bicycle shops). Of the many attractions of this sparkling port city, its renowned zoo is probably the most famous. The zoo is part of Balboa Park, which also houses an excellent fine arts gallery. In the center of town is the Old Town Plaza, around which are some houses dating from the early nineteenth century, and reflecting the strong Spanish influence on the city. Also in San Diego is a section of the Pacific Coast Bicentennial Route, which runs from the Mexican to the Canadian border. Leaving town you follow this route for a little ways. Head south on Harbor Dr. to National City. Continue south from here on Cleveland Ave. to 24th St. Turn left on 24th St. to Hoover Ave. Turn right (south) on Hoover to 33rd St. Turn left on 33rd St. to National Ave. Turn right (south) on National Ave., which becomes Broadway. Follow to the center of

Chula Vista (5 miles; grocery, restaurants, motels, bicycle shop). In Chula Vista you will leave the Pacific Coast Bicentennial Route and head eastward into the foothills of the Laguna Mountains. To make this eastward turn you follow Broadway to an intersection with L St. Turn left (east) on L St., climbing some grades. L St. becomes Telegraph Canyon Rd., which you follow for about 8 miles to a junction with Otay Lakes Rd. Bear right on Otay Lakes Rd., rolling through open country and past Lower Otay Lake. A recent fire has denuded the landscape, but the plants are rapidly growing back, with chaparral and other scrub flourishing in the ashes. Continue up a valley on a road partially shaded by generous oak trees to a

Junction, California 94 and Otay Lakes Rd., (21 miles). Turn east (right) on Calif. 94. You soon begin a 7-mile climb up the side of a canyon, winding past small ranches and second homes to a crest at Milepost 32. From here you swing down sharply, descending about 600 feet to Barrett Junction. After crossing a small creek you begin a climb of about 4 miles to

Potero (18 miles; general store, camping). This little village is set in a valley with stands of live oak and eucalyptus, some of which offer shade along the route. This may be welcome here; around this point you begin losing the tempering effects of the ocean breezes, and if you're riding in summertime, things will begin to heat up. Continue east on Calif. 94 through country where heat-resistant digger and ponderosa pine do well, mixing in here with predominating oaks. Climbs are moderate and you run alongside a little stream to

Campo (13 miles; grocery, café). You leave the valley floor here and begin a hard climb that lasts nearly 12 miles. Much of this is on a relatively shadeless canyon wall, and if you are taking the tour during the warm season, you should try to cover this stretch early in the morning. The road is narrow and winding, so use caution. Climb to a crest (3,500 feet), which you hit just 2 miles before Boulevard, at the junction of your route and the Tierra del Sol Rd. From this junction you have a chance to relax as you coast into

Boulevard (14 miles; grocery). There are some lovely stretches of old road here, as old Highway 80 was once the major east-west route through this region. You pass from the oak-studded countryside into terrain that is more arid, and the vegetation changes into desert cactus, yucca plant, and spiny grasses. Continue to

Jacumba (5 miles; grocery, café, hotel). The hot springs hotel here could be used as a setting for a Tennessee Williams play, with its seemingly failing efforts to retain its former luxurious façade. As you leave town you pass by a little airstrip, then begin a rolling climb for 4 miles to a crest where you cross under Interstate 8. A service station a few hundred yards down the hill has water. From here you must use the Interstate shoulder for a 10-mile downhill run to the desert floor. The descent is steep, and you must be very careful of sidewinds in the rocky, treeless canyon. Arriving at the bottom, you will have dropped some 2,000 feet in about 10 miles. You must leave the Interstate at Exit 8, then go into

Ocotillo (14 miles; café, grocery), Junction with County Road S2. The little village is nothing more than a scattering of houses in the desert, but is a good water source and perhaps a snack stop. Head north on Co. Rd. S2, which has fair paving. You climb very gradually through sandy terrain where you will see many varieties of cacti growing. In spring, the long-stemmed cactus sends forth delicate red blossoms. After about 8 miles you pass into the boundary of Anza-Borrego Desert State Park, the largest state park in the West. You are also on the approximate route of one of the first stagecoach lines going west from St. Louis, passing via the south to avoid the Sierra, which was impenetrable in winter. Markers commemorate a number of the old stations, which were spaced 20 miles apart. Beginning at MP 52.5 you have a steep downgrade of 4 miles into a canyon. Continue past a campground at MP 47, then on to

Agua Caliente (25 miles; grocery). There is a hot spring here. The Vallecito Stage Station is about 4 miles from here (grocery, camping). Typical desert growth continues, with durable mesquite trees and cactus. Climb upward into

Butterfield (10 miles; café, grocery, camping). This little resort is named after John Butterfield, hard-driving founder of the stage line that bore his name.

Junction, Calif. 78 and Co. Rd. S2 (10 miles; no services). You must make a short jog right here, then left again on Co. Rd. S2. The road widens out considerably, and is better paved. You start up a broad valley, with a number of private ranches on both sides of the road. Continue on an uphill grade to

San Felipe (11 miles; grocery), then just a half-mile beyond cross a high point (3,636 feet) at MP 6. Descend through oak and pine forests to

Junction with Calif. 79 (6 miles; no services). Turn west (left) on Calif. 79 and go to

Junction with Calif. 76 (4 miles; no services). Turn north (right) on Calif. 76 toward Oceanside. You enter a broad valley and begin working your way upward again, past Lake Henshaw (grocery), then near MP 48 you begin a steep 6-mile downhill. From here the route rolls up and down, past the La Jolla Indian Campground (MP 41.5), where you start another climb to MP 39. You drop quickly down a steep, winding road, vegetation changing from desert plants and oaks to cultivated orchards of citrus and avocado.

Rincon Springs (20 miles; grocery, restaurant, motel). At this point you have reached the broad Pauma Valley, cut by the San Luis Rey River, not far off the tour route.

Mission San Antonio (12 miles; grocery, camping 1 mile down the road). Traffic will pick up here, so be alert, particularly on weekends when people travel to Lake Henshaw. You cross Interstate 15, and continue through a wide valley where you may experience strong headwinds from the ocean. Just beyond the junction of Calif. 79 and Co. Rd. S13 you have a short, final climb, after which you pass into urbanized areas, past the Mission San Luis Rey, founded in 1798. It is regarded as one of the most impressive of all California missions, showing Spanish, Moorish, and Mexican architectural influences. Continue to

Oceanside (24 miles; grocery, restaurant, motels). You intersect the Pacific Coast Bicentennial Route here. North of you lies Camp Pendleton, through which you may ride. Stop at the gate for permission and a map. Other than Camp Pendleton, however, the rest of the Pacific Coast Bicentennial Route both north and south of Oceanside passes through highly urbanized terrain, and you may wish to return to your starting point, or head off in another direction, via bus or train.

TOUR #2: SANTA BARBARA—PINE MOUNTAINS—CUYAMA VALLEY

Distance: 237 miles.

Terrain: Steep climbs leaving Santa Barbara and making your way into the Pine Mountains. Gentler terrain along the Cuyama Valley, then mostly hilly riding, with one major pass back to Santa Barbara.

Roads and Traffic: Generally light to moderate on two-lane roads.

Season: March through October.

Weather: Spring and fall rides are subject to rain and cold temperatures in the mountains. Otherwise temperate along the coast, warmer inland. Dry from June through September.

Special Features: For a tour so close to civilization, there are surprisingly long stretches where you are miles from towns or other signs of civilization. Very scenic riding through the elegant foothill area behind Santa Barbara, with good mountain riding in the Pine Mountains.

Connecting Transportation:

Santa Barbara: Greyhound, Amtrak, air service.

It is rare in highly congested southern California to pass quickly from urban areas into wilderness; yet that is precisely what happens in this tour. Within half a day of leaving the coastal city of Santa Barbara, you arrive at mountain reaches far from the nearest house. The contrast is accentuated by your trip out of Santa Barbara, where you pass some of the most opulent real estate in the West. You cross

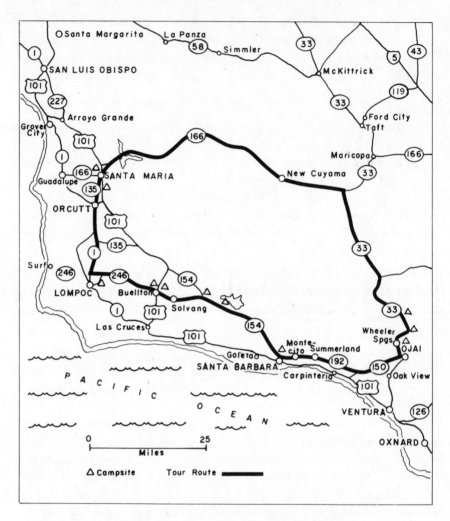

Tour #2   Santa Barbara—Pine Mountains—Cuyama Valley

a small summit and descend to the Ojai Valley, then it is only a short distance to the Los Padres National Forest, where you leave civilization behind, and enjoy a stretch of more than 60 miles where houses, as well as other visitors, are rare. The climb is steep, but you will shake off some of the heat characteristic of the interior valleys as you climb higher. From a pass just above 5,000 feet you descend to the Cuyama River, which you follow for many miles, past ranches and irrigated fields, finally arriving again in the lowlands at Santa Maria. From here you work an up-and-down route back to Santa Barbara, and civilization once again.

For all the advantages of getting off on your own, you ought to realize that the mountains are very challenging riding, and you must be equipped to travel stretches through which you will find only limited services, and in one case, a 55-mile stint with no services at all.

Santa Barbara (grocery, restaurant, motels, camping, bicycle shops). There is much to see and do in this wealthy city built on a shelf between the Santa Ynez Mountains and the sea. Spanish priests and soldiers arrived here in 1782, and the flavor they imparted to it predominates still, with beautiful stuccoed buildings with red-tile roofs visible through the trees. There is a good museum in town, and of course the Santa Barbara Mission, built in 1815 by the padres, using Canalino Indians as laborers, after an earlier structure was destroyed in an earthquake. Just behind the city lie the mountains and extensive sections of the Los Padres National Forest. To begin the tour you must climb to the upper parts of town where you intersect California 192. Head east (parallel to the coast) on Calif. 192, which twists and turns many times as it makes its way up and down small ridges, past luxurious homes and heavily forested estates. The route is well posted, but watch turns carefully, as the road changes name frequently. (Foothill Rd., Stanwood Dr., Sycamore Canyon Rd., East Valley Rd., Foothill Rd. again, Casitas Pass Rd.) For the most part, there are no shoulders, but traffic is restricted primarily to residents living on or near the tour route. Continue along Calif. 192 though the small communities of Monticito and Summerland, past numerous citrus and avocado orchards, then drop down to a valley and

Junction, Calif. 150 and 192 (16 miles; no services). Turn east (left) on Calif. 150 toward Ojai. The road winds up through beautiful forests of live oak, following a clear mountain stream. You must cross Casitas Pass (1,155 feet), then continue to

Ojai (18 miles; grocery, restaurant, motel, bicycle shop). Junction, Calif. 33. Your turnoff on Calif. 33 comes before you enter the main part of Ojai, and you may want to continue into town instead to shop. Your next full services are in New Cuyama, 69 miles away, although there are some small cafés after you reach the Cuyama Valley. The first of these cafés is 38 miles away. If you have gone into Ojai to restock, return to the tour route and go north on Calif. 33. After 5 miles you pass the little resort of Wheeler Springs (café). By this time you have climbed out of the agricultural valley and are in pine forests. The climb becomes steeper the farther you go, and you crest a hill at Milepost 27, drop down and cross Sespe Creek, then begin climbing again, but this time more gradually. Near MP 40 you start another steep climb, with a hard 3-mile stretch to a summit at 5,058 feet (MP 43). This is the highest part of the tour, and certainly the hardest. From the high point you have excellent views of all the Coast Range. You drop down very steeply for 5 miles on road surface that is only fair, so use caution. At the bottom you pass a ranger station (MP 48), a good source for water. From here you have an essentially level ride down the Cuyama River valley. There is a café near MP 50, and another after you cross the Santa Barbara County line at MP 3. Continue on an easy ride past cultivated fields to

Junction, Calif. 166 and 33 (57 miles; no services). Turn west (left) on Calif. 166 toward Santa Maria. You continue following the Cuyama River, which makes a sweep westward here. The first part of this long and somewhat uninteresting country is through open fields, largely devoid of trees. Pass through Cuyama and on to

New Cuyama (12 miles; grocery, café). You should restock here, as the next services are 55 miles away. As you leave town, you swing down along the Cuyama River, which you then cross several times. Some of this terrain is rugged and steeply rolling. Once past Twitchell Reservoir you must make a left turn on Suey Rd. This comes about 3 miles before the junction of Calif. 166 and U.S. 101. (Suey Rd. floods in wet weather, and if this is the case, continue on down Calif. 166 to a junction with U.S. 101. Ignore the sign prohibiting bicyclists and walk your bicycle on the southbound lane of the freeway to the first exit.) Either route will bring you to

Santa Maria (55 miles; grocery, restaurant, motel, camping). You may want to rest awhile in the park on the north end of town, and luxuriate in some of the services that have been so rare since leaving Ojai. At Santa Maria you pick up Calif. 135 south toward Orcutt. There is an excellent shoulder once you leave town, then the road becomes four-lane divided. Continue to the southbound exit to Calif. 1. Leave the freeway and go south on Calif. 1. From here you begin a climb up a narrow, rocky canyon, pedaling hard for 1.5 miles to a crest at MP 28. You descend into a broad valley and come to

Junction, Lompoc-Casmilia Rd. and Calif. 1 (20 miles). Turn left at the traffic signal on Lompoc-Casmilia Rd., heading toward La Purisima Mission, which you may visit. Just past the mission you have a junction with Calif. 246. Bear left on Calif. 246 and after an easy stretch arrive at

Buellton (14 miles; grocery, restaurants, motels). You pass by a well-known restaurant at this intersection; people come from miles around to eat Andersen's Split Pea Soup. If you are not inclined to indulge in this delicacy, continue straight on Calif. 246 to

Solvang (3 miles; grocery, restaurants, motels). It is hard to tell what is authentic about this entire town built to resemble, theoretically, a Danish village. You may wish to wander past its numerous tourist shops. Leave east, continuing on Calif. 246 to a junction with Calif. 154, 6 miles from town. Turn right on Calif. 154 toward Santa Barbara. Traffic picks up here, particularly on weekends. You have a 2-mile run to where you cross the Santa Ynez River, then a good ride through stands of live oak to Lake Cachuma (camping). Beyond the lake, at MP 20, you begin a 4.5-mile climb up over San Marcos Pass. It is hard. You cross the summit at MP 24.3 (2,225 feet). From here you have a very steep downhill, and you may experience a temperature change as you enter the maritime weather system of the coast. Descend for about 6.5 miles, using caution as the surface is so-so and following traffic may be heavy. Go to

Junction, Calif. 192 and 154 (37 miles). Turn left on Calif. 192, cross under the freeway, then begin a rolling ride that will eventually take you back to

Santa Barbara (5 miles; grocery, restaurants, motels, camping, bicycle shops). The Pacific Coast Bicentennial Trail connects here, and you may go north or south, although the southerly arm becomes very congested as you near Los Angeles.

TOUR #3: MONTEREY—BIG SUR— SANTA LUCIA MOUNTAINS

Distance: 304 miles.

Terrain: Short but steep hills almost the entire tour route. Moderate grades in the San Benito Valley.

Roads and Traffic: Moderately heavy but slow-moving traffic along the coast through Big Sur. Quiet two-lane roads in the Santa Lucia Mountains and in the San Benito Valley.

Season: Mid-April to November. Fall and spring are the best seasons.

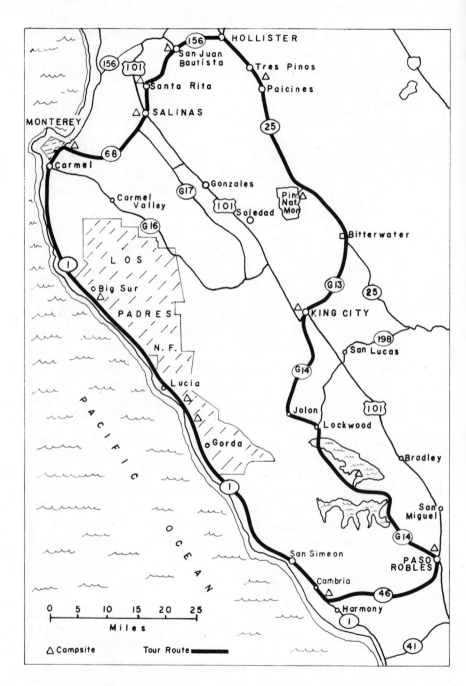

Tour #3   Monterey—Big Sur—Santa Lucia Mountains

Weather: Cool maritime weather with a chance of fog along the coast. Hot and dry inland.

Preferred direction: South along the coast from Monterey, north through the interior valleys.

Special Features: Big Sur is probably the most photographed and well-known stretch of coast in the western United States. You ride high above swirling waves, azure seas, and the white of foaming salt water. The tour route allows you to make a circle back to your starting point via interesting, but less spectacular, scenery in the foothills of the Santa Lucia Range.

Connecting Transportation:

Monterey: Greyhound, air services; Amtrak from Salinas, 18 miles away.

The 100-mile stretch of coastline from Monterey south to the Hearst Castle at San Simeon is among the most scenic in the world. The ride through this region, known as Big Sur, is difficult. With rare exceptions, you are either climbing or going down. The hills are not long, mostly under 2 miles in length, but they give you little rest. The rewards, however, are considerable. You are in almost constant view of the ocean, which combines with the plunging cliffs of the Santa Lucia Range to produce thousands of coves, small beaches, and countless rock formations of great beauty. For the most part you ride high above the sea; as the cliffs slope downward toward the south, you have direct views downward to the swirling waters below. Most of the terrain is open, with grasses and chaparral covering the hillsides. What few trees that you do see—mostly Monterey pine, Monterey cypress, and a scattering of eucalyptus—are tortured by the wind into fantastic shapes, many clinging to the soil with desperate tenacity.

Near the end of the route along Big Sur you come to the remarkable castle constructed by newspaper giant William Randolph Hearst. San Simeon eventually got too cumbersome for even this wealthy family to handle, and is now a state park. It may be visited, but reservations are absolutely necessary (see Appendix 4 for address of California State Park system and information on making reservations).

Just beyond San Simeon, you turn inland, with dramatic change in scenery and temperature, although the terrain stays steep and hilly. From the valley town of Paso Robles, once on the King's Highway north from Spanish Mexico, you head into the sharp foothills of the back side of the Santa Lucia Mountains. There are two lakes that offer recreation and camping opportunities, and a number of quiet, excellent rides through high valleys. You cross the Salinas Valley, then head into more forgiving terrain to make your way northward through the San Benito Valley—not flat, but much easier riding. Beyond Salinas, at the upper reaches of your route, you swing westward for a brief run down to your starting point at Monterey.

Although the coast road is very popular, much of it is protected from development, and you need to pay attention to your next supply points. This is even more true of the Santa Lucia Mountains and the ride down the San Benito Valley. Because motels are scarce there, the latter half of the tour is recommended for camping cyclists only. Those requiring motels may wish to restrict their tour to the Big Sur portion and make their way back to their starting point via U.S. 101 and frontage roads.

Monterey (grocery, restaurant, motels, bicycle shop). Much changed from the days when John Steinbeck immortalized it in his novels *Tortilla Flat* and *Cannery Row*, Monterey still holds a great deal of charm and interest, particularly its old waterfront, and even the modern Cannery Row is still worth a stroll. You can also spend a good many hours along the working-boat waterfront, with its flotilla of small fishing craft. Leave Monterey south via Munras Ave., which joins California 1 on the outskirts of town. Ride the shoulder of Calif. 1 toward

Carmel (4 miles; grocery, restaurants, motels). The main part of town lies to the right of the tour route. Carmel is one of those nearly perfectly picturesque spots which have managed—in spite of all the tourism connected with it—to hold onto its original character and charm. Spend an hour or so walking down its streets, and to its crescent beach. Rejoining Calif. 1, you begin a steep descent amidst usually heavy traffic toward Carmel Valley. Most of the heavy traffic now turns inland at this point, but the coast road is sufficiently popular to insure an adequate supply of cars at all times, including very wide motor homes. Be particularly cautious, as much of the next 94 miles is over narrow, twisting road. In addition to having a wind advantage by taking the tour north to south, you also have the advantage of riding the edge of the road closest to the water. This is superb for views, but leaves you little room for improvisation if you get caught in a squeeze.

The route is not easy riding. With few exceptions, you are either climbing or going down. Most of these grades are short

—the longest continuous ones less than 3 miles—but their constant occurrence is fatiguing. The rewards are more than adequate. You are constantly in view of the sea. Sometimes it is 800 feet below you, swirling amidst tortured rock formations. Sometimes it is only a few feet away, as you swing around a hairpin turn and discover a beach hidden to everyone's eyes but your own. Supply points are fairly well distributed for the first 30 miles from Carmel, after which they become scarce. There are also numerous state-park and national-forest campgrounds, some of which are very scenic themselves. The first of these is

Pfeiffer–Big Sur State Park (27 miles; camping), inside the Los Padres National Forest. There is a special walk-in camping section here set aside for bicyclists and hikers. Spaces are limited to twenty-five persons, so it is a good idea to stop by mid-afternoon. There are excellent examples of coastal redwoods to be explored. Continuing on the tour route past the state park you have a steep 2.5-mile climb. The small cluster of buildings and services at the crest (Milepost 44) (grocery, restaurant, and camping area) is the most complete set of service facilities you will find until you arrive in Gorda, 36 miles away, although there are a number of small cafés between you and there. As you descend from this high point, the road is carved out of a cliff, the sea churning about 800 feet below you. Stopping and taking long looks is better than riding and taking short, hurried ones—not to mention safer. You may want to pull into one of the numerous turnouts built out onto the cliff. You descend steeply for a mile and a half, then more gradually. From the bottom of the hill you then climb and descend on a rolling route to Lucia (restaurant), past a small café and grocery at MP 16, then on to

Gorda (36 miles; grocery, restaurant). From here you swing down almost to the level of the water, then have two final steep climbs, the second one ending just after you pass out of the Los Padres National Forest. From the top of the latter hill you descend down to near sea level, where the ride is much easier across Piedras Blancas Point to

San Simeon (31 miles; no services). The Hearst Castle is about 5 miles east of the highway, uphill. To tour the castle, which is a state park, you must have reservations. You should make these several weeks in advance through Ticketron (see the

white pages of a telephone book) or directly through the state
park system (telephone numbers and address in Appendix 4).
If you are not visiting the castle, continue south on Calif. 1 to
Cambria (9 miles; motel, restaurant, grocery). A community built
largely on the tourist industry generated by San Simeon. Motels are crowded. Continue to
Junction, Calif. 46 and 1 (3 miles). You leave the coast at this point
and turn east (left) on Calif. 46. This is a wide highway with
excellent riding shoulders. After 5 miles of gentle, rolling upgrade you begin a 4-mile climb that crests at MP 9.2 (1,762
feet). You wind down 2 miles over moderate grades, past vineyards and a scattering of oaks to
Junction, U.S. 101 and Calif. 46 (22 miles). Take the frontage road
on the near side of the freeway (South Vine). You are not
permitted on U.S. 101, and this is the only alternative. Go
north on South Vine to
Paso Robles (3 miles; grocery, restaurant, motel). Once in town, jog
right on First St., go one block to Spring St. (Business U.S.
101). Turn north on Spring to the far edge of town to 24th St.
Turn left on 24th St., which is also County Road G14. The
next 24 miles is almost all hilly terrain, and although grades
are not exceptionally long, many of them are quite steep.
There is also some recreational traffic, particularly on weekends, into Lake Nacimiento, so use caution during these periods. You have an initial climb out of Paso Robles of about
2 miles, and then the road begins a series of ups and downs,
with almost no level riding. You cross the bottom end of Lake
Nacimiento (camping, minimal groceries off the tour route),
then turn sharply left, following Co. Rd. G14 up a steep hill.
You then have a ride along a high ridgetop looking down into
Lake Nacimiento and out across the higher peaks of the Coast
Range. There is a long downhill, then the terrain becomes
more moderate as you cross back into Monterey County.
Continue on an easy ride to
Lockwood (37 miles; grocery, café). Turn left at the intersection and
continue following Co. Rd. G14 through a level valley, then
climb through a range of hills separating you from the Salinas
Valley, into which you descend, and go to
King City (25 miles; grocery, restaurant, motel). This is an important place for you to restock, as your next supply point is a
general store in the little town of Paicines, 52 miles away. If
you are planning an overnight stay at Pinnacles National Mon-

ument, 31 miles away, you should shop here, as there are no supplies available at the campground. Leave King City via Broadway, which becomes Co. Rd. G13, and follow east toward the hamlet of Bitterwater (water available). You wind up through rounded hills, almost devoid of any tree cover, and which are golden brown most of the year.

Bitterwater (17 miles; water available), Junction Calif. 25 and Co. Rd. G13. Turn north (left) on Calif. 25 toward Pinnacles National Monument. You wind down the San Benito Valley over rolling terrain, then to a turnoff to

Pinnacles National Monument (14 miles; camping). This is a small preserve of towering rock spires and lovely canyons. The camping area is about 4 miles in off the route on a paved road. If you choose not to go into the monument, continue on Calif. 25, climbing alongside a stream whose banks support generous stands of live oak—the first consistent tree cover you will have seen for some time. Climb to a high point at MP 26.5, then start a gradual descent. The State Forest Fire Station on your left just down from the hillcrest has drinking water. As you drop further down into the valley you pass extensive fields of Almadén winery, a major producer of table wines. Some of the whites are excellent. Continue to

Paicines (21 miles; general store). Supplies may be limited here, and there is a more complete grocery store down the road at

Tres Pinos Park (5 miles; grocery, restaurant, camping). The road widens out considerably here and has a good shoulder. Traffic picks up considerably, much of it related to the wine industry.

Hollister (7 miles; grocery, restaurants, motels, bicycle shop). An old valley town with a number of excellent parks for relaxing in the shade. Some of the older residential streets are pleasantly tree-lined, with solid turn-of-the-century homes set back across green lawns. Leave via Calif. 156 west to

San Juan Bautista (8 miles; grocery, restaurant, motel, camping). The old mission, founded in 1797 by the followers of Father Junípero Serra, may be visited. It was an important step in the chain of missions that stretched northward from San Diego to San Francisco Bay. Just at the south edge of town take Salinas Rd., heading southwest toward Salinas. You make your way up a canyon, the last 2.5 miles of which are a steep climb to a crest near MP 29. You then have a 2.5-mile downgrade that is steep, winding, and over poor surfaces. Use caution. Your route changes its name to San Juan Grade, and you follow this to a junction with Main St., where you turn left and continue into

Salinas (17 miles; grocery, restaurant, motels). This is an important center for the lettuce-growing region of the state. Your tour route joins Business U.S. 101, which you follow to a junction with Calif. 68 at South Main St. Turn right on Calif. 68, which is a wide four-lane highway with good shoulder. You have a few small grades to go over, then a long downhill to a junction with Calif. 1 and your starting point of

Monterey (18 miles; grocery, restaurants, motels, bicycle shop). You are not permitted on Calif. 1 in Monterey, so you must make your way back via residential streets. You intersect the California Pacific Coast Bicentennial Route here (Del Monte Ave.), which you may follow northward along the coast.

TOUR #4: SACRAMENTO—GOLD-COUNTRY FOOTHILLS—LAKE TAHOE

Distance: 364 miles.
Terrain: Primarily mountain terrain. Tour starts and ends in Sacramento Valley, which is all level riding.
Roads and Traffic: Light to moderate traffic over most of route; heavy traffic in Lake Tahoe region.
Season: May to October.
Weather: Warm and sunny. Cool nights in mountains. Hot days in Sacramento Valley.
Special Features: Opportunity to explore some of the Gold Rush towns of the Sierra foothills; beautiful high mountain scenery; half a day along Lake Tahoe.
Connecting Transportation:
    Sacramento: Greyhound, Trailways, Amtrak, air service.

In this tour, you can retrace some of the most important elements in California's history, as well as explore some of the scenic beauty that attracts visitors and new residents still. Although the first settlers in California were ranchers and missionaries, gold brought the greatest wave of immigration. Beginning in Sacramento, a city built largely by traders supplying the early prospectors, you make your way into the Sierra foothills, where early fortune-seekers crawled up canyons and mountains in search of ore. Most came back broke, or spent what they did find, but the onslaught was enough to launch California's popu-

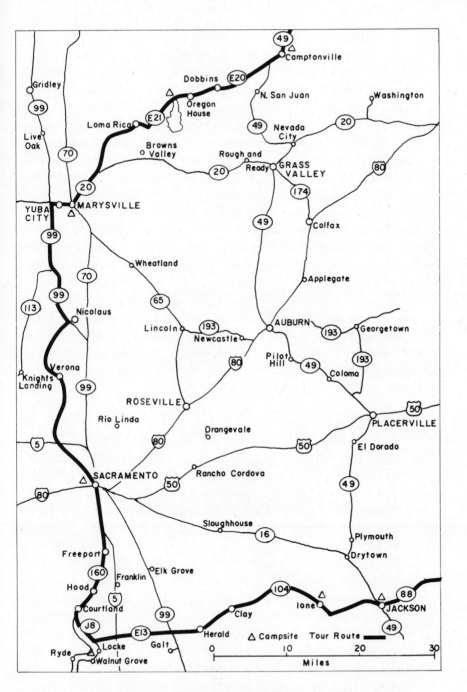

Tour #4   Sacramento—Gold-Country Foothills—Lake Tahoe (Section one: Sacramento to Camptonville and end of tour)

lous reputation. In some ways, the towns left by the early prospectors still have the rough-and-tumble—if not romantic—air they wore a century and more ago. False-fronted buildings, the inevitable river or stream where gold was panned or whose water was used to placer-mine the substance out of adjoining digs, board sidewalks, and wooden balconies are still well preserved. Newer residents wearing western clothing seem to provide a modern replacement for the appearance of the original settlers. From the old mining towns of Camptonville, Downieville, and Sierra City, you make your way to the eastern side of the Sierra and to Lake Tahoe, a 6,000-foot-high lake of unfathomable depths that attracts hundreds of thousands of visitors the year round. You avoid some of the congestion by taking a separate bicycle path around the first part of the lake, then share a winding roadway with a good bit of motor traffic the rest of the way, the bother of the cars alleviated a good bit by the spectacular views you have of the lake. From here you get to explore some high alpine country, making your way over 8,700-foot Carson Pass, then down lovely high mountain lakes to another town spawned by the mining boom, Jackson. From here you drop back down into the Sacramento Valley, making your way through fruit and nut orchards bordering the Sacramento River back to the tour's starting point.

Sacramento (grocery, restaurant, motels, youth hostel, camping, bicycle shops). This tree-shaded city is an excellent starting point for tours; it's near the center of the state and has the additional advantage of having its western side almost completely undeveloped, allowing quick access to the flat countryside of the Central Valley. Bicyclists may wish to visit the newly restored state capitol building or the restored Old Sacramento before leaving on the tour. Leave north via 16th St. (California 160), which becomes a divided highway as it crosses the American River. Just after crossing the river take the first exit, the Northgate exit. Continue a few hundred yards to a junction of Del Paso and Northgate. Follow Northgate half a mile to a junction with the Garden Highway. Turn left on the Garden Highway, which follows the levee built to contain the waters of the Sacramento River, which used to flood regularly. Continue northward along the river, past a number of new homes fronting on the water to

Verona (16 miles; grocery). From here the road follows the levee, then drops off, going past rice fields and a number of rich

orchards. One mile before you reach the small town of Nico-
laus, you cross under an underpass that is the

Junction, Calif. 99 and Garden Highway (9 miles). Turn right, go up
to the highway, then turn right again on Calif. 99 toward
Yuba City. You cross the Feather River and ride through flat
orchardlands. The road has moderate traffic but has a good
riding shoulder. Continue to the junction where Calif. 113
joins Calif. 99, and continue on toward Yuba City. Traffic increases as you near town. The buttes rising from the floor of
the Central Valley strike a sharp contrast to the level valley
floor.

Yuba City (17 miles; grocery, restaurants, motels, bicycle shop). Turn
east (right) on Calif. 20 toward Marysville. You wind through
a quickly developing metropolitan area, cross the Yuba River
and continue to

Marysville (3 miles; grocery, restaurants, motels, bicycle shop). Continue on Calif. 20 out of town. You wind along the base of a
levee beside the Yuba River. Traffic is normally moderate to
heavy, but the ride is level and there is a good riding shoulder.
Continue to

Junction, Loma Rica Rd. and Calif. 20 (7 miles). Turn left on the
road to Loma Rica. You begin rising a bit off the valley floor,
passing pastureland that normally is golden brown throughout
the summer.

Loma Rica (9 miles; grocery). There is a junction here, and you continue straight, staying on Loma Rica Rd. toward Dobbins.
The route is well marked, and you will have little trouble following it as long as you follow the signs toward Dobbins. You
roll through brown foothills of the Sierra. Pavement is often
rough but improves shortly. Continue to

Junction, County Road E21 (Marysville Road) (6 miles). Turn left
on Co. Rd. E21 toward Dobbins. You pass Collins Lake (camping) then continue to

Junction, Co. Rds. E20 and E21 (3 miles). Turn right on Co. Rd. E20
toward Dobbins and Oregon House. You are properly in the
foothills now, and riding increases considerably in difficulty.
As a payoff you begin to lose some of the heat typical of the
Central Valley. Continue past Oregon House (grocery) then
on to

Dobbins (9 miles; grocery). The next section of the route is difficult,
as you gain elevation rather quickly. You will notice a change

in vegetation as you leave behind the grasslands and valley oaks typical of the hot valley and enter regions studded with the tall, reddish-barked ponderosa pine. This sturdy tree, with the soft bed of needles it spreads around itself, is found throughout the West and is the prime source of yellow-pine timber for the region. You cross Bullard's Bar Reservoir on the road doing a tightrope act on the top of the dam, then have another hard climb toward Camptonville. There is an excellent campground one mile past the cutoff road to North San Juan, if you want to gather your resources. Otherwise continue on Co. Rd. E20 to

Junction, Calif. 49 and Co. Rd. E20 (10 miles). Turn left on Calif. 49 and follow it 1 mile to

Camptonville (1 mile; grocery, restaurant). This is one of many old mining towns typical of this part of California. The main part of town lies up from the highway, and it is worth the short climb to go up for a walk around. There has been no great effort to "restore" Camptonville; thus much of what you see is original. From Camptonville continue on Calif. 49, following a rolling ride with a number of climbs, then descend to the Downie River. There are numerous national forest campgrounds along the river, and it is an excellent place to spend the night, but your next grocery point is Downieville, 21 miles away. Shop and plan accordingly. The ride along the Downie River is one of the best in northern California, with the blue water tumbling and churning just off to your right. Swimming is excellent, the water warming up nicely by midsummer.

Downieville (21 miles; grocery, restaurant, hotel). This old mining town is set in a deep cleft carved by the river. Although it has experienced some growth recently (some of the attention sparked by a find of large nuggets just below the town bridge), it still bears very much the atmosphere of an original mining town. You might want to stop for a walk past the old buildings, most of which have resisted being turned into antique shops and fern bars, at least at this writing. Cross the river and wind up a steeper section of the route to

Sierra City (13 miles; grocery, restaurant, motel). This is about as high as serious mining activity reached on the river. It is a good place to stock your pack, as you have only a small grocery at Howard Creek, 6 miles up the road, before your climb over a 6,700-foot summit at Yuba Pass. The summit climb itself is one of the easier in the Sierra, with grades generally moderate.

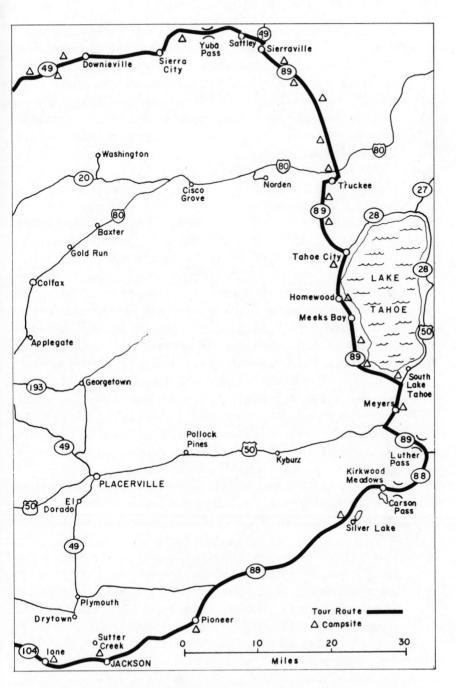

Tour #4 (Section two: Downieville, Lake Tahoe, Jackson—see section one for end of tour)

You reach the highpoint at Milepost 41.2. From here you begin a steep, winding downhill run of 6 miles. You have excellent views of the high valleys on the eastern side of the Sierra. Continue down to

Junction, Calif. 89 and 49 (17 miles). Turn right on Calif. 89 toward Sattley. You will have bottomed out by this time. Continue on the valley floor to Sattley (grocery), then past high mountain pastureland to

Sierraville (5 miles; grocery, restaurant, motel). You continue out of Sierraville on Calif. 89. You soon leave the valley, and must make some moderate climbs as you cross one watershed and move on to another. There are numerous national forest campgrounds along this stretch, all within easy reach. A few miles before you reach Truckee, you pass a rest area and picnic grounds on your left, which mark the site of where part of the ill-fated Donner party waited out 12 feet of snow during the winter of 1848, most of the group dying of starvation before rescue came in the springtime. As you near Truckee, you cross over Interstate 80, then descend to town.

Truckee (24 miles; grocery, restaurants, motels). Calif. 89 is not particularly well marked through town. After descending the road running beside the lumbermill, you reach an intersection. Continue straight at the intersection, following the Donner Pass Rd. through town. After about 1 mile you come to a junction of Calif. 89 and the Donner Pass Rd. A large Safeway store is on your right. Follow Calif. 89 by turning left toward Lake Tahoe. A well-marked bicycle lane is provided on the right shoulder of the road. You follow the Truckee River upstream on an easy ride past Squaw Valley (restaurant, motel) and on to

Tahoe City (14 miles; grocery, restaurant, motels). You start an incredibly beautiful ride around the west shore of Lake Tahoe at this point. Much of the first part of the route is on separate bicycle path, as far as Sugar Pine Point State Park, beyond Homewood. Most touring bicyclists are used to paces which, in our opinion, are a bit fast for this type of bikeway. You share it with joggers, people on roller skis, and other riders. Most important, automobiles crossing the bicycle lane to turn into driveways may not be on the lookout for you. All of this is meant to say that you should slow up and use great caution, being particularly on the lookout for automobiles and other vehicles turning into your path. Continue to

Homewood (7 miles; grocery, motels). Regain the bicycle path, winding through forests surrounding the lake. After Sugar Pine Point State Park, you rejoin the roadway. Use caution, as there are many narrow spots, and although traffic is slow, it normally is heavy. For ultimate enjoyment of the lake, it is best to cover this stretch early in the morning. You skirt Emerald Bay, the waters surrealistically blue and green, the tiny island at its center punctuating the beauty of the spot. Riding is hard here, as you climb a considerable distance from the water. There are a number of state and private campgrounds all along the lake, but they are crowded in summer, and you'll probably have difficulty getting a spot unless you have reservations (see Appendix 4 for reservation information).

Lake Tahoe City (21 miles; grocery, restaurants, motels), Junction U.S. 50. Turn southwest on U.S. 50, which is a busy road but has a good riding shoulder. As you leave the lake area you shake off the worst of the local traffic. Continue through Meyers (grocery, restaurant, motel), then to

Junction, Calif. 89 and U.S. 50 (5 miles). Turn southeast (left) on Calif. 89. Shortly you begin the first of two pass climbs, this one by far the more benign. After leaving the intersection you have a short level stretch, then begin climbing near MP 6. The ride is mostly moderate in difficulty to the summit of Luther Pass (7,740 feet) at the county line (MP 0). You then have a long descent where you lose some 700 feet in elevation to the floor of Hope Valley. Continue to

Junction, Calif. 88 and 89 (12 miles). Turn southwest (right) on Calif. 88 toward Kirkwood Meadows. The next stretch is the hardest of the tour. You begin with a climb over Carson Pass, one of the highest in California (8,573 feet), then have a series of other hard climbs as you make your way from one alpine lake to another. You start the climb up to Carson Pass near MP 11. After some preliminary rolls, you begin climbing in earnest, the last 4.5 miles very hard. You crest MP 5, then have a long coast down to Kirkwood Meadows (grocery, café, motel). After crossing the meadow, you have another 1.5-mile climb, then a run down to Silver Lake and Kit Carson (restaurant, motel, camping). You climb up from Silver Lake, then have a rolling ride through beautiful high country. There are a number of small resorts along the way, beginning with Hams Station (café), about 20 miles from Kirkwood. Most of these have cafés and lodging. Continue past Cooks Station (gro-

cery), Black Station (café), Amador Pines (restaurant, grocery), Oak Creek (motel, café), Buckhorn (grocery, café,
motel) to

Pioneer (53 miles; grocery). At this point you have come out of the
high Sierra and are in the foothills again. Traffic picks up here,
and you must use caution, as the riding shoulder is narrow. If
possible, avoid this stretch on weekends, particularly Sunday
afternoons and evenings, when vacationers are returning from
Lake Tahoe. Continue to the historic mining town of

Jackson (15 miles; grocery, restaurants, motels, bicycle shop). Recently favored by people seeking to escape the urban areas of
the Sacramento Valley, Jackson has undergone considerable
restoration. You may wish to take a break from the long downhill run and stroll through the old section of town. Continue
west on Calif. 88 out of town through rolling foothill country
to

Junction, Calif. 104 and 88 (9 miles). Turn onto Calif. 104, losing
most of the traffic, which normally is rather heavy around
Jackson. Follow it past thinly wooded countryside to the old
town of

Ione (2 miles; grocery, restaurants). This is a pleasantly genuine place,
with untouched false-fronted buildings, old-fashioned hardware stores, and a main street that must look very much as it
did fifty years ago or more. High above the town lies Preston
Castle, an imposing brick structure that has served a number
of uses, most recently as a school of industrial arts. After
climbing up past the castle, you have a gradual descent then
a gently rolling ride through brown grasslands. You pass immediately by the somewhat ominous towers of the Rancho
Seco nuclear power plant, feeling as we did, perhaps, to be a
little better off once you are on the windward side of it. Continue on an easy ride to

Junction, Co. Rd. E13 and Calif. 104 (24 miles). Continue straight
west on Co. Rd. E13, crossing over Calif. 99, heading toward
Walnut Grove. The terrain here is in marked contrast to the
high mountains you have just covered; the only hills in sight
are the ones you have just come down.

Vorden (7 miles; grocery, restaurant). Turn north on Co. Rd. J8 toward Courtland. This last stretch of the route is something of
a repeat of the first stages of the tour, as you make your way
along the lower reaches of the Sacramento River. The road
follows the top of the levee, then drops down through pleasant

fruit orchards. Just outside Courtland (grocery, restaurant) Co. Rd. J8 joins Calif. 160, which you follow back to the tour's starting point at

Sacramento (25 miles; grocery, restaurant, motels, youth hostel, camping, bicycle shops). You intersect Tour 5 here, which takes you through Lassen National Park and on to the north part of the state. Tour 6 also originates in Sacramento, and makes a long loop northward, cutting in through the Coast Range, then swinging down through California's famed redwood forests.

TOUR #5: SACRAMENTO VALLEY—LASSEN NATIONAL PARK—YREKA

Distance: 342 miles.

Terrain: An easy ride up the Sacramento Valley to Chico, then high mountain travel with numerous passes and summits in the California Cascades. Highpoint is on the flank of Mount Lassen at 8,512 feet. Moderate riding from there to tour end.

Roads and Traffic: Mostly quiet two-lane roads; two brief stretches where you use Interstate shoulder.

Season: Late June through September. If you skirt the climb through Lassen, you can extend the season from May to mid-October.

Weather: Hot rides in the Sacramento Valley, moderate temperatures in the mountains. Some chance of scattered afternoon thundershowers in the mountains, otherwise dry and sunny.

Special Features: The ride is dominated by two of the most beautiful mountains in the West, both of which are volcanic. You climb one, and the other (Mount Shasta) dominates the scenery for a hundred miles.

Connecting Transportation:
Sacramento: Greyhound, Trailways, Amtrak, air services.
Yreka: Greyhound, Trailways.

Two of the most striking volcanic peaks in the West dominate this tour: beautifully symmetrical Mount Shasta and the still-active Mount Lassen, which last erupted in 1914, but which reminds us constantly that all is not still inside, as numerous geothermal spoutings dot the national park that surrounds the peak.

The ride begins in the agricultural Sacramento Valley, and you pass a quiet day or two making your way upriver near the banks of

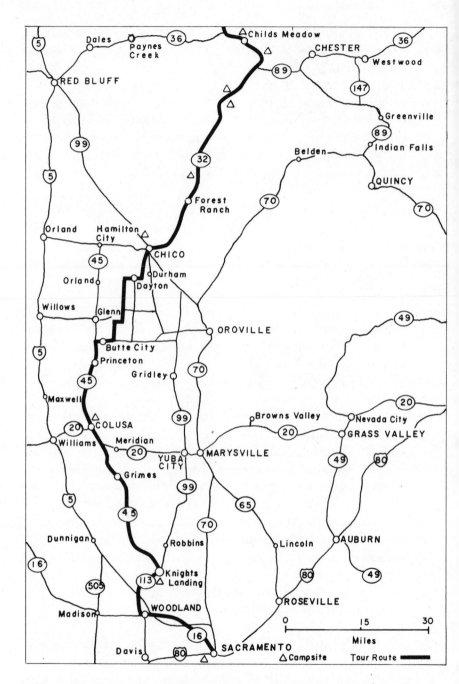

Tour #5   Sacramento Valley—Lassen National Park—Yreka   (Section one: Sacramento to Childs Meadow)

the Sacramento, although you are close to the water only a few times. After a largely backroad ride up to Chico, you leave the valley and begin a long but exceptionally pretty climb up deep, shaded canyons to the volcanic plateau on the flank of Mount Lassen. You shortly begin climbing again, entering the park boundary, then commence a twisting, spectacular ride up the flanks of the mountain, with a chance at one point to park your bicycle and trek to the summit on foot, if you wish. If not, your road reaches a high point at 8,512 feet, far above timberline, and although it is not all downhill from here, the first good bit of it is.

After leaving the park you begin a ride through fairly gentle terrain, following bubbling Hat Creek, then pass within what seems like an eyelash of Mount Shasta, 14,162 feet high. To climb this one you need snowshoes or mountaineering skis, even in late summer, as snow covers all the upper slopes. The shadow—or at least the dominance— of this mountain follows you as you cross high but more moderate terrain to the end of the tour in Yreka.

Sacramento (grocery, restaurants, motels, youth hostel, camping, bicycle shops). The capital of California, Sacramento still retains some of the atmosphere it had when it was a medium-sized valley town, particularly in its shady downtown area. The oldest part of town is being meticulously restored to its mid-nineteenth-century appearance, and is the largest restoration of its kind in the West. The West's largest railroad museum is located nearby. Leave Sacramento on California 16 (I Street), and cross the Sacramento River. The route rejoins the river on the other side of West Sacramento, and you ride alongside it much of the way to

Woodland (15 miles; grocery, restaurants, motels, bicycle shop). Woodland is typical of many towns in the Sacramento Valley, built originally around agricultural interests, and now growing rapidly. The old parts of town have excellent examples of Victorian architecture. Leave via Calif. 113 north to

Knight's Landing (12 miles; grocery, restaurant, motel, camping). Early river boats pulled in here where now a bridge spans the Sacramento. Leave north via Calif. 45, which touches the river at several points, but generally weaves a course through open fields. Continue to

Grimes (26 miles; café, motel). A sleepy village near the river. Continue out of town on Calif. 45 through fields, some of which are used for the cultivation of rice, an important crop in this part of California. In summer, when the fields are flooded, the water adds humidity to the normally dry air, cooling things a bit. Frog hunting is a favorite evening sport. Continue to

Colusa (12 miles; grocery, restaurants, motels, camping). There is an excellent state park here on the Sacramento River, where you can go for a swim to cool off or for a night's stay. Colusa is a fine old town, with many lovely nineteenth-century houses. Continue north on Calif. 45; the route runs on the west side of the river levee. Continue through Princeton (grocery) to

Junction, Calif. 162 and 45 (18 miles). Turn east (right) on Calif. 162 and cross the river toward Butte City (grocery). Follow Calif. 162 east (straight) for 3 miles to a left-hand junction with Road Z. Turn north (left) on Road Z, which changes its name but is well posted, toward Chico. Continue to a junction with Ord Ferry Rd. Turn east (right) on Ord Ferry Rd. and follow it 3 miles to a junction with Dayton Rd. Turn north (left) on Dayton Rd. toward Chico, winding through immaculately tended nut orchards to

Chico (27 miles; grocery, restaurants, motels, bicycle shop). The deep shade of the trees was an early—and still effective—form of air-conditioning. Leave town north via Calif. 32 through a natural arcade created by stately old elms. As you leave Chico you get views of the mountains that form a backdrop to the valley town. Cross the eastern side of the Sacramento Valley on a level ride for about 3 miles, then begin a climb from near Milepost 12 up one of the ridges, which will lead you up into the high mountains. Much of the initial stages of this climb is in treeless country, and should be negotiated early in the morning. The views west across the valley to the Coast Range are striking as you make a 12-mile, rolling climb to

Forest Ranch (15 miles; grocery, restaurant). The elevation here is just above 2,000 feet, and much of the intense valley heat is dissipated. The complex of stores on the left side of the road provides the last services for 43 miles, although there are numerous campgrounds and water sources over the next stretch. Although you are making your way into the mountains, the route is not constantly uphill, as there are a number of important dips where you plunge down into canyons, from the bottom of which you must regain all the elevation you lost. You crest a long 10-mile climb near MP 37. Shortly thereafter you have one of two long descents, bottoming out as you cross a creek near the Tehama County line. You have another long

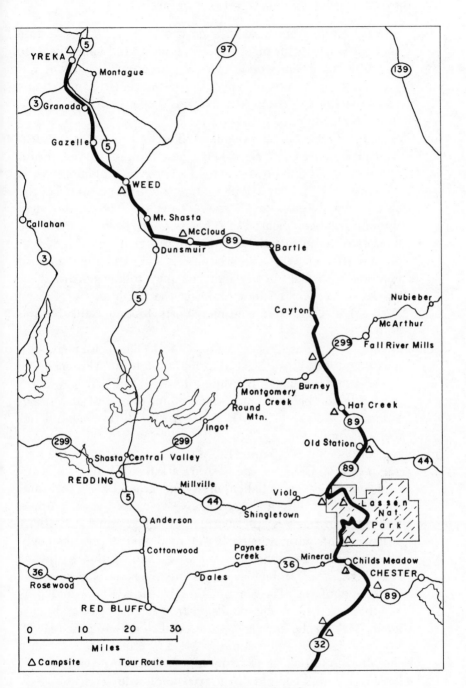

Tour #5 (Section two: Childs Meadow to Yreka)

upward climb from here to a crest at MP 7.75. The terrain
changes from digger pine, which can withstand valley heat, to
stands of red fir and ponderosa, the canyon walls blocking out
the sun at many points. Finally after another dip into Loma
(no services) you climb to a spacious meadow that provides a
short level ride to

Junction, Calif. 89, 36, and 32 (41 miles). The tour route turns northwest (left) onto Calif. 89 and 36. There is an unmarked cluster
of buildings 2 miles down the road where you will find services
(grocery, café, motel; MP 98). (If you don't want to make the
climb over Lassen, or if you're traveling before the road
through has been cleared of snow, you can detour around the
mountain by turning right at this intersection of Calif. 89 and
36 and sticking with 36 through Chester, and then on to a
junction with Calif. 44, which you may follow northwest to
where you rejoin the tour route on the north side of Lassen
Park.) The basic tour continues northwest on Calif. 89 and
36 to

Childs Meadow (7 miles; grocery, café, motel). This is a lovely high
meadow typical of the California Cascades. The meadow
stretches to the flanks of Mount Lassen itself. After a short
level ride you begin a hard 9-mile climb to a crest at Morgan
Summit (5,750 feet) at MP 88. There is a little downhill run
for half a mile to

Junction, Calif. 36 and 89 (5 miles). Calif. 36 goes west here; the tour
goes north on Calif. 89, the Lassen Park Road. It offers a beautiful, winding—and challenging—ride around the south and
east flanks of California's most active volcano. Lassen erupted
in 1914, and there is still considerable geothermal activity at
various points within the park. The road winds upward steeply
from the junction to the park entrance, then continues upward
still. You have spectacular views out over the Cascade and
Sierra mountains. The summit crests near MP 7.5, and it is
possible to go from this point via trail to the peak of Lassen
itself. Back on the bicycle, you descend steeply to near MP 24,
then you have a 3-mile climb to MP 27.5, then a descent into
the Manzanita Lake area (camping, groceries). From here you
have a downhill run out of the park and on to

Junction, Calif. 89 and 44 (34 miles). Turn northeast (right) toward
Hat Creek and Old Station. You have a short, half-mile climb
to Eskimo Hill Summit (5,933 feet), then a downhill run, steep
at first but tapering off after the first 4 or 5 miles, and into

Old Station (12 miles; grocery, café, motel, camping). From this
point on the road rolls through nearly uniform ponderosa
forests, crosses Hat Creek a number of times, which offers
numerous opportunities for camping. Just after Old Station
you branch left on Calif. 89 and drop down through rock-
strewn countryside that testifies to the extent of Lassen's past
eruptions. Continue down into the Hat Creek Valley, which
offers a beautiful, nearly level ride on good highway to

Junction, Calif. 89 and 299 (23 miles; restaurant). Continue straight,
past McArthur–Burney Falls State Park (camping) then over
steeper terrain as you make your way around Lake Britton.
The little grocery store at MP 26, about 4.5 miles past the
junction, is the last place for supplies until you reach McCloud,
42 miles away. About 4 miles beyond the grocery store you
begin a climb to Dead Horse Summit (4,513 feet) at MP 43
on the Siskiyou County line. From here the route is exceptionally pleasant as you drop through shady ponderosa forests to
Bartle (café), then down to the old mill town of

McCloud (42 miles; grocery, café, motel, camping). McCloud, just off
to the north of the route, is worth a visit. The closing of the
mill left the town isolated economically, but the beautiful
setting has brought some prosperity back in the form of country homes and tourism. Much of the feeling of the "company
town" is preserved in the tiny, uniform houses and the old
company store. From McCloud you have a 5-mile climb with
some steep pitches to a summit at 4,470 feet (MP 29.5), then
a descent with excellent views of the upper Sacramento Valley,
the Trinity Alps, and Mount Shasta, which looms impressively
close to the north, snow-covered even in summer. Continue to
the end of Calif. 89 (MP 34.15). Turn north (right) here on
South Mount Shasta Blvd. and continue 3 miles to downtown

Shasta City (13 miles; grocery, restaurants, motel, camping, bicycle
shop). This little logging town is completely dominated by
the mountain towering behind it, so large it sometimes appears
to be a stage backdrop rather than a real mountain. Yet real
it is, all 14,162 feet of it. The peak is about 10,000 feet above
you, although only a few miles away. Leave town via North
Mount Shasta Blvd. to a junction with Interstate 5. You take
the Interstate, riding on the shoulder up a moderate climb to
Black Butte Summit (3,912 feet) near MP 11, then drop down
to

Weed (11 miles; grocery, restaurant, motels, camping). The main street, just off the tour route, retains much of its nineteenth-century feeling, and Weed still is heavily dependent upon the logging industry for its economic survival. The old company store has been turned into an interesting emporium. After looking at Weed continue on Interstate 5. Ride the wide paved shoulder of the Interstate to

Edgewood-Gazelle Exit (3 miles; no services). Leave the Interstate, cross underneath, then head north on the old highway toward Gazelle. The road winds very gradually uphill across an open plain, where you can experience strong headwinds from time to time. Traffic is light. Pass through

Gazelle (8 miles; café) and continue through open country on this high plain, with excellent views of Mount Shasta behind you, and the high peaks of the Trinity Alps off to the left. The ride is an easy upgrade to

Yreka (18 miles; grocery, restaurants, motels, camping, bicycle shop). Resting at the base of the Siskiyou Mountains, Yreka is an old logging and mining town. The main street is authentic, the town having lain in a state of economic decline for many years; it only recently underwent an economic revival based largely on its charm and unspoiled buildings. Bus transportation is available back to the starting point of the tour, or you may continue an exploration of northern California by following our tour of the Klamath and Trinity Rivers (Tour 7). You can also cross Siskiyou Pass via Calif. 263 and Interstate 5 and go a short distance to the town of Ashland, Oregon, where we commence our tour of southern Oregon and Crater Lake (Tour 8).

TOUR #6: SACRAMENTO VALLEY—COAST RANGE— COASTAL REDWOODS—NAPA VALLEY

Distance: 583 miles.

Terrain: Flat valley riding north of Sacramento, steep grades and long climbs in the Coast Range, rolling and level rides through the redwood forests of coastal California.

Roads and Traffic: Mostly quiet two-lane roads. Summer tourist traffic moderate to heavy, but slow-moving along the Avenue of the Giants (coastal redwoods).

Season: May through October.

Weather: All extremes—hot valleys, temperate mountain temperatures, cool and sometimes foggy rides along the coast. Northwest winds in coastal area and upper Napa Valley, normally
southerly winds in Sacramento Valley. Usually dry from June
through September. Some chances of rain in preceding and
following months.

Preferred Direction: Local wind patterns (see section on California
weather earlier in chapter) make it advantageous to follow tour
route as written, leaving north through the Sacramento Valley
and turning south along the Pacific coast.

Special Features: Level easy rides in the Sacramento Valley, quiet
roads through the Coastal Range, an unmatched ride through
the redwoods, then opportunities for wine tasting in renowned
Napa Valley wineries.

Connecting Transportation:
Sacramento: Greyhound, Trailways, Amtrak, air service.

Coastal redwoods, deep mountain forests, clear bubbling streams,
and wine in world-famous Napa Valley tasting rooms—all are part of
the image California presents to the rest of the world. The portrait
is largely true, and this long tour allows you to sample generous
proportions of each of these images. You start in the Sacramento
Valley, where everything from soup to nuts (almost literally) is
grown. At the northern end of the Sacramento Valley you head up a
quiet road into an unspoiled portion of the Coast Range. Heading
past isolated digger pines and valley oak, you then move into heavy
fir and pine forests, with excellent views of peaks in the Coast Range
that will still be snow-clad through late July or August. The Coast
Range is tough cycling, but you will be rewarded with one of the
most lightly traveled roads in California and with excellent opportunities to camp or picnic along some blue-ribbon mountain streams.
As you drop westward out of the high mountains, you enter into an
area heavily influenced by cool Pacific weather. It is a perfect climate
for the Sequoia *sempervirens*—the coastal redwood—and perhaps
the highlight of the trip is a tour down the Avenue of the Giants,
nearly forty miles of virgin timber of a size unequaled anywhere
outside of California. After crossing back over the Coast Range on a
route less strenuous than the first, you make your way into wine
country. This is the Napa Valley, known throughout the world for its
production of great wines. You have some opportunity for sampling,
as you will pass by numerous tasting rooms. Leaving the wine coun-

try, you pass through forests of oak and pine, then out into the Sacramento Valley for a short ride on bicycle paths to your starting point at Sacramento.

Sacramento (grocery, restaurants, motels, youth hostel, camping, bicycle shops). For description see Tour No. 5. Leave Sacramento northwest via California 16 toward Woodland. After passing through a small urban district called West Sacramento you come into open fields and go past orchards, all typical of the first leg of your trip through the highly productive valley. In time the route draws close to the Sacramento River and then on to

Woodland (16 miles; grocery, restaurants, motels, bicycle shop). Woodland has some fine old nineteenth-century houses, and you may wish to deviate from the tour route to cruise some of the residential streets before leaving north on Calif. 113. Cross Interstate 5 and after 1 mile turn left on County Road 18/18B. This connects with old U.S. Highway 99, once the main north-south route through the state, but now replaced by Interstate 5. As a result, the old road is pretty much deserted, and offers absolutely level, very quiet riding north. You pass a number of small towns and crossroads, most of which wear a somewhat worn and bedraggled expression, as if still at a loss to explain the emptiness of the streets, the new highway carrying all important traffic. Services between Woodland and Red Bluff are evenly spaced out, but stores often have only minimal supplies. Williams and Willows are the best equipped. Continue north on a very quiet ride through Yolo, Dunnigan (café, camping), Arbuckle (café) and on to

Williams (40 miles; grocery, restaurant, camping). The elaborate metal arch spanning the main street into town may promise a bit more than the town can deliver, but it is a good place to restock. Continue north out of town through Maxwell (grocery, café, camping), then on to

Willows (26 miles; grocery, café, camping). Here again you will find more complete supplies and services than some of the smaller towns to the north or south. Continue to

Orland (16 miles; grocery, restaurant, camping, motel, bicycle shop). A pleasant valley town settled in the mid-nineteenth-century. One of the first homes in this part of California was built just north of town; a plaque notes the site. The valley floor begins

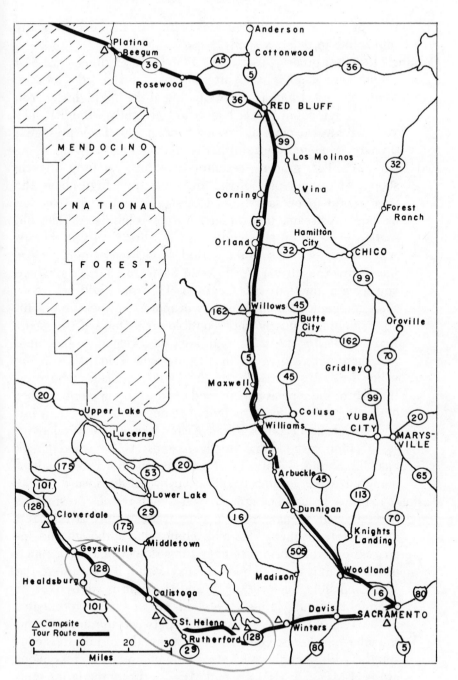

*Tour #6 Sacramento Valley—Coast Range—Coastal Redwoods—
Napa Valley (Section one: Sacramento to Platina and end
of tour)*

to slope gently upward from this point, but the effect is nearly impossible to define visually. Go to

Corning (12 miles; grocery, restaurant, motel). In Corning, turn east (right) on Solano St., then after one block turn north (left) on Road 99 West, which is a continuation of the old highway. You pass through country that begins to roll gently—the first hills you will have experienced since Sacramento. They presage a dramatic change in terrain that commences just beyond

Red Bluff (21 miles; grocery, restaurant, motels, camping, bicycle shop). The upper part of the town was built high above the Sacramento to be safe from flooding. With the construction of dams upstream, this threat is largely eliminated. The old section of town on the high banks is quite lovely, its houses typified by gracious porches and large, overhanging oaks. Leave town north via North Main St. to the outskirts, where you have a junction with Calif. 36. This route will be a constant companion for the next day or more. Turn west on Calif. 36, beginning a nearly imperceptible climb toward the Coast Range. The first 12 miles is through pastureland, dotted here and there with a grayish digger pine, which flourishes in the valley heat. It's named after the Digger Indians, who used the nuts of the pine as a main food source. As you climb further out of the valley the normally hot temperatures subside a bit, and the grade becomes stiffer. Near Milepost 14 you have a steep climb, drop down briefly to cross Cottonwood Creek near the Shasta County line, then have another hard climb of 3 miles to MP 9. From here it is a short coast downward to

Platina (42 miles; grocery, camping). You should restock on supplies here, as well as make certain your water supply is full. You immediately begin an 8.5-mile climb, and although the increased elevation brings temperatures down somewhat, much of that climb is through open country with full exposure to the sun. If possible, an early start from Red Bluff is advised, or an overnight stay at Platina. The climb out of Platina terminates at the Trinity County line at MP 0. Between this summit and the village of Forest Glen, 23 miles away, the terrain rolls constantly, with a number of 1- to 5-mile climbs. You cross major crests at MP 35.5, MP 33.3, and MP 27.2. From the latter summit you have a nice, long downgrade of 9 miles to

Forest Glen (31 miles; grocery, camping). This is a good stopping place for the night, as the next 43-mile stretch is rugged riding on narrow, winding roads, with some hard climbs. The rewards

are considerable, however, as you have spectacular views of the
Coast Range, including the Trinity Alps to the north. You are
in dense forest, and because the road winds as much as it does,
motor traffic is at a minimum. Use caution on the turns though,
and listen for approaching traffic, including logging trucks.
Climb out of Forest Glen for 8 miles to a crest at MP 10. Although there are some short climbs from here onward, they
are easier than what you have done already. After crossing the
highpoint, which lies above 4,000 feet, you have beautiful
views of the Mad River below you, as well as some high volcanic peaks off to the south. Descend to MP 4.2 in the Mad
River Valley, then continue to the little hamlet of

Mad River (15 miles; grocery, lodge). Once beyond this resort you
have a short but steep climb over a ridge separating you from
the Van Duzen River. You then drop down and run alongside
the Van Duzen on an easy ride to

Dinsmore (7 miles; grocery, café, motel, camping). Lying at the head
of the Van Duzen River valley, you have excellent views upward of many surrounding peaks. You have a hard 3-mile
climb from here to a crest at MP 39.36, then a steep descent
along a very narrow road, not well paved. Use caution on the
turns and keep your speed down. At the end of the downhill
you cross a valley, then have a short climb to MP 33, after
which is a long, steep downhill of about 7 miles to

Bridgeville (19 miles; grocery, café). You deserve a rest in this little
hamlet lying on the Van Duzen River, as you have just crossed
one of the most rigorous stretches to be found in California—
or the West, for that matter. The little café in Bridgeville
boasts excellent homemade pie. From Bridgeville you make
your way through redwood forests, then across more open,
pastoral land to Hydesville (grocery, café), then on down to

Alton (25 miles; café), Junction, U.S. 101. In the transition from
mountains to coast, you have also changed climates, as the narrow band of land in which you find yourself has a weather
system all its own. Cooled by air masses off the Pacific, temperatures on land seldom rise above 80 degrees, and more
often than not—particularly in summer—fog banks move in
off the frigid waters of the ocean and hang over the land well
into mid-morning. On many summer days the fog never disappears at all; you can ride in cool 50-degree and rather drippy
weather while someone inland may be roasting in temperatures
approaching 100. The most spectacular product of this climatic

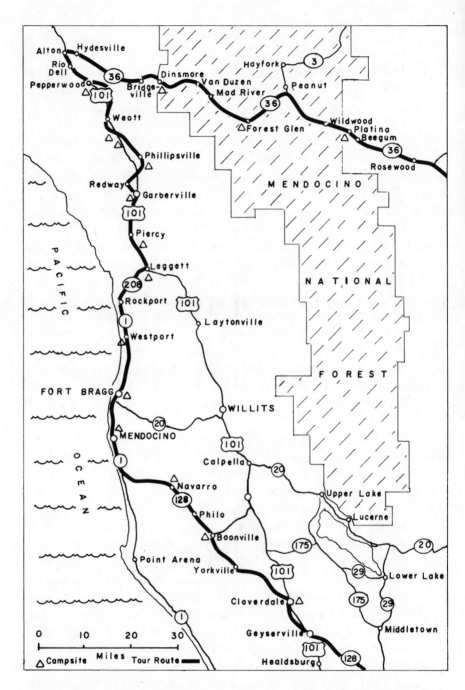

Tour #6 (Section two: Platina to Sacramento—see section one for termination of tour)

phenomenon is the coastal redwood. The ride
beyond Fort Bragg is dominated by these pond
lent giants. Through much effort, money, an
largest of these largest living things have been s
of being turned into lawn furniture.

As you turn south (left) on U.S. 101 from Alton, you have
a stretch of busy highway, but with a wide shoulder. At Rio
Dell (grocery, restaurant, motel) you can leave the main road
and cruise down Davis Street, then back on U.S. 101 through
Stafford to

Junction, Calif. 254 (Avenue of the Giants) and U.S. 101 (12 miles).
Leave the freeway at this point and begin following the route
marked AVENUE OF THE GIANTS. This scenic road puts you into
contact with some of the most impressive redwood trees found
in the state, with numerous opportunities for camping and for
further exploration on foot. Traffic is moderate, and moves
fairly slowly, but because of the dense shade and the dark soil,
you need to wear bright clothing and keep to the right of the
road. Grades are generally gradual, and you cross or run
parallel to the main highway at points. For the most part, however, you are in deep, silent, forest. Services, including campgrounds and motels, are numerous, although state park
campgrounds are always crowded. The Burlington Campground 4 miles north of Meyers Flat is your best bet, as it has
a bicyclists-only area with spaces for twenty-five riders at 50¢
a night each. Go through Redcrest (grocery, café, motel, camping). Along the route you will notice some high-water marks
posted during the flood of the Eel River in 1964. Some of these
are 30 feet above you. When that great flood receded, some
villages had completely vanished. Continue past local produce
stands set out on the highway, where you can buy fresh fruit
and vegetables in season, to

Meyers Flat (22 miles; grocery, café, motel, camping). For the curi-
ous who have never bicycled through a redwood tree, it's
possible to have the experience here—for a fee. If you wish to
forgo this adventure, continue south through Miranda (grocery, restaurant, motel, campground) and Phillipsville (motel,
restaurant) at the end of the Avenue of the Giants. Rejoin
U.S. 101 south for 3 miles to the Redway exit, where you leave
the freeway to go through Redway (grocery, café, motel),
then follow the Eel River on a quiet back road edging along
the east bank to

Garberville (19 miles; grocery, restaurants, motels, camping). From here south you follow U.S. 101 again, with terrain considerably steeper than in the redwood groves you have just come through. For the most part there is a good riding shoulder, but there are some sections with little or no shoulder, and you should use caution. This section of U.S. 101 is on the Pacific Coast Bicentennial Route, so there are signs warning motorists to be on the lookout for you. If it's foggy, wear bright clothing and use lights if you have them. Climb out of Garberville for 1 mile to a crest at MP 9.84, then down and over a level stretch to the Mendocino County line, where the road rolls through stands of redwood, juniper, cedar, and fir. Go through Benbow (grocery, café, motel, camping) before the county line, climb again to Piercy (grocery), then follow a rolling course to

Leggett (24 miles; grocery, motel, café, camping). You have a junction here with Calif. 208. Turn west (right) on Calif. 208, a two-lane road with light to moderate traffic. The shoulder varies from nothing to 2 feet. As you leave Leggett you drop down momentarily to cross the Eel River, then begin a long climb in which you gain more than 1,000 feet in elevation. You are constantly in heavy forest, but with good views through to the Coast Range from time to time. You have a 4-mile climb from the Eel to a highpoint at MP 10, then a winding descent through Hales Cove (café) and then on down to where you reach the coast. Route 208 changes to Calif. 1 at this point. After a brief but hard climb, you come to

Westport (28 miles; grocery, café, motel, camping). From here south to Fort Bragg you ride directly along the ocean, with excellent views of the surf just off to your right. Winds normally are strong here, but blow in mainly from the northwest. The best place for beachside camping is at MacKerricher State Park, 4 miles north of Fort Bragg. Continue on to

Fort Bragg (15 miles; grocery, restaurants, motels, camping, bicycle shop). This is a fishing port and lumber town. The old company store of the local lumber company has been turned into a contemporary general store, and is interesting to spend a moment or two strolling through. Continue south on Calif. 1, which has a wide shoulder at this point. You pass through arbors of wind-beaten juniper, its normally whitish bark bleached even whiter by the fierce salt air. The road rises and falls, but climbs are short to

Mendocino (11 miles; grocery, restaurants, motels, camping). This
charming north-coast community is just off the new highway,
and you may wish to take a break from the wind and stroll
down some of its fine old residential streets. Mendocino is
something of a haven for escapees from city life, and is an
active, yeasty community. Continue south through Little River
(grocery, motel, camping) where there is another state park
campground. The road becomes very narrow along here, and
you need to exercise caution, particularly on blind turns and
when climbing or descending the numerous short hills. Signs
warn motorists of your presence. At

Junction, Calif. 128 and 1 (10 miles) you leave the coast highway.
Turn southeast (left) on Calif. 128 toward Boonville. You begin an easy uphill ride along the north fork of the Navarro
River, passing through deep redwood forests and alternating
pastures and vineyards. Winegrowers are discovering that the
cool coastal valleys are good locations for growing premium
wine grapes, and you will see a number of small wineries along
this section of the route, and even greater numbers of them as
you cross the crest of the coastal range and head into the Napa
Valley.

Navarro (14 miles; general store) is a little hamlet set deep in the
redwoods. Continue through Philo (grocery, café, motel) then
past more vineyards and fruit orchards to

Boonville (15 miles; grocery, restaurant, motel). From Boonville you
begin a climb into the coastal range, and if the weather has
been foggy, it is often here that you begin to break clear. Go
on a rolling climb to Yorkville (grocery, café), after which you
have a rolling downgrade for about 4 miles. You then begin a
final climb to the Mendocino-Sonoma County line at MP 50.9.
Descend steeply to

Cloverdale (27 miles; grocery, restaurants, motels, camping). Located
on the Russian River, Cloverdale is a good spot to relax and
warm up from the coastal fog, as temperatures are usually
high here in summer. Leave on a section of U.S. 101 to Asti
Rd. Exit and follow Asti Rd. to Dutcher Creek Rd. Follow
Dutcher Creek southward, paralleling the freeway to Canyon
Rd. Turn east (left) on Canyon and follow to

Geyserville (12 miles; grocery, restaurant). The name of this town
reflects the considerable geothermal activity in the area, including the world's largest geothermal power plant located nearby.

But Geyserville is making more of a name for itself these days with another product—wine. You will see evidence of this as you continue south. Leave south via Calif. 128 following a route up the Alexander Valley, where crops of mustard are interspersed with premium wine grapes. You crest a hill at MP 25.16 and descend on a narrow but very pretty route that takes you under shady oak trees until you reach the outskirts of Calistoga. Here you have a junction with Calif. 29 (Lindon St.). Turn left on Calif. 29 and go into the town of

Calistoga (21 miles; grocery, restaurants, motels). This is a good spot to get off and stroll. Calistoga has been noted for its hot mineral baths from the time the upper Napa Valley was first settled. There is a pleasant combination of early-frontier atmosphere combined with the elegance of the old mineral baths. Leave town northeast on Calif. 29 for about 1 mile to a junction with the Silverado Trail Rd. Turn south (right) on Silverado Trail Rd., which is somewhat busy but has an excellent shoulder. You pass through rich wine country, where some of the best wines in the world are being cultivated. Several wineries along the route invite tasting. Lena Emmery and Sally Taylor's *Grape Expeditions* (see Bibliography) is designed for the bicyclist who wishes to sample Napa Valley terrain—and its wines. Go past the back side of St. Helena and continue another 4 miles to

Junction, Calif. 128 and Silverado Trail (13 miles; no services). Turn east (left) on Calif. 128. Here you begin a 40-mile ride through hilly terrain. The road is narrow in spots, and winds considerably. Although traffic is usually light, there are stretches around Lake Berryessa where cars will be pulling boat trailers. Pitches are steep around Lake Berryessa, and around a smaller lake, Hennessey Lake. Between these two lakes are some lovely rides through valleys with groves of live oak, which keep their green holly-shaped leaves the year round. The only replenishment point along the route is the junction of Calif. 128 and 121 (grocery, café), about midway between your turnoff from the Silverado Trail and the town of Winters. Beyond Lake Berryessa (camping) you follow Putah Creek downstream, with a number of good picnicking spots off to your right. From here the road is level to

Winters (40 miles; grocery, restaurant). There are some old Victorian homes in this town founded in the latter part of the nineteenth century. Leave Winters via Co. Rd. E6 toward Davis. Co. Rd.

E6 changes to Co. Rd. 31, which has either good shoulders or a marked bicycle lane most of the way to

Davis (13 miles; grocery, restaurants, motels, bicycle shops). You cross the northern part of town. Davis probably has the highest ratio of bicycles to people of any place in the country. When classes let out at the University of California, there are veritable bicycle jams on the streets. Co. Rd. 31, which you have been following, changes its name to Covell St. in Davis. There are separate bicycle paths or marked bicycle lanes on the street. As Covell St. takes a long sweep to the right, it becomes Mace Blvd., which also has a well-distinguished and posted bicycle lane. Just before the road rises to cross the Interstate, turn left on Co. Rd. 32A. You parallel the interstate on Co. Rd. 32A (marked clearly as a bicycle route) for about 2 miles, then there is a turnoff to your left onto a bicycle lane. As this is part of the main bicycle route between Davis and Sacramento, the turn is well marked. Follow this separate bicycle path, which parallels the freeway through open fields, for several miles until it brings you to West Capitol Ave. in West Sacramento. Follow West Capitol straight through a built-up section of trailer parks and fast-food services, then cross the Sacramento River and arrive back at the tour's starting point in

Sacramento (17 miles; grocery, restaurants, motels, youth hostel, camping, bicycle shops). From Sacramento you may continue your exploration of northern California on the Sacramento Valley and Lassen National Park tour (Tour 5) or you may connect with the tour of the Sierra Nevada, Lake Tahoe, and Gold Country (Tour 4).

TOUR #7: REDDING—TRINITY AND KLAMATH RIVERS—YREKA

Distance: 392 miles.

Terrain: Gentle grades along the Trinity and Klamath Rivers, hard climbs in the Siskiyou Mountains.

Roads and Traffic: California 299 out of Redding heavy to moderate, with traffic decreasing after Weaverville. Light traffic on two-lane roads the rest of the tour route.

Season: May to October.

Weather: From June to October very dry, daily maximum temperatures in the 70s to low 80s.

Special Features: Beautiful rides along two of northern California's
  most scenic rivers, the Trinity and less-well-known Klamath.
  Spectacular views of nearby Trinity Alps and Mount Shasta.
Connecting Transportation:
  Redding: Greyhound, Trailways, Amtrak, air service.
  Yreka: Greyhound, Trailways.

   Two rivers and two alpine landmarks dominate this tour. The
Trinity River makes its way westward through the mountains of
northern California, passing close by the fabled Trinity Alps, whose
beauty first attracted prospectors in search of gold, and now attracts
many backpackers who wish to explore the Salmon–Trinity Alps
Wilderness Area. Because of the justly deserved reputation of both
the Trinity River and the Trinity Alps, the first part of the tour route
is through popular country, although the highways are normally wide
or have good riding shoulder. Once beyond Willow Creek, however,
where California 299 goes westward and our tour route takes a turn
to the north, traffic becomes light and remains so for the rest of the
trip. You make your way down the Trinity to a confluence with the
Klamath, then turn east and head upriver. Blue herons wade gingerly
along the edge of the shore, heads dipping alertly in search of fish.
Deer clamber up the sides of hills and disappear into the forest. You
pass through little villages with a handful of houses and a few small
stores and café where you can get food. But most of the latter part
of the tour route is away from civilization, with only you and the river.

Redding (grocery, restaurants, motels, camping, bicycle shop). This
  rapidly growing city at the upper end of the Sacramento Valley
  is also one of the warmest places in northern California, so you
  may find the weather a bit on the hot side. But you soon begin
  leaving the growing population and the heat behind, as you
  begin climbing into the Coast Range just out of town. The
  first miles on California 299 are gradual hills, past the historic
  mining town of Shasta, with nineteenth-century brick buildings now part of a state park. After one of these rolling grades
  you drop down to
Whiskeytown Lake (10 miles; camping), which has a number of excellent swimming beaches near the campground at the far end.
  Once beyond the campground, you begin a 9-mile climb to
  Buckhorn Summit. The last 4 miles are the hardest, and about
  a mile before you reach the crest, you have a welcome spring

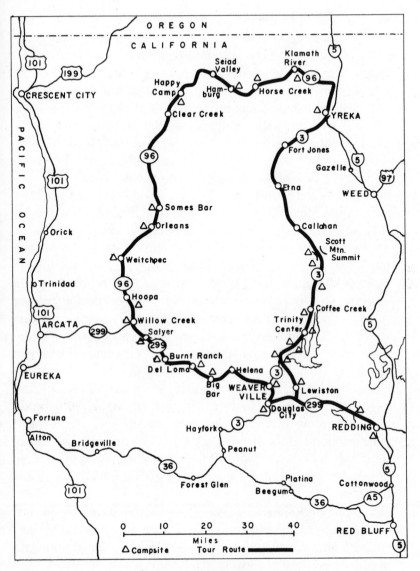

Tour #7   Redding—Trinity and Klamath Rivers—Yreka

off to the left of the road. The summit (3,213 feet) is at the
Trinity County line, therefore Milepost 0. You have a steep
downgrade, then must climb some rolling hills to
Douglas City (29 miles; grocery, café, motel, camping), a small resort village on the Trinity River. Your route runs alongside
and crosses this clear mountain stream, with excellent fishing
and a few places where you can easily get down the bank for

a swim. Out of Douglas City you leave the river, climb a hill, then go on to

Weaverville (6 miles; grocery, restaurants, motels, camping, bicycle shop). This historic mining town has been carefully preserved, and has an interesting state historic museum dating to the days when Chinese laborers were imported to work in local mines. The Chinese scrupulously kept their own way of life and their own religion, and their beautiful Joss House, a place for religious ceremony, is a testament to their great persever- ance in the face of discrimination and sometimes abusive con- ditions. Guided tours of the Joss House are offered by a state park ranger on a scheduled basis. Other than the Joss House, Weaverville maintains many of the buildings from its past when it was a mining camp, including a beautiful gazebo in a small town park. As you leave on Calif. 299, you have a climb to Oregon Mountain Pass (2,888 feet) near MP 48. After a sharp descent you wind along the Trinity River again, passing through a series of small communities that offer basic services: Junction City (grocery, café, camping), Helena (grocery, café, motel, camping), Big Bar (grocery, café, camping), Del Loma (grocery, café, motel, camping), and the small hamlet of Cedar Flat (café, motel). From here you cross the Trinity and begin a hard 2-mile climb up its southern bank, with heady views down off the right side of the road if you want to drift close enough to take them. Near MP 11.5 you pass a cluster of buildings known as Burnt Ranch (grocery, camping), then descend to Salyer (grocery, camping), after which you follow the Trinity to

Willow Creek (58 miles; grocery, cafés, motels, camping). Lying just to the south of the Hoopa Valley Indian Reservation, Willow Creek is one of your better supply points, as most stores are small between here and Happy Camp, nearly 90 miles from here. At Willow Creek you leave Calif. 299, and much of the traffic behind. Turn north (right) on Calif. 96, first following along the Trinity, then beginning a substantial climb up over a headland, the climb terminating just beyond MP 5. The road rises and falls more or less continually to

Hoopa (12 miles; grocery, café, motel, camping). There is an Indian museum in town, as you are now on reservation land. Hoopa is also an important logging center. You must exercise increas- ing caution from here north, as logging-truck traffic increases.

The trucks can be heard from some distance, and your best defense is to keep a more or less constant ear out. As the road winds and has little or no shoulder, be particularly alert against getting caught in a "squeeze"—being passed in two directions at the same spot. Remember, too, that logging-truck drivers are normally paid by the load, and are losing money if they chug along behind you on stretches where it is difficult to pass. Pull off and allow them to get by. Large groups need to be particularly aware of this. Your ride continues through rolling country along a highway where you are completely out of sight of houses, telephone wires—and even litter. Herons and other birds may be glimpsed from time to time fishing diligently in the Trinity.

Weitchpec (10 miles; grocery) lies at the confluence of the Trinity and Klamath Rivers. Be alert for an expansion grate at the far end of the bridge. The gaps in the joint are an absolute disaster for bicycle wheels. After crossing the bridge turn east (right) on Calif. 96 toward Happy Camp. The next stretch of the route from here to near Yreka is one of the prettier river rides in northern California. You are almost completely removed from signs of civilization, except for the roadway itself. You are climbing upward, but most grades are gradual or of only moderate difficulty. From time to time you may catch glimpses of rafts floating by, and if the water looks inviting, you can get down at a number of points for a swim.

Orleans (15 miles; grocery, motel, café, camping). The markets in town are fairly large, so restock here—there are only limited services in Somes Bar (grocery, camping), then a 41-mile stretch with none. The road has long stretches where it brings you next to the river.

Happy Camp (49 miles; grocery, cafés, motel). This is a busy logging town built on the banks above the river. A mill at the far end of town provides employment, and nights will find the local bars filled with loggers, who do much in their own way to preserve the image they have of rollicking drinkers. Fortunately, most of them are congenial. Outside of town you have a 2.5-mile climb up Cade Mountain Summit. Continue down to Seiad Valley (grocery, café, camping), then a moderate upgrade through Hamburg (grocery, café, camping, motel) and Klamath River (grocery, café, motel, camping). At

Junction, Calif. 263 and 96 (59 miles; no services) you cross, then

leave the Klamath River via Calif. 263, beginning a moderate
climb up a steep-walled canyon, with a stream and an old road
far below you. You round a curve and are presented with a
startling view of Mount Shasta, its snow-white dome seeming
to hang in the sky. The view appears and disappears with
tantalizing unexpectedness as the road winds through gorges
cut in the rock. You will notice a marked change in vegetation
as you make your way up over a rise then begin a moderate
descent into

Yreka (6 miles; grocery, restaurants, motels, camping, bicycle shop).
This is an historic old town whose residents have done much
in recent years to restore its original appearance and ambiance.
The main street has examples of restored mining-day architecture, as do many of the residential streets. Leave town south
via Calif. 3. You cross an open plain for several miles, then at
MP 45 begin a 3.5-mile climb up a 7 percent grade to a summit
(4,097 feet) at MP 41.5. You look down on the historic Scott
Valley, and in the distance out to the Trinity Alps. Descend
into the valley and to

Fort Jones (13 miles; grocery, café, motel). There is an Indian
museum in town, which was once on the stagecoach trail between Redding and Grants Pass, Oregon. Continue down the
valley, once filled with miners panning and placer-mining for
gold. The telltale rock piles are mine tailings from some of the
larger operations, and at one point you pass an abandoned
stamping mill, where rock was crushed and the dust processed
to float out the gold. Continue through Etna (grocery, café) to

Callahan (24 miles; café, grocery). The historic Callahan Ranch Hotel
was built in the 1880s, when this was an important stop on the
stage route into Oregon. The rooms are being restored, but are
not for rent. Leave Callahan on Calif. 3, crossing a small stream
in a few miles, then beginning a 7-mile climb to Scott Mountain Summit (5,401 feet). The climb brings you extensive
views of the dry grass of Scott Valley and the green slopes of
the Trinity Alps. At the summit (MP 0) is a campground. You
wind down a steeper grade than the one you ascended, with
numerous switchbacks and blind turns calling for caution.
There is considerable change in the vegetation; this side is
much more verdant than the northern slope. You wind down
for 5 miles through a forest of pine and fir, then a more gradual
descent where you join the Trinity River once again. A dam
has been built downstream, and at the upper end of the result-

ing lake you'll see extensive traces of large-scale placer mining, evidenced by the round rocks in the tailings. At

Coffee Creek (26 miles; grocery, café, motel, camping) you have a chance to restock on supplies and relax a bit before continuing downriver to

Trinity Center (8 miles; grocery, cabins, camping). There is a good museum here with displays and memorabilia of pioneer life, including kitchen utensils and hand-operated wooden washing machines. For the next 22 miles, from Trinity Center to the junction with the Lewiston Road, your route is a constant up and down as you make your way along Clair Engle Lake. Services are well spaced out. Along the route you get closeup views of the Trinity Alps, some of the finest mountain scenery in the West. Several roads, most of them unpaved, lead up into the wilderness area from the tour route. Continue your up-and-down ride around the lake, then a final climb to MP 38, where you find a

Junction, Lewiston Rd. and Calif. 3 (22 miles). You turn east (left) on the Lewiston Rd. toward Lewiston. You have a nice ride along one of the tributaries to the Trinity River, going through pine and fir forests to MP 264.8, where there is an old metal bridge off to your right. Cross the bridge and go into

Lewiston (10 miles; grocery, café, motel, camping). This old mining town has been revived recently with refugees from metropolitan life, and there is considerable new building going on. Climb out of town to an intersection with the main highway (unmarked) and turn south (right) toward Redding. There is a 1-mile climb to make, then you go down to a

Junction with Calif. 299 (5 miles; no services). You rejoin your original tour route at this point. Turn east (left) toward Redding, and begin a climb back over Buckhorn Summit, the grade a bit easier this way. The MP at the top is 72.5 when coming from this direction. From here continue back to the end of the tour at

Redding (30 miles; grocery, restaurants, motels, camping, bicycle shop). If you want to continue your exploration of northern California, you may swing south from here 31 miles to the town of Red Bluff, and intersect our tour of the Coast Range and Redwoods there (Tour 6). The best route out of Redding is via Calif. 273 to Anderson, then either take Interstate 5, or go via Balls Ferry Rd. and Jelly's Ferry Rd. to Red Bluff. For further exploration into the California Cascades, you can in-

tercept our tour at Mount Shasta and Lassen National Park
by taking Calif. 44 east out of Redding to Lassen National
Park (see Tour 5 for details).

TOUR #8: SOUTHERN OREGON—CRATER LAKE—WILLAMETTE VALLEY

Distance: 401 miles.

Terrain: Rolling, short hills near the starting point of Ashland, long
climbs into the Cascades to Crater Lake (7,100 feet), the last
section a hard ascent. Downhill runs to the upper Willamette
Valley, gentle terrain into Eugene.

Roads and Traffic: Most of the route follows quiet two-lane roads.
There are three short stretches of freeway riding to avoid dirt
roads or as the easiest route over summits. Light to moderate
traffic from Crater Lake to the Willamette Valley, and a short
stretch of urban traffic into Eugene.

Season: Mid-June through September.

Weather: July and August are the best months, with little chance of
rain. There may be snow on the ground at Crater Lake through
June.

Connecting Transportation:
Ashland: Greyhound, Trailways.
Eugene: Greyhound, Trailways, Amtrak, air service.

In a little over 400 miles, this tour covers nearly every condition,
kind of terrain, climate, and scenery that you will experience in southwestern Oregon, except for the Pacific coast. And that isn't far away.

The tour starts in the Shakespearean Festival town of Ashland, just
on the northern edge of the Siskiyou Mountains, and a short hop from
California. You explore some of the rolling terrain and lovely valleys
in this part of the state, including the historic mining town of Jacksonville, which still wears most of the appearance it did a century ago.

The climb to Crater Lake is long, but the pull is not nearly as hard
as it may appear, as most of the grade is gentle; only when you reach
the area near Crater Lake National Park boundary does the climbing
resemble true pass difficulty. Once at the rim of the lake, you have
one of the most spectacular views in the West—a scintillating, blue
lake set within the oval rim of an old volcano crater. You can choose
one of two routes around the rim of the lake; our route takes the

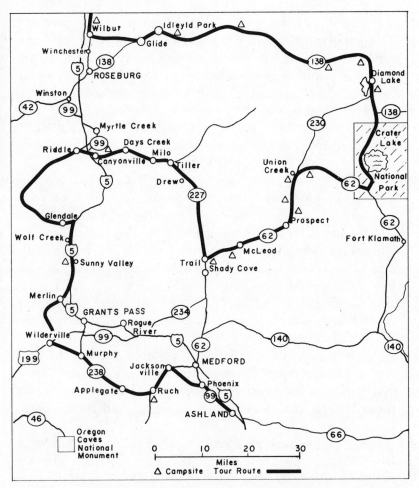

Tour #8 Southern Oregon—Crater Lake—Willamette Valley (Section one: Ashland to Wilbur)

shorter western side. Once past a highpoint on the crater rim, more than a thousand feet above the surface of the lake itself, you plunge downward through a region peppered with volcanic debris from many years ago, then pass picturesque Diamond Lake with Mount Bailey looming across the water, the mountain peak snow-capped most of the summer. A long ride down the Clearwater River, past sentrylike spires that are volcanic plugs, brings you down to a point near the watershed of the Willamette Valley. You wind through old agricultural towns into Eugene, from which a number of connecting routes are available that will take you as far as the East Coast if you are so inspired.

Ashland (grocery, restaurants, motels, bicycle shop, camping nearby).
This popular little town has made a justifiably deserved reputation for itself with its Shakespearean Festival. Dramatic pro-
ductions include more modern plays as well. Tickets should
be secured well in advance during the summer season. A small
university and houses climbing steep hillsides grace the town
as well. Leave north via U.S. 99, a busy four-lane highway
with a bicycle path much of the way along the west side of the
road to

Phoenix (7 miles; grocery, motel, restaurants). The old town has been
largely swallowed up with development, and you'll be eager
to turn off west (left) onto the Stage Road South on the far
edge of town. Head northwest toward Jacksonville. The road
you are on was the first important inland link between the
agricultural riches of Oregon and the mineral wealth of California. You wind through orchard country for several miles,
then begin a short but hard climb to just above Jacksonville.
From here you have a steep downhill through stands of live
oak to the old town of

Jacksonville (8 miles; grocery, restaurants, motels). This is a charming
restored mining town. It is worthwhile to lock up your bicycle
and spend an hour or two exploring. Leave via Oregon 238
toward Ruch. You immediately begin a hard 3-mile climb.
Continue to

Ruch (8 miles; grocery, camping nearby), then follow the Applegate
River through pastureland and rich farm country. The surrounding hills form a green corridor for you through the hamlet of Applegate (grocery, café, camping) and on to

Murphy (20 miles; grocery, café). Just inside Murphy turn west on
Wilderville Rd. and follow the signs to Wilderville. You pass
through shady stands of oak and pine, then up a valley with a
moderate climb to

Wilderville (7 miles; grocery), Junction, U.S. 199. Turn east (right)
on U.S. 199 and follow 1 mile to a junction with Merlin Rd.
Turn north (left) and follow the west bank of the Rogue River.
The road passes a fragrant mint farm, then through nicely
wooded country. Continue to a bridge where you cross the
Rogue, then turn right on the east bank and continue a short
distance to Robertson Bridge Rd. Turn left on Robertson
Bridge Rd., up a short but very steep little hill, then a longer
descent to

Merlin (12 miles; grocery, café). This was the site of an Indian massacre in 1855, when native Americans rose in protest against white intrusions into their territory. Several settlers were killed here and at various spots along the Rogue. From Merlin you follow a series of small roads up to the junction with Interstate 5. To get to the Interstate from Merlin, turn left on Stratton St., cross the railroad tracks and continue to a T intersection with Pleasant Valley Rd. Turn left and continue to

Junction, Interstate 5 (4 miles). You join the Interstate at this point, turning north toward Roseburg. Using the shoulder, you begin a climb toward the first of three summits you must cross. The stretch of Interstate is 14 miles in all. Your first climb is about 2.5 miles to Sexton Mountain Pass (1,960 feet). You have a steep descent to Sunny Valley (grocery, camping), then begin a 2-mile climb to Smithhill Summit at 1,730 feet. You drop down again, then begin a final climb, which is less difficult, to Stage Road Pass (1,830 feet). Continue down 1 mile to the Glendale exit. Leave the Interstate at this point and follow the road west (left) to

Glendale (16 miles; grocery, restaurant, café). This once-thriving lumber town has seen better days, but people still remain refreshingly open, hearkening back to simple times. You may need to stock up in town, as the next services are 38 miles away, and even though you are following the river downstream, you have a number of hard climbs over ridges. The grocery stores are actually a bit beyond your turnoff, so if you want to shop you have to continue into town, then double back to the bridge across Cow Creek and turn toward Riddle. You begin a long, rolling climb that has some difficult sections, through a pretty canyon. The road climbs and falls for about 10 miles, until you reach a highpoint above Cow Creek. You then descend to the level of the stream and begin a much easier ride, for the most part staying next to the water. There are a number of primitive campsites along the way, but you must supply your own drinking water (or boil streamwater rapidly for at least five minutes). Continue past some hopeful weekend-prospector dredging rigs to

Riddle (38 miles; grocery, café). The economy of the town rises or falls on lumber demand, and when we passed through it was low. There is a nice, homespun café or two in town. Continue through town and head out on the road toward Canyonville,

climbing a short hill, then going down and crossing the Interstate and on into

Canyonville (6 miles; grocery, restaurant, motel; camping 2 miles
north on Oreg. 99). A pleasant little town, and the grocery
stores here are more complete than most you will find until
you reach Prospect, over 70 miles away. Leave Canyonville via
Oreg. 227 east toward Tiller. You begin a gentle ride up a
canyon, with pastureland and farms on either side of the road.
Continue through Days Creek (grocery) and Milo (no services) to

Tiller (24 miles; grocery, café). The grocery store is relatively well
stocked. You leave the South Umpqua River here, continuing
on Oreg. 227 up through a narrow gorge where you hug the
left flank, then you come out into a more open valley and
pass by Drew (no services), after which you begin a hard
climb to a summit at 3,500 feet. You move out of the grasslands
typical of the valley and are in deep stands of pine and fir.
Descend down a long rolling ride to

Trail (26 miles; grocery). Turn east (left) on Oreg. 62, which carries
moderate traffic at this point—some of it is logging traffic, with
the trucks often fully loaded and moving fast. This and other
traffic thins out beyond Prospect, 21 miles up the road. You
parallel the Rogue River until you reach Casey State Park
(no camping), where you begin a hard 2-mile climb up around
Lost Creek Reservoir. The road along the lake is moderate
until you cross its east end, then you have another short but
steep climb up out of the lake basin. After that, the riding is
considerably easier across a wide, green valley, where you may
see a few head of buffalo grazing on the right side of the road.

Prospect (21 miles; grocery, hotel, café). This small town is set just
off the highway, and has a wonderful old hotel facing the
schoolhouse. Next to the hotel is a country general store worth
the side trip just to visit. There are a few small stores and
cafés on the road between Prospect and Crater Lake, but the
most complete supplies are found in Prospect. Continue east
on Oreg. 62; shortly you enter the Rogue River National Forest, where you will start to cycle through dense stands of
Douglas fir, ponderosa, and western red cedar. The upgrade is
gentle as you begin a climb that will last to Crater Lake. Pass

Union Creek (10 miles; grocery, café, motel), a small cluster of
buildings next to a National Forest campground, and your

last supply stop before Crater Lake. Two miles beyond Union Creek you reach a junction with Oreg. 230; stay right on Oreg. 62. After passing Milepost 60, some 18 miles beyond Prospect, you will notice the road becoming steeper. This gradient will continue to sharpen until you come to the Crater Lake Turnoff, near MP 70. Turn left at the junction, and you have a short gradual descent, then begin climbing again to the park headquarters. From here you can see a sharp hill off to your left, which you begin climbing. You go about 1.5 miles over a very steep grade, with a number of switchbacks. Once over the top you have a short but well-earned coast to

Crater Lake Lodge (23 miles; grocery, restaurant, lodge). Rest here and enjoy some of the best views of the lake just across the road. You'll see more of the lake, but you'll have to climb to do it, as the road begins winding around the west rim, going up a series of sharp rises and then a final 2.5-mile climb until you reach an unmarked highpoint of 7,100 feet. From here you get views off as far away as the Coast Range, and exceptional glimpses of the Cascades. You drop down and shortly leave the rim, heading north rather than continuing around on Rim Drive. Continue your descent down a long hill to Pumice Desert at about 6,000 feet. The desert is a flat, nearly barren landscape formerly bombarded with fallout from the volcano that created the gaping hole in the mountain. You have a short climb out of this volcanic basin, then a steady downhill run to a junction with Oreg. 138, which you follow north to

Diamond Lake (24 miles; grocery, camping, lodge, restaurant). This is a popular resort on a lovely alpine lake. Mount Bailey lies just across from you at 8,363 feet. There are numerous national forest campgrounds along the east side of the lake. The road around has a good shoulder. Traffic is normally light to moderate but increases on weekends and holidays. Five miles beyond Diamond Lake, Oreg. 138 turns westward and begins a descent along the Clearwater River. This ride becomes more spectacular the farther down you go. Near MP 66 the shoulder disappears and you begin a steep downhill, winding through impressive rock-walled canyons and spires. The latter were once volcanic plugs, the softer rock surrounding them having eroded away. There is a small general store at Dry Creek, which is 9 miles from Steamboat. When you reach the latter point, you have come out of the high mountains and are run-

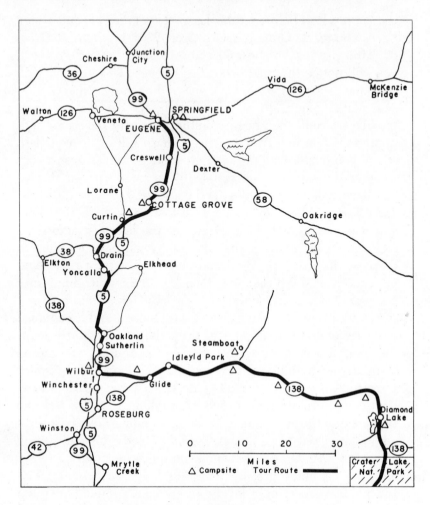

Tour #8 (Section two: Wilbur to Eugene)

ning along the North Umpqua River, famous for its trout
fishing, and a favorite spot for Western writer Zane Grey.
Continue down a gently sloping valley to

Idleyld Park (57 miles; grocery, restaurant, motel). From here the
road runs through open pastureland, presaging the Willamette
Valley. Continue to

Glide (3 miles; grocery, restaurant), a community strung out along
Oreg. 138, which has become busy by this point. Just on the
outskirts of Glide you leave Oreg. 138 by turning north (right)
on the Wilbur Rd. (County Road A200). Although you follow the Umpqua River downstream, the route rises and falls
over a series of steep spines leading down the river, and riding

is moderate to hard. The valley is broad where you enter it, but soon you are high on a grassy slope on the east bank of the river. Continue to

Wilbur (16 miles; grocery). You join Oreg. 99 at this point, which used to be the major north-south highway through the state. There is a charming wooden church in town, and a cedar-shake mill that seems to produce its own crop of ready-for-the-market moss as part of its product. Head north (right) on Oreg. 99, on an easy ride up through the valley to

Sutherlin (5 miles; grocery, restaurants, motels, bicycle shop). This is one of the larger towns on this part of the tour route. Leave north via Oreg. 99 to

Oakland (2 miles; grocery, restaurants). A totally different town of tidy brick buildings dating back to the 1890s. First established in 1851, the town was moved to its present site some twenty years later when the Oregon Central Railroad Company laid its tracks through here. Fire destroyed earlier wooden structures, and the present brick buildings replaced them. (From here there is an alternate route to Yoncalla which passes via Elkhead. It involves a steep climb, and as we were weary of that activity by this point, we decided to storm up the freeway instead.) Your route leaves Oakland via Oreg. 99 to Interstate 5, which is an easy ride for about 4 miles; then you climb a few small hills over the next 4 miles to

Rice Hill Exit (10 miles; motel). Leave the Interstate at this point and rejoin Oreg. 99. The road follows an easy route over the old highway to Yoncalla (grocery, café), then past some old farms, the barns of which still have their sides painted with advertisements advocating the curative powers of liver pills and other nostrums. You scallop some small, interesting hills dotted with live oaks, then drop down into

Drain (8 miles; grocery, motel, restaurant). This town is located near the watershed between the Rogue River valley and the Willamette Valley. The route here is joined by Oreg. 38 from the coast, and the next stretch is rather busy. You have a good shoulder for a few miles outside of town, then it disappears. (Just before you reach Interstate 5 there is a dirt road toward the little town of Lorane. You can use this as a cutoff into Eugene. The dirt lasts for about 9 miles. We don't like to ride on dirt, though.) Our route continues straight to

Junction, Interstate 5 (7 miles; grocery, restaurant, motel, camping). Go north on I-5. A short and moderate climb brings you over the ridge separating the two valleys mentioned earlier. Stay on the Interstate for 5 miles, then turn left off Interstate 5 at the Cottage Grove exit. Use great caution here, although if you are prudent there is no real difficulty in getting off easily. Continue through the appropriately named village of Divide and on to

Cottage Grove (10 miles; grocery, restaurants, motels, camping, bicycle shop), which marks the upper reaches of the Willamette Valley. Cottage Grove may have received a blessing in being bypassed by the freeway, as it is a well-laid-out town with a good homespun feeling. Continue north on Oreg. 99 through Saginaw (grocery), the route passing up over gentle hills with the Coast Fork of the Willamette River off to your right. Pass through Creswell (grocery, restaurant). Near Eugene, Oreg. 99 joins Oreg. 126. You turn west (left) and follow 126 through typical urban traffic into

Eugene (19 miles; grocery, restaurants, motels, camping, bicycle shop). See Tour 9 for description of Eugene. You have a number of alternatives out of Eugene for connecting tours, with options open to the coast, the Cascades, or north through the Willamette Valley.

TOUR #9: WILLAMETTE VALLEY TO THE COLUMBIA

Distance: 200 miles.

Terrain: Easy riding in the upper Willamette Valley, with some hills around Brownsville. Two significant climbs in the low mountains separating the Willamette Valley from the Columbia.

Roads and Traffic: Light traffic for almost all the tour route, but normal city congestion in Eugene and Salem.

Season: April through October, but the midsummer months of July and August are the driest.

Weather: Moderate temperatures; occasionally cloudy or rainy days, depending upon month.

Special Features: Good variety from rich farmlands to moss-covered timber country, quiet roads.

Connecting Transportation:

Eugene: Greyhound, Trailways, Amtrak, air service.

Rainier: Greyhound; Amtrak at Longview, just across the Columbia River.

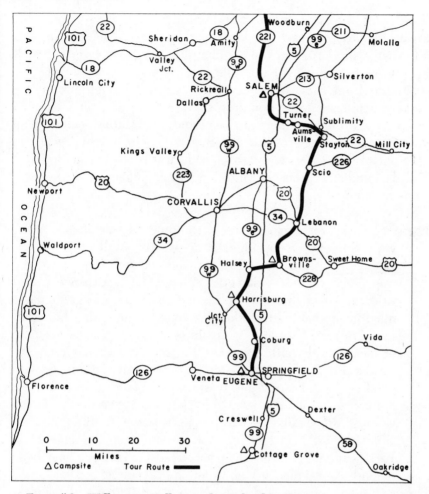

Tour #9 Willamette Valley to the Columbia (Section one: Eugene to Salem)

We originally developed this tour in an effort to find a route of varied terrain up through the Williamette Valley, and also to provide a corridor that avoided ash fallout from the eruptions of Mount Saint Helens during the summer we were exploring the region. We were more successful in finding the varied terrain than in avoiding the ash, but both experiences proved interesting, if not always pleasant. Barring further activity from the volcano, your ride should have all the benefits and none of the disadvantages.

The route passes from the table-flat farmlands of the upper Willamette Valley near Eugene into the rolling foothills that bulge on the eastern flank of the valley. Crossing it, see many of Oregon's oldest towns, the most authentic and untouched of which is probably Brownsville. As you reach the lower part of the Willamette the tour route veers westward, and you begin a pleasant and not very difficult stage through some low-lying hills and mountains separating the Willamette from the Columbia. After passing through productive forests of hemlock and fir, you drop sharply down into the Columbia River valley. From here there are numerous possibilities, including an intersection with the Oregon Loop Bicycle Trail, by which you can swing out to the sea or double back southward into Portland. There are also a number of other tour intersections at Eugene, and the lower end of the tour.

Eugene (grocery, restaurants, motels, camping, bicycle shop). Along with the city of Springfield across the Willamette River, Eugene is an important cultural and economic center for the upper end of the Willamette Valley. There are some placid rides on bicycle trails along the river, and spacious green parks filled in summer with students, picnickers, and other bicyclists taking a rest. City streets are busy, and you can get a map of local bicycle paths from the Eugene city officials (see Appendix 1). Eugene is also on the Trans America Trail, with good connections east and west on route summarized in Tour Summary 1, found later in this chapter. Leave north via the Coburg Rd. Traffic is heavy near town, but thins out considerably within a few miles. Continue past Armitage State Park (camping), where the marked bicycle lane you have been on ends. Continue through quiet countryside to

Coburg (8 miles; grocery, café), which has a little park for picnicking. Leave town via the North Coburg Rd. to a junction with Pole Line Rd. just at the edge of town. Turn north (right) toward Harrisburg. Continue through level farm country on a quiet road through Harrisburg (grocery, café, motel, camping) where you intersect Oreg. 99E, a busy road which you follow 9 miles to

Halsey (21 miles), Junction, Oreg. 228. Turn east (right) on Oreg. 228 toward Brownsville. The ride is absolutely level except for a slight hump in the road as you cross Interstate 5. Most of the fields are in wheat and rye grass. After crossing the Interstate continue another 4 miles to the Brownsville turnoff. Turn north (left), cross an old bridge, and follow into the center of

Brownsville (7 miles; grocery, restaurant, motel, camping). This is one of Oregon's oldest communities, settled in the mid-nineteenth century by farmers coming to make a new start in rich valley land. The population remains predominantly agrarian. Considerable efforts are being made to preserve buildings reflecting the town's rich history. There is a park and a free campground just over the hill from city hall. Leave north via County Road 425, the Brownsville-Lebanon Road. The next section of the route is well posted with signs to Lebanon, but there are a number of alternatives. Take those following paved roads. After leaving Brownsville you abandon the level terrain of the Willamette Valley for a picturesque ride over some short but steep hills, with good views westward. There are numerous fields of hay and rye grass, and a charming deserted one-room schoolhouse to the left of the road. Continue into

Lebanon (15 miles; grocery, restaurants, motels). This is a large, busy town, and a good supply point. Leave Lebanon northwest via U.S. 20 to Airport Rd. Turn right on Airport Rd. toward Scio. Continue 8 miles to a junction with Oreg. 226. Turn east (right) and continue for 6 miles to

Scio (14 miles; grocery, café). This little town is perched on a rolling ridge above Thomas Creek. Leave north on the road to Stayton. You must cross a dividing ridge between Thomas Creek and the North Fork of the Santiam River. Pass through forested land alternating with cleared pasturelands of grass crops through Stayton (grocery, restaurant). Leave north from Stayton for 2 miles to

Junction, Oreg. 22 (7 miles). Turn west (left). This is a busy highway but with a good shoulder. Continue up a gradual hill then down about a mile to a junction with Mill Creek Rd., which you take and go into

Aumsville (4 miles; grocery, café). This is a sleepy little town with a pleasant park on the far edge where you can dip into a genuine old-fashioned swimming hole. If you are not so inclined, continue on through Turner (grocery), where you leave by West 3rd St. toward Salem. The road scallops a number of little rounded hills that separate small streams flowing down toward the Willamette River. The route is well signposted until you reach

Salem (13 miles; grocery, restaurant, motels, camping, bicycle shop). The history of Salem predates the arrival of white settlers, as there were a number of Indian villages near here. In early settlement days the town of Oregon City at the falls of the Willamette was more important, but today Salem is the capital of Oregon, a thriving, active city. Leave town via Marion St., walking your bicycle across the bridge spanning the Willamette. Continue to a junction with Oreg. 221 (Wallace Rd., where you turn north (right) toward Dayton. Continue on Oreg. 221, which parallels the Willamette River, passing through farmlands that have provided much wealth to this part of the state since the early white settlers arrived.

Dayton (20 miles; grocery, café). Continue north out of Dayton to a junction with Oreg. 18. Turn west (left) for one mile to a junction with Lafayette Rd. Turn north (right) toward

Lafayette (5 miles; grocery, café). Turn left on 3rd Street, then within a few blocks turn right on Bridge St. toward Gaston. There is a sign on Bridge St. indicating a Trappist Abbey, which you pass on your right about 2 miles from town. The road commences to roll as you leave the flat basin formed by the Willamette. The rest of the tour is over much hillier terrain. Continue 6 miles to

Junction, Oreg. 240 (6 miles). Turn west (left) toward Yamhill. The road winds through pretty farm country, the hills carefully controlled to guard against soil erosion. There are a few exquisitely kept horse ranches on this part of the route.

Yamhill (6 miles; grocery, café). Turn north (right) on Oreg. 47, and begin a gradually rolling ride up another pretty valley. The road carries moderate traffic, but has a good riding shoulder. When we toured here in 1980, a fine coating of volcanic ash blew up in our faces each time a heavy truck passed, and we practiced short, vigorous dashes with our mouths closed and our eyes in slits. Continue through Gaston to

Forest Grove (17 miles; grocery, restaurants, motels, bicycle shop). This town, heavily hit by ash from the second eruption of Mount Saint Helens, mounted enormous efforts to rid itself of the residue. Our son played merrily in 3 inches of powder around the swings in the town park. Leave town north via Oreg. 47, on which you will stay for some time. Traffic thins out considerably as you pass· immaculately kept farms owned by descendants of the first Dutch settlers in the region. One evening we slept in a pasture with a good bit of ash, and were a big attraction for a herd of Guernseys, who kept poking our bicycles over with their noses and stealing water bottles out of their wire racks. A rambunctious leader then pranced

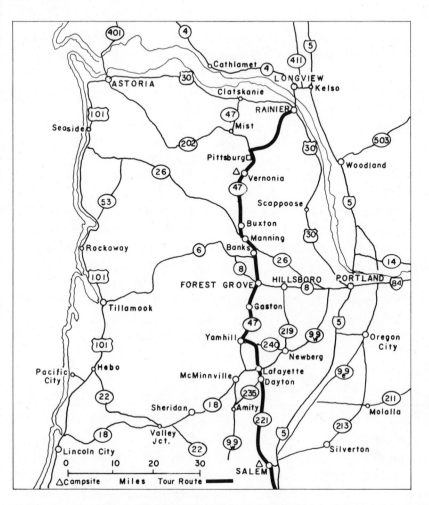

Tour #9   (Section two: Salem to Rainier)

threateningly toward our tent. As city folk, we conceded the
victory to the steers and moved across a fence where they
couldn't join us. Soon you reach

Banks (6 miles, grocery, café). Just beyond town you (and Oreg. 47)
turn west (left) onto U.S. 26, which is exceptionally busy but
has a wide shoulder. The stretch is not long—about 4 miles—
until Oreg. 47 splits off to the north. You turn with it. As you
head up the valley you begin climbing moderately, making
your way up through dense cedar and deciduous forests to a
highpoint about 5 miles from Buxton. You then descend and
continue through typical coastal forests to the logging town of
Vernonia (21 miles; grocery, restaurants, motel, camping). This little

town marks the change from the agrarian economy of the valley to the timber-oriented hills. Leave via Oreg. 47 following Rock Creek in a pleasant valley past Pittsburg (café) then 4 miles to

Junction, Apiary Rd. (9 miles; unmarked). The turnoff is clearly signposted to Rainier. Turn right and begin winding up through dense forests for about 2 miles, after which you start a harder climb of 4 miles, the last mile of which is difficult. From this point you descend to the Clatskanie River valley. Once in the valley you intersect old U.S. 30, which is used as a part of the Bikecentennial organization's Oregon Loop Bicycle Trail. (Details are given in Tour Summary 5.) To follow the present tour continue on toward Rainier, climbing out of the river valley past the high school, then down a steep series of switchbacks to

Rainier (21 miles; grocery, restaurant, motel). At Rainier you are along the Columbia, which is exceptionally wide at this point. If you wish to continue northward into Washington, you may cross into Longview on the bridge. Washington 411 provides a good corridor northward toward Puget Sound.

TOUR #10: EUGENE TO SISTERS VIA SANTIAM PASS

Distance: 163 miles.

Terrain: Rolling riding through a part of the Willamette Valley, then a long climb to Santiam Pass. Most of the climbing up to the pass is moderate, but the last several miles are hard. A long downhill run to Sisters, on the eastern side of the Cascades.

Traffic: Quiet through most of the Willamette Valley, moderate to heavy as far as Detroit Lake, moderate to light from there to Sisters.

Season: June through September.

Weather: Normally dry, but some chances of rain, particularly through early summer.

Special Features: Nice riding through some of the oldest settlements in Oregon's Willamette Valley, a beautiful ride through the Cascades. Good opportunities for connecting routes with other tours.

Transportation to Starting and Terminating Points:
>   Eugene: Greyhound, Trailways, Amtrak, air services.
>   Sisters: Trailways.

Connecting Tours:

Eugene: Tour 9: Willamette Valley to the Columbia.
Tour 8: Southern Oregon—Crater Lake—Willamette Valley.

This tour started as something of a busman's holiday for us. Having a day of free time while camping at Oregon's Detroit Lake, we decided to take a ride. We ended up climbing over Santiam Pass. As the little town of Sisters, just a short ride down from the pass, has always been one of our favorite places, we decided to put everything together in a tour that would connect the western and eastern side of the Oregon Cascades.

Not far from our minds were the advantages such a route would have in making connections with other routes, both our own and those developed by Bikecentennial. The Trans America Trail, which touches both Eugene and Sisters but goes via McKenzie Pass, allows for a convenient—and beautiful—round trip. The starting point of our tour in Eugene corresponds to a number of other routes of our own as well as those developed by the Oregon Department of Highways.

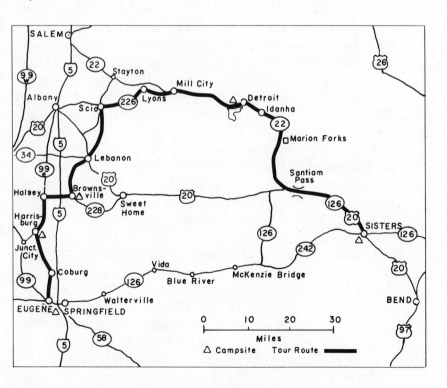

Tour #10   Eugene to Sisters via Santiam Pass

We hope you'll be as pleased as we were with our "rest-day ride." In Sisters, we asked a little girl how she liked the place, and she replied in the most emphatic voice: "I *love* Sisters." We think you will too.

Eugene. See Tour 9 for description of first 63 miles of trip, to

Scio (63 miles; grocery, café). Scio overlooks one of the tributaries flowing down from the Cascades. Turn east (right) on Oreg. 226 toward Lyons. The road is level until you reach the hamlet of Jordan, where you begin some moderate climbs out of the Willamette Valley. Continue to

Lyons (14 miles; grocery, café), a small town dependent upon the lumber industry. Oreg. 226 veers north here, but you may take a quieter alternative by leaving Lyons via County Road 6, the Lyons–Mill City Rd. Continue up a pretty valley on an easy run to

Mill City (7 miles; grocery, café, motel). Here you join Oreg. 22, which lies just across the river and up a little pitch of a hill. Traffic on this road is normally moderate, but on weekends there is a great deal of vacation traffic going to Detroit Lake, a popular resort with a large National Forest campground. The shoulder is narrow to nonexistent, so weekend travel is hazardous. Traffic thins out considerably above Detroit Lake. Continue through Gates (grocery, café, motel), winding up Santiam Canyon. This area was originally settled by farmers, but they soon discovered that lumber was a more lucrative crop. A rest area above Gates has displays explaining this part of the region's history. Continue on a moderate climb to a point just below Detroit Lake Dam, where you begin a short but hard ascent to get up to the level of the lake. You have a pleasantly level run on the north shore on a good road with wide shoulder. The National Forest campgrounds lie between you and the little village of

Detroit (17 miles; grocery, café, camping, motel). Stay on Oreg. 22 and follow the upper end of the lake and the Santiam River. Pass through the logging town of Idanha (grocery). You have some excellent views of Mount Jefferson (10,495 feet) ahead of you. The climb is moderate for about 10 miles from Detroit, when you begin climbing more steeply. Continue past the little mountain resort of Marion Forks (restaurant). Begin a hard climb at Milepost 74 that lasts, with only a few brief

respites, until you climb to Santiam Pass. You pass some interesting old lava flows off to the right of the road near MP 80,
then continue on to a junction of Oreg. 22 with U.S. 20. U.S.
20 is a spur of the Trans America Trail and will connect you
with the route over McKenzie Pass, a tougher climb than the
one you are on. The climb from this junction is 6 hard miles to
Santiam Pass (37 miles; youth hostel). The hostel is set off to the
north side of the road, and is one of the more scenic you'll find
in the West. From the summit, which you reach at MP 80
(4,817 feet), you begin a long descent past some pretty alpine
lakes, edge past 6,000-foot Black Butte, then down through
the drier forests of the eastern slope to the little town of
Sisters (25 miles; grocery, restaurants, motel, camping). Beautifully
located just to the east of the Mount Washington Wilderness
Area, it gives you excellent views back of the Cascades, including the picturesque Three Sisters, all over 10,000 feet.
You have a choice of continuing east on the Trans America
Trail or going back to Eugene on another part of the same
route (see Tour Summary 6).

TOUR #11: EVERGREENS AND ISLANDS OF PUGET SOUND

Distance: 235 miles, not including ferry travel.
Terrain: Moderate hills, easy valley rides.
Roads and Traffic: Mostly quiet roads, but congestion near Deception
Pass State Park and on entrance back into Seattle.
Season: May to October, but July and August are the best months.
Weather: Generally little rain in July and August, measurable pre-
cipitation on from 10 to 14 days a month in spring, early sum-
mer, and autumn.
Special Features: Beautiful island rides, ferry-hopping through Puget
Sound, lovely agricultural valleys in western Washington.
Connecting Transportation:
Seattle: Greyhound, Trailways, Amtrak, air service.

Western Washington offers the bicyclist the unique opportunity to
explore one of America's most picturesque waterways by combining
riding with low-cost ferry travel. Your ferry travel begins the ride, as
you leave from downtown Seattle on the Bremerton Ferry for an

hour's ride across the gray-green expanse of Puget Sound. After debarking at Bremerton, you begin a trip past tiny fishing coves and uninhabited inlets of the sound. Within a day or so of ferry riding and bicycling, you arrive at Port Townsend, a beautifully kept nineteenth-century town on a spit of land jutting out into Puget Sound. You may want to explore a bit, or hop a convenient ferry to Whidbey Island, one of the largest in the West. Highpoint of your visit to the island is a ride across the bridge spanning Deception Pass, a deep cleft separating Whidbey from Fidalgo Island. The sea swirls mercilessly against the rocks far below, pulled by immense tidal forces. A short ride brings you to the mainland, and a tour high above Samish Bay on Chuckanut Drive, leading you into Bellingham. From there you turn southward and pass through some of western Washington's pastoral scenery, with green meadows edging up to dense forests of hemlock and fir. You have the opportunity to continue an exploration of Washington when you reach Sedro Woolley, as you intersect our tour of the North Cascades National Park and northern Washington (Tour 12) at this point. If you wish to return to Seattle, follow the tour route down a series of valleys, then finally through a heavily built-up area for the last 20 miles or so of the tour. You need to plan this last stretch for noncommuter hours, or if possible for a weekend morning.

Seattle (grocery, restaurants, motels, camping, youth hostel, bicycle shops). This beautiful city, set amidst steep hills, deep freshwater lakes, and a sinewy arm of the Pacific Ocean, has excellent possibilities for day excursions. Chuck Steward's *Bicycling Around Seattle* (see Bibliography) will help you with routes. One nonbicycling excursion you should treat yourself to is the Pike Place Market, a labyrinth of the exotic and mundane along Seattle's waterfront. When you've spent enough time there, it's only a short ride to the ferry terminal at Pier 52, where you can slip on board the Bremerton Ferry. After securing your bicycle to a bulkhead, remove all valuables and go upstairs for a scenic crossing of Puget Sound. The ferry wends its way through Rich Passage, past the densely covered hillsides of Bainbridge Island, and then docks at

Bremerton (grocery, restaurants, motels, bicycle shops). Bremerton is a busy town, the economy of which is centered on the Sound and the naval shipyards there. The U.S.S. *Missouri*, on which the Japanese surrendered to end World War II, rides at anchor

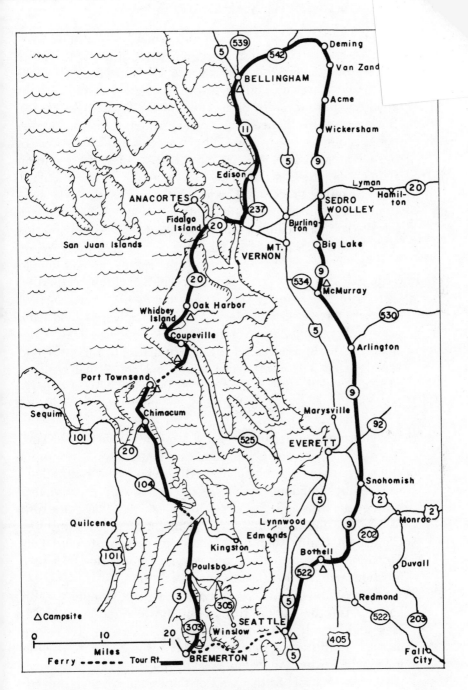

Tour #11   Evergreens and Islands of Puget Sound

in the harbor and may be visited. Bremerton is a hilly town, and you'll get a good bit of exercise in short order. Leave north via Washington 303 toward Brownsville. (Local traffic is heavy for the first few miles out of town. To avoid this you can take an alternate route from Bremerton, on the Brownsville-Illahee Rd., passing by Illahee State Park [camping].) From higher points along the route you will get exceptional views west of the Olympic Range, and on clear days, you will see Mount Rainier and the Cascade Range to the east.

Brownsville (7 miles; grocery). This is a little harbor on Burke Bay. Continue north on Wash. 303 through deep fir and hemlock forests. You must climb a number of short hills. At the junction with Wash. 308 (Keyport Turnoff), stay left toward Wash. 3. When you reach Wash. 3, turn north (right) and continue to

Poulsbo (10 miles; grocery, restaurants, motels, bicycle shop). Settled in 1883 by Norwegians, this fishing town still retains much of the spirit of its early settlers. A Viking festival is held each May to commemorate Norwegian Independence Day. Continue on Wash. 3 north for 4 miles to a turnoff for the Hood Canal Ferry. This short trip across the Hood Canal replaces the damaged floating bridge just to the north. After debarking you begin a long, uphill climb of moderate difficulty on Wash. 104 to

Junction, Chimacum–Port Ludlow Rd. (8 miles; no services). Turn north (right) toward Chimacum. You begin a quiet ride up a valley typical of the northwest, with deep green pastureland watered by abundant rainfall. As the ferry south of you makes subsequent trips and discharges other vehicles, you get a rush of cars buzzing by you every 15 minutes or so. Pass through Chimacum (café, camping), following the signs toward Port Townsend. Beyond Chimacum go via County Road 12 to a junction with Wash. 20. Continue north to

Port Townsend (17 miles; grocery, restaurant, motels, camping, youth hostel). You can explore this seaport town of red-brick buildings and stately Victorian houses by following the route marked by the seagull signposts. There is also a state park in town where you can camp. When you are ready to leave, wheel your bicycle to the head of the line of cars waiting for the Keystone Ferry. You'll be put on first. The crossing to Whidbey Island will take about half an hour. Land at Casey State Park (camping) and continue to

Coupeville (7 miles; grocery, café, motel). The road winds up over gentle hills and past prosperous dairy farms. As you approach Oak Harbor, traffic begins to pick up, and the shoulder varies from 3 feet to nothing. Early starts, bright clothing, and avoiding weekends are all advised. Continue to

Oak Harbor (13 miles; grocery, restaurant, motels, camping). From here you begin a pretty but congested ride toward Deception Pass. The road rises and falls, and thick forests of hemlock and fir press in on both sides of you. Continue on a narrow but ridable shoulder to Deception Pass (café, grocery, camping). This narrow strait is spanned by a bridge, and the view downward is thrilling. Sea waters churned by the tides swirl past stark rock formations far below you. The next 6 miles of roadway has little or no shoulder, and traffic is heavy. Continue on Wash. 20, picking up a good shoulder as you cross a short passage of water, then you have good riding conditions to

Junction, Bayview–Edison Rd. (36 miles; restaurant). Turn north (left) off of Wash. 20 toward Edison. You ride through level country, the small back road affording excellent views of Puget Sound. Continue to Edison (grocery, café), then on to a junction with Wash. 11 (Chuckanut Drive). Follow Chuckanut, which twists far above Samish Bay. It is a popular route with motorists, but signs tell them to look out for you. Moreover, the turns keep traffic slow. It is one of the more picturesque routes in this part of Washington, and a favorite of local bicyclists. Go past Larrabee State Park (camping), then after a final crest descend to downtown

Bellingham (25 miles; grocery, restaurants, motels, camping, bicycle shops). The university has made this port town a haven for bicyclists, with marked bicycle lanes and good bicycle shops. Leave Bellingham via Wash. 534. You climb a series of broad hills of only moderate difficulty. Farms are spread out on both sides of the route. Ten miles outside of Bellingham you cross the Nooksack River and meet Wash. 9. Turn right (southeast) and continue to

Deming (15 miles; grocery, café). Start up the south fork of the Nooksack River, which has cut a broad valley. There are pastures in the foreground, with steep wooded hillsides and waterfalls forming a green-and-silver backdrop. Continue on Wash. 9 to Van Zandt, which has an interesting little general store with a decidedly upbeat proprietorship. Go through

Clipper (grocery), then you leave the valley and begin a rolling ride that brings you to the railroad-and-mill town of

Sedro Woolley (24 miles; grocery, restaurants, motels, bicycle shop). The main street and shopping area lie off to the south of the highway. Leave Sedro Woolley on Wash. 9. You cross the Skagit River, following a wide road with well-paved shoulder on an easy ride to

Clear Lake (3 miles; grocery, café). There is a rustic old shake mill in town. From here you begin passing through rolling hills with a number of small natural lakes on the sides of the road. Traffic is light, and the route combines excellent northwest riding conditions with occasional glimpses of stalwart mountains looming out of an often misty foreground. The road passes through forests of white-barked alder, fir, and hemlock as you pass between the towns of Big Lake (grocery), McMurray, and Bryant.

Arlington (23 miles; grocery, restaurant) is a small town on the Stillaguamish River. Continue south on Wash. 9, a good stretch of road with wide shoulder. You climb a number of moderate grades, passing out of the cultivated valley into forests.

Snohomish (20 miles; grocery, restaurant, motel, bicycle shop) is both a logging and farming center. From here on south congestion becomes a problem, and you need to use caution. The shoulder is 6 to 8 feet wide and in fair condition.

Junction, Wash. 522 and 9 (10 miles; no services). Wash. 9 ends here, and bicycles are not permitted on this section of Wash. 522, although you'll be taking this highway into Seattle. Here, take the old Woodinville-Snohomish Rd. to the south, keeping along the railroad track to a junction with the Woodinville-Duvall Rd. Turn west (right) and go through Woodinville to Woodinville Dr., which you follow (it changes to Riverside) into

Bothell (5 miles; grocery, restaurant, motels, camping, bicycle shop). This once-small town has been absorbed into greater Seattle. You join Wash. 522 from here into Seattle. It is a busy four-lane highway with gravel shoulder. Commuter traffic is exceptionally busy here, and you should cover this part of the route at midday if possible. Just beyond the suburb of Lake Forest Park you can leave Wash. 522 by turning south (left) on 35th Ave. N.E.; proceed to

Seattle (12 miles; grocery, restaurants, motels, camping, youth hostel, bicycle shops).

TOUR #12: NORTH CASCADES NATIONAL PARK—NORTHERN WASHINGTON—SANDPOINT, IDAHO

Distance: 404 miles.

Terrain: There are five passes to cross in the state of Washington, with interesting valley rides through pastureland and orchard country.

Roads and Traffic: Moderate traffic at the beginning of the tour route, mostly light traffic thereafter.

Season: June to mid-September.

Weather: Chances of rain on the west side of the Cascades, diminishing in July and August. Mostly dry and warm east of the Cascades.

Special Features: North Cascades National Park and the peaks just east of it are among the most beautiful in the West. You cross rock summits, with snowfields hanging high above you in midsummer, then a series of less challenging passes into the lake country of Idaho.

Connecting Transportation:

Sedro Woolley: Greyhound; Trailways serves Mt. Vernon, 10 miles away.

Sandpoint: Greyhound, Amtrak.

The five major passes you must cross in following Washington 20 across the state may at first appear forbidding. Indeed, there are some hard climbs, and cyclists proceeding at a normal pace will have at least one major climb every few days. If it were not for the extraordinary beauty of the land, we would admit that the climbs were more of a detriment than they are. But for the effort you expend—and not all the passes are of maximum difficulty—you are more than rewarded with quiet roads and unspoiled scenery. The highpoint of the tour is undoubtedly in the first few days, when you make your way up into North Cascades National Park. The best of the mountain scenery actually comes after you have passed through the park area and are on its eastern side. Here, we will match the mountain scenery against any you will find in the West. Beautiful sculptured peaks break the skyline. Snowfields and hanging glaciers seem to hover above you. Green, clear mountain streams rush by. Best of all, the road is very well graded, has a wide shoulder, and in spite of the beauty of the region, is still not exceptionally heavily traveled.

Tour #12   North Cascades National Park—Northern Washington—
Sandpoint, Idaho (Section one: Sedro Woolley to New-
halem)

After passing through the Cascades, you cross a number of lesser ranges, dropping into the intervening valleys, some of them offering a bounty of lush irrigated orchards. The last section of the tour is along the gentle land surrounding the Little Pend Oreille River, dotted with lakes that anticipate the scenery awaiting you in the Idaho Panhandle at the tour's end.

Sedro Woolley (grocery, restaurants, motels, bicycle shop). This old
mill-and-railroad town lies in the Skagit Valley north of Seattle. (Cyclists coming from Seattle may find a routing in Tour
11.) You leave east from Sedro Woolley, and you have two
choices. Washington 20—which you'll be taking all the way
to the Idaho border—is at this point a wide but busy highway
until you reach the town of Concrete, 23 miles away. If you
wish to avoid this, cross to the south side of the Skagit River
and take the South Skagit Highway, which follows the river

more closely than does Wash. 20, and is of course much quieter. On either ride you pass through deep evergreen forests with views of the river through openings in the trees.

Concrete (23 miles; grocery, restaurant, motels). Aptly named, this small town was once a huge concrete factory, producing raw materials for the dams built by the municipal electric company of Seattle on the Skagit River. Now only abandoned shells of the plants remain. Continue east on Wash. 20, with some lessening of traffic. Almost immediately you begin to climb some small rises that run down to the river.

Rockport (9 miles; grocery, café, motel; camping nearby at Rockport State Park). Beyond Rockport is a bald-eagle sanctuary, and the birds can often be seen rising off the waters, intently searching for fish below.

Marblemount (8 miles; restaurant, sleeping rooms, camping). At this hamlet you can visit Blackie's Tavern, which bills itself as the last watering spot of its kind for the next 89 miles. Unpainted lap-sided houses set in the woods nurture various shades of green moss. Continue on a generally easy ride through deeper and deeper forest to

Newhalem (15 miles; grocery, camping). This tidy community of company houses was built to shelter employees of the several power projects upriver. The general store is well stocked, and is your last chance to get groceries until you reach Winthrop, 74 miles away. Two passes must be crossed in the interim. Unless you are a strong rider, the best thing to do is camp midway, preferably near or on the other side of the two passes. From there it is an easy morning's ride into Winthrop, which has well-stocked stores and numerous restaurants. Leaving the bright yellow houses of Newhalem behind you, you begin climbing for 1.5 miles up a steep canyon, the road cut into the canyon walls with good views down. The best view comes when you cross a deep gorge on a bridge whose surface is made of steel latticework, allowing you an unsettling view of the river churning hundreds of feet directly below your bicycle wheels. Streams of silver waterfalls streak down the opposite walls of the canyon. You drop down to the level of the lake formed by Diablo Dam, then begin a series of steep climbs. These lead you around the south end of Ross Lake. As you leave the lake, you start up a gradual grade alongside Granite Creek. It is here that the views become more and more spectacular. Small circular snowfields and glaciers hang on the

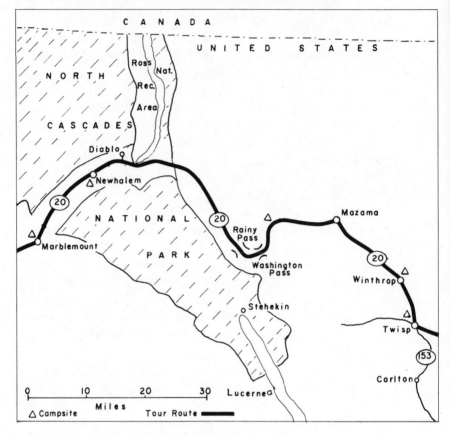

Tour #12   (Section two: Newhalem to Twisp)

cliffs high above you. At each turn a new peak of incredible beauty reveals itself to you, its rock summit etching jagged lines against the sky. The last 4-mile climb to Rainy Pass is hard. The summit (4,860 feet) is at Milepost 158. You descend a mile, then begin another climb to a second pass—Washington Pass, at 5,744 feet (MP 162). From this vantage point you see Whistler Peak on your left, and then Mount Silver Star. Other mountains rear rugged heads as far north as you can see. Once over Washington Pass you have a series of very steep switchbacks along the flank of a U-shaped, glaciated valley. Vegetation becomes more sparse on the drier eastern slopes. You have a good 5-mile run down, then more gradual downhill to a broad valley carpeted in pasture grasses. The Methow River cuts a course against the bank of hills to the right of you.

Winthrop (74 miles; grocery, restaurants, motels, camping). You may

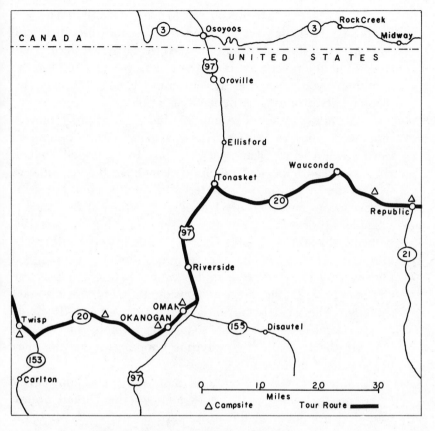

Tour #12   (Section three: Twisp to Republic)

want to stop for a breather in the shaded park just on the edge of town. The center itself has an authentic enough rough-and-tumble appearance. Winthrop used to be near the end of a paved road, and was largely neglected until 1972, when the road you have just passed over was cut through the Cascades. The economic stimulus of being close to the north Cascades has tended to diminish some of the town's former authenticity, but it is still pleasurable to stroll along the board sidewalks or examine some of the curios for sale in the antique stores. Continue down the Methow River on Wash. 20 to

Twisp (9 miles; grocery, restaurants, motel, camping). Somewhat larger than Winthrop, Twisp is a good place to stock up, including water supplies, as your next large stores are a little over 30 miles away, and there is a hard pass climb separating you from them. A few miles outside of Twisp, Wash. 20 leaves the Methow River valley and you begin a climb toward Loup

Pass (4,020 feet), which you reach near MP 214.5. The last 5 miles of that climb are hard. As you descend the other side, you enter forests denser than those covering the western slope, something of a reversal of the normal pattern. As you leave the mountains you enter the agricultural Okanogan Valley, famous for its produce, particularly its apples.

Okanogan (29 miles; grocery, restaurant, motels, camping, bicycle shop with minimal parts). There is a historical museum in town. Each August, Okanogan plays host to a stampede, which emphasizes an important ranching element in the economy as well as the typical lore associated with such events. For a bit of variety, go north out of Okanogan on Wash. 215 toward

Omak (4 miles; grocery, restaurants, motels, camping). From this point north, Wash. 20 joins U.S. 97, a main north-south route into Canada. Prospectors and fortune hunters once plugged northward along the same route, known in the 1860s as the Caribou Trail. Traffic increases considerably, but there is good shoulder. The road is currently being repaved. At Riverside (grocery, café) there is a nice shaded park where you can cool off from the typically high daytime temperatures in this part of the state. Continue to

Tonasket (24 miles; grocery, restaurants, motels, bicycle shop). Fruit from this growing country goes all over the United States. Camping privileges in the town park do not apply to tents, unfortunately, as the police chief informed us just as we were nestling down for the night. The adjacent swimming pool is a welcome relief from the heat, in any case. As you leave Tonasket you begin a climb along Bonaparte Creek, which leads you out of the hot valley into more verdant and cooler terrain. Services over the next 40 miles are limited to a small store in Wauconda, 24 miles from Tonasket. After an initial 4-mile climb of moderate difficulty, you enter a broad valley where the grade is more gradual. Some of the ranches here date to mid-nineteenth-century homesteads. Original log buildings and outbuildings poke disheveled and roofless heads up out of the waving brown grass. At places touched by irrigation water, lush grass and alfalfa meadows spring up. Near MP 275 are some Indian petroglyphs drawn on a rock face just off to the left of the road. After leaving this valley you climb through sparse ponderosa pine, the nearby stream broadened out by beaver dams.

Wauconda (24 miles; grocery, café—limited supplies). Set in one of the broad valleys that were so attractive to homesteaders, there are some beautiful examples of two-story log houses off the road. In early summer yellow, purple, and red wildflowers add their own dash of color to the landscape. You have a final climb to Wauconda Summit (4,305 feet) at MP 289. Then you start a steep 3-mile downgrade through dense forests, after which you have a more rolling descent to

Republic (16 miles; grocery, restaurant, motel, camping). Located on the Sanpoil River, Republic has known raucous days as a mining town, and more recently has served as something of a haven for escapees from complexities of urban life. The downtown seems to go at its own pace, wearing much the same face it has for years. Drop down across the river, then begin still another long climb up into the Kettle River Range, which separates you from the Columbia River basin to the east. Services are nonexistent for the next 40 miles, and you must cross Sherman Pass in the interim. The first 4 miles of that climb, beginning near MP 309, are moderate. The rest is harder. You crest at MP 319.5 (5,575 feet). This is followed by a steep 5-mile drop, then a more gradual descent along Sherman Creek through deeply forested country until you get down near the Columbia River basin itself, where vegetation thins out. The final run brings you along the flank of the Columbia, across a bridge, and into

Kettle Falls (40 miles; grocery, restaurants, motel, camping), a mill town on the edge of the Columbia. There is a pleasant park at the water's edge. Continue on a gentle uphill grade through wheatfields in the Colville River valley to

Colville (10 miles; grocery, restaurants, motels, camping, bicycle shop). Set in a lovely, broad valley, Colville is the last important town—and bicycle shop—you will pass until you reach the end of the tour in Sandpoint, Idaho. Shortly after leaving town you leave the valley cut by the Colville River and make your way over your last highpoint, this one much more benign than the earlier ones. You make this climb in short segments, leveling off as you cross a valley, then climbing again. About 20 miles outside of Colville you reach the Little Pend Oreille River, and although you will continue to climb, the upgrade is minimal. You pass small natural lakes surrounded by forests of aspen and lodgepole and ponderosa pine. There are a number of small resorts and campsites. Beaver Lodge near MP 379 has a small grocery store, and some of the resorts just off the

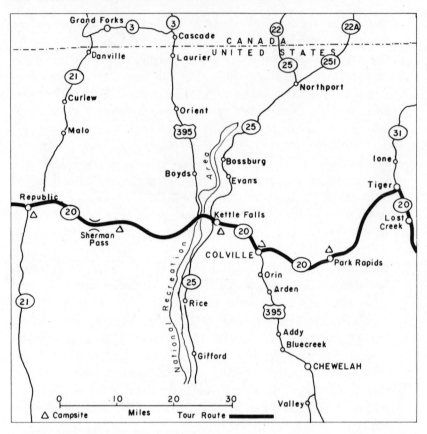

Tour #12   (Section four: Republic to Tiger)

road sell minimal supplies. Near MP 386, with almost no visual change in terrain, you pass a last highpoint, then shortly after begin a steep 4-mile downgrade that will eventually bring you to the Pend Oreille River at the uninhabited town of

Tiger (36 miles; no services, including water). From this point you have a lovely, level ride down the valley carved by the gentle Pend Oreille. Continue through a number of small resorts to

Blue Slide (8 miles; grocery). Continue on downriver with a short climb or two over ridges to the small town of

Usk (23 miles; grocery, café). Go into town and cross the Pend Oreille River. Just downriver you will see numerous log boom pilings with interesting-looking tops. These are bald eagle nests, and you probably will see a good many of these giant creatures floating above the river looking for food. At the end of the bridge turn south (right) on a road through the Kalispell Indian Reservation. Continue along the river to

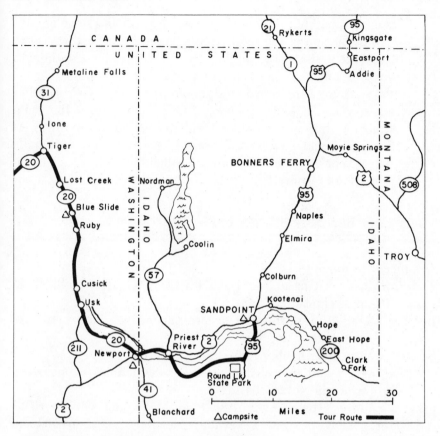

Tour #12   (Section five: Tiger to Sandpoint)

Newport (16 miles; grocery, restaurant, motels, camping). (You inter-
cept a leg of our Idaho Panhandle tour here [Tour 14].) Newport has a tiny railroad museum. As you cross the state line,
Wash. 20 ends, and you are on U.S. 2. Head east on U.S. 2
toward Sandpoint. This is a busy east-west route, but you have
only 6 miles of it, and that with wide shoulder, to

Priest River (6 miles; grocery, restaurant). Leave U.S. 2, turn right
into town and cross the Pend Oreille River. Immediately upon
reaching the south bank, turn east (left) on a country road.
The route rolls through pastureland, juts away from the river
after several miles, then passes Round Lake State Park. Just
past the park you reach a

Junction with U.S. 95 (19 miles; no services). Turn north (left) and
head toward Sandpoint. The road is very busy, but has a good
shoulder until you reach the bridge just outside of town. This
span, which carries you across an arm of Pend Oreille Lake,

is narrow and has no shoulder. A good sprint and some aggressive possession of the right-hand portion of the roadway seem to be the best way of handling the 1-mile stretch. Continue to Sandpoint (11 miles; grocery, restaurant, motels, camping, bicycle shop). Here at the north end of one of Idaho's most beautiful lakes, you can easily spend a day strolling down the main street or through the older residential districts of town. At Sandpoint you have connections with our Idaho Panhandle tour (Tour 14) and our tour from Sandpoint to Glacier National Park (Tour 15).

TOUR #13: RENO—VIRGINIA CITY—LAKE TAHOE

Distance: 214 miles.

Terrain: Mostly flat or rolling, but with two very steep, difficult 8-mile pass climbs.

Road and Traffic: Light through eastern part of loop, heavy in Lake Tahoe, Carson City, Reno areas.

Season: May to mid-October.

Weather: Warm and sunny. Cool evenings. Sometimes strong westerly winds in Nevada basins.

Special Features: Historic gold-rush town of Virginia City; agricultural valleys of western Nevada; ride along east shore of Lake Tahoe.

Connecting Transportation:
   Reno: Greyhound, Trailways, Amtrak, air service.

   Although much of Nevada is arid, forbidding land—even to lovers of the desert and solitude—its western portion has had a rich history, and one of the greatest water treasures of the West, Lake Tahoe, is shared equally by Nevada and California. The tour explores the historic mining town of Virginia City, where the famous Comstock Lode was mined, creating probably as many fortunes as any mine in the West. It possessed the richest silver vein ever discovered. After visiting Virginia City, the tour route takes you through some of Nevada's sagebrush desert, a vast, treeless land of solitude. Where water is available in Nevada, lush farm crops are possible, and this is demonstrated in the surprisingly green agricultural valley around Yerington, where the tour follows a branch of the Walker River. Swinging westward, you come—after an incredibly hard climb—to the shores of

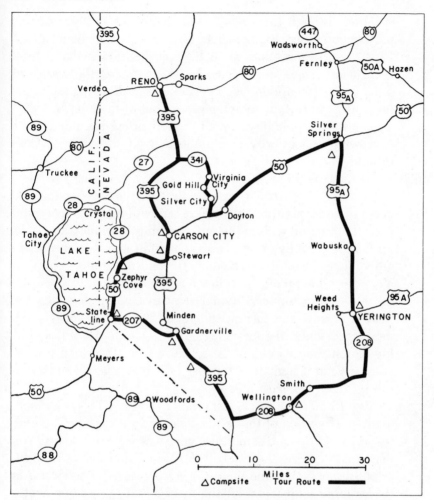

Tour #13   Reno—Virginia City—Lake Tahoe

Lake Tahoe. The Nevada side, in spite of the concentration of gambling casinos, is much less developed than the western side, with better opportunities for good views and private swims. The tour returns to its point of origin via Carson City, Nevada's capital.

Although most of the terrain is rolling or flat, there are two pass climbs, each of which is 8 miles long. They are exceptionally steep, and should be undertaken by riders in good condition only. Water is generally available throughout the tour, but carry extra supplies.

Reno (grocery, restaurants, motels, camping, bicycle shop). You may want to secure your bicycle some place and spend an hour strolling through the casinos, where inveterate slot-machine players and other gamblers hold forth twenty-four hours a day. First-time visitors, and some like ourselves who have been there many times, never cease to be amazed at the wealth of hope (not to mention money) expended in these places. Leaving with your fortune intact, go south out of town on U.S. 395, a busy four-lane highway with a good riding shoulder. Reno is growing very quickly, and traffic is always heavy here. Continue to

Junction, Nev. 341 and U.S. 395 (12 miles). Turn east (left) on Nev. 341 toward Virginia City. One mile past the intersection you come to a complex of stores where you will find a grocery and café, the last you will find before reaching Virginia City. Stock up here, especially on water, as the climb ahead is exceptionally difficult. Almost immediately beyond the stores you begin a winding ride up off the valley floor, and grades are steep. Be on the lookout for recreational vehicles coming down, as the road is narrow and has no shoulder. The higher you go, the more spectacular the views are. After a climb of 8 miles, during which there is almost no reprieve from the steep grades, you arrive at a summit (Milepost 1.6). From here you have a rolling ride over bare hills to

Virginia City (13 miles; grocery, restaurants, motels). This is a much-made-over version of the original, with a great deal of emphasis on the wild—and sometimes gory—aspects of its past. You may want to visit the Bucket of Blood Saloon or other such establishments, but the more interesting parts of town are in the restored homes just off the main street. A visitors' center housed in an antique railroad car can provide you with details of what to visit. You climb briefly upward to the top end of town, then start a very steep plunge down Nev. 341 through Gold Hill (restaurant) and Silver City. It was near these two hamlets that the famous Comstock Lode, the richest silver vein ever discovered, was mined. Some active, although small-scale, mining is still going on. Continue down, perhaps stopping periodically to sightsee, as the grade is very steep and your brakes will heat up. Continue to

Junction, U.S. 50 and Nev. 341 (8 miles; café, motel). If places such as Virginia City typify the mineral aspect of Nevada's history, the valley you are about to traverse typifies Nevada's geography. Almost all of Nevada is part of the Great Basin, and the

flat valley floor alternates with high, stark mountains. Turn
east (left) on U.S. 50, passing some new bedroom communities
serving Carson City, to

Dayton (3 miles; grocery, café). Nearby is Dayton State Park. The
town was founded in 1864 as part of the Silver Rush. Continue out on the Carson Plains past Stagecoach (grocery) to

Silver Springs (21 miles; grocery, motel), Junction, U.S. 95A and 50.
This is a good place to stock up, as there are no services over
the next stretch. Turn south (right) on U.S. 95A toward Yerington. You cross a treeless stretch with a moderate grade to
Wabuska (no services), then down into the Walker River valley. No matter how much of a desert-lover you are, it is always
pleasant to see the green of pastures. These are all irrigated by
the Walker River, and the valley stands in contrast to the bleak
gray hills surrounding it. Continue to

Yerington (24 miles; grocery, restaurants, motels). This prosperous
town was built on agricultural interests, one of the earliest settlements in Nevada. The cottonwood trees providing some
shade along the route are rare in the state. At the center of
Yerington you reach a junction with Nev. 208. Turn south on
Nev. 208 toward Wellington. You follow the West Walker
River, a clear mountain stream that attracts trout fishermen
from around the region. Make your way up the West Walker
River, through a pretty canyon of reddish rock, and out onto
open plain. There is a rest area off to the right of the road
where you can get water and picnic.

Smith (21 miles; general store). A farming hamlet. Continue on Nev.
208 to

Wellington (5 miles; general store, café, camping). Campgrounds are
rare in this part of the state, and you may wish to avail yourself of this one. Otherwise, camping out on the desert (out of
sight if possible) is always possible. You have a 1.5-mile climb
out of Wellington, then drop into a broad valley at the base
of the Sierra. You have a long and often steep descent to

Junction, U.S. 395 and Nev. 208 (10 miles; grocery, camping). Turn
north (right) on U.S. 395. This is a busy road, but it's wide
and has a consistently well-paved shoulder. You start a climb
of moderate difficulty, passing through fragrant stands of juniper and pine—none large enough, however, to provide
shade. You cross a highpoint at MP 9.5, then have a long downhill to

Gardnerville (26 miles; grocery, café, motel). Turn south on Nev. 207, cross the East Fork of the Carson River, then proceed west toward Kingsbury Grade. After crossing the valley floor you arrive at a junction. Continue straight ahead toward Kingsbury Grade and Lake Tahoe. At the junction you begin one of the toughest climbs you will find anywhere in the West. The summit is 8 miles away, and you switchback up the side of what seems to be a canyon wall in order to get there. The last quarter-mile may need to be walked. There is no mile-post at the summit, but it is recognizable when you reach the complex of buildings named, appropriately enough, Incline Village. Continue down on a steep 3-mile descent, with good views of Lake Tahoe directly ahead of you to

Stateline (17 miles; grocery, restaurants, motels). Turn north (right) on U.S. 50. You must thread your way through dense traffic here, most of it slow-moving. Some of the first part of the route has a separate bicycle path. The rest is wide four-lane highway. You have excellent views of Lake Tahoe, this side of the lake much less developed than the western side. There is a state campground at Nevada Beach. Continue past Zephyr Cove (grocery, café, motel), then on a wide highway bordering the lake. About 9 miles beyond Zephyr Cove the road veers away from the lake, and you begin a climb of moderate difficulty that takes you across a ridge separating Lake Tahoe from the basins of western Nevada. You have a long, steep descent to the Carson valley and

Junction, U.S. 395 and 50 (22 miles). Turn north (left) on U.S. 395, using a good shoulder to ride on to

Carson City (2 miles; grocery, restaurant, motel, camping). The state capitol on your right is a superb example of nineteenth-century public architecture. Continue north on U.S. 395, which has a good riding shoulder. Wind often is a factor here, so if possible cover this stretch in the morning. Thirteen miles north of Carson City is Bowers' Mansion, built by Lemuel Bowers from the fortune he made on the Comstock Lode. It may be visited. There is a state campground (Davis Creek) nearby. Continue over long rolling hills with moderate climbs past Steamboat (Hot Springs), then rejoin the tour route at the junction of Nev. 341 with U.S. 395. Continue north on 395 to the tour's end at

Reno (30 miles; grocery, restaurant, motels, camping, bicycle shop).

SUMMARIES OF OTHER ROUTE GUIDES

A number of route guides have been developed by various departments of transportation and cycling groups. Some of them, particularly those that intersect our own tours and allow bicyclists to explore a given region more thoroughly, or to create circular tours, are given below. We say where to get each guide; only with a guide can you follow the route in detail. Costs are current in 1981. If you join Bikecentennial, you save a considerable percentage of the cost of their materials.

TOUR SUMMARY #1

Title: Pacific Coast Bicentennial Route.
Area covered: Pacific coast from Oregon border to Mexico.
Source: Caltrans (see Appendix 4 for address).
Cost: $1

Developed by Caltrans, the highway department for the state of California, this booklet is designed to fit into the map compartment of your front pack. It gives two-color maps of the route, accompanying description, and route profiles. Also noted are the California state parks en route that have special camping areas for bicyclists. You order the map directly from Caltrans.

SUMMARY: Route may be followed in either direction, but it is written from north to south. Start at Brookings, Oreg. U.S. 101 south to California border. Ocean View Dr., Sarina Rd. to Smith River. Fred Haight Dr. and brief sections of U.S. 101 to Fort Dick. Lake Earl Dr. to Crescent City. U.S. 101 to Klamath, Arcata, Eureka (detailed routing through Eureka given in tour booklet). U.S. 101 south through Scotia, Rio Dell Garberville, Leggett, Calif. 208 south from Leggett, then Calif. 1 south through Rockport, Fort Bragg, Little River, Point Arena, Anchor Bay, Ocean Cove, Fort Ross, Bodega Bay, Valley Ford, Tomales, and Marshall. Outside of Marshall, Calif. 1 to Point Reyes Station, then Petaluma Point Rd., Platform Bridge Rd., and Sir Francis Drake Blvd. through Fairfax, San Anselmo, Ross (detailed routing from Ross through San Francisco via Golden Gate Bridge given). South out of San Francisco on Calif. 35 and residential streets and frontage roads to Calif. 1, just north of Moss Beach. Calif. 1 south to El Granada, then Calif. 92 for short stretch to bypass Half Moon Bay. Then Calif. 1 through San Gregorio, Davenport, Santa Cruz (detailed routing given). Castroville, Fort Ord, Marina. Bicycle path from Marina to Sand City. (Detailed route through Monterey given in tour booklet.) South on Calif. 1 from Monterey to Carmel. (From Carmel to just beyond San Simeon, guide follows same route as our Tour No. 3.) Calif. 1 through Lucia, San Simeon, Cambria, Harmony to just before Cayucos. Ocean Blvd. through Cayucos, rejoining Calif. 1 to San Luis Obispo (detailed routing through San Luis Obispo given). South from San Luis Obispo via Higuera St., San Luis Bay Dr., Palisades Rd., Shell Beach Rd., Dolliver St. to Pismo Beach, Grover City, then rejoin Calif. 1 outside Oceano. Calif. 1 through Guadalupe, Orcutt, Lompoc to junction with U.S. 101. Follow U.S. 101 to Hollister Ave., north of Santa Barbara (detailed routing through Santa Barbara given). From Sea Cliff follow Old State Highway and bicycle path, Main St. to Ventura (details of routing through Ventura given). Rejoin Calif. 1 in Oxnard, follow to Santa Monica. (Detailed route provided from Santa Monica through Torrence, Manhattan Beach, Hermosa Beach, Redondo Beach.) Rejoin Calif. 1 outside Redondo Beach, follow through Laguna Beach, Dana Point, to San Clemente (detailed route through San Clemente and Camp Pendleton provided). Through Oceanside via Pacific St., Carlsbad Blvd. to County Rd. S. 21. Follow S. 21 south to La Jolla, then detailed route given in tour booklet from La Jolla through San Diego, Chula Vista, to Mexican border.

TOUR SUMMARY #2

Title: Southwest America Bicycle Trail.
Area covered: Yuma, Arizona, to San Juan Capistrano, California. Rest of route (summarized in Chapter 8) continues to Larned, Kansas.
Source: Southwest American Bicycle Trail, a YMCA Affiliate Program, 816 Van Buren, Amarillo, Tex. 79101.
Cost: Available from Bikecentennial (see Appendix 2 for address) at $2.75 members; $3.25 nonmembers.

The Southwest America Bicycle Trail was developed in 1974 and 1975 by several YMCAs in order to provide a southwestern connection with the Trans America Trail developed by Bikecentennial. The entire guide covers the area from San Juan Capistrano to Larned, Kansas. Parts of the route from Oceanside through the Anza-Borrego were instrumental in our own exploration of that area, and a more complete discussion of those sections is found in our Tour 1.

SUMMARY: Leave San Juan Capistrano via El Camino Real South and old Highway 101. Go via the Bicycle Trail through Camp Pendleton. Maps available at gate. Calif. 76 between Oceanside and Lake Henshaw to Calif. 79 below Lake Henshaw. Follow Calif. 79 south to junction Calif. 76. Go east on Calif. 76 to County Rd. S2. South on S2 through Anza-Borrego State Park to Ocotillo, where you have a brief section of I-8 to Calif. 98, then east on Calif. 98 through Calexico. Continue on Calif. 98 to junction with I-8, follow I-8 to Yuma. See Tour Summary No. 16 for continuation through Southwest.

TOUR SUMMARY #3

Title: Oregon Bike Routes.
Area covered: All the Pacific coast from California border to Astoria (several other routes given; see following summaries).
Source: Oregon Department of Transportation, Travel Information Section, Salem, Oreg. 97310.
Cost: Free.

This is a one-sheet, three-color set of maps detailing bicycle tour routes in Oregon. Some were developed by the Oregon Department of Transportation, some were developed by Bikecentennial and outlined on the map. The following summary allows the cyclist to explore the coastal region of Oregon following U.S. 101. Campgrounds and location of bicycle repair shops are noted. Route profiles are given.

SUMMARY: Start at Brookings, Oregon. Follow U.S. 101 north through Gold Beach, Port Orford, Bandon. Outside of Bandon follow county road (unnamed in guide) to Cape Arago. Follow Empire Blvd. to Coos Bay. Through Coos Bay on Newmark, Broadway, Virginia Ave. to junction U.S. 101. Follow U.S. 101 north through Winchester Bay, Florence, Waldport, Newport, Tillamook, Garibaldi, Manzanita, Cannon Beach, Seaside, then Business U.S. 101 to Astoria.

TOUR SUMMARY #4

Title: Oregon Bike Routes.
Area covered: Willamette Valley from Eugene to Portland.
Source: Oregon Department of Transportation (address in Summary
   3).
Cost: Free.

This one-sheet map provides a number of routes. We used the first few miles of the following route in constructing our own tour of the Willamette Valley. After that, most of the routing is different, and will allow the rider to fashion a circular tour of the Willamette Valley by combining it with sections of our Tour 8.

SUMMARY: Start at Eugene. Leave north via Coburg Rd. to Coburg, then county road to Harrisburg. North on county road (unnamed in guide) which runs west of and parallel to Oreg. 99E to Corvallis. Through Corvallis via Oreg. 34 to Oreg. 99W. North on Oreg. 99W through Monmouth to Rickreall. East from Rickreall via bicycle lane paralleling Oreg. 22 to Salem. Leave north from Salem via Oreg. 219 to Champoeg State Park. Follow county roads (unnamed) east to Canby. North from Canby on county roads (unnamed) to West Linn. Northeast on county roads to Lake Oswego. Detailed routing from Lake Oswego to downtown Portland given on map.

TOUR SUMMARY #5

Title: The Oregon Loop Bicycle Trail.
Area covered: Circular route from Portland, along the Columbia to
   Astoria, down the Pacific coast, then inland to Portland.
Source: Bikecentennial, P.O. Box 8308, Missoula, Mont. 59807.
Cost: $3.95 members; $4.95 nonmembers.

Bikecentennial is a member-supported, nonprofit organization, which has been extremely active in developing a number of high-quality route guides for all parts of the United States. The current guide was one of their earlier ones, first published in 1977. Maps are single color and do not give details of topography. Detail is provided for intricate sections of the route and for the Portland area.

SUMMARY: Leave north from Portland on N.W. Nicolai St./U.S. 30. Follow U.S. 30 through Linnton, Holbrook, Scappoose, to Warren. Just beyond Warren take Old Portland Rd. to St. Helens. Return to U.S. 30 and follow to Deer Island. Leave U.S. 30 at Deer Island and take Canaan Rd., Meissner Rd., and Apiary Rd. to Old U.S. 30. Turn left on Old U.S. 30 and follow through Alston to Inglis. Turn south and rejoin U.S. 30 at Clatskanie. Follow U.S. 30 along Columbia River through Westport, Svenson, Fern Hill to Astoria (detailed route through Astoria given). Leave Astoria via U.S. 101/26 south through Seaside, Nehalem, Garibaldi to Tillamook. From Tillamook take Three Capes Scenic Route along the coast through Sandlake to Pacific City. Head inland from Pacific City to rejoin U.S. 101, follow south to Oretown and Neskowin. Outside Neskowin take unsigned road on north side of Neskowin Creek, head inland toward Otis. At Otis join Oreg. 18, follow east through Rose Lodge, Boyer, Grand Ronde and to Fort Hill for junction Oreg. 22. Follow Oreg. 22 east through Buell to Rickreall. Separate bicycle route available from Rickreall to Salem. Leave Salem via Oreg. 219 north to Butteville, then follow Arndt Rd. to Canby. Leave north via town of West Linn to Lake Oswego. Details of route are provided to downtown Portland.

A "Camping Alternative" details a route out of Scappoose via county roads to Oreg. 47 and 202 to Astoria.

TOUR SUMMARY #6

Title: Trans America Trail. Coast–Cascades.
Area covered: West-to-east route from Astoria, Oregon, to the Idaho border. Remainder of route described in Chapter 7 in Tour Summaries 7 and 8.
Source: Bikecentennial (address in Summary 5).
Cost: $7.95 members; $10.95 nonmembers.

Bikecentennial organized and developed the first thorough route guides for long-distance cycling in the country. The following is taken from a portion of the first volume of their Trans America Trail and takes the trail from the Pacific coast to Missoula, Montana. The guide fits in the front pack map compartment, and when used with accompanying descriptive guidebook, gives complete detail of route, historical, geological, cultural, and incidental information. Also noted are locations of camping facilities and names and addresses of motels. Locations of basic food services are also noted.

SUMMARY: The route begins with two separate spurs from the coast, one starting in Astoria, the other in Reedsport. Both routes join in Eugene. The Astoria leg leaves via U.S. 101, then follows back roads detailed in guide to Seaside. Follow U.S. 101 south to Cannon Beach. Follow U.S. 101 south through Manzanita to Nehalem. Beyond Nehalem take Oreg. 53 and back roads detailed in guide to Tillamook. From there a series of back roads leads to Cape Lookout State Park and then to Pacific City. Outside Pacific City turn south on U.S. 101 to Neskowin. Outside Neskowin back roads lead to Otis, then east on Oreg. 18 through Grand Ronde, then via Oreg. 22 and back roads to Buell. Rejoin Oreg. 22 to Rickreall, then bicycle lane and backroads to Monmouth. From here backroad route brings you to Corvallis, then south through Peoria, Harrisburg, and Coburg to Eugene.

The other spur leaves Reedsport via backroads along the Smith River to Oxbow Divide, then down to Willamette Valley and Eugene.

The route leads east from Eugene via backroads and joins Oreg. 126. Follow Oreg. 126 to McKenzie Pass, or if closed by snow, via Santiam Pass (see our Tour 10 for route details over Santiam Pass to Sisters). Continue to Sisters. Follow Oreg. 126 to Redmond, north on U.S. 97 to Prineville Junction, then east toward Prineville via backroads. U.S. 26 east out of Prineville, cross Ochoco Summit, to Mitchell, John Day, Prairie City, Austin. After Austin via backroads and Oreg. 220 to Oreg. 7 to Baker. Take Oreg. 86 east from Baker to Idaho state line.

SEVEN

The Mountain States:

Colorado, Idaho, Montana,

northern Utah, and Wyoming

COLORADO

Colorado, with an average elevation of 6,800 feet, is the highest state in the nation. It is split nearly down the middle by the Rocky Mountains, creating two clearly distinct regions.

TERRAIN

In the east—everything lying east of Denver—is a gradually sloping, semi-arid prairieland that extends into Kansas and Nebraska. Receiving about 12 inches of rain a year, it is sparsely populated, and except where the horizon is broken by occasional hills and sandy bluffs, is level, open riding.

To the west of Denver, rising almost without warning or intervening foothills, are the Rockies. They are a series of mountain ranges running in generally north and south, but with many spurs, high valleys, and east-west ridges that break up the overall pattern. The farther west one moves from Denver, the less imposing the mountains become, although for sheer massiveness of its high mountain ranges, none of the lower forty-eight states compares with Colorado. Within the western half of the state are some 830 mountains between 11,000 and 14,000 feet. Of the 81 peaks in North America above 14,000 feet, Colorado has 51.

This great collection of peaks and ranges makes bicycling in Colorado different from bicycling in any other state in the country. Almost without exception, mountain riding in the western United States normally means climbing a single range, crossing a pass, then descending the other side. Usually, it is a day's work to get over and down. The Rockies sharply break this pattern. Just in the sheer number of mountain passes you can cross, no state comes close to Colorado. Here, you can climb three and four passes within a day or two, and never drop below 8,000 feet. The road system is well enough developed that you can spend weeks, rather than days, in the high mountains. There are dozens of pass roads, most of them above 8,000 feet. Many exceed 10,000 feet, and a good handful of them are over 11,000 feet. Finally, there is Mount Evans, which although not a pass, has the highest paved road in the country, where you can bicycle to an elevation of 14,260 feet above sea level. It is no wonder that Colorado is a center for high mountain touring, attracting not only local cyclists, but others from every part of the country, and from abroad, as well.

Some geographic terminology will help you understand this extremely complex mountain topography. The first term is "Front Range." This refers to the mountains which rise abruptly from the eastern prairies. Interstate 25, running north and south through Colorado, lies at the base of the Front Range, and Colorado's major cities are found there—Pueblo, Colorado Springs, Denver, Boulder, Greeley, and Fort Collins—all lying in a more or less straight north-south line on or near the Interstate. About 80 percent of Colorado's population lives in this narrow strip.

The second useful term is "park." Parks are high mountain basins or valleys that lie just west of the Front Range. Although high, the parks are relatively level areas completely surrounded by high peaks. There are three important parks in Colorado—North, Middle, and South Parks. North Park lies behind the Front Range just south of the Wyoming line. It is a land of gentle, rolling terrain, having much in common with the dry regions of Wyoming. It is an important cattle-raising area. Middle Park lies west of Denver. It has more varied terrain, and is a popular tourist region; visitors come from all over to enjoy the scenery and recreation around such towns as Breckenridge and Granby. South Park lies west of Colorado Springs, has elevations of 8,000 to 10,000 feet, and slopes gently eastward toward the town of Pueblo.

These three parks, separated from each other by east-west ranges, are connected by pass roads to form a north-south corridor immediately behind the Front Range, allowing passage between Wyoming and New Mexico. Although the parks themselves can be easy riding, the passes separating them are hard. Hoosier Pass, for instance, which separates Middle from South Park, is a stiff, unforgiving, 11,541-foot pass.

To the west of the row of parks lie other high mountains. Although not as imposing as the Front Range, they are nearly as high. Mount Antero, Mount Elbert, and the Mount of the Holy Cross all top 14,000 feet, and there are other examples as well.

In the very westernmost part of the state, one leaves the grip of the high mountains. The strip of land lying along the Utah-Colorado border is generally rolling sagebrush desert, used either for dry-farming or cattle-raising. In south-central Colorado, north of the town of Antonito, is the gentle San Luis Valley, which has become an important agricultural region primarily through irrigation. U.S. 285 traverses this valley, and our Denver-to-Santa Fe tour makes use of it.

CLIMATE

As one would expect, Colorado's mountains create wide differences in climate between the western and eastern parts of the state. The eastern prairies have uniform weather. Summer brings daytime temperatures well into the high 80s and low 90s. Nights are pleasantly cool, but not cold. What rain there is falls mostly in the summer, usually in the form of afternoon thunderstorms. These can be violent in nature, bringing high winds and hail.

Winds across the prairies are primarily southeasterly to southwesterly, and blow at about 8 miles per hour. Near the Front Range itself winds are more variable, depending upon local topography.

Climate in western Colorado depends on which slope you're on and how high. As air masses from the Pacific move into the state, they already have been drained of much moisture. Because of this, the high mountains receive the heaviest amounts of rainfall, and the parks, the eastern sagebrush deserts, and areas such as the San Luis Valley are comparatively arid; cyclists crossing Rocky Mountain National Park will notice the eastern slopes are much drier, and undergrowth more sparse, than on the western side. As you pass from valley to high pass, you will see this variation clearly. Sagebrush gives way to stands of lodgepole. Higher up come stands of ponderosa, which in turn give way to colorful aspen trees, and at the highest elevations there will be stands of alpine fir.

Some precipitation figures will help illustrate this point. Steamboat

Springs, lying at about 6,000 feet on the western side of the Rockies, receives 1.4 inches of rain in July. Leadville, lying farther east at about 10,000 feet, gets almost twice as much.

Mountain temperatures in western Colorado fluctuate widely. Daytime temperatures, depending on elevation, will range from the high 60s to the mid 80s. Nighttime lows at the highest elevations, such as at Leadville, are often near freezing throughout summer. Some areas of Colorado theoretically have no growing season, as frost is a factor the year round, with average lows below 32 degrees. Cyclists in the mountains must be prepared for these cold nights, and must plan on getting later starts in the morning.

Wind in the high mountains depends on numerous local factors, although westerlies prevail throughout the western half of the state. Riders will note a funneling effect of the wind in narrow canyons. This can be particularly hazardous when it catches you from the side, one reason among many why descents in the mountains should always be undertaken with full control of the bicycle, and with great caution.

ROAD NETWORKS AND BICYCLE ROUTE GUIDES

Colorado's road system owes much to the discovery and exploration of precious and semi-precious minerals; miners opened roads in places no one would otherwise have dreamed of building them. The wealth returned to the state by the extraction of these resources also left enough money to maintain the roads. The result is a system of mountain roads that is more extensive than in most mountainous regions of the West.

The eastern prairies, by contrast, reflect the low population density and the difficulty of intensively cultivating the land. There are relatively few roads, and towns are often 50 miles apart. This, and the feeling among many cyclists that eastern Colorado is far less scenic than the western mountains, have made it much less popular for riding. There are, however, three important bicycle route guides which traverse eastern Colorado, which we will cover shortly. These allow the cyclist to explore some open, relatively untracked territory, where rewards of solitude and easy riding mitigate the rather uniform, unbroken terrain.

Traffic conditions on Colorado's western roads follow population trends. It is difficult to find quiet riding near the Front Range cities of Denver, Colorado Springs, and Boulder. The farther you move from these places, the better traffic conditions become, although you must still be cautious about using routes between these cities and popular mountain recreation areas. U.S. Route 40, which runs east-west in the northern part of the state, is a good example. In western Colorado, traffic on U.S. 40 is moderate to light, the long distance between towns diminishing vehicle intensity. But once moving into the mountains, traffic picks up considerably, and increases proportionately the closer you come to Denver. U.S. Route 285, running southwest out of Denver toward New Mexico, is another case in point. Traffic here is heavy within a hundred miles of Denver, then thins out.

Generally speaking, the high mountain roads, particularly the state routes, have good riding conditions, again with the caveat about popular resort areas. Colorado Route 9, running north to south through the three parks, is part of the Trans America Bike Trail, and generally offers quiet riding; so do numerous other state routes in the north, west, and south.

Fortunately, the great popularity of Colorado among both native and visiting bicyclists has led to the creation of numerous route guides and tour itineraries to help you in making road choices. Our tour over the Rockies from Boulder to Steamboat Springs uses quiet roads, or roads with good shoulders, with the exception of the portion through Rocky Mountain National Park, where traffic is nearly always heavy, though slow. Our route from Denver to Santa Fe cuts through the southern Rockies, and the lower portions of that tour have relatively light traffic, primarily because they are far from cities. In the next chapter you will also find a tour that starts in Santa Fe and takes you through southern Colorado via Durango to Mesa Verde National Park.

In addition to these, the four route guides developed by the Colorado Department of Highways, which we discussed in Chapter 3 and which we summarize at the end of the chapter, allow the cyclist to use major Interstate corridors fanning out from Denver. These combine use of frontage roads, old highways that the Interstates have replaced, and short stretches on the Interstates themselves. Riding is not always quiet, but the guides indicate very precisely where hazardous areas are, and in some instances advise cyclists to cover short stretches via some other means.

The Trans America Bike Trail also follows a good route through Colorado, entering the state from the north near the town of Walden, then making its way through North, Middle, and South Parks before

turning eastward toward Pueblo. From Pueblo the route heads eastward across the prairielands. Bikecentennial's members have created
a route guide that gives a brief summary of a loop out of Boulder
through Rocky Mountain Park. This duplicates in great part our own
tour of that region.

A number of books give details of day tours in Colorado, many of
which start and end in the cities along the Front Range. Route guides
and useful books are detailed in Appendix 1.

IDAHO

Until 1927, anyone living in southern Idaho who wanted to visit the
north part of the state had to get there through either Montana or
Washington, because an enormous uplift of the earth's crust makes
the center part of the state nearly impenetrable. In fact, the road cut
in 1927 (U.S. 95) is still the only north-south route through Idaho.
There are still no east-west routes through the rugged interior.

Whatever difficulties this massive uplift and its resulting mountain
ranges make for the cyclist, they do allow the state to be divided
rather neatly into three distinct regions for purposes of discussion.
These are the Panhandle in the north, the mountain ranges of the
center, and the relatively flat, dry, Snake River plain in the south.

PANHANDLE

Terrain.   The Panhandle, a triangular area that extends south from
the Canadian border for some 120 miles, is most often characterized
by its lakes and river systems. The three largest lakes of the Panhandle—Priest, Pend Oreille, and Coeur d'Alene—cover some 150,000
acres, and there are many smaller lakes.

Most of the lakes were formed when glaciers from the last ice age
retreated, their debris clogging streambeds to form natural dams. The
result of this glacial action, and the relatively low elevation of the
area, have left Panhandle topography much more gentle and easier
cycling than the middle part of the state. Elevations of most towns
are around 2,000 feet, and the predominant impression of the land
is a pleasant softness. Climbs are moderate, usually less than 4 miles,
and most commonly under 2 miles.

The only real limitation to the terrain of the Panhandle is its size—

it is only 50 miles wide at its northern end and about 120 miles long from north to south. Any tour that stays within the Panhandle must be tightly designed. Heading west from Coeur d'Alene you encounter the rolling, dry wheatfields of Washington. Going eastward toward Montana, you encounter pretty, but eventually more rugged, riding. To the south lie the formidable barriers of central Idaho.

Climate. All of Idaho is influenced by the air arriving from the Pacific Ocean, felt most acutely in the Panhandle. Moist air travels up the Columbia River gorge relatively unobstructed, bringing rain and snow to the undulating hills and low mountains. As a result, the north is heavily forested, and logging has always been economically important since shortly after the arrival of the first white settlers. This precipitation is heaviest in winter, but there is still a good deal of summer rain, particularly in June and September. Coeur d'Alene receives 1.93 and 1.35 inches respectively during these months, although July and August are only about half as rainy (0.66 and 0.72 inches). Most of these storms are cyclonic—that is, related to warm or cold air masses moving through the state. Typically they last only a day or two, then move on.

Temperatures in the north are moderate in summer, although days when it goes into the 90s are not uncommon. Average temperatures in Coeur d'Alene during June and September are 61 and 60 degrees respectively, and 69 and 68 degrees in July and August. What this means is pleasant bicycling temperatures most days, with the possibility of hot days during July and August—we rode into Coeur d'Alene one July day and watched the temperature on a bank's flashboard rise from 104 to 110 degrees within 45 minutes' time. Nighttime temperatures are pleasant, rarely too hot for comfortable sleeping.

Road Networks. Road networks in the Panhandle are fair. Many of the paved roads are important national routes (U.S. 2, 95, 10, and Interstate 90). Bicyclists wishing to venture off onto unpaved roads have a much better choice, but this is rigorous travel, calling for special bicycles and the ability to pedal long distances between supply points. Road surfaces are fair, and shoulders inconsistent. In general, a bicyclist traveling into Idaho from Washington will notice a deterioration of road quality. People arriving from the east will notice some improvement, since Montana takes the booby prize for road maintenance. If at all possible, bicyclists should avoid extensive travel on U.S. 2 and 95, as both carry heavy traffic and neither has consistently paved shoulders.

Our tour of the Idaho Panhandle takes advantage of most of the region's quieter secondary roads.

CENTRAL IDAHO

Terrain. The vast middle area of Idaho, stretching from a line running eastward from Lewiston to a curved line running eastward from Boise, is composed of a series of mountain ranges with particularly descriptive names—the Crags, Hells Half Acre, the Sawtooths, the Seven Devils. Lewis and Clark made their way across this region in 1805, following an old Indian trail along the Lochsa River. But it was only in 1962 that a paved road was completed along the same route (U.S. 12).

The middle part of central Idaho is still completely without paved roads, and as such is of prime interest to backpackers and whitewater enthusiasts, but is best avoided by bicyclists. This leaves only the northern and southern parts of central Idaho open to bicycling.

In the north, the main city is Lewiston, on the Washington-Idaho border along the Snake River. The Lewiston area is more like the warm palouse of neighboring Washington than anything else. Heading eastward from Lewiston, however, the cyclist soon begins to encounter more rugged terrain, first the Crags, and beyond them the long Bitterroot Range forming the border with Montana. The main route through this region is U.S. 12.

South-central Idaho is characterized by the Sawtooth Mountains, the Pioneer Mountains, the Lost River Range, and the Lemhi Range. All of these ranges run more or less northwest-to-southeast, and the highest mountain in the state is here, 12,655-foot Borah Peak. Many other mountains reach 11,000 to 12,000 feet. It is rugged terrain, but the rather consistent orientation of the mountains does leave a number of routes open to riding.

Climate. The high mountains of central Idaho attract more rainfall than other areas of the state. Naturally there are also greater variations in daily temperatures in the mountains. Average daytime highs will be in the 70s, with nighttime temperatures sometimes dropping down to near freezing. The region is not as often stormy as the north, but there is always the possibility of afternoon thundershowers. Winds can be a problem, particularly in the valleys, opening up to the Snake River plain in the south.

Road Networks. For all the challenges of terrain and climate in central Idaho, the road network and the possibilities for touring are rather good. A section of the Trans America Bike Trail makes its way through the state, entering southern Idaho from Oregon near Cambridge, then moving north to just below Lewiston, where it follows U.S. 12 toward Missoula, Montana. In the south-central portion of the state, a number of roads follow the valleys, some of them running alongside very beautiful mountain peaks. Bicyclists who have explored this region have developed route guides that are available from Bikecentennial (see Appendix 1). We summarize some of these at the end of this chapter.

SOUTHERN IDAHO

Terrain.   The southern part of Idaho is as different from the other two regions as one could imagine. The chief characteristics of the south are the Snake River and the plains that extend on either side of it to the north and south. The Snake forms a nearly perfect "smile" in southern Idaho, entering in the east not too far from Idaho Falls, dipping south, then heading back north toward Boise. Along its banks in either direction is a region of little rainfall, hot summer temperatures, undulating lava beds, and sagebrush plains. By using the Snake as a source of irrigation water, however, the south of Idaho has become the breadbasket—or, more properly, the potato basket—of the state. About 90 percent of Idaho's famous russet potatoes are grown here. Sugar beets, hay, and alfalfa are other important crops.

Not surprisingly, this crescent is also the most heavily populated in the state, and the towns of Boise, Twin Falls, Pocatello, and Idaho Falls are all located along or near the Snake. In general, the region is the easiest cycling within Idaho, although there are important limitations put upon this by high summertime temperatures and the relative lack of road networks in some sparsely populated regions of the south.

The one important deviation from this fairly level, dry terrain is found in the southeast corner of Idaho, below Pocatello. This is a region of mountains and rolling hills that separate the Snake River plain from the Great Basin of Utah. Although relatively dry, the tree cover increases in the valleys and along ridgetops. Mormons moving up from Utah were the first settlers in this part of Idaho, and their mastery of agricultural technique and their industry is still seen today in the farms that carpet the valleys and sweep partway up the hills.

Climate.   The Snake River valley is the hottest and driest part of Idaho. Boise has an average high temperature of 91 degrees in July, and Pocatello, at the other end of the state, nearly matches it with 90. Average summer lows range from the high 40s to low 50s. Temperatures are more moderate in June and September, reaching only the high 70s at both Boise and Pocatello.

July and August are dry as well as hot. Boise gets only 0.15 and 0.30 inches during those months, and Pocatello only a little more. Of all the summer months, rain is most likely in June, averaging over 1 inch along the Snake. September and even October have less than an inch of rain. Because of these rainfall and temperature patterns, the cycling season in the Snake River valley lasts from mid-May to mid-October.

Winds can be a problem, though. The winds blow mainly from the northwest and southwest, and average more than 10 miles per hour in the eastern part of the valley near Pocatello. Winds do tend to become more moderate during the high summer months, however.

Road Network and Bicycle Route Guides. Because of the higher population density and the emphasis on farming, there are more roads in southern Idaho than further north. Interstate 15 crosses the region from east to west, but a number of subsidiary routes on either side of it are good bicycling roads. The mountainous southeast corner of the state also has a good network of secondary roads. Our Tour 17 from Salt Lake City to Jackson, Wyoming, at the south entrance to Grand Teton National Park, takes advantage of these roads. Bikecentennial members have explored some routes paralleling Interstate 15 in the area between Raft River and Bliss, and details of their routes are available from that organization (see Appendix 2).

Not recommended is the road running from Twin Falls to Ketchum (U.S. 93 and Idaho 75). We also advise you to keep off U.S. 26, connecting Twin Falls to Craters of the Moon National Monument. It is narrow and carries heavy tourist traffic.

MONTANA

A swath of mountain ranges fills the western two-fifths of Montana, angling southeastward from the Canadian border to Yellowstone National Park. These ranges, some of them beautifully sculpted by glaciers during the last ice age, determine not only the topography of western Montana, but its climate, pattern of settlement, and economic base as well. The eastern three-fifths of the state are markedly different. The mountains diminish into rolling prairie, a dry land well suited to cattle-grazing and abundant, rippling wheatfields, more characteristic of the plains states than the mountains. Thus it is most convenient to look at Montana's two segments independently.

WESTERN MONTANA

Terrain.   In general, the cyclist in western Montana will find the mountain ranges—and the roads that traverse them—more forgiving than in some other areas of the West, such as Colorado. This is due to the relatively low elevations of the mountains and the fact that roads take advantage of the numerous northwest-to-southeast valleys; this allows the cyclist the satisfaction of seeing mountains without actually having to cross them constantly. Most peaks in western Montana are between 6,000 and 10,000 feet, yet the roads lie considerably lower, often running down valleys at about 4,000 feet. This ability to combine the best of two worlds has led to Montana's popularity as bicycling territory.

Certainly the jewel of the state's high mountain scenery is Glacier National Park, with its elegant, sweeping valleys and imposing rock walls scoured by centuries of glacial action. But there are other impressive areas of western Montana which, if less known than Glacier, are often all the more welcome to the bicyclist because of the lack of crowds and automobile traffic. The Swan River valley south of Glacier, the Bitterroot Valley south of Missoula, the Clark Fork Valley just inside the Idaho border in the north part of Montana are a few examples. There are also a number of excellent mountain rides south of Helena and Butte, which, although less spectacular than the northwest part of the state, are less crowded and more open to quiet riding.

Climate.   The mountains of western Montana play a determining role in the state's climate. The area above Missoula is within the influence of the Pacific maritime climate, and rainfall is heavier here than in the rest of the state. The resulting forest cover is much denser. As the mountains rake off moisture on their western slopes, this creates a rain-shadow effect on the eastern side. Some storage gauges in Glacier National Park indicate an average annual precipitation of nearly 120 inches. By contrast Helena, in the rain shadow of the Rockies, gets less than 15 inches.

The rainiest month in western Montana is June; Kalispell, just outside Glacier, gets 2.56 inches of rain. Billings, Great Falls, and Helena all get between 2.25 and 3.11 inches in June. Precipitation in all four places drops sharply in July, August, and September. Kalispell gets just a little over an inch of rain per month from July through September, with Missoula, Billings, and Helena getting even less.

Winds are moderate in the mountainous west, most stations reporting average velocities of less than 7 miles per hour for the summer months. As this entire region is influenced by Pacific wind flows, most wind will blow in from the west or northwest, but local topographic features will vary this pattern considerably. In cycling between Glacier and Yellowstone, for instance, riders will notice a consistent northwest wind. This makes it advantageous to take the tour from north to south.

Southwestern Montana, which includes the region south and west of Helena, is considerably drier than the northwest. Roadways through the southwest usually traverse sagebrush plateaus or valleys, although good tree cover is usually found on the higher peaks.

Temperatures in western Montana are moderate during the daytime, and pleasantly cool in the evenings. Daytime highs usually range in the high 70s and low 80s. As you move south through the state, daytime temperatures get correspondingly higher. Kalispell, for instance, has an average high of 81 degrees in July, Missoula 85, and Helena 84.

EASTERN MONTANA

Terrain and Climate.   Although drained by two important rivers, the Yellowstone and Missouri, eastern Montana is much drier than the west, and the topography mirrors this relative aridity. The rolling prairies are given over mostly to dryland farming, and are the homes of the great cattle spreads. Except for an occasional range of hills, some buttes and gorges cut by the Missouri and Yellowstone, and an occasional grain elevator or oil rig, the horizon is level and unbroken. Very sparsely populated, the region has an attraction for the bicyclist in providing quiet, even tomblike, roads, but imposes demands in terms of distance between supply points and a relative dearth of campgrounds and other amenities.

Weather in eastern Montana is what is called continental, strongly influenced by weather systems sweeping down from the north, particularly in the winter. During the summer, daytime highs usually are in the high 80s or low 90s. Miles City has an average maximum of 90 degrees in July, Billings 89 degrees. Nights cool off, however, temperatures usually hovering in the mid-50s, so sleeping is pleasant.

Eastern Montana receives most of its rain during the summer months, which helps account for its suitability as a wheat-growing region. Great Falls has consistent summer rains that add up to an inch or more per month from July through September. Often these rains come in the form of afternoon thundershowers. July and August particularly have short but violent storms, often with high winds and hail. Other than this, winds are predominantly westerly, and stronger than in the western part of the state; many stations report average velocities in excess of 10 and 11 miles per hour during the period from May through September.

ROAD NETWORKS AND BICYCLE ROUTE GUIDES

Montana's road network is concentrated in those areas where money could be earned most easily—the mineral- and timber-rich western portions of the state. The great mountain chains that extend from the Canadian border down to Yellowstone have attracted settlers from the days shortly following Lewis and Clark's historic expedition up the Missouri in 1805. Fur trappers, then miners in search of gold, then giant mining operations such as found at Anaconda and Butte all played their role in developing the western part of the state. As a result of this development, a good network of paved roads runs like rivulets from northwest to southeast, down the many valleys between mountain ranges. The routes down the Swan River valley, the Bitterroot Valley, and the Clark Fork in the northwest have already been mentioned. But the southwest also has a good road network connecting lesser-known areas such as Helena, Dillon, Three Forks, and some of the now-deserted gold towns such as Virginia City and Nevada City, which lie to the west of Yellowstone.

Because these roads take advantage of natural valleys, riding is relatively easy, given the overall topographical features of the region. This pattern is disrupted in southwestern Montana, however, where the orientation of the ranges becomes less clear. Cyclists here will find themselves climbing and falling more; some of the hills run from 4 to 6 miles, making the ascents the equivalent of mountain passes whether marked as such or not.

While Montana does not have large cities, and what towns there are do not cluster close together, tourists clog certain justifiably renowned areas. The two focal points of this traffic are Glacier National Park and to a lesser extent Yellowstone.

Glacier particularly poses a problem for the cyclist. On the western side, in the Kalispell-Whitefish area, a number of roads funnel down to one major route entering the park. On the eastern side, there are more paved roads going into the park, but only one of them is a through road, the Going-to-the-Sun Highway over Logan Pass. Just to the south of the park, scalloping its southern boundary, lies U.S. 2, a busy east-west road.

In addition to the traffic, road surfaces in and around Glacier are poor, and road shoulders have a way of disappearing when you need them most—when you are closest to the park. What all this means is that a cyclist wishing to enter Glacier—and it is worth the trip—must plan early morning rides anywhere near the park boundaries. Within the park itself, Going-to-the-Sun Highway is closed to cyclists from 11:00 A.M. to 4:00 P.M. between Apgar, on the west side of the park, and Logan Pass. Anyone wishing to cross the pass must do so before eleven.

The roads into Yellowstone pose less of a problem, both because there are more of them, and because they enter from different points of the compass, dispersing traffic. Still, the great popularity of the park demands care in riding to it, and particularly inside it. We give a full discussion of riding Yellowstone in our Glacier–to–Grand Teton tour.

There are a number of excellent route guides available for western Montana, but the eastern part of the state is relatively ignored. Two of our own tours trace routes through western Montana, Tour 15 connecting Sandpoint, Idaho, with Glacier National Park, and Tour 16 connecting Glacier with Grand Teton. The former enters the state from the Idaho Panhandle and features a pretty, relatively easy ride down the Clark Fork River and up the eastern side of Flathead Lake. The Glacier-Teton tour runs down the scenic Swan River valley, then passes via Helena and the historic Three Forks area southward into the west entrance of Yellowstone.

The Trans America Bike Trail enters Montana near Missoula, then swings southward down the Bitterroot Valley. It then cuts eastward over several passes to enter Yellowstone on the west side.

The Bikecentennial organization has also developed a Great Parks Tour, the northern section of which connects Missoula to Jasper, Alberta. Much of the southern part of this route is the same as our own tour of the Swan River valley. The northern part of the Great Parks tour splits into two sections at Glacier, one going through the park, the other skirting its western edge, passing via Whitefish and Eureka along route U.S. 93 to the Canadian border. Details of our own tours, and a summary of the others, are found at the end of this chapter and are indexed in Appendix 1.

NORTHERN UTAH

Although Utah is most often classified as one of the Mountain States, only the northwest part of it closely resembles the others in that group. Southern Utah is much more a part of the Southwest, both in terms of its climate and topography. Northwestern Utah is clearly part of the Great Basin, but for simplicity's sake we will include it here. Southern Utah will be dealt with in Chapter 8.

TERRAIN

There are two important ranges which, with their foothills, fill most of northeastern Utah. The first of these are the Wasatch Mountains, running north-south just east of Salt Lake City, Provo, and Ogden. The second range is the Uinta Mountains, which run on a line east from Salt Lake City to the Colorado border.

Both ranges play a great role in defining the character of this part of Utah, not only in the obvious effect upon topography, but in trapping enough moisture to produce tree cover and to provide irrigation water to the farms along their bases.

Still and all, the amount of moisture gleaned from the predominantly westerly winds is not great, and both ranges have harsh erosion patterns visible on their lower reaches. These are particularly noticeable along the western side of the Wasatch Mountains to the east of Salt Lake City and Ogden. The mountains rise behind these basin towns like immense fluted barriers, the lower portions totally without tree cover. Only in the higher elevations are the effects softened by stands of aspen, fir, and pine.

The Uintas are higher than the Wasatches, and following the normal pattern of moisture increasing with elevation, are greener and have a much more developed series of small lakes and streams. Utah's highest peak is found here, 13,528-foot King's Peak. So also is one of the state's most lovely areas, the High Uintas Primitive Area, accessible on foot or pack animal only. Cyclists coming into Utah from the north have the best chance of observing the Uintas, visible from a considerable distance from Wyoming. A part of the range is crossed in our tour from Brigham City to Dinosaur National Monument (Tour 18).

Much of the rest of northern Utah is filled with the Great Salt Lake and its accompanying basin. The land portion of this region is lonely, desolate country, nearly roadless. Only in the state's northwest tip are the vast level spaces broken. Here, the Grouse Creek Mountains rise near the Idaho border. Utah Route 30 and a few other secondary roads go up into the mountains. The rest of the region is untracked.

CLIMATE

As has been indicated, neither the Wasatch or Uintas receive much moisture. At the most, a few sections of the Uintas receive about 40 inches of rain a year, which is quite modest in comparison to other mountain ranges. But there are summer storms that move in from the west and last a day or so. We experienced this while riding out of Flaming Gorge across the Uintas, getting pinned down for two days while waiting out storms. But for the most part, the weather threatens and clouds more than it rains; our experiences were exceptional. Salt Lake City receives 1.3 inches of rain in June, the rainiest month, but considerably less than an inch for all the other months through September. Vernal, at the southern base of the Uintas, receives only 0.72 inches in June, 0.54 in July, 0.80 in August, and 0.67 in September. Rainfall increases the higher one goes, and the uppermost reaches of the Uintas receive enough rain to create a pretty area of small lakes in and near the High Uintas Primitive Area.

Temperatures vary with elevation. In the Salt Lake City area, about 4,300 feet, summer temperatures reach into the 90s in July and August, and most summers have days when temperatures soar over the 100 mark. July and August are the hottest, with average highs of 93 and 90 respectively; June and September have average highs in the low 80s. Vernal, about 1,000 feet higher, has a correspondingly lower temperature. As you climb into the mountains from either Salt Lake City or Vernal, temperatures drop into the high 70s or low 80s, making pleasant daytime cycling. Nights are cool, but hard freezes are not a problem in the mountains during the summer.

Winds in northern Utah are fairly strong during the summer, especially in the Salt Lake Basin. Salt Lake City's winds all through the summer average about 9 miles per hour. At times, particularly in late afternoon, air rising off the Salt Lake Basin will funnel up through narrow canyons; these winds reach high velocities and can be hazardous for cyclists speeding downhill.

ROAD NETWORKS AND BICYCLE ROUTE GUIDES

Because of the dense population in the Salt Lake City–Ogden area, and because the Uintas have relatively few roads, cycling possibilities are not as abundant in northern Utah as they are in some other parts of the state. A number of roads run up through the canyons of the Wasatch Mountains from the populous lowlands; some of them make good cycling routes, particularly those north of Ogden. Utah Route 39 out of Ogden and U.S. 89 out of Brigham City are good, and U.S. 89 is used in a tour in this chapter. Cyclists trying to thread their way in the strip of land between the Great Salt Lake and the Wasatch Mountains will have some difficulty however. This strip is highly populated, and even with local or county maps, route-finding is tedious. After much searching, we found that the least painful route was U.S. 89, which has a good shoulder, although is mostly four-lane highway with heavy traffic. With diligence, the cyclist can also spot frontage roads along 89 that alleviate the problem of traffic for short stretches.

The only roads through the Uintas are at the ends of the range. State Route 150 winds south from Evanston, Wyoming, and passes near the western end of the High Uintas Primitive Area and a series of small lakes, then turns west toward Salt Lake City. State Route 44 comes south from Flaming Gorge on the Wyoming border, passes a relatively easy summit at about 8,000 feet, then plunges down deeply eroded canyons into Vernal. Both roads are hard riding, but have excellent scenery and light traffic. U.S. 40, which runs east-west along the southern edge of the Uintas, is a busy but ridable road; traffic thins out the farther one gets from Salt Lake City. But a quieter —albeit more difficult—ride can be made by using lesser routes north of U.S. 40; Utah Routes 35, 87, and 121 serve as good connecting links to Vernal.

There are a number of route guides available for this part of the state. Our tours from Salt Lake City to Jackson, Wyoming (Tour 17), and from Brigham City to Dinosaur National Monument (Tour 18) take advantage of some of the pretty canyon rides and agricultural scenery of northern Utah. Another segment of the Brigham-Dinosaur Tour reenters Utah from the Flaming Gorge National Recreation area, crosses the Uintas, and ends in Vernal. An excellent tour in *The American Bike Atlas and Touring Guide* traces a loop out of Ogden, going up challenging Ogden Canyon, then connecting with Logan Canyon above Bear Lake in the very northernmost part of the state. Part of that route is contained in our Tour 18.

WYOMING

Wyoming comes from a Delaware Indian word meaning "plains" or "end of the plains." The name is particularly apt. Even though Wyoming has some spectacular mountain scenery (Yellowstone and the Grand Tetons top the list), the plains make up well over half of the state, and the cyclist who travels very far in Wyoming will most likely remember them most vividly. These plains, or more properly basins, have long been a primary attraction of the area, luring first tribes of Sioux, Shoshone, Crow, and Cheyenne in search of buffalo and antelope, then later serving as major pathways for white settlers moving west. These plains are high (the mean elevation of Wyoming is near 6,700 feet), but are relatively easy to cross. Historic South Pass, just south of present-day Lander, was the only route west where wagons could cross the Continental Divide without using extra teams of oxen or mules or taking the wagons apart. It is still an important pathway, crossed by Wyoming Route 28.

Wyoming's plains are cut up by a number of high mountain ranges. These drain off enough rainfall to produce good forests, primarily of lodgepole pine. These ranges are scattered, with no single pattern that makes them easy to describe. The Rocky Mountains cross the state from the northwest to the south center. But they're most mountainous in the northwest part of the state, which have Wyoming's two most renowned tourist attractions, Yellowstone and Grand Teton parks. But there are also significant ranges in north-central Wyoming (the Big Horn Mountains) and in the south (the Medicine Bow and Laramie Ranges). Given this somewhat random pattern of plains separated by high mountains, the clearest way to discuss terrain is to locate the state's three main basins then briefly discuss each. The discussion of mountains in Wyoming can be relatively brief, since most roads skirt them; only Yellowstone and the Big Horns have significant road networks.

BASINS

Terrain. The largest of Wyoming's basins is found in the eastern part of the state. With the exception of the Black Hills on the South Dakota border and the Laramie Mountains west of Cheyenne, most of the east belongs to this basin. At its heart is the Thunder Basin National Grassland, a rolling prairie whose thin topsoil and sparse rainfall permit little plant growth. Many of the early homesteads in the region lie abandoned, and some unwise exploitation of the land led at one time to Dustbowl conditions. Although the riding is level here, the great distances between towns make the area somewhat formidable for bicycling.

The second large basin is in north-central Wyoming, just to the west of the Big Horn Mountains. The town of Worland is about the geographical center of the basin, which is cut in half by the Bighorn River flowing north. Almost all of this rolling terrain lies at about 4,000 feet, with imposing mountain barriers rising on all sides, surrounding an area about 70 to 90 miles in diameter. Riding is easy, most of it through grasslands and sagebrush broken up by irrigated fields of sugar beets, beans, grains, and alfalfa.

The third important basin in Wyoming is in the south, somewhat west of the center. As the Continental Divide makes its way into this section of Wyoming, it appears to lose its way, and ends up doubling back on itself in a large circle. The interior of this circle is a basin out of which there is no drainage. It's called the Great Divide Basin or, more descriptively, the Red Desert. What little rainfall the area receives cuts shallow washes, then usually disappears. There are no important towns within this basin; Rawlins stands outside its eastern and Rock Springs near its western end. Interstate 80 skirts its southern border, and travelers who have covered this route by either bicycle or automobile remember it as being particularly barren.

Climate.   Weather in Wyoming's basins is semi-arid. Casper, in the east at an elevation just over 5,000 feet, gets 1.25 inches of rain in June, 1 inch in July, and less than an inch in each of the remaining summer months. Cheyenne, in the southeast and about 1,000 feet higher than Casper, gets more rain—2.41 inches in June, 1.82 in July, 1.45 in August, and just over an inch in September. Other stations on the various basins report similar patterns—June being the wettest month, then rainfall decreasing thereafter.

Much of this rain comes in scattered afternoon thundershowers. Whether you are hit by them is a matter of chance. Until we got used to this hit-or-miss pattern in Wyoming, we always rode in some uncertainty; it often appeared that we were going to get rained on, but the showers ended up striking elsewhere. Often you will be treated to a brilliant lightning display but remain perfectly dry yourself.

Summer temperatures on the plains are warm, but not torrid. The hottest months are July and August, when you can expect temperatures into the mid-80s most days. Nights cool down to the mid-50s. June and September highs are in the mid-70s over most of the basins.

The most consistent factor about Wyoming's weather is the wind —particularly on the rolling prairies and basins, where there are few mountains or trees to break the wind's velocity. These winds are predominantly westerly, and average from 10 to 12 miles per hour throughout the summer. But these averages are deceptive; they include the relatively calm hours of night. Wind typically builds as the day goes on. This calls for early riding, and if you are a late starter, you usually will find Wyoming tough going—particularly if you are heading westward. By 11:00 A.M., winds will be strong, and they just get stronger during the afternoon.

MOUNTAINS

Terrain. Wyoming's mountains will stand comparison with those in any part of the West, although except for Yellowstone and the Tetons, most of the ranges are little known. This is probably due to the state's small population and the fact that most major roads do not cross the ranges, but rather follow the more accessible paths in the valleys between them or along the plains. Of most interest to the cyclist are the Big Horn Mountains, a north-south range in north-central Wyoming, and the mountainous area in the northwest that includes Yellowstone and Grand Tetons National Parks.

By far the most thoroughly explored part of Wyoming is Yellowstone. The park has a road network with two linked circles and five main roads to the various entrances. Most of Yellowstone lies at elevations above 7,000 feet, and the roads skirt beautiful alpine meadows, travel around or alongside numerous streams and rivers, as well as take you to Yellowstone's geysers and hot springs. But the bicyclist is likely to remember not geysers but the fantastic high alpine scenery, which will stand comparison with any such terrain in the world. It is simply stunning.

The price one pays for this is having to share it with a good many others. Motor traffic is heavy, although slow-moving. Also, there are some hard pulls. Our tour through Yellowstone (Tour 16) takes you across the Continental Divide three times in very short order. Although not all three crossings are equally strenuous, the general elevation (above 8,000 feet) can take its toll.

Cycling through the Grand Teton National Park, just south of Yellowstone, is considerably easier. In part this is due to the lower elevation (nearer 6,000 feet). Also, roads there follow routes around several lakes, where riding is gentle, or swing out onto the sagebrush prairies, where it is easy.

The Big Horns, lying just to the west of the towns of Sheridan and Buffalo, are more challenging riding for the cyclist. Elevation goes from about 3,500 feet to nearly 9,000 feet in just a few miles. For your efforts you are treated to some of Wyoming's best scenery, including Cloud Peak in the Cloud Peak Wilderness Area, a mountain rising to 13,165 feet above sea level.

Climate. Weather in the mountains follows the general rule that higher elevations attract more rainfall. The region just south of Yellowstone is the wettest area of the state, getting about 31 inches of precipitation a year. In summer, storm fronts moving over the mountains bring rainy periods of a day or so. As in the basins, the wettest month is June; Yellowstone gets 2.26 inches of rain that month. July, August, and September receive about 1.25 inches of rain each.

Because of the high elevations, you can also expect cold weather. After being pinned down by rain for two days in Yellowstone during August, we managed to get down to lower elevations just before a 2-inch snowfall. These snows don't last, but they are not uncommon, particularly as September advances. Generally speaking, however, you can expect pleasant cycling weather all summer, with highs in the 70s and lows around 50 degrees. Wind is less of a problem in the high mountains than it is on the plains.

ROAD NETWORKS AND BICYCLE ROUTE GUIDES

Because of Wyoming's low population and its distance from other important population centers, it does not have many roads to choose from. On the other hand, the low population makes for light traffic, except on the roads leading into Yellowstone and Grand Teton parks. U.S. 14 in the north between Sheridan and Yellowstone is crowded in June, July, and August. U.S. 89 coming in from the south to Grand Teton is also crowded, although less so than U.S. 14. Interstate 80, which runs east to west through the south of the state, has very heavy traffic, but in some instances is the only through road between points. We suggest using a short stretch of this in our tour from Salt Lake City to Jackson, Wyoming, and the Trans America Trail uses another short section in the central part of the state. Riding is safe, but not particularly relaxing.

The great popularity of the two national parks in Wyoming has prompted a number of route guides for bicyclists. Our tour of the

Great Parks (Tour 16) winds through Yellowstone and terminates in Jackson, just south of Grand Teton. Another tour we offer (Tour 17) starts in Salt Lake City and ends in Jackson, allowing a linkage for bicyclists arriving from the south. In addition, the Trans America Trail features a ride through Yellowstone and part of the Tetons, then heads southeast through the Wind River canyon, onto the southern plains, then into Colorado.

In addition to these tours which relate essentially to the parks, our tour between Brigham City in Utah and Vernal, Utah (Tour 18) cuts through the southwestern corner of Wyoming, and includes a ride through Flaming Gorge National Recreation Area. Much of this is across rolling sagebrush desert, although the ride starts to pick up some of the spectacular scenery of Flaming Gorge just as the route leaves Wyoming and veers into Utah near Manila. Details of these and other routes just mentioned are given later in this chapter, and indexed in Appendix 1, along with tour books that provide route information.

ROUTE GUIDES

TOUR #14: THE IDAHO PANHANDLE

Distance: 272 miles.

Terrain: Easy to moderate; the sharpest hills are on the southern and eastern sides of Coeur d'Alene Lake.

Roads and Traffic: Most of the tour is on quiet secondary roads, or uses good ridable shoulders on short sections of U.S. 95. There is an 11-mile segment between the top end of Coeur d'Alene Lake and the city of Coeur d'Alene on U.S. 10. This is an exceptionally busy road with poor shoulder, although construction is under way to widen it. Travel this section with extreme caution.

Season: Mid-May to October.

Weather: Generally warm and sunny, but subject to occasional rain.

Special Features: Beautiful natural lakes and rivers. Suitable for beginning tourists because of the moderate terrain and the wide choice of camping spots and motels. Excellent swimming.

Connecting Transportation:
Sandpoint: Greyhound, Amtrak, air service.
Coeur d'Alene: Greyhound.

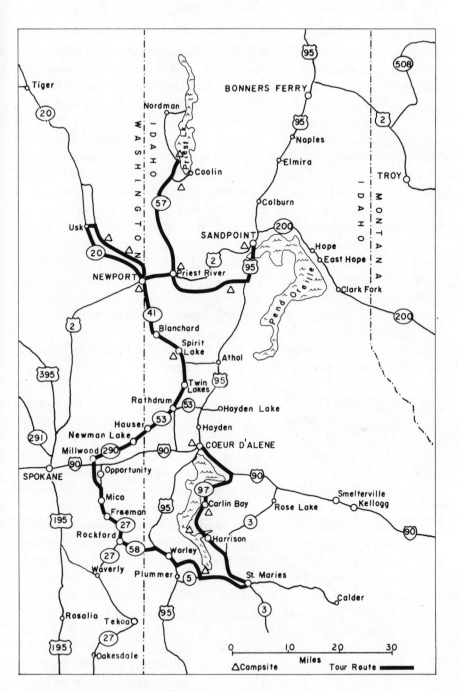

Tour #14   The Idaho Panhandle

No area of the West combines all the features of the Idaho Panhandle. At elevations above 2,000 feet, the Panhandle is densely wooded, and pocketed with beautiful natural lakes of all sizes and shapes. Clear rivers connect the lakes. Unlike many high, cold Western lakes, the Panhandle lakes will beckon in the most finicky swimmer. Waters are warm, yet clear. The lakes are natural, and don't have the disturbing bathtub ring of mud and blackened tree stumps that mark most man-made lakes. The area receives a considerable number of tourists, both from adjoining states and from Canada, just to the north. In spite of this, most of the tour route follows quiet roads. Best of all, the riding is easy to moderate—which in itself is unusual for a wooded, well-watered area of the West.

We developed this tour as part of a short bicycling vacation taken with a sister and brother-in-law who had never bicycled before. Both were in their early 50s. The relatively short distances between possible stopping points made it an excellent choice; most days we covered 20 to 35 miles. Experienced cyclists can cover the 276 miles much faster, of course, but we encourage you to take this tour at a slow pace, allowing yourself time to swim and relax amidst some of the West's most enticing lakes and soft, natural scenery.

Sandpoint, Idaho (grocery, restaurants, campgrounds, motels, bicycle shops). Sandpoint is a pretty town at the tip of Pend Oreille Lake. It has a museum and an active downtown where all services are available. There is an excellent bicycle shop just on the outskirts of town, should you need equipment or a last-minute repair. To begin the tour, you must leave to the south on U.S. 95, a busy highway with little or no shoulder for the first few miles. Just outside Sandpoint a narrow bridge crosses Pend Oreille Lake. Once across this, a moderate 2-foot shoulder develops, which gradually widens to about 6 feet. You catch good views of Pend Oreille Lake off on your left. Continue to

Junction, DuFort Rd. and U.S. 95 (11 miles). Turn west (right) on DuFort Rd. There is a sign at the intersection pointing toward Round Lake State Park. This park surrounds a beautiful small lake, with an excellent swimming beach. It is a good stopping point for newcomers to the Panhandle who want to try one of its nicer state parks and beaches. Water is clean and temperature mild. Past the park, continue on DuFort Rd. toward the town of Priest River. The road joins the Pend Oreille River some two miles beyond Round Lake State Park, and generally follows the river at a distance of a half mile to two miles. Traffic is light. There are a few hills of moderate difficulty, but none with over a mile's climb. Cross the Pend Oreille River and into the town of

Priest River (19 miles; grocery, restaurant). This small town, apparently in the process of mild decay, hugs the Pend Oreille River. Climb a little grade up from the town, cross U.S. 2, and head north on the road to Priest Lake (Idaho 57). This is a lovely section of the tour, on a road that alternates between dense stands of lodgepole pine and nicely cleared pastureland. The road has been recently paved, and traffic is light to moderate, although it peaks on busy weekends. There are some moderate hills between Mileposts 3 and 7, and a short series of hills as you near the bottom end of

Priest Lake (24 miles; grocery, campgrounds). There are a number of National Forest campgrounds on the west side of Priest Lake. The nearest is at Outlet Bay. There are two small grocery stores in the vicinity, the best stocked one just a few hundred yards before the turn off to Outlet Bay Campground. The small town of Coolin, on the southern tip of the lake (turnoff 22.5 miles north of Priest River, then 5 miles on Coolin Rd.) has a good store and a restaurant. Priest Lake is a long, narrow lake, set prettily in the midst of round, wooded hills. There is a good, small beach at Outlet Campground. The only paved road leading back to Priest River is the one you came on; a gravel road leading out of Coolin eventually connects with the paved road. We recommend doubling back on Idaho 57 to

Priest River (24 miles; grocery, restaurant). Turn west on U.S. 2 toward Newport. This section of highway is busy, but there is a wide shoulder. Just before you get to Newport you reach a bridge crossing the Pend Oreille River. Cross over the bridge on the sidewalk and continue into the town of

Newport, Wash. (6 miles; motels, restaurants, grocery). This is a charming, typical Western town with no frills about it. People are friendly and helpful. There are hardware stores with a few bicycle parts. A number of small cafés offer down-to-earth homemade food, and a small museum awaits you near the railroad station. From Newport, turn north on Washington 20. This road runs close to the slow-moving Pend Oreille River (a dam is just downstream). There are a number of small resorts along the river's edge, and you can get down for a swim in a number of spots. Off to the west are pleasant farms and pasturelands. Continue to the town of

Usk (16 miles; café, general store). Usk has a nice wooden American gothic church. The Kalispell Indian Reservation is just across the river. The most compelling attraction is the bald-eagle sanctuary on the Pend Oreille River. The eagles build nests on the old log-boom pilings, many of which are quite close to the bridge crossing the river. You can't go into the sanctuary, but you can see the birds lift off and begin their graceful, soaring arcs in search of fish. Cross this bridge at Usk; once over the river, turn south (right) on the county road leading toward the Pacific Northwest Geophysical Observatory. Follow the river south, on the opposite shore from your northbound road, returning to

Newport (16 miles; motels, restaurants, grocery). Follow signs to Idaho 41, which begins just outside Newport. Follow Idaho 41 south toward Spirit Lake. As you leave Newport you begin a 1-mile climb of a 6-percent grade, which takes you out of the river basin to rolling countryside of dense stands of lodgepole pine interspersed with cleared pastureland. Pass through Blanchard (café, grocery) to

Spirit Lake (18 miles; grocery, café, camping), a town on a ridge overlooking the lake of the same name. To get to the lake, head west down the main street and drop down a short but steep grade. There are a number of resort motels and campgrounds along the lake. The town of Spirit Lake has an excellent early wooden church, and a short main street complete with western saloon. If you camp on the lake, you must shop in town. Leave Spirit Lake south on Idaho 41 to

Rathdrum (11 miles; grocery, café). Rathdrum has a nice city park good for picnicking. Leave south on Idaho 41 again, and you will notice a change in topography, away from the densely wooded hills to more open pastureland and cultivated fields. The country continues to flatten as you follow the road toward Spokane. Pass through

Hauser (10 miles), near the Idaho-Washington line, where the road becomes Wash. 290. Follow it, amidst increasing traffic, to the town of

Millwood (11 miles; grocery, restaurant, motels), a suburb of Spokane. In Millwood turn south on Argonne Rd., toward Mica. The road becomes the Dishman-Mica Rd., then joins Wash. 27. Pass through Mica, then Freeman (grocery), following a road which winds past beautifully contoured wheat fields to

Rockford (16 miles; grocery, café). This is a small farm town with a nice city park offering some shade. At Rockford, you leave Wash. 27 and take the road to Worley. This changes to Idaho 58 at the Idaho line. Leaving Rockford, the road follows a nice stream, and the countryside becomes wooded again. Continue to

Junction with U.S. 95 (10 miles). Turn south on U.S. 95, which will be busy, but which has a minimal shoulder for riding. Follow it in a southerly direction to Worley, then to

Junction, Conkling Park Rd. and U.S. 95 (4 miles). Turn east (left) and follow a rolling, quiet road toward Heyburn State Park. Just before you get to the park, you have a sharp 1.5-mile downgrade, bringing you to Coeur d'Alene Lake and

Heyburn State Park (6 miles; camping). From the state park to the town of St. Maries, you pass along the south bank of the St. Joe River, the highest navigable waterway in the world (2,307 feet). The St. Joe forms a series of lakes—Round Lake, Lake Chatcolet, Lake Benewah. Upon leaving Lake Benewah, you have a steep mile climb (7-percent grade) that crests at MP 133. From here you can see the town of St. Maries, down in the valley to the east of you. The ride is pretty, amidst nice stands of ponderosa pine.

St. Maries (13 miles; grocery, motels, restaurants) is a logging town built on a hill above the St. Joe River. It is a good place to re-stock, as there are no stores of any great size between here and Coeur d'Alene. Leaving St. Maries, you pick up signs indicating the White Pine Highway, named in honor of the lumber ex-tracted from this area. Cross the river, following Idaho 3 to the north. The road hugs the north bank of the St. Joe, then rises and falls over a series of small hills. Near the base of one of these is the site of the Mission of the Sacred Heart, estab-lished in 1846 to serve the local Indians. At MP 92, you com-mence a 3-mile 5-percent grade that is one of the harder pulls on the trip (crests just beyond MP 95). Beyond the crest there is a junction with Idaho 97, which you take to your left toward Harrison. After a 4-mile stretch of rolling hills you begin a sharp downgrade to the little lake town of

Harrison (18 miles; grocery, café, motel). At one point Harrison was an important logging town; logs were floated up Lake Coeur d'Alene and milled here. Leave northward on Idaho 97. Just outside Harrison you begin a 1.5-mile climb (crest at MP 71).

The downgrade on the other side is 2 miles long at 7 percent. Continue on through the little settlements of Carlin Bay (grocery, camping) and Turner Bay (grocery, café). At MP 91, you begin a mile's climb, cresting near a rest area just short of MP 92. At MP 96 you come to

Junction, U.S. 10 and Idaho 97 (28 miles; camping nearby). Route 10 is in the process of becoming part of the Interstate system, but at present is a busy, narrow route that is dangerous. There is shoulder most of the way, but use caution. Follow U.S. 10 to

Coeur d'Alene (11 miles; grocery, restaurants, motels, camping, bicycle shop), a pretty town at the north end of Coeur d'Alene Lake. There are an excellent bathing beach and public park in the downtown area. Lying on one of the first east-west routes through the region, Coeur d'Alene has been an important town from early settlement times though it never grew large. It enjoyed prosperity as a lumber town and also as a mining center. Silver and lead are still mined extensively in or near a number of small towns lying to the east.

If you wish to return to the starting point of the tour in Sandpoint (47 miles), you can travel north on U.S. 95. This is a busy road, with varying shoulder. Bus transportation is also available between Coeur d'Alene and Sandpoint.

TOUR #15: SANDPOINT, IDAHO—CLARK FORK—GLACIER NATIONAL PARK

Distance: 250 miles.

Terrain: There are short hills, usually less than a mile long, down both the Clark Fork River and along the eastern side of Flathead Lake. Between Flathead Lake and Glacier, the terrain rolls a good bit, but with some level riding across the agricultural plain near Kalispell.

Road and Traffic: There is heavy traffic for the first few miles out of Sandpoint. Traffic thins as you go up the Clark Fork River. Traffic is light until you approach Flathead Lake. The road up the east side of the lake has moderate traffic, and fair to poor surfacing. Shoulders are inconsistent. As you leave Flathead Lake and approach Glacier, traffic becomes heavy, and you are advised to cover this stretch as early in the morning as you possibly can.

Season: Mid-May to mid-September.

Weather: Warm, temperatures in the high 70s or low 80s. Chance of
some rain, although storms usually last only a day or so.

Special Features: The road along the Clark Fork River is one of Montana's premier cycling routes, with a ride of only moderate
difficulty contrasting with the sharp mountain ranges rising on
either side. The end point in Glacier National Park presents the
cyclist with some of the finest glaciated scenery in North
America.

Connecting Transportation:
Sandpoint, Idaho: Greyhound, Amtrak, air service.
West Glacier: Amtrak.

The ride between Sandpoint, Idaho, and the west entrance to Glacier National Park connects one of the West's more pleasant towns with
one of its most spectacular parks. These two end points alone would
justify the trip. But the ride in between is as lovely as you will find
in this part of the West, featuring a very relaxing ride up the Clark
Fork River, then a ride along the east shore of Flathead Lake, where
the Mission Range plunges down into one of the largest lakes in the
western United States. During midsummer you can enjoy the deli-
cious cherries for which the Flathead Lake area is famous. They are
sold at numerous roadside stands and make an excellent opportunity
for stopping.

In addition to these two water-oriented sections of the tour, there
is another interesting section across rolling grasslands, where you
pass within a few miles of the National Bison Range. A short side trip
allows you to view some of the largest herds of buffalo left in the
West.

At the end of the tour, of course, is spectacular Glacier National
Park (part of Waterton-Glacier International Peace Park) with its
wide, U-shaped valleys, crystalline Lake McDonald, the option of
a challenging ride over Logan Pass. Cycling in the park is best done
in the early-morning hours before tourist traffic picks up. Bicycles are
not allowed on the road between Apgar on the west side of the park
and Logan Pass between 11:00 A.M. and 4:00 P.M., but you will still
have ample opportunities to take short rides along Lake McDonald,
all around which you can see the imposing rock walls and high peaks
for which the park is famous. There are numerous campgrounds
around the lake to serve as base camps for such day excursions.

Sandpoint, Idaho (grocery, restaurants, camping, motels, bicycle
shops). Sandpoint is one of those cities which has maintained

all the advantages of a small town with all the amenities of a larger city. Situated at the north end of Lake Pend Oreille, it has a softness about it contributed by the lake and the densely wooded hills to the north and east. Leave Sandpoint on U.S. 95 north, a short but busy stretch of highway to

Junction, Idaho 200 and U.S. 95 (2 miles). Here you turn east (right) toward the small towns of Kootenai and Ponderay (the latter, incidentally, a reasonably close phonetic transcription of the word Pend Oreille). As you move away from Sandpoint, traffic will diminish, although you are advised to cover this initial stretch in the morning if possible. After turning onto Idaho 200 you catch glimpses ahead of you of the Cabinet Mountains,

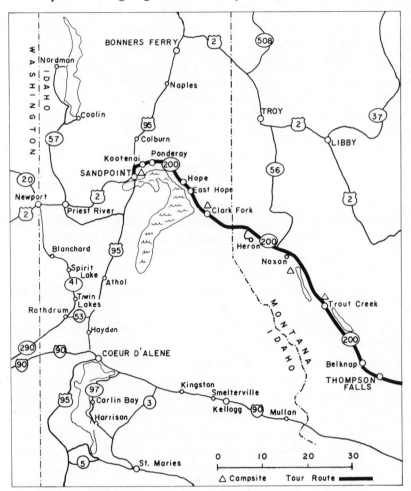

Tour #15   Sandpoint, Idaho—Clark Fork—Glacier National Park
(Section one: Sandpoint to Thompson Falls, Montana)

which look (and are) imposing. Your route, however, will take you alongside them, not over them. On your right is Lake Pend Oreille, formed some 10,000 to 20,000 years ago when a large glacial sheet retreated. An earlier lake covering this area was some 800 to 1,000 feet deep. Continue through Hope, where you have a nice vantage point of the lake to

East Hope (17 miles; grocery, motels). Just south of East Hope, David Thompson established one of the earliest trading posts in the old Northwest Territory, which he called Kullyspell House, after the tribe of local Indians. There are a number of campgrounds near East Hope, and you can readily get down to Pend Oreille Lake for a swim. The lake is one of the most dramatic of the Idaho Panhandle's lakes, with islands rising out of the water and hillsides plunging steeply downward. Blue herons can usually be seen fishing in the shallow water. Continue to the town of

Clark Fork (10 miles; grocery, café, campground, motel). Here the terrain begins to change as you leave the lake and start following the Clark Fork River. The road rolls up and down; most hills are only moderately difficult and less than a mile long. About 4 miles south of the town of Clark Fork you pass some imposing rock cliffs. About 7 miles south of town you climb a sharp hill a mile long (crest at Milepost 63) that brings you into Montana and past the Cabinet Gorge Dam. Road surfaces are fair to poor, and the road shoulder inconsistent. If you wish to get supplies there is a bridge across the river, which you may cross to reach

Noxon (26 miles; grocery, café, motel). There is a small park here if you want to picnic. Cross back over the bridge to Montana 200 once again, passing one of several narrow reservoirs built on the Clark Fork. The scenery is less spectacular, and your vistas broaden out. Pass through

Trout Creek (14 miles; grocery, café, motels), which is a nice town set along the east bank of the river; you get good views of the Cabinet Mountains to the east. On the other side of the road are the foothills of the Bitterroot Mountains, which from this vantage point appear softer and more subtle than the Cabinets. Between you and the ranges are stands of thin lodgepole pine and carefully tended pastureland. Near Belknap (general store) you pass through some pretty canyons cut by the Clark Fork. Continue on to

Thompson Falls (20 miles; grocery, restaurant, motels), named after the explorer and trapper David Thompson. On leaving, you sweep around some lovely pastures, then into canyons formed by the river. The ride rolls considerably, and there are some sharp hills around MP 55 and 56. Small ranches block out parts of what valley bottom there are, and a persistent railroad track separates you from the river. The scenery, however, is among the best of the tour.

Plains (24 miles; grocery, café, camping, motels) is a small, pleasant town which invites you to camp free in its city park. Pick out a grassy area near the pavilion, under which you can cook and eat if you wish. The trains roll within a few hundred feet of you during the night, so be prepared! On leaving Plains, the valley broadens, and the dense stands of timber give way to much drier grasslands and dry wheat farms. A few miles past

Paradise (4 miles; café, general store) there is a junction with Route 135. You do not take this turnoff, but a few miles upstream is a commercial hot springs and just beyond that a National Forest campground. You can stop and visit or continue on Mont. 200, this time following the Flathead River, which winds through open range country. You pass the small settlement of Perma (no services) to

Dixon (28 miles; general store); just outside of town is a junction, Mont. 212 and 200. Turn north (left) on Mont. 212 toward the National Bison Range. Since shortly after Paradise you have been on the Flathead Indian Reservation, where you may camp and fish only by permit. Continue north on Mont. 212 to

Moiese (5 miles; general store). Near here is the entrance to the National Bison Range, where substantial herds of these animals, once so numerous, are now fenced and protected. You can bicycle into the range, about 2 miles off the road, for a firsthand glimpse. Leaving Moiese, you begin to glimpse the Mission Range ahead of you. Road surfacing improves considerably after Moiese, and terrain levels off to large, flat fields. Continue to

Charlo (7 miles; café, camping). This is a collection center for the local wool trade, and you often can see pickup trucks lined up at the railhead with enormous sacks of wool bulging from the truckbed. The campground in Charlo is free. As you leave, you have increasingly clear views of the Mission Range, whose sharply eroded valleys run east and west, opening up toward you. Continue on Mont. 212 to

Junction, U.S. 93 and Mont. 212 (5 miles). Turn north (left) on U.S. 93 toward Ronan. This is a major highway with heavy traffic, but there is a wide shoulder. The width of this shoulder diminishes as you get toward Flathead Lake, and its surfacing deteriorates. Exercise caution, and if possible, travel this section to Flathead Lake on weekday mornings.

Ronan (5 miles; grocery, restaurants, motels). This is one of the larger towns you will pass through in some time, so is a good supply point for major items, although there is an increasing frequency of services the closer you get to Glacier National Park. Just beyond Pablo (grocery) the shoulder on U.S. 93 narrows, and the paving is very bad. As you near the junction

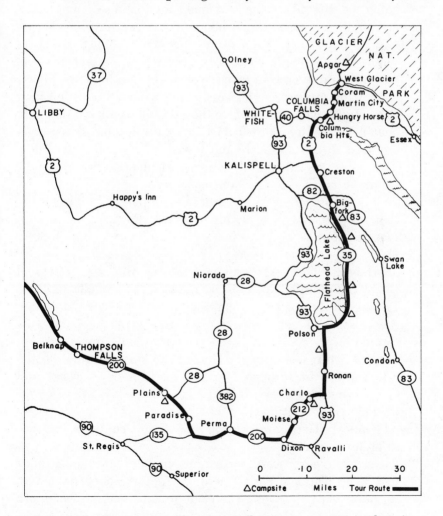

Tour #15 (Section two: Thompson Falls, Montana, to West Glacier)

with U.S. 93 (at MP 59), you get a good view of Flathead
Lake to the north, ahead of you. The lake is 28 miles long and
15 miles wide. You descend a steep, short hill to the

Junction, U.S. 93 and Mont. 35 (12 miles; restaurants). Turn east
(right) and begin skirting the bottom end of Flathead Lake.
The great dimensions of the lake allow for good winds to pick
up velocity, and they can be a problem. The farther you get
from U.S. 93 the less traffic there will be, although it will remain moderate all the way up the lake. The road rolls considerably, and is rarely level, except for a few stretches of several
miles where you ride right next to the lake. There are a number
of small stores, cafés, and private and public campgrounds
along the east side of the lake, and supply and stopping points
are numerous. One special bonus if you are traveling during
mid-July to early August are the stands along the road
selling succulent Flathead Lake cherries. Some orchards will
permit you to pick your own if you wish. Continue to

Bigfork (32 miles; grocery, restaurants, motels), which is just off your
route. Just beyond Bigfork, on the next hill, is a large shopping
center. From Bigfork to Glacier the roads become increasingly
crowded. Ride cautiously and use shoulders when available.
Two miles beyond Bigfork you pass a junction with Mont. 82.
Continue north through Creston to

Junction, U.S. 2 and Mont. 35 (14 miles). Kalispell is 7 miles off the
tour route to the west of this junction, and has a number of
bicycle shops as well as other services. The tour route follows
U.S. 2 to

Columbia Heights (11 miles; restaurant, motels). You begin a gradual
rise off the Kalispell Plain toward the mountains of Glacier Park.
From here the road rolls increasingly, the pitches sharpening
the closer you get to the west entrance of the park. Pass
through Hungry Horse (grocery, restaurants, motels, camping), which is near Hungry Horse Dam, about 6 miles off the
tour route. Pass through Martin City (motels, grocery) and
Coram (motel, grocery, restaurants). About MP 148 you start
up a long hill. Continue to

Apgar (14 miles). Here you turn off U.S. 2 and continue into the
small town of

West Glacier (2 miles; grocery, restaurants, motels) and the entrance
to Glacier National Park. There are Amtrak connections here
for points east and west. The campgrounds within Glacier are

crowded all through the summer, and campsites are on a first-come, first-serve basis. Your best way to get a site is to arrive in the morning, which is also the best time of day to cover the very heavily traveled roads into the park. If all campsites are filled, a standard procedure is to cycle around looking for other bicyclists or sympathetic travelers who will share their space with you. You should pay part of the fee. There are excellent evening programs given at various campgrounds. Lock your bicycle securely, and take money and all valuables with you. The National Park Service has done an excellent job of dealing with habitual problems posed by bears, but they can do it only if you follow their instructions carefully.

TOUR #16: THREE GREAT PARKS: GLACIER, YELLOWSTONE, AND GRAND TETON

Distance: 531 miles.

Terrain: There are a number of important and difficult passes, and much of the route lies at high elevations. The tour should be take by experienced bicyclists, or if by inexperienced riders, then in the company of experienced cycle tourists.

Roads and Traffic: Heavy traffic around Glacier and in both Yellowstone and Grand Teton National Parks. Other than these points, there are many miles of quiet riding on two-lane highways.

Season: June through mid-September.

Weather: Chances of rain are better in the north than in the southern parts of the tour, although the high elevations of each park increase the chances of rain, particularly in the afternoon. Nights can be cold in all the parks but normally temperatures do not go below freezing.

Preferred Direction: Consistent northwesterly winds make a north-to-south route best. It also saves much of the harder riding until last.

Special Features: The parks are justly well known, and each very different from the others. Glacier with its broad, imposing valleys, Yellowstone with its high alpine scenery, Grand Teton with its jewel-like peaks are major attractions. In between, much pretty riding, and some soulful long spaces.

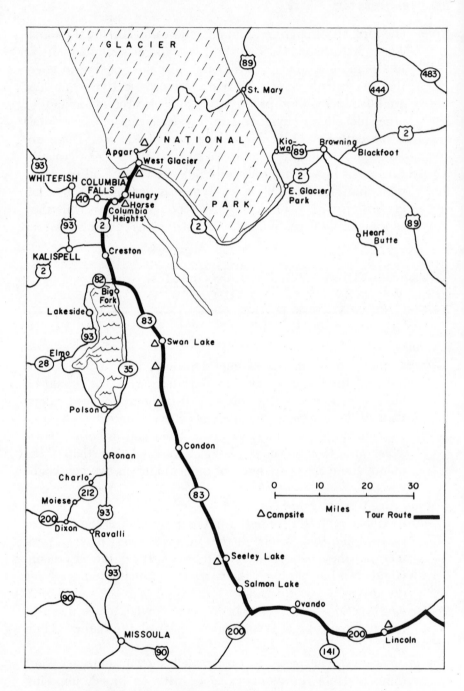

Tour #16   Three Great Parks: Glacier, Yellowstone, and Grand Teton
(Section one: West Glacier to Lincoln, Montana)

Connecting Transportation:
>West Glacier: Amtrak.
>Jackson, Wyoming: Greyhound, air service.

To bicycle through Glacier, Yellowstone, and Grand Teton National Parks is one of the high points for a cycle tourist in the West. These are among the best loved of all national parks. Each is distinctive; all emphasize preserving what was once truly wild about the West—rugged scenery, spectacular, often impassable terrain, and safe territory for fast-disappearing species of wildlife, including grizzly bear and moose.

As popular as the parks are—and they are popular with bicyclists as well as other visitors—the ride connecting them has numerous attractions in its own right. It well represents Western scenery, weather, plants, and wildlife. The spectacle of the parks is matched by rigorous passes, long, dry plateaus, an interlacing of startlingly clear streams and rivers, stark remnants of deserted towns, and a great deal of broad Western sky. If the parks are crowded, the spaces in between are most often empty, and the bicycle tourist will have plenty of time for contemplation and solitude.

After leaving the spectacles of Glacier, the tour follows the Swan River valley, a lovely ride in northern Montana that is not particularly difficult and keeps beautiful mountain ranges in sight. Out of the long valley, the terrain switches rather quickly into broad, semi-arid land where a variety of grass crops are raised. The tour goes through the historic town of Helena, where gold brought miners from all over the country to pick and sluice for the elusive wealth the mineral could bring. South of Helena, the cyclist may feel echoes from white America's earliest days, as the tour route is not far from that taken by Lewis and Clark in their epic journey up the Missouri in 1805. Then, after Three Forks, the tour winds over the largely treeless hills up the Madison River, one of the best-known trout streams in the country, attracting anglers from all over the world. Near the source of the Madison, the cyclist passes into Yellowstone National Park, well known for its geysers, but we think even more attractive because of its exquisite high alpine meadows and meandering, sharply clear and cold streams. In Yellowstone the Continental Divide is crossed three times (you will already have crossed it once farther north), then there is a long, 2,000-foot drop to the borders of Jackson Lake, across which rise—so magnificently that first-time visitors have difficulty believing the spectacle—the Teton Range. Nearly constantly in view, the Tetons seem to grow higher and higher the farther one goes along.

Shortly after leaving Grand Teton National Park, the cyclist reaches Jackson,Wyoming, and the end of the tour.

Glacier National Park. The town of West Glacier has a grocery store, restaurant, and motels. There are several campgrounds in the Lake McDonald area, but you need to check in early to get a spot. If you can't find a vacancy, circle through the camps looking for other bicyclists who may be willing to share a spot with you. Logan Pass, about midway on the Going-to-the-Sun Highway, is a hard climb, but cyclists can make it if they start very early in the morning. Cyclists are not permitted on the highway between Apgar and the pass from 11:00 A.M. to 4:00 P.M. Mornings are the best time for exploring the area around Lake McDonald on a bicycle. Tourist traffic gets very heavy (although it moves slowly) by early afternoon. Leave the park through West Glacier and

Junction, U.S. 2 (2 miles). Turn west on U.S. 2 toward Columbia Heights. The road rolls downward through a number of tourist towns—Coram (motel, grocery, restaurants), Martin City (motels, grocery), and Hungry Horse (grocery, restaurants, motels, camping). As traffic is very heavy on this road, it is best to start out from Glacier early in the morning, preferably by first light. Continue on U.S. 2, which has a good shoulder after Columbia Heights to

Junction, Montana 83 and U.S. 2 (37 miles). Turn southeast toward Swan Lake. You lose most of the tourist traffic at this junction, and begin a gentle downgrade until you intersect the Swan River. You then start a gentle upgrade along the east bank of Swan River and Swan Lake, a narrow, pretty lake where you may catch glimpses of blue herons busily fishing. The road rolls somewhat once past the lake, with a moderate grade near Milepost 75. Continue to the town of

Swan Lake (22 miles; grocery, motels, camping). This pleasant little lake town is an important supply point for you. Although you will pass several small grocery stores and cafés, the next place to buy substantial groceries is in Seeley Lake, 55 miles south. Swan Lake is at MP 70; you pass the following supply points as you move southward: MP 45.5, Condon (grocery); MP 42, Swan Center (café, grocery); MP 37.5 (grocery); MP 36 (grocery); MP 26 (camping).

As you leave Swan Lake you begin a series of gradual climbs, all under a mile in length. The forest closes in around you, and from time to time there will be breaks in the tree cover that will allow you to see the Swan Range off on your left. The Bob Marshall Wilderness is back within the range, and you will pass several outfitters who arrange pack trips into the wilderness area. On the west side of the road is the Swan River, and behind that, seeming to move closer to the road the farther south you go, is the Mission Range. This is truly one of the loveliest rides in Montana, and a favorite with many local bicyclists.

Near MP 34, you begin a sharp climb of about 2 miles, then pass a rolling watershed separating the Swan River and the Blackfoot River drainage basins. Several small, pretty lakes border the road. There are a number of campgrounds, but some have no water supply. Usually you can get water from someone in an RV or trailer. Continue to

Seeley Lake (55 miles; grocery, restaurants, motels, camping), a busy tourist town by a lake of the same name. From Seeley Lake southward you will notice an increase in tourist traffic and a deterioration in road quality. Continue south to

Clearwater Junction (15 miles; grocery, café) where you hit Mont. 200. Turn east (left) at the junction. There is a marked change in both terrain and plant growth. You leave the verdant lake-and-river country and enter into more open grasslands. The Blackfoot River is to the south of you. Beyond the river you get good views of the Garnet Range. Traffic through here is moderate, but drivers normally have ample opportunity to see you. Continue on an easy ride to

Ovando (13 miles; general store, café), which lies off the road. This tiny agricultural hamlet contains some interesting original log houses and buildings. There is a small café on the main highway. Past the junction of Mont. 200 and 141 (you stay on 200) you will notice a lessening of traffic, and you enter into a very scenic canyon cut by the Blackfoot River. High rock walls rise several hundred feet above you on your left, and the Blackfoot River runs on your right. Shortly after you leave the canyon you enter a broad, open grassland with several horse ranches. Continue to

Lincoln (27 miles; grocery, restaurants, motels, camping). Lincoln is a good-sized town, and an excellent place to restock—your next major stop is Helena, 58 miles away, and there is only one general store along the way, in Canyon Creek, across the Continental Divide. The city park in Lincoln has free camping.

We were picnicking there when we encountered a Dutch couple who were bicycling to Argentina—having started in New York. Sharing cold cuts with them in the park, we became convinced they had the wherewithal to make it. We've never heard. Leave Lincoln and continue east on Mont. 200 to Junction, Mont. 279 and 200 (12 miles). Turn southeast (right) on Mont. 279. You enter a narrower valley than the one you have been in, and start climbing almost immediately toward a cross-

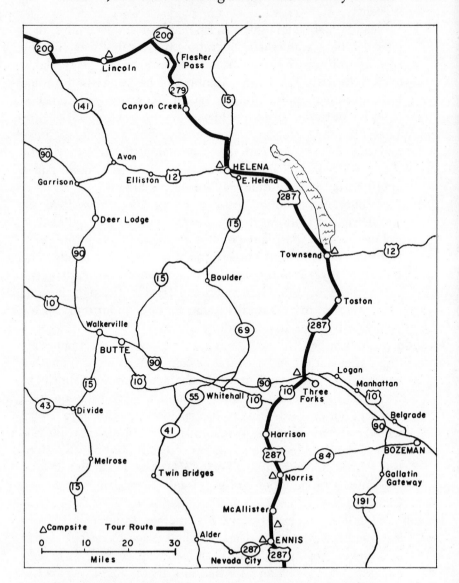

Tour #16 (Section two: Lincoln, Montana, to Ennis, Montana)

ing of the Continental Divide. There is an excellently preserved two-story log farmhouse on your right. The hard climb toward Flesher Pass begins near MP 33.5, and you can see the road switching back and forth on the hill ahead of you. The stiffest climb occurs on these switchbacks and up to the summit, near MP 30. There is a marker at the Continental Divide giving the elevation as 6,131 feet—which is about 200 feet shy of most map indications. For cyclists coming in the other direction, the hard climb begins about MP 27. Continue down the other side of the pass, through forested regions and into dry grasslands. As you approach Canyon Creek, you ride along a rolling basin that is actually an arm of Montana's enormous eastern prairies. Tree cover diminishes considerably, and between here and Yellowstone you will be primarily in semi-arid terrain. Lewis and Clark often complained bitterly in this area that their two worse enemies were mosquitoes and the prickly pear. Continue to

Canyon Creek (24 miles; general store), which is little more than a momentary collection of buildings amidst rolling ranchlands. The road rises and falls gently, passing by shallow but steep-walled canyons cut by brief but hard rains. Continue to

Junction, North Montana Ave. (15 miles; grocery), a frontage road for Interstate 15, which you will be able to see directly ahead of you. Turn south on North Montana Ave. toward

Helena (7 miles; grocery, restaurants, motels, camping, bicycle shops). Although it's the capital of Montana, Helena has a small-town atmosphere, and makes considerable effort to preserve signs of its beginning as a strike-it-rich gold town. Set at the base of a sharp line of mountains, the town lies just above 4,000 feet. You can still visit Last Chance Gulch, where a group of miners decided, fortunately for them, to give it one last chance. In Helena, your last supply point for 33 miles, you intersect U.S. 287, which you take south. Although busy, it has an excellent shoulder. Off to the east, out of sight, lies the Missouri River, up which Lewis and Clark came in their flatboats (towing them with great difficulty at this point) into uncharted territory. The explorers were eager to get to the source of the Missouri, which they had been following from its confluence with the Mississippi. They finally arrived at the commencement of the Missouri at Three Forks, near which your route passes. Continue along a gently rolling ride, past Canyon Ferry Lake, to

Townsend (33 miles; grocery, restaurants, camping, motels), a tidy little town lying near the Missouri. The campground is just to the north of town. You should restock at Townsend, as it is your last real town until you get to Harrison, just over 50 miles away. If necessary, you can get supplies in Three Forks, which is off your route. There is also a small café in Toston, 11 miles south of Townsend. Between Townsend and the junction with U.S. 10, you follow the Missouri more closely than before. It is an undulating ride, with some traffic bound for Yellowstone. After crossing the Missouri near Toston, you lose the wide riding shoulder you have had since Helena. You pass large fields of wheat on the open prairie. Continue to

Junction, U.S. 10 and 287 (32 miles). Near this point the Madison, Jefferson, and Gallatin Rivers join to form the Missouri. Clark, leading an advance party, arrived here in the summer of 1805, and decided to follow the Jefferson, as it was the largest and seemed to offer the most direct route into the mountains. From a hill to the side of the road you can glimpse the three rivers, and decide for yourself which you might have chosen to follow. Near the intersection is a KOA campground, which is your last water source (unless you go into Three Forks) until you get to Harrison, 20 miles away. You follow U.S. 10 and 287, climbing and descending over short hills within sight of the Jefferson River. Continue to

Junction, U.S. 287 and 10 (11 miles; no services). Turn south on U.S. 287 toward Ennis. You soon cross the Jefferson River and begin a hard 3-mile climb that crests at MP 79. The mountains off to the south are the Tobacco Root Mountains. You descend 3 miles into the town of

Harrison (9 miles; grocery, café, motel). From Harrison you climb and descend over a series of steep hills, none of which is as long as the one you climbed just before getting to town. After the crests of one of these hills you drop into a valley to

Norris (10 miles; grocery, café, camping). Shortly after leaving town you begin another hard climb of about 3 miles, the hill cresting at MP 60. From the top of the hill you can see a broad valley running right and left, with the town of McAllister off in the distance. The descent into the valley floor is quite steep. (For persons coming from the other direction, there is an exceptionally steep 1-mile pitch, followed by rolling climb, then a hard climb to the hillcrest at MP 60.) Continue to

McAllister (10 miles; grocery, restaurant, motels), located in a valley where irrigation has made possible the cultivation of alfalfa, which stands as a pleasant relief to the brownish grasses and sage on the surrounding hills. From McAllister you will follow the Madison River all the way into Yellowstone National Park, and the worst of your climbing is over, although the road up into the park climbs moderately. Continue to

Ennis (7 miles; grocery, restaurants, motels, camping). Another good place to restock, as this is the largest town for some time and a stop on the Trans America Bike Route. Leaving town, you cross the Madison, which bears the title of a blue-ribbon trout stream, with authenticated tales of superb catches. It is a beautiful, clear, shallow stream. Continue on a generally easy ride to

Cameron (11 miles; café, grocery, motel). The road into Cameron lies in former bottomland cut by the Madison. You can see the escarpments on your left. The roadside rest at MP 16 has drinking water. The Madison has cut some nice canyons off to the west of the road. Continue along a gradually uphill ride to

Junction, Mont. 87 and U.S. 287 (30 miles). From here you can look southwest toward Raynolds Pass, first explored in 1860 by Jim Bridger. It presents an exceptionally easy crossing of the Continental Divide. Your route, however, continues on U.S. 287. Shortly after leaving the junction you pass into the area rocked in 1959 by a sharp earthquake, which did much to re-arrange the topography near the west side of Yellowstone. Hebgen Lake dropped 9.5 feet after the quake. You pass Hebgen Lake, near which is an Earthquake Area Visitors' Center, climbing a hill to get up around the dam. Once at lake level, the ride is easy into Yellowstone. There are a number of motels and campgrounds along the lake.

Junction, U.S. 191 and 287 (22 miles). Turn south (right) on com-bined U.S. 191 and 287, passing through dense forests of lodge-pole pine, to

West Yellowstone (8 miles; grocery, restaurants, motels, camping). This is a somewhat frantic resort town catering to the mobs of tourists funneling into Yellowstone. Turn east (left) on U.S. 287 and head directly into the park. There are a number of possible routes through the park other than the one we detail here. Remember that Yellowstone is one of the most popular of our National Parks, and you share it with a good bit of

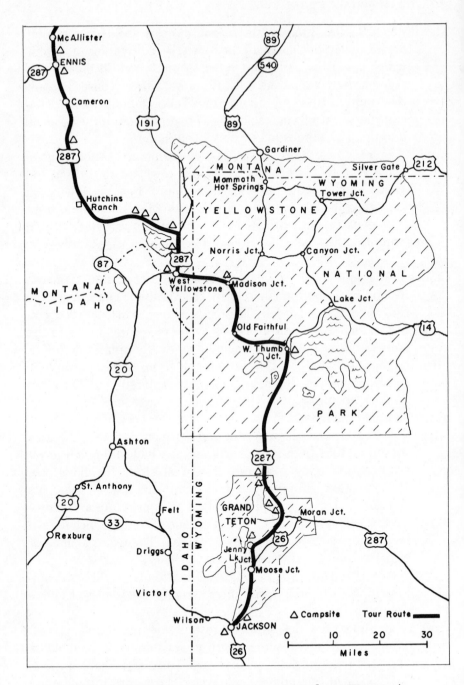

Tour #16 (Section three: Ennis, Montana, to Jackson, Wyoming)

motor traffic. Our advice is to schedule your riding in the early morning hours, then pull in during early afternoons. In addition to the traffic, keep in mind that Yellowstone is high—much of the time you will be well over 7,000 feet. Evenings can get cold.

One bonus for cyclists is the setting aside of special areas within campgrounds where you pay only a minimal camping fee. Currently that is 50¢ a night, administered on the honor system. Do pay the fee, and fill out the envelope, as this demonstrates that cyclists are using the areas—the only sure way to argue for the expansion of such a system.

After entering the park, you have an easy ride along the Madison River to

Madison Junction (14 miles; camping). Turn south (right) toward Old Faithful. Soon comes one of a number of climbs you'll make in the park, this one about 1.3 miles long. After reaching the crest of the hill you have an easier ride along the Firehole River. The road shoulder disappears about 4 miles past Madison Junction, and extra caution is needed from this point until you leave the park at the south entrance. Continue on an easy-to-moderate ride past Fountain Paint Pot, Great Fountain Geyser, and Midway Geyser Basin to

Old Faithful (16 miles; grocery, restaurant, hotel). You must leave the main road to get back to the geyser. You may wheel your bicycle right up to the edge of the geyser viewing area if you don't want to leave it unattended. (Remember that Yellowstone draws a broad variety of people, some of whom are unfortunately thieves. Use caution in popular areas such as this and in campgrounds.) Leave the Old Faithful area southward. You soon cross the Firehole River and begin one of three crossings of the Continental Divide. After crossing the Firehole, you climb sharply for 1.5 miles, roll gradually upward across a plateau, then begin another sharp climb of three-quarters of a mile to the Continental Divide at Craig Pass (8,261 feet). There are no mileposts within the park to help you gauge these distances. Leaving Craig Pass you drop sharply down for 1 mile to De Lacy Creek, then begin another climb of 3 miles to the second crossing of the Divide (8,391 feet). Only the last mile of this climb is hard. You then have a long, winding descent of about 4 miles to

West Thumb and Grant Village (17 miles; grocery, camping). This is a complex of facilities on Yellowstone Lake. The campground at Grant Village has a special bicyclists' area. Turn south at West Thumb toward Jackson. Soon you begin a relatively easy uphill ride to a third crossing of the Continental Divide (7,988 feet). Once across the Divide, you follow the Lewis River, which cuts a deep gorge off to the east of the road. You have a long, rolling descent to

South Entrance (22 miles; elevation 6,886 feet). After leaving the park, you have a gradual downhill ride, then a 1.5-mile climb just before you reach

Grand Teton National Park Entrance (7 miles). The imposing peaks of the Teton Range, rising more than a mile above the Wyoming prairies, create one of the most dramatic sights in the West. Immediately in the foreground are a number of lakes, and the combination of flat lake surface and the sharp pyramidal upthrusts of the mountains is very striking. After entering the park, you have a 2-mile descent to Jackson Lake (6,772 feet). Several campgrounds line the eastern side of Jackson Lake, but these get crowded during the summer, so early arrivals are important. Continue around Jackson Lake, with good views of the Tetons, to

Colter Bay Village (9 miles; grocery, restaurant, camping). From Colter Bay southward there is a paved bicycle lane 3 ft. wide, average surface quality. The route takes you away from the lake, which you rejoin at

Jackson Lake Junction (4 miles; restaurant, motel). Take the road south to Jenny Lake, probably the prettiest area of the park, with Grand Teton (elevation 13,770 feet) and its sibling Middle and South Tetons directly across from you. Continue to

North Jenny Lake Junction (8 miles). Turn onto the one-way road that takes you down to Jenny Lake. This is probably the highlight of a trip through Grand Teton, the imposing peaks nearly within reach just across Jenny Lake. Come out at

South Jenny Lake Junction (6 miles; grocery, camping), an important headquarters for climbers and backpackers. From South Jenny Lake Junction head south toward Jackson. As you move away from the lake you swing out onto the prairies, with a distinct change in vegetation and terrain. Pass the Moose Entrance Station, and go south on an easy ride on U.S. 89 and 187 to

Jackson (16 miles; grocery, restaurants, camping, motels, bicycle shop). Jackson is a bustling tourist town, drawing much of its economic support from visitors to the two great parks to the north. If you've been hankering for a good restaurant meal and a choice motel bed, this is a good place to enjoy both.

TOUR #17: SALT LAKE CITY TO JACKSON, WYOMING

Distance: 288 miles.

Terrain: Mostly moderate hills, but with some sharp 3- and 4-mile climbs at various crossings of the Bear River and near Grays Lake in Idaho.

Roads and Traffic: Heavy traffic from Salt Lake City to Brigham City (56 miles), although much of the route follows U.S. 89, which has a wide riding shoulder. Light to moderate traffic the rest of the tour, with the exception of a 14-mile stretch on U.S. 89 just inside the Wyoming state line, also with a wide shoulder.

Season: Mid-May to October.

Weather: Mostly sunny, although subject to short rain squalls from time to time. Hot days in the Salt Lake Basin, but moderate weather thereafter.

Special Features: This is an excellent connecting tour for people starting out from the Salt Lake City area who wish to visit Grand Teton and Yellowstone National Parks (see below). But the route north has many attractions in its own right, including some picturesque farming villages in northern Utah that have remained essentially unchanged since the nineteenth century, and a pretty ride up the Grand Canyon of the Snake, just south of Jackson.

Connecting Transportation:
Salt Lake City: Greyhound, Trailways, Amtrak, air service.
Jackson: Greyhound, air service.

Although we originally intended this tour as a connecting link between Salt Lake City and our tour to Grand Teton and Yellowstone National Parks, we discovered to our delight that the tour route was actually very attractive all by itself. The ride to northern Utah is generally easy, and takes you through some of the oldest towns in the region, with many prize pieces of Victorian architecture. Later, the tour winds up through dry hilly country past one of the West's most important wildlife sanctuaries, Grays Lake National Wildlife Refuge, located on a high basin in southern Idaho. You might see a variety of birds lifting off from the swampy grasses bordering the lake, including cranes and Canadian geese. Finally, the tour route winds up through the Grand Canyon of the Snake, where stiff rock walls rise a thousand feet or more above you. This is a fitting prelude to the town of Jackson, a gateway to Grand Teton and Yellowstone National Parks.

Salt Lake City (grocery, restaurants, motels, camping, bicycle shops), the world center of Mormonism, is an interesting mixture of theological and cultural influences. The Mormons were driven here from Illinois and Missouri in the mid-nineteenth century, and the mark of these early settlers is still the most powerful one seen and felt. The Mormon Tabernacle, a marvel of nineteenth-century ingenuity, is visited by hundreds of thousands of people yearly. Salt Lake City has also developed an active secular life. There is a new downtown performing-arts center, where the Utah Symphony and Ballet West appear, a professional basketball team, and an increasingly active night life. Traffic in Salt Lake City and along the first 56 miles of the tour route is heavy. Cyclists arriving from other areas with their bicycles already in cartons may wish to go north via bus (Greyhound or Trailways) to Brigham City, and start the tour from there. Riding from that point onward is in light or moderate traffic. If you're bicycling out of Salt Lake City you may wish to pick up your own route north by using a Davis County map, although we found it simpler to take Utah 106 north through Bountiful and continue on to

Junction, U.S. 89 and Utah 106 (19 miles). Turn north (right) on U.S. 89, a busy four-lane road with a wide shoulder. The route rises and falls along the lower foothills of the Wasatch Range, and off to the west are good views of the Great Salt Lake. Continue to

Ogden (16 miles; grocery, restaurants, motels, bicycle shops, camping). Another city settled by Mormons, and a clean, well-laid-out town today. Continue north on U.S. 89, which has about a 3-foot shoulder, to

Brigham City (21 miles; grocery, restaurants, motels), a pleasant city with tree-lined streets. Rising behind the town are the Wasatch Mountains. Continue north on U.S. 89 until the edge of town, where you reach a junction with Utah 69. Turn north on Utah 69 toward Honeyville, Deweyville, and Collinston, all hamlets with tiny stores where you can buy supplies if necessary. The Wasatch Mountains diminish in height the farther north you

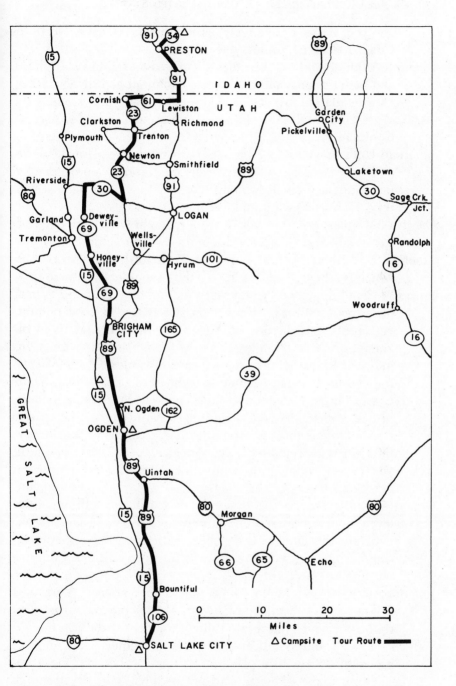

Tour #17   Salt Lake City to Jackson, Wyoming   (Section one: Salt Lake City, Utah, to Preston, Idaho)

go; you make a relatively easy crossing shortly. North of Collinston about 2 miles, you come to

Junction, Utah 30 and 69 (21 miles). Turn east (right) on Utah 30, and begin a long rolling climb to a summit at Milepost 106.5. During the climb you leave the cultivated valleys along the Wasatches, and enter into dry grasslands and hilly terrain. Continue to

Junction, Utah 23 and 30 (7 miles). Turn north (left) on Utah 23, and begin a relatively easy ride up through more irrigated farmlands and small farming towns dating from the last century, such as Newton and Trenton. At

Cornish (21 miles; grocery) you reach a junction with Utah 61. Turn east (right) and continue through Lewiston (grocery) to

Junction, U.S. 91 and Utah 61 (7 miles). Turn north (left) on U.S. 91, which is a busy road but has a riding shoulder. Continue to

Preston (11 miles; grocery, restaurants, motels, bicycle shop), a busy little town with a pleasant main street. It is a good point to get supplies, as the next grocery store (a small one) is in the hamlet of Niter, 38 miles away. At the north end of town you intersect Idaho 34; take it northeast. Six miles outside of Preston you have a sharp 2-mile descent to the Bear River. There is a primitive campground here (no water) just north of the bridge. We spent a windy night here, eating fresh fish supplied by kindly neighbors to whom we had gone for water. Beyond the river is a steep 3-mile climb, peaking at MP 16. From here, you have a rolling ride with some sharp pitches, past Niter (grocery) to

Grace (42 miles; grocery, café, motel), at which point the road has leveled out considerably. You may note the intensive effort to cultivate the land in this valley, with beautiful examples of contour plowing reaching partway up steep hillsides. Continue north out of Grace to

Junction, U.S. 30 and Idaho 34 (5 miles; no services). Turn east (right) on the combined highways. U.S. 30 is a major east-west route, but which has a safe riding shoulder for the trip to

Soda Springs (7 miles; grocery, restaurants, motels, camping), a growing town with a pleasant city park for picnicking. Continue on Idaho 34 northward out of town, past dry farms of wheat and rye, then onto high, arid hills of sage and grasses. After topping one of these rises you will see Blackfoot Reservoir and the minute community of

Henry (24 miles; grocery), which has one of the oldest standing

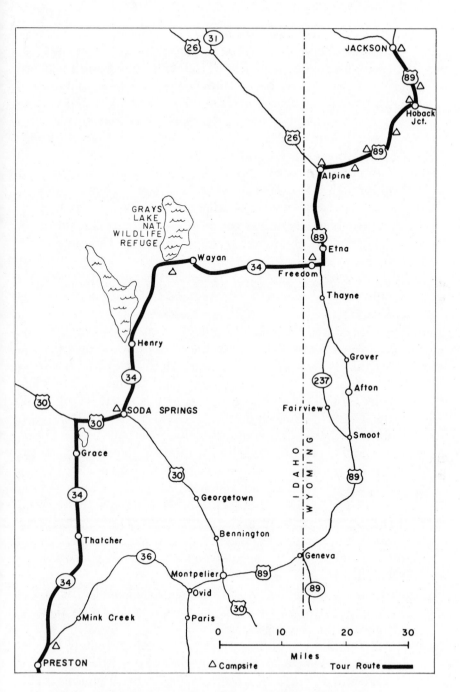

Tour #17 (Section two: Preston, Idaho, to Jackson, Wyoming)

buildings in the area, a quaint log cabin that serves as a general
store. Continue on, climbing up above the reservoir until you
reach a large, circular valley. Stretching to the north is a very
shallow lake, Grays Lake, which is a wildfowl sanctuary. Canadian geese and whooping cranes may be seen lifting off in a
flurry from the high grasses. There is a National Forest campground about 4 miles off the road; the turnoff is about 3 miles
before you reach the town of

Wayan (15 miles; grocery). Out of Wayan you start a 4-mile climb
up through grass and sage hills. The ascent is hard; summit is
at MP 98. Going down the other side you must be particularly
careful about unmarked cattle grates. The farther down the
valley you go, the more forested it becomes. Continue to the
Mormon town of

Freedom (20 miles), which is just inside the Wyoming state line. The
route number changes to Wyoming 239. Continue a short distance to

Junction, U.S. 89 and Wyo. 239 (2 miles). Turn north (left) on U.S.
89 toward Alpine. You are in the Star Valley, known particularly for its Swiss cheese. Pass through the town of Etna (café,
grocery), one of the many small dairy towns in the valley.
Traffic is moderate to heavy, but there is a safe riding shoulder. The Salt Range is on the east, and the Salt River runs to
the west of you. Continue to

Alpine (14 miles; grocery, restaurants, camping, motels). From this
junction up to Jackson, you will be in the Snake River valley.
The most immediate attraction is the Grand Canyon of the
Snake. The impressive walls rise 1,000 feet above the riverbed.
The best views are off to the north (left). The canyon itself is
forested in stands of lodgepole, ponderosa, and aspen. Traffic
is moderate, and the shoulder appears and disappears at in-
tervals. At

Hoback Junction (23 miles; grocery, campground, motel), continue
on U.S. 89 toward Jackson. There is a good riding shoulder
from this intersection to

Jackson (13 miles; grocery, restaurants, camping, motels, bicycle
shops). Jackson is an important gateway to the Tetons and
Yellowstone Park, and is well supplied with all touring amenities. Set at the base of a long plain, it is surrounded by attractive, rolling hills. You can connect here to our Tour 16,
taking the hard way, in reverse order, or only as far as the
southern parks.

TOUR #18: BRIGHAM CITY, UTAH—FLAMING GORGE— DINOSAUR NATIONAL MONUMENT

Distance: 323 miles.

Terrain: Hard climbs in Logan Canyon in Utah and very difficult climbs at the south end of the Flaming Gorge National Monument. There are stretches of 40 to 60 miles without services. Easy to moderate riding in parts of Utah and Wyoming.

Roads and Traffic: Moderate traffic about a quarter of the ride; otherwise light.

Season: Late May to mid-September.

Weather: Usually warm and dry. There may be afternoon thundershowers in Wyoming.

Preferred Direction: West to east. Prevailing westerlies in Wyoming.

Special Features: Beautiful canyon rides in Utah, and very scenic rides through red-and-ochre-walled gorges at the south end of Flaming Gorge National Monument. Dinosaur Monument has the largest deposits of dinosaur fossils in the world.

Connecting Transportation:

Brigham City, Utah: Greyhound, Trailways.

Vernal, Utah (19 miles from Dinosaur National Monument): Trailways, air service.

Although it may not appear so at first glance, this particular tour takes you through as representative a region as you will find in the Mountain States. Elevation varies from just above 4,000 feet at Brigham City (north of Salt Lake City) to a high pass at 8,428 feet just outside Flaming Gorge National Recreation Area. There are expanses of mountain scenery, with dense stands of ponderosa pine, larch, lodgepole pine, and juniper. There are also rolling sage-and-jackrabbit deserts, where clusters of antelope bend into neat arcs while grazing on the sparse vegetation. There are also the abrupt changes in vegetation typical of the Mountain States, where you pass in a few miles from arid plateau to deeply wooded mountain or from deep red gorges glutted with color to smooth, worn sandstone with twelve geological ages locked inside.

The ride is typical also in the span of riding conditions, from very hard mountain riding to the graceful sweep of semi-arid desert. Temperatures vary from crisp mornings to blazing heat in the area around Vernal, Utah.

Finally, there are the demands that the Mountain States make upon you as a rider. There are stretches of 40 miles or more where water is difficult to find, so you must plan your ride carefully. At the same time with a few exceptions, roads are quiet, and you will have many hours to immerse yourself in the great dome of the sky, often with many miles between you and the next human being.

Brigham City, Utah (grocery, restaurants, motels). Named after the Mormon leader who led the initial group of settlers to Utah, Brigham City bears the unmistakable mark of a Mormon town, with its temple, tree-lined streets, and the cheerful bustle of its inhabitants, Mormon and non-Mormon alike. You start your tour by heading south out of town to an intersection northbound with U.S. 89. Turn east (left) toward Logan. You immediately begin an 8-mile climb, first past grassy hills, then into heavier stands of timber. The road is busy, but there is a good riding shoulder. The road peaks at Milepost 380, dips down for a mile, then climbs another mile to a second summit at MP 382. You then descend 5 miles to a fertile valley floor that you follow to

Logan (24 miles; grocery, restaurants, motels, bicycle shop). Leave Logan northeast via U.S. 89, passing the University, then enter Logan Canyon. This ride, one of the prettier ones in northern Utah, takes you slowly up a timbered canyon, the road running alongside a lively stream. This was once the site of a deep freshwater lake, and you can see the marks of earlier erosion patterns high on the canyon walls. There are a number of National Forest campgrounds along the road, as well as a good many sites for ad hoc camping along Logan River. There is an excellent water source at Rick's Spring, which issues from the base of an arched cave. It is a welcome sight on typically hot days. The ice-cold water is essentially snowmelt from much higher elevations trapped between rock layers to reemerge at this point. Beginning at MP 437, you commence a 7-mile climb that peaks at 7,800 feet at MP 430. From here you get a view of Bear Lake lying nearly 2,000 feet below you, its deep blue a contrast to the rather colorless landscape surrounding it. You wind down a very steep series of switchbacks (a hard stretch for people coming the other direction) to

Garden City (40 miles; grocery, café, motel). Turn south (right) on Utah 30. There are three general stores along Bear Lake, and the most complete is at Garden City. There is a small store at

Pickleville, just a few miles away, and another small store at Laketown, 10 miles on. The next supply point after Laketown is Kemmerer, Wyoming, 56 miles away. Continue along Bear Lake to

Laketown (13 miles; general store). Just outside Laketown, you begin a hard climb up a narrow, winding canyon. The grades are 6 and 7 percent. The crest is at MP 130.5. From the summit you look down on a large valley cut by the Bear River. You begin a long, rolling descent to the valley and

Sage Creek Junction (12 miles; no services). Continue east on Utah

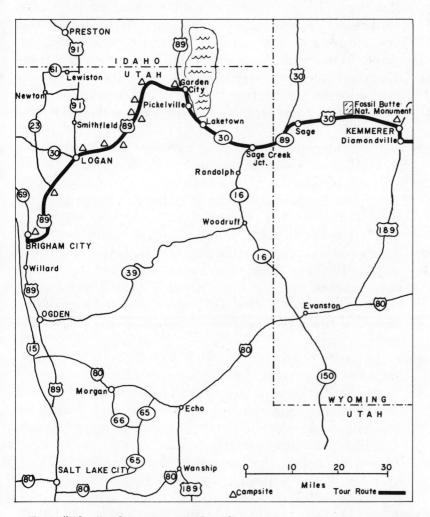

Tour #18   Brigham City, Utah—Flaming Gorge—Dinosaur National Monument (Section one: Brigham City, Utah, to Kemmerer, Wyoming)

30 toward the Wyoming state line. The valley is used for cattle grazing, the Bear River supplying vital water. The countryside is sagebrush, rabbitbrush, greasewood, and thin grasses. There are also a variety of cacti; be careful when wheeling your bicycle off the road, as spines and thorns can penetrate your tires. A bad dose will ruin a tire, as you can never find all the thorns. As you cross the border, Utah 30 changes to Wyoming 89, which you follow to

Junction, U.S. 30 and Wyo. 89 (10 miles; no services). Turn south (right) on U.S. 30, a rather busy truck road, but with wide shoulders. The great distances tend to space out the trucks, so they are not particularly bothersome. As you ride along, you will see a number of interesting and colorful buttes, primarily to the north. Most notable of these is the Fossil Butte National Monument, where fossils of many different ages are embedded in sedimentary rock. You occasionally get good views of the Uinta Mountains to the south and east. Follow U.S. 30 to

Kemmerer (25 miles; grocery, restaurants, motels). Kemmerer started as a coal-mining town in the late nineteenth century. The recent rise in the value of coal and the discovery of natural gas in the area have brought about an economic resurgence in the area. There is a small museum in the town park, where local artifacts and memorabilia are displayed. The nearby town of Diamondville (grocery, restaurant, motels) is your last supply point until Green River, 68 miles away, although there are a restaurant and motel in Little America, located on Interstate 80, 47 miles away. Follow U.S. 30 east out of Diamondville along the Hams Fork, past tiny crossroads places called Opal and Granger to

Junction, Interstate 80 and U.S. 30 (49 miles). Cross over the Interstate and head east on I-80 toward Green River. As with all freeway riding, stay on the shoulder and be particularly careful when crossing exits, stopping if necessary until there is no following traffic which might turn off and cut into your path. Continue past Little America (good water source, also restaurant and motel), then leave the Interstate at MP 72, Westvaco exit. Follow a frontage road paralleling the main road to a junction with Wyo. 374, which you take to

Green River (24 miles; grocery, restaurants, camping, motels; bicycle shop in Rock Springs, 15 miles off the tour route on I-80). The town takes its name from the river here. In 1869, John

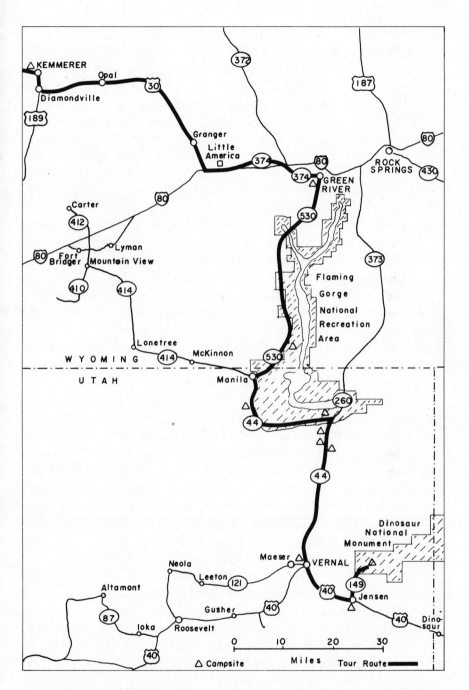

Tour #18   (Section two: Kemmerer, Wyoming, to Dinosaur National Monument, Utah)

Wesley Powell and his men began their historic exploration of the Green and Colorado Rivers from this point. Coming into town, you'll see an impressive display of eroded rock spires and cliffs on the east bank of the river. Once in town cross over the Green River on Wyo. 530 toward Flaming Gorge Recreation Area. You immediately begin a 5-mile climb that is hard, cresting at MP 5.5. Much of the rest of the trip through the recreation area is through the so-called "badlands" of Wyoming, although for that matter terrain and vegetation are really typical of much of the state. Before modern roads were cut, its remote gullies and canyons did provide sanctuary for desperados such as Butch Cassidy. There are a number of campgrounds along the route, and the road rises and falls over rolling terrain, crossing arms of Flaming Gorge Reservoir. Not all campgrounds have water, so check for latest information at the Flaming Gorge Recreation Area Visitors' Center just outside of Green River. Continue on Wyo. 530 to the Utah line, where the route changes to Utah 44, and takes you to

Manila (45 miles; grocery, café, motels). This is a good supply point. The next place to buy groceries is Vernal, 64 miles away, although you may be able to get basic supplies at Red Canyon Lodge, at the south end of Flaming Gorge Reservoir, just off the tour route. Just out of Manila you cross a meadow, then begin one of the more difficult sections of the tour, climbing some exceptionally steep grades. The first of these starts on the far side of the meadow, climbs 4 miles to a crest at MP 58. Shortly thereafter you have a steep 8-percent downgrade through fantastically colored rock strata, cross a stream, then begin an even more difficult climb, this one lasting 4.5 miles and cresting at MP 51.5. From here the grades become less oppressive, although you will continue climbing at hard-to-moderate levels until you cross a summit 25 miles outside of Vernal. As you work toward that point, you will notice a marked change in vegetation, as the nearly treeless plains of Wyoming give way to dense stands of ponderosa, larch, and aspen. At MP 49 you pass a rest area that has drinking water, descend another hill, then begin a climb to a hillcrest at MP 44. Although you will still climb, grades are only moderate from this point on. Continue to

Junction, Utah 260 and 44 (28 miles). Turn south (right) still on Utah 44 toward Vernal, climbing a moderate grade through a pretty meadow to a rather painless crossing of a summit at

MP 25.7 (8,428 feet). From here you roll over terrain which becomes barren again, with the exception of creases in the hills that collect enough water to support trees. At MP 20 you cross a final highpoint, then begin a 10-mile descent, winding past sandstone formations on either side of you. Be careful, as there are a number of unmarked cattle grates. There are incredible views as you descend, first of a deeply cut gorge on your right, then of a vast panorama that stretches for 30 miles or more and includes mountains, bluffs, treeless hills, and a scattering of lakes. A roadside sign says that some twelve different oceans have covered this area. The descent bottoms out near MP 10, then you have another hard but short climb to a crest at MP 9, after which you have an easy ride to

Vernal (35 miles; grocery, restaurants, camping, motels). There is a pleasant park in town with good shade and picnic tables. A town museum adjacent to the park has examples of dinosaurs and other creatures that once roamed the area. Vernal is on U.S. 40, a road busy with local traffic until you get a few miles from town. Turn east (left) on U.S. 40, which has a narrow shoulder you can ride on. Continue past pasturelands and irrigated fields to

Jensen (12 miles; café, grocery, camping). Turn north (left) here on Utah 149 for an easy 7-mile ride to the Visitors' Center of Dinosaur National Monument. The ride in gives you an excellent view of pretty rock cliffs cut by the Green River. You appreciate the difficulties the landscape and heat presented to early paleontologists who explored the area.

Dinosaur National Monument (7 miles; camping). This park contains the most impressive collection of dinosaur fossils in the world. You view the cliff of the most important dig from the shelter of an air-conditioned building, and you can view workers meticulously chipping away to expose even more fossils. A tram from the Visitors' Center takes you up to the dig, saving some hot and steep riding. You must leave the monument via the same road you came in; if you camp there you'll have to bring your groceries with you. The campgrounds do have water. Bus and air services are available at Vernal.

TOUR #19: BOULDER—ROCKY MOUNTAIN NATIONAL PARK—STEAMBOAT SPRINGS

Distance: 227 miles.

Terrain: Long pass climbs in Rocky Mountain National Park and over Gore Pass.

Season: Mid-June to mid-September.

Weather: Usually dry with moderate temperatures, but chances of rain and cold weather at high elevations in Rocky Mountain National Park. Cool or cold nights at high elevations.

Special Features: Spectacular high mountain scenery, crossing the highest paved pass road in the U.S., and the longest ride on paved roads above timberline in the country. Lovely meadows, alpine lakes, and interesting old mining towns on the tour route.

Connecting Transportation:

Boulder: Greyhound; air service at Denver.

Steamboat Springs: Trailways, air service.

The ride through Rocky Mountain National Park is unique. Not only do you cross the highest paved pass road in the country, but you have an 11-mile stretch of road where you are consistently more than 12,000 feet above sea level.

The climb is long, but the grades are not unusually steep, never over 6 percent. Nonetheless, it is a significant challenge, and should be undertaken only by riders in good condition who are well equipped to handle the contingencies of mountain travel (see Chapters 4 and 5).

You will also find a significant amount of motor traffic moving through the park with you. But this usually moves slowly, and although bothersome at times, is not particularly dangerous. Outside the park you will be on roads with either light or moderate traffic.

Beyond the spectacular ride at heights normally reached only by hikers and climbers, this tour has other attractions. From Boulder, with its prominent signs warning motorists that bicyclists have the right to use the full right-hand lane, you pass through some lovely foothills area before approaching the park. After your ride over Trail Ridge Road, you descend to elevations of about 8,000 feet, with a quiet ride through some relatively unvisited alpine scenery, culminating at Gore Pass. Then, once out of the high mountains, you descend the Yampa Valley, with its historic—and unvarnished—old mining towns of Phippsburg and Oak Creek. You end the tour in Steamboat Springs, a pleasant resort town at the western base of the Rockies.

Boulder (grocery, restaurants, camping, motels, bicycle shops, youth hostels) is almost a bicyclist's heaven. In addition to being a manufacturing center for bicycle equipment (Cyclist's Touring Shop, Kirtland), the city hosts the Red Zinger Mountain Road Race, which annually attracts top national and international competition. There are numerous examples of stately

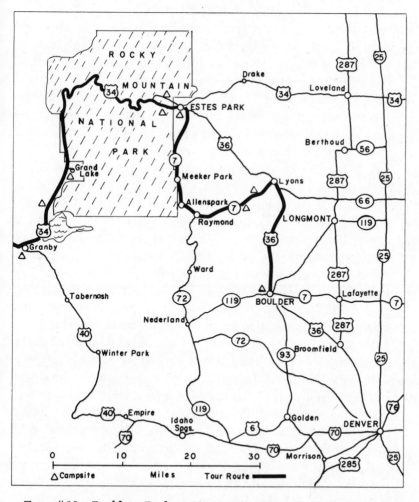

Tour #19   Boulder—Rocky   Mountain   National   Park—Steamboat
Springs (Section one: Boulder to Granby)

Victorian architecture, and perhaps the fastest-moving bicycle traffic anywhere in the world. Leave town north via U.S. 36 toward Lyons. The road is busy but has a good shoulder. At

Lyons (17 miles; grocery, café) turn southwest (left) on Colorado 7, and begin a lovely canyon ride up the South Saint Vrain Canyon. The stream flows alongside you, and you pass through nice stands of ponderosa. Continue through Riverside to

Raymond (15 miles; grocery). Stay on Colo. 7, which angles northward and becomes a section of the Peaks-to-Peaks Highway, a rolling road with excellent views of the Rockies to the west. In general, you have a fine riding shoulder on the highway, and traffic is light to moderate. There are a number of long climbs, most of moderate difficulty. Climb to

Allenspark (6 miles; grocery, restaurant, motel), an interesting old hillside town, now a tourist center with several original log buildings still in excellent condition. Leave Allenspark, climb through Meeker Park, until you reach a final crest at Milepost 12, near Wind River Ranch. You pass a number of National Forest campgrounds along the route. From the summit, you have an 8-mile downhill run to a junction with U.S. 36, which you follow less than a mile to

Estes Park (17 miles; grocery, restaurants, motels, youth hostel, bicycle shop). This is a full-blown tourist town catering to Rocky Mountain National Park visitors. Set in a magnificent valley directly below the towering 14,000-foot peaks of the park, it is one of the most attractively situated cities in the West. Since the ride through the park should be started as nearly after dawn as possible, most bicyclists will stay in or near Estes Park. The closest campground to the tour route inside the park is Moraine, not far from Park Headquarters. (Aspenglen Campground is on a road off our tour route, but this road, U.S. 34, intersects the tour route inside the park at Deer Ridge Junction.) Our tour leaves Estes Park via U.S./Colo. 36 to

Beaver Meadows Entrance (4 miles; camping nearby), where you can pick up a map of the park and pay the 50¢ entrance fee. From this point, High Point is 23 miles away. Almost without exception, all of this 23 miles is climbing, although the first 14 miles are the most difficult. There are no mileposts within the park, so you must use landmarks to give you an idea of your progress. Climb out of the Beaver Meadows, by the entrance station, to Deer Ridge Junction (U.S. 34 and Colo. 36). From here you begin the most strenuous part of the climb. You begin by winding up a long valley, then switchbacking up one of its flanks. This is a long, difficult climb. Finally, you round the prow of a hill and break through timberline, pass through a forest of dead lodgepole pine on your left, then sweep gradually upward along Trail Ridge Road proper. The road follows a beautifully contoured route through alpine tundra, a delicate ecosystem of plants clinging desperately to the thin soil. If it is early in the year, you will usually see snowbanks along the road. Around you are peaks that break upward so numerously that the entire horizon seems splintered with rock and snow. Winds are usually strong, and will batter you from various angles as you ride. Keep a low profile, and watch against being blown out into the traffic lane. High Point (12,182 feet) is unmarked—so many motorists were stopping that the Park Service took down the sign. But gravity will tell you when you have arrived. You start a downhill swing into the flank of the ridge, pass a visitors' center (your only shelter on the crossing), pass Fall River Pass (11,796 feet) and Milner Pass on the Continental Divide (10,758 feet). These may be the only two passes in the country which you cross (in this direction) without turning a pedal! After Milner Pass, you go down through a series of six sharp hairpin turns until you gain the floor of Phantom Valley. Here, the road runs gently downhill along the valley cut by the North Fork of the Colorado River, whose source lies only a few miles up this valley. There is a campground at Timber Creek. Continue to

Grand Lake Junction (48 miles; a mile off the route is Grand Lake, with grocery, restaurants, motels, camping, youth hostel). Stay on U.S. 34 past Shadow Mountain Lake, a beautiful alpine lake with steep mountains rising from the far side, then past Lake Granby. There are numerous motels, campgrounds, and restaurants along the route to

Junction, U.S. 40 and 34 (14 miles; a mile to the east is Granby, with grocery, restaurants, motels, youth hostel, bicycle shop). There are a few grocery stores and cafés at the intersection if you do not wish to go into Granby. Turn west (right) on U.S. 40. You ride here through sagebrush country over a busy road to

Hot Sulphur Springs (11 miles; grocery, restaurants, motels). This little town hugs a bank of the Colorado River. Just beyond town you enter a steep-walled canyon, and the road has narrow shoulders. Use caution in covering this stretch to

Parshall (5 miles; grocery), a small fishing town lying off the road.

Once past Parshall you parallel the Colorado River through
open country, considerably drier than the mountains from
which you have come. Riding is easy to
Kremmling (12 miles; grocery, restaurants, motels), a junction with

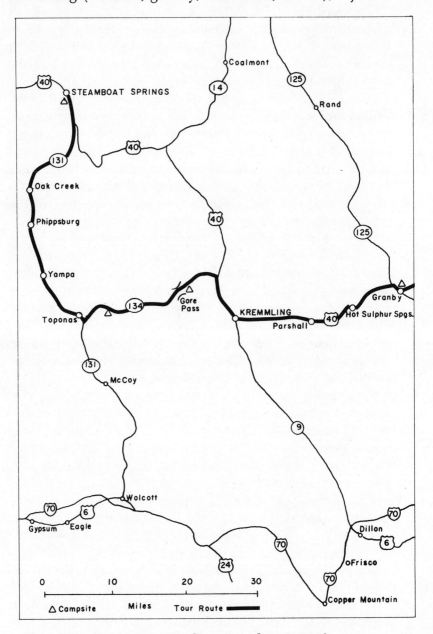

Tour #19   (Section two: Granby to Steamboat Springs)

the Trans America Bike Route and a good supply point. Towns are small from here to Steamboat Springs. There is a nice town park with a minuscule museum. Stay on U.S. 40, heading west to

Junction, Colo. 134 and U.S. 40 (6 miles). Turn west (left) on Colo. 134 and begin a hard climb to Gore Pass. You wind first up a dry canyon, the gorge cut by the stream lying off to your left. The hillsides are covered mostly in sage, with small clusters of juniper. You cross a nice, open meadow, the only real breather in the climb, then start up again over a number of steep pitches. You reach Gore Pass at MP 16 (9,524 feet). There is a campground at the summit. Once over the top, you wind down through nice alpine meadows, with beaver ponds linked together in interesting strands. There are several campgrounds along this stretch, should you wish to stop for the night. At MP 8 you start climbing out of the valley, cresting at MP 7. From here it is a straight downhill run to

Junction, Colo. 131 and 134 (27 miles). Turn north (right) on Colo. 131 toward Toponas, just a mile away (general store). Continue down a gentle valley with interesting rock spires on the south side of the road. The country, except beside the stream you follow, has reverted again to sage and grasses, and is used almost exclusively for grazing. Continue through Yampa (grocery, café, motel), then to the little town of

Phippsburg (19 miles; grocery). Beyond Phippsburg the valley closes in more markedly, and you pass from agricultural land to land first exploited for its coal. Oak Creek (grocery, café, motel) is the most interesting of these towns, with some wonderful old hardware stores and bars. It has undergone a revival recently, and we were caught up in a lively town festival in late summer, escorted out of town by a pickup-truck load of exceedingly happy participants. The road winds past old coal tipples, then through a broad agricultural valley to

Junction, U.S. 40 and Colo. 131 (21 miles). Turn northwest (left); it is a short ride along a busy stretch of U.S. 40 to

Steamboat Springs (5 miles; grocery, restaurants, motels, camping, bicycle shops, youth hostel). This ambitious ski resort wears a more homespun atmosphere than do some of Colorado's posher establishments. But you'll find here all the amenities you want, particularly if you feel up to celebrating after taking one of the highest mountain tours in the country.

TOUR #20: DENVER TO SANTA FE

Distance: 372 miles.

Terrain: Within the first 145 miles out of Denver there are four major passes to climb, and within the last 80 miles between Taos and Santa Fe in New Mexico you are in the Sangre de Cristo Mountains, with a number of hard climbs. There are a few stretches of 40 miles or more in southern Colorado and northern New Mexico where there are no services.

Roads and Traffic: From Denver to Bailey (45 miles), traffic is heavy, only part of the ride has good shoulder. Beyond Bailey, traffic thins out the farther south you go. The rest of the route has either wide, ridable shoulders or is on quiet backroads.

Season: Mid-May to the end of September, unless you are taking the tour south to north. In that case, be out of the Rockies by mid-September.

Weather: Mostly sunny with moderate temperatures, but with chances of rain and cold weather in high mountain areas. Drier and warmer in New Mexico.

Special Features: There is beautiful mountain riding in Colorado, and an interesting change in culture as you go south. You pass from Western frontier influence in the Rockies to a mixture of ancient Pueblo, Spanish, and contemporary Hispanic cultures in New Mexico. Northern New Mexico is uncrowded, and surprisingly green. The Sangre de Cristo Mountains are hard but interesting riding, through some of North America's oldest settlements.

Connecting Transportation:

Denver: Greyhound, Trailways, Amtrak, air service.

Santa Fe: Greyhound, Trailways, Amtrak.

In many ways, this is a tour of great contrasts. The first is that of terrain—running from the high Rockies to the Rio Grande Valley in the southwest. It is also a contrast in cultures—Denver, the burgeoning metropolis, firmly established as the financial capital of the Mountain States, and Santa Fe, the oldest capital city in the United States, and cultural home to the oldest societies in the country. Between these two important centers, the tour route takes you from some of the most striking mountain scenery in Colorado to the fragrant forests of juniper and piñon typical of the Southwest. Even the colors are in contrast, from the deep green of high alpine fir to the reddish soil of New Mexico.

The tour presents some physical challenges. Shortly after you leave Denver, you come to the first of the four mountain passes you must

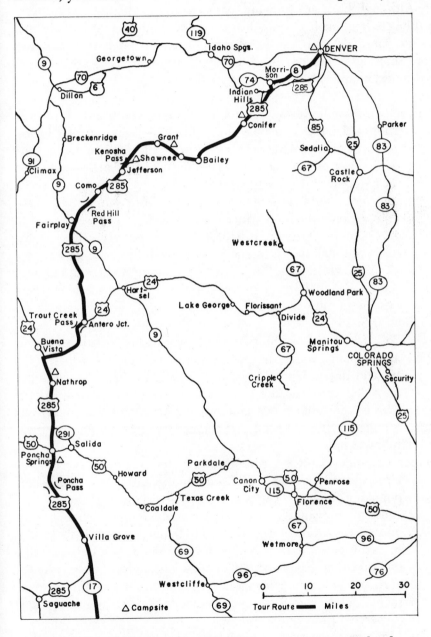

Tour #20   Denver to Santa Fe (Section one: Denver, Colorado, to Villa Grove, Colorado)

cross before you leave Colorado. There are also some steep climbs out of Taos, as you make your way up into the Sangre de Cristo Mountains of New Mexico.

Finally, there are the attractions of two old cities, Taos and Santa Fe. Although both are growing, each can be navigated comfortably by bicycle, and each reveals distinct cultures not found outside this region. Santa Fe is also an excellent jumping-off point for tours that more thoroughly explore the Southwest. Many of these are detailed in the next chapter.

Denver (grocery, restaurants, camping, motels, youth hostel, bicycle shops). Denver is a busy city, and a bicyclist wishing to explore its many attractions should use the bicycle route map available from the Denver Planning Office (see Appendix 1). Leave Denver by going west on Yale Ave., then take a short jog to the right on Hoyt, then left on Morrison Rd. This becomes Colorado 8, on which you climb to

Morrison (17 miles; grocery, restaurants)—an old town, with many of its original buildings and houses carefully restored. Stay on Colo. 8, which jogs through town; leaving Morrison, climb a mile and a half through beautiful red-rock formations, then descend a mile and a half to

Junction, U.S. 285 and Colo. 8 (3 miles). Turn south (right) on U.S. 285. This is a busy four-lane highway; it has a wide shoulder at this point, which disappears at Indian Hills Rd. A half-mile beyond Indian Hills Rd., leave U.S. 285 and take the old highway that runs parallel to it through Tinytown and Fenders. This is a hard but pretty climb up Turkey Creek Canyon. After 8 miles on the old road you rejoin U.S. 285, which you then follow 3 miles to

Conifer (11 miles; grocery, restaurants, motel). Located on a wide alpine meadow, this little community and Aspen Park are popular commuter towns for people working in Denver. Because of this you lose some traffic at this point, although you must use caution until you reach Bailey, after which traffic thins out considerably. As you leave Conifer, you begin a rolling ride that has some difficult ascents. Pass through Silver Springs (grocery, café, motel), then continue climbing to a point 2 miles from Bailey, where you begin a steep downgrade (7 percent) for 2 miles into

Bailey (15 miles; grocery, café, motels). This little town straddles the North Fork of the Platte River. The grocery store is on a side street to your right just as you enter town. Continue on U.S. 285, which runs alongside the river. The stream has scalloped flatlands out of the hillsides, and these are used for grazing. The ride is considerably easier and traffic is lighter. Ride through the hamlet of Shawnee (grocery) and on to

Grant (12 miles; grocery, motel, restaurant). Two miles beyond Grant you leave the river and begin a hard 6-mile climb to Kenosha Pass (10,000 feet). The middle part of the climb is the worst, the top becoming less steep. Crest is at Milepost 203.5. This is the first of four passes you must cross before leaving Colorado; each succeeding one is a bit lower and easier to cross. Go down a 2-mile hill, which brings you into sight of one of Colorado's parks, a broad, high basin with fairly easy riding.

Jefferson (10 miles; grocery, café) is a tiny village set on the eastern edge of the park. Ride on good shoulder and easy terrain until you reach the base of Red Hill Pass. You have a 2-mile climb, cresting at MP 186.5 (9,993 feet). You'll be able to see the pretty red-rock formations after which the pass is named, off to your right. Drop down a rolling 4-mile run to

Fairplay (16 miles; grocery, cafés, motels), just off the tour route. It is a picturesque old mining town, the courthouse a masterpiece of intricate design, an anomoly in a place that grew so rapidly. The main street, just a block off Colo. 9, has a number of original buildings. The Bikecentennial Trans America Bike Trail intercepts the tour route here. Your next support point after Fairplay is Buena Vista, 36 miles away. Leave Fairplay via U.S. 285 toward Antero Junction. The ride along this stretch is relatively easy; you make your way through rolling parkland, with alternating sage-and-grass plains and forested uplands. The high peaks are constantly in view all around you. Continue to

Antero Junction (22 miles; no services). Stay on U.S. 285 and begin a climb to

Trout Creek Pass (1 mile)—not a particularly difficult climb. The pass crests at MP 226 (9,346 feet). You begin a long downhill run, moderately steep for the first 4 miles, then steeper through rock canyons with impressive pinnacles jutting upward. Finally, near MP 214 you bottom out onto a beautiful valley, set below spectacular peaks on all sides. Continue to

Junction, U.S. 285 and 24 (13 miles; grocery, café, camping, motel). The town of Buena Vista is 2 miles north of the tour route. If you do need to go into town, turn south (left) on U.S. 285. The river on your left is the Arkansas, considerably different in character here from the dammed-up stream it becomes farther to the southeast. The ride is easy along a busy highway with a wide shoulder. As you approach

Poncha Springs (14 miles; grocery, cafés, motels), you begin climbing again. The climb is hard for 7 miles and peaks at Poncha Pass (9,010 feet), near MP 119. Poncha Pass, the last of your four passes in Colorado, is a demarcation point. To the south of you lies the San Luis Valley, a long, narrow corridor leading south toward New Mexico. From the top of the pass and until you reach Taos, tree cover virtually disappears from the tour route. Mountain fir and pine give way to sagebrush and cactus. So also does the character of the people change—although population is sparse. More often than not, Spanish is the tongue you will hear spoken on the streets, and the largest building in town is apt to be a Roman Catholic church, not the town hall or the post office.

You see the Sangre de Cristo range off to your left, forming a jagged border to the San Luis Valley. By name, and by its geographical location, this too announces a change for you. The range extends clear to Santa Fe, and was named by the earliest Spanish explorers to the region. As you descend from Poncha Pass, although you are still in Colorado, you have entered another land. Continue on an easy ride to

Villa Grove (22 miles; grocery). The store is in the town's only gas station, and has minimal supplies. You may need to stock up here. Hooper, 35 miles distant, is the next grocery. Continue south to

Junction, Colo. 17 and U.S. 285 (5 miles; no services). Turn south (left) on Colo. 17 toward Hooper. This is sparsely populated land, although there is a scattering of farms which, through the use of deep wells, have been able to irrigate grass crops and alfalfa. Otherwise sage and cactus dominate. There are good views of the Sangre de Cristo Mountains off to the east, the highest peaks reaching 14,000 feet or more.

Hooper (30 miles; grocery), whose buildings indicate more prosperous days past, is just off the road to your left; the grocery, though, is on the main highway. Continue south on Colo. 17. Six miles south of Hooper, near the town of Mosca (motel, café), is a turnoff for the Great Sand Dunes National Monument. You can see the dunes off to your left, but the entrance

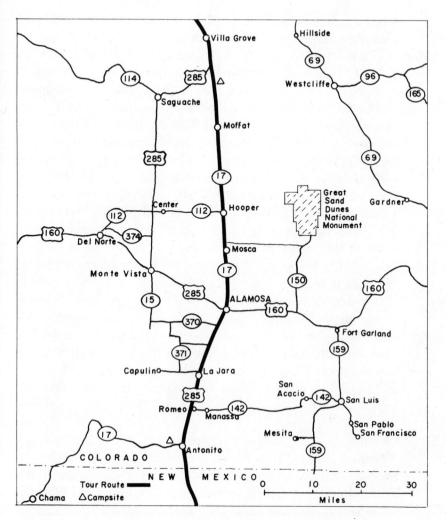

Tour #20 (*Section two: Villa Grove, Colorado, to Antonito, Colorado*)

to the monument is 22 miles off the tour route. There is a campground there. If you decide against the 44-mile round trip into
the monument, continue south to

Alamosa (19 miles; grocery, restaurants, motels, bicycle shop; campground near town on Colo. 160). Alamosa is a large town,
and a good point to resupply. Rejoin U.S. 285 and follow it
south to

La Jara (14 miles; grocery, café, motel). There is a turnoff here to
Pike's Stockade State Historical Monument, where Zebulon
Pike built his stockade before he was arrested by the Spanish
for intrusion into their territory. As you go south, another in-

teresting historical point is Manassa, the hometown of Jack Dempsey, three miles off the tour route.

Antonito (14 miles; grocery, café, motel; campground 5 miles west on Colo. 17). This is an important supply point, since your next real grocery store will be in Taos, 60 miles away, although you will find two cafés in Tres Piedras. Antonito is one of the terminuses for the Cumbres and Toltec Scenic Railroad, constructed in the 1880s to connect the rich mining camps in the area. Excursions are available daily during the summer and early autumn. As you leave Antonito and head south on U.S. 285, you begin a gradual climb with a large, round mountain looming ahead of you—San Antonito Peak (10,908 feet). There are stands of juniper and pine dotting the landscape, particularly on the higher ridges.

Tres Piedras (31 miles; café). You may need to get water and snacks here, as it is 29 miles to Taos. You also leave U.S. 285 at this point. Turn east (left) on U.S. 64 toward Taos. You roll down an undulating valley, past some of the largest cattle spreads in the West, toward the Rio Grande. You cross the river on a marvelous bridge, arching hundreds of feet above the waterway. There is a rest stop before the bridge where you get a good view of it. Water is available there also. Continue southeastward, climbing gradually all the while, until you reach

Taos (29 miles; grocery, restaurants, camping, motels, bicycle shop). Founded in 1617, Taos is rich in Spanish traditions, as well as an even older Native American culture. Today it is an important cultural and artistic center. Streets, houses, and lifestyles all reflect the influences of past ages. Nearby is Taos Pueblo, one of the oldest continuing communities in North America. There are a number of museums in Taos reflecting a lively interest in local art. Leave town via New Mexico 68 to

Ranchos de Taos (3 miles), Junction, N. Mex. 3. Turn south on N. Mex. 3 toward Talpa, passing typical adobe houses reflecting Mexican influence in the area. For the next half-day you will be following one of the earliest roads in the area, laid out by Spanish settlers in the eighteenth century. You have a series of hard climbs in the Sangre de Cristo Mountains, as the roads connecting these old valley settlements are separated by steep ridges. The first climbs 12 miles, beginning from the intersection of N. Mex. 68 and 3. You pass through fragrant sections of juniper and piñon pine, then rise higher into ponderosa

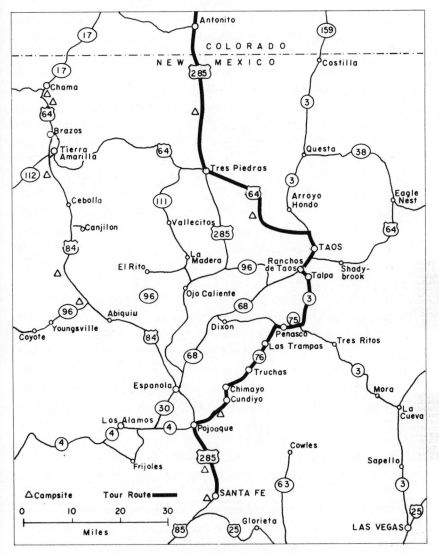

Tour #20   (Section three: Antonito, Colorado, to Santa Fe, New Mexico)

forests. This first climb, which gets you well up into the mountains, is the equivalent of a pass, although it is not marked as
such. You crest at MP 61.5, then descend into a lovely valley
where you reach

Junction, N. Mex. 75 and 3 (16 miles; no services). Turn sharply west
(right) on N. Mex. 75 and go down a narrow valley to

Peñasco (6 miles; grocery, café). Continue on a rolling up-and-down
ride, then another long hill that crests at the National Forest
boundary. From there you run down into another valley to

Las Trampas (6 miles; small cantina). Las Trampas is the site of an old mission church built in 1751 to serve 12 families who came to settle here from Santa Fe. A sign indicates where you can find the caretaker in order to see the church. Leaving Las Trampas you have another climb to

Truchas (8 miles; café), an interesting little town perched on a high ridge overlooking the Rio Grande Valley. From Truchas you begin a 7-mile descent, skipping from ridgetop to ridgetop to the town of

Chimayo (7 miles; grocery, café). Founded in 1720, Chimayo is an important weaving center. You can visit a number of weaving shops in town, where superb examples of this ancient craft are on display. The local weavers, whose families have plied their craft here for many generations, will be happy to discuss their works with you. Leave via the road to

Cundiyo (4 miles; no services) after which you have a final climb in the Sangre de Cristos of about a mile's length. After the summit of this short hill you roll along N. Mex. 4 through rich, reddish landscape deeply eroded by seasonal rains, making your way down to the Rio Grande basin to

Pojoaque (11 miles; grocery, restaurants), Junction, U.S. 285 and N. Mex. 4. There are several important pueblos nearby, including the Nambe, Santa Clara, Pojoaque, and Tesuque. At the little town of Pojoaque, you rejoin U.S. 285, which you have followed on and off from Denver. At this point it is a busy four-lane highway, but has a good riding shoulder. There is one final climb before you reach Santa Fe, cresting near MP 238. Off to your right is the Santa Fe Opera, known for its fine summer opera festival. Continue down into

Santa Fe (28 miles; grocery, restaurants, motels, camping, bicycle shops). Founded in 1610, Santa Fe is the oldest capital in the United States. The Old Palace of the Governors (1610), the San Miguel Mission (1621), the Loretto Chapel, and the Plaza are all among the oldest landmarks in the country. The adobe houses of the city lie mostly hidden among piñon pine and juniper, and downtown Santa Fe is one of the few state capitals still comfortable to explore by bicycle. Santa Fe's charm is very contagious, and you may wish to pass several days here walking the small streets, enjoying its restaurants, mission, plaza, and unique cultural ambiance. For further exploration of the Southwest, see the following chapter.

SUMMARIES OF OTHER ROUTE GUIDES

The popularity of the Mountain States has led to the development of a number of route guides. Below are summaries of some of those routes, along with information on cost and where to order them. For those routes developed by the bicycling organization Bikecentennial, it is a distinct advantage to join the organization, as you save on the cost of their publications. Bikecentennial is also an excellent source for other route guides not summarized here which have been developed by fellow members. These are indexed by state in Appendix 1.

TOUR SUMMARY #7

Title: The Trans America Trail: Coast–Cascades.
Area covered: The Coast–Cascades book covers an area from the Oregon coast to Pueblo, Colorado. The following summarizes that part of the route from the Oregon-Idaho border to Missoula, Montana.
Source: Bikecentennial, P.O. Box 8303, Missoula, Mont. 59807.
Cost: $7.95 members; $10.95 nonmembers.

This section of the Coast–Cascades guide to the Trans America Trail takes the rider from the Oregon-Idaho border across Idaho to Missoula, Montana. For the western section of the Coast–Cascades route see Tour Summary 6.

SUMMARY: Start at Cambridge, Idaho. Leave north on U.S. 95 through New Meadows, White Bird, to Grangeville. From Grangeville leave east via Idaho 13 to Kooskia. Take U.S. 12 from Kooskia northeast along the Selway and Lochsa rivers. Go through Lowell, Lolo Hot Springs, to U.S. 93. Turn north on U.S. 93 and follow to Missoula, Montana. For continuation to Pueblo, Colorado, see Tour Summary 8.

TOUR SUMMARY #8

Title: Trans America Trail: Rocky Mountains.
Area covered: Missoula, Montana, to Pueblo, Colorado.

Source: Bikecentennial (address in Summary 7).
Cost: $7.95 members; $10.95 nonmembers.

The Rocky Mountain guide and book detail the Trans America Trail route through Montana, to Yellowstone and Grand Teton National Parks, through Wyoming and into the upland parks of Colorado to Pueblo. This section of the Trans America Trail is one of the most popular and scenic, with an excellent route through the Rockies. For an alternate route through much of the same territory see our Tours 16 and 19.

SUMMARY: Start at Missoula, Montana. Leave south via U.S. 93 and secondary roads detailed in route guide through Lolo, Florence, to Junction, Mont. 269. Follow it through Stevensville, Corvallis, to Hamilton. Take U.S. 93 south through Darby, Sula, to Junction, Mont. 43. Go east over Lost Trail Pass, Chief Joseph Pass to Wisdom, and Mont. 278. Follow it through Jackson (no services, including water, for next 43 miles) and over Big Hole Pass, Badger Pass, to U.S. 91. Turn north through Dillon, to Twin Bridges. Take Mont. 287 southeast through Sheridan, Laurin, Alder, Nevada City, Virginia City, to Ennis. Leave Ennis on U.S. 287 (do not confuse with Mont. 287) to West Yellowstone. Follow U.S. 287/89 through Yellowstone National Park, Grand Teton National Park, to Moran Junction. Leave east via U.S. 287/26 through Dubois to Lander. Take Wyo. 789 over Beaver Divide, through Sweetwater Station, Jeffrey City, Lamont, to Rawlins. Leave Rawlins on Interstate 80 to Wyo. 130, south to Saratoga, then south to Wyo. 230. Take that to Riverside, Colo., then to Colorado state line then Colo. 125 to Walden. Leave southwest on Colo. 14 to Muddy Pass. Turn south on U.S. 40 to Kremmling. Leave south on Colo. 9 through Silverthorne, Dillon, Breckenridge; cross Hoosier Pass to Fairplay. Leave south on U.S. 285/Colo. 9 to Canyon City and Hartsel (last water and food supply for 50 miles). Take Colo. 115 from Canyon City to Florence. From Florence take Colo. 67 south to Wetmore, then take Colo. 96 east to Colo. 45. Go left on Colo. 45, which becomes Pueblo Blvd. Follow to U.S. 50. Turn right on U.S. 50, ride under I-25 and onto Colo. 47. Follow Colo. 47 to U.S. 50. Go east on U.S. 50 to Pueblo. Detailed route through Pueblo provided. For continuation of Trans America Trail through Colorado to Kansas state line, see following summary.

TOUR SUMMARY #9

Title: Pueblo, Colorado, to Kansas state line segment of Trans America Trail: Plains–Ozarks.
Area covered: Pueblo, Colorado, to Tribune, Kansas. (Guide continues through Kansas and Missouri to Ste. Genevieve, near the Illinois line.)
Source: Bikecentennial (address in Summary 7).
Cost: $7.95 members; $10.95 nonmembers.

The following route summary includes only a small portion of the route found in the Plains–Ozarks guide part of the Trans America Trail—from Pueblo and across the Colorado plains in an easterly direction to the Kansas state line.

SUMMARY: Leave Pueblo (detailed route through city provided) on U.S. 50/Colo. 96, then stay on Colo. 96 after it splits from U.S. 50. Follow to Boone City, Sugar City, Ordway, Arlington, Haswell, Galatea, Eads, Sheridan Lake, Towner, then cross Kansas state line and continue on Kans. 96 to Tribune.

TOUR SUMMARY #10

Title: Great Parks Bicycle Route: Northern Section.
Area covered: Missoula, Montana, through Glacier National Park to Canada. (Rest of guide details routing through Canadian national parks.)
Source: Bikecentennial (address in Summary 7).
Cost: $5.95 members; $8.95 nonmembers.

This route guide is the first of two which detail routes through national parks, both in the U.S. and in Canada. The guides provide three maps which indicate terrain and services available. A separate service directory lists campsites, groceries, restaurants, and bicycle shops.

SUMMARY: Leave Missoula, Montana, via Broadway toward East Missoula and Montana 200. Follow that to Clearwater Junction, then turn north on Mont. 83. Go through Seeley Lake and Swan Lake, to

Mont. 209. Take that north to Bigfork, where you take Mont. 35 to Mont. 82, which you take to Kalispell (detailed route through Kalispell given). Leave Kalispell via Whitefish Stage Rd. and U.S. 93 to Whitefish, then to Mont. 40. Follow that through Columbia Falls to U.S. 2; take that through Glacier National Park to Saint Mary. Leave Saint Mary northward on Mont. 89 through Babb, then to Mont. 17, which take north to Canada. (Guide continues through Canadian national parks.)

TOUR SUMMARY #11

Title: Great Parks Bicycle Route: Southern Section.
Area covered: Steamboat Springs to Durango, Colorado, via Rocky Mountain and Mesa Verde National Parks.
Source: Bikecentennial (address in Summary 7).
Cost: $6.95 members; $8.95 nonmembers.

This is the second of Bikecentennial guides that allow the bicyclist to explore some of the great national parks of the West. The book features three-color maps and a guide that details all services. Information on weather and sights en route is included.

SUMMARY: Leave Steamboat Springs via U.S. 40 over Rabbit Ears Pass, Muddy Pass, to Colo. 14. Turn north to Walden, then from Walden go south on Colo. 125 to Granby. (From here the Bikecentennial route takes you through Rocky Mountain National Park. Our own Tour 19 details the same route—reverse order. The Bikecentennial guide also gives an alternative around the park, which we summarize here.) Leave Granby via U.S. 40 through Tabernash and Winter Park, cross Berthoud Pass, continue to Berthoud, then to I-70/U.S. 6. Use short sections of I-70, then U.S. 6 through Georgetown, over Loveland Pass, to Keystone. Take County Road 1 to Colo. 9. Follow through Breckenridge, over Hoosier Pass, to Alma, to Fairplay. Take U.S. 285 south over Trout Creek Pass to Johnson Village, Nathrop, and into Poncha Springs. (This section from Fairplay to Poncha Springs is detailed in our own Tour 20.) Take U.S. 50 through Maysville and Garfield, over Monarch Pass, down to Parlin, Gunnison, Sapinero, to Montrose. Take Colo. 789 south from Montrose through Ridgeway. Go west on Colo. 62 to Placerville. Turn southeast on Colo. 145 to Colo. 14. Take Colo. 14 over Lizard Head Pass, go through Rico, Stoner, Dolores to Cortez. Turn east on U.S. 160 to Mesa Verde National Park. Continue east on U.S. 160 through Mancos, Hesperus, and into Durango. (At Durango you intersect our Tour 21.)

TOUR SUMMARY #12

Title: Bicycle Colorado: Across-the-Rockies Route.
Area covered: The route follows the I-70 corridor from the Utah-Colorado border into Denver.
Source: Colorado Department of Highways, 4201 East Arkansas Ave., Denver, Colo. 80222.
Cost: Free.

The strip maps developed by the Colorado Department of Highways follow a number of linear routes that have Denver as a common focus. The route summarized here follows the I-70 corridor from near Parachute, Colorado, over the Rockies and into Denver.

SUMMARY: Start Utah state line. Go east on old U.S. 6 to Mack, Loma, to Fruita. Take frontage road along I-70 to Grand Junction. Take I-70 Loop through Clifton, then east on U.S. 6 to I-70 (Exit 44). Ride shoulder of I-70, then U.S. 6 to Parachute. Section of U.S. 6 narrow and dangerous. Use great caution or cover by other means. From Parachute take U.S. 6 east to I-70 at Exit 87. Take I-70 through Canyon Creek to Exit 114—West Glenwood. Exit and follow frontage road to Glenwood Springs. Leave east on 6th Street, ignoring Dead End sign, through opening in fence to bicycle path. Rejoin I-70 to Dotsero, then U.S. 6 through Gypsum, Eagle, Walcott, to Edwards. Take I-70 to Exit 173—West Vail. Leave I-70, follow frontage road to Vail Interchange—176, then via service road on south side of I-70 past Gore Creek Campground. Use Recreation Trail, then up 14-percent grade (!) to Vail Pass. Continue to Colo. 60. Go north to Copper Mountain. Take bicycle path to U.S. 6, which you follow through Frisco, to Colo. 9. Take Colo. 9 and then frontage road past Heaton Bay campground on Dillon Reservoir. Turn right on U.S. 6 to Loveland Pass, go to I-70, which you follow to Bakerville. Take frontage road to Silver Plume, then I-70 through Georgetown. Exit Interchange 233—Lawson, follow service road through Lawson to Idaho Springs. Take bicycle route east to Exit 243—Hidden Valley. Follow I-70 to U.S. 6, to Colo. 40. Follow that to I-70, rejoin I-70 to Exit 254. Rejoin U.S. 40 to Colo. 26. Take that to Denver. (Detailed routing through Denver given.)

TOUR SUMMARY #13

Title: Bicycle Colorado: South Platte Route.
Area covered: Follows the South Platte River from Denver to Nebraska state line.
Source: Colorado Department of Highways (address in Summary 12).
Cost: Free.

This tour takes you through the little-populated regions of eastern Colorado. While scenery is not as spectacular as in the rest of the state, spaces are open and riding is easy.

SUMMARY: Leave Denver by detailed route provided. Take U.S. 85 to Colo. 52. Take that east to Fort Lupton and Hudson. Leave on frontage road paralleling I-76 to Keensburg. Join I-76 to Roggen. Leave on I-76 and use shoulder for 14 miles to Exit 60. Cross under I-76, continue east on frontage road to Exit 64, cross under I-76 and continue east on U.S. 6 to Wiggins. Leave on U.S. 6 for 1 mile, cross I-76 to frontage road, rejoin I-76 to Exit 75, join U.S. 34 to Fort Morgan, then to Junction with U.S. 6. Follow U.S. 6 east to I-76, rejoin I-76 to Exit 95. Leave Interstate, continue on frontage road to U.S. 6 at Hillrose. Continue on U.S. 6 through Merino, Atwood to Sterling. Leave via U.S. 138 toward Proctor, Crook, Ovid, to Julesburg.

TOUR SUMMARY #14

Title: Bicycle Colorado: The Front Range Route.
Area covered: Raton, New Mexico, to Cheyenne, Wyoming.
Source: Colorado Department of Highways (address in Summary 12).
Cost: Free.

The Colorado Front Range Route follows the I-25 corridor from south to north, connecting New Mexico to Wyoming. Although you're not in the mountains, you're never far away; the Rockies lie just to the west of you. Because the route goes through Colorado's most populous region, it's essential to use the strip maps in the guide.

SUMMARY: Leave Raton, New Mexico, on I-25 to Raton Pass, then down to Starkville. Leave I-25, follow frontage road to Trinidad, rejoining Interstate at junction with Colo. 239. Ride shoulder to Exit 27—Ludlow. Take frontage road to Aguilar, rejoin I-25 to Exit 42. Follow frontage road to Walsenburg. Rejoin I-25 at Exit 50, follow through Apache to Cedarwood. Exit, following Verde Rd., then rejoin the Interstate again from Exit 87 to Exit 91. Follow frontage road into Pueblo. Follow signed bicycle route through the city and rejoin I-25 at Exit 104, follow I-25 to Pinon, exit, cross underneath, follow frontage road to Exit 114. Ride Interstate shoulder to Fountain. Leave Interstate here, and follow detailed route around Colorado Springs and Denver. North of Denver, join Colo. 51 to Brighton, then via U.S. 85 to Platteville and to Colo. 60. Turn north on Colo. 60 and follow 5 miles to Co. Rd. 396; take that east to U.S. 34. From this point take specified backroads back to U.S. 85, which you follow through Pierce, Nunn, and Rockport to Wyoming state line and into Cheyenne.

TOUR SUMMARY #15

Title: Bicycle Colorado: Over-the-Plains Route.
Area covered: Denver to Kansas state line near Burlington, Colorado.
Source: Colorado Department of Highways (address in Summary 12).
Cost: Free.

The tour guide uses the I-70 corridor from Denver to Kansas, passing across open prairies. Riding is easy, but may be hot and windy in summer.

SUMMARY: Leave Denver by route detailed, east on U.S. 40 and Tower Rd. Take frontage road of U.S. 40 for 5 miles, cross under I-70 in the suburb of Watkins, which is on U.S. 36. Continue east on U.S. 36 through Bennett to Byers. Take U.S. 40 out of Byers for 23 miles to Agate. Join I-70 for 21 miles to Exit 354—River Bend. Follow U.S. 40 to Limon, then pick up frontage road of I-70 toward a tourist attraction called The Tower. Continue to Genoa. Leave town on frontage road to south of I-70, continue through Arriba, Flagler, and to Seibert. Leave east on U.S. 24 through Vona, Stratton, Burlington, then to Kansas state line.

EIGHT

The Southwest: Arizona, New Mexico, and southern Utah

ARIZONA

The stranger to Arizona is in for some pleasant surprises. Much of the promotional literature from the state emphasizes the Sunbelt cities of Phoenix and Tucson, with their desert locations, abundant sunshine, and year-round golf courses. Much of Arizona is actually high, from 5,000 to 8,000 feet; a good bit of this high country is heavily timbered and could easily be mistaken for parts of northern California or even southern Oregon. And while much of southern Arizona is excellent for winter riding—summer temperatures are too high for most cyclists—at least two-thirds of the state has moderate summertime temperatures and offers excellent touring in June, July, and August.

The scenic parks, monuments, and recreation areas located within Arizona emphasize the wide range of cycling possibilities, with high-elevation areas such as the rim of the Grand Canyon better visited in summer or autumn, while low-lying areas such as Organ Pipe Cactus National Monument or Saguaro National Monument provide excellent wintertime or early-spring touring. Here's a more detailed look at Arizona's topography, climate, and the variety it offers the bicyclist.

TERRAIN

Arizona may be divided into three main topographical areas. In the northeast is a high plateau, with elevations from 5,000 to 7,000 feet.

Cutting this plateau in two parts is the Colorado River. The disparity between the elevation of the plateau and the gorge cut by the Colorado is so great that the river is bridged by highways in only two places—one at Page, near Glen Canyon Dam near the northern border, and the other just a dozen miles downstream at Marble Canyon. For the rest, the Colorado is unassailable until it turns southward below the Grand Canyon to form the boundary between Arizona and its two western neighbors, Nevada and California.

Although the plateau through which the Colorado cuts bears the same name as the river, it has been parceled out into a number of regions, each of which has its own name and character. The region to the north of the Grand Canyon is called the Kaibab Plateau and that to the south is termed the Coconino Plateau. But in spite of these local variations in name and in specific detail, the Colorado Plateau is of a piece geologically, and there is more uniformity to it than there is diversity. Much of it is level and tree-covered. Cyclists on our tour from Zion National Park to Flagstaff (Tour 23) pass through some of this forest cover near the Jacob Lake area. Other visitors traveling to the north rim of the Grand Canyon will get an even greater exposure to it. For the most part this tree cover varies in type and density depending upon elevation. On those parts of the Colorado Plateau between 5,000 and 6,000 feet, there is mostly sagebrush and scattered stands of juniper. At higher elevations are dense forests of piñon pine, then uniform stands of stately ponderosa. Finally, at the very highest locations are intrusions of aspen, their brilliant yellow-and-orange leaves crowning the autumn landscape.

Although the northeast quadrant of Arizona is also a land of high plateaus, its character is considerably different from the Colorado Plateau. Some of this difference is topographical, with less abundant tree cover and more openly exposed dry washes, buttes, and canyons. But much of it is also cultural, as the entire section of the state is part of the Navaho and Hopi Indian Reservations. Streaked with narrow mountain ranges that run southwesterly toward the Little Colorado River, it is a dry land, and although the road network is no more sparse than in other parts of the state, its reservation status has limited the size and number of settlements found there. The Canyon de Chelly National Monument, a rugged, beautiful sandstone canyon located near the New Mexico border, is one of the primary tourist attractions in this part of the state.

The second general topographical area of Arizona consists of a series of mountain ranges running from the southeastern corner toward Flagstaff. These ranges merge with the high Colorado Plateau north of that city. Peaks in these ranges rise to elevations of 12,000 feet or more; Humphrey Peak (12,670 feet), just north of Flagstaff, is the tallest. Although there is a great deal of variety in the peaks that make up this range, they form an important green belt in the state, and a good deal of Arizona's timber reserves are found here. These mountains also supply the water that has made it possible for places such as Phoenix and Tucson to flourish.

Part of this mountainous region is a 200-mile clifflike configuration called the Mogollon Rim. It runs from a point a hundred miles south of Flagstaff in an easterly direction toward New Mexico. Traveling the few roads that actually cross the rim gives the cyclist a steep downhill rush, as elevation is lost very rapidly, and there are decisive changes in vegetation and temperature, as one passes from the cool greenery of the mountains to blast furnace of the desert within a few miles. As long as you stay in the uplands, though, the mountains of this massif provide excellent summer cycling. The area south and southeast of Flagstaff is pocketed with lakes and small streams. In the southeast corner, just outside Tucson, the mountains offer colorful spring and autumn riding, especially parts of the Coronado National Forest, the Chiricahua National Monument, and historic sites such as Tombstone.

The third topographical area of Arizona is the best known—the low-lying desert of the southwest, with Phoenix on its eastern edge. Much of this region is really a continuation of the Sonora Desert of Mexico—the land of the saguaro cactus, the organ pipe cactus, the rolling, seemingly lifeless dunes of sand. But even here one can find breaks in the uniformity of the desert and excellent winter riding. The Gila River runs west through the region, and its waters irrigate cotton fields, nut orchards, and in the area around Yuma, citrus plantations. A few low-lying mountain ranges break the level horizon, but for the most part riding here is easy, as the land slopes toward the Colorado River, which at the southwestern corner of the state has fallen nearly to sea level.

CLIMATE

As you'd expect, climate follows the great geography patterns. The Colorado Plateau, being high, has a relatively moderate summer climate. Daytime average high temperatures at the rim of the Grand Canyon are about 82 degrees in summer, with lows in the low 50s. Flagstaff's summer highs are in the 70s and low 80s.

As you move south and lose elevation, temperatures rise. Average highs in Yuma, in the southwest at an elevation of 141 feet, soar well into the 100s during June, July, and August. September cools off to a relatively temperate 100 degrees! Even in April, highs reach 86. Phoenix, more moderate, lies at about 1,100 feet, but its daytime temperatures are in the 100s all summer long. Tucson, higher still, averages highs of 98 and 99 in June and July, with only an insignificant drop in the months before and after.

What this means for most bicyclists is, stay away in summer. Even native riders usually restrict their summer riding only to the morning hours.

It may seem surprising that the chances of getting rained on during the summer—at least at higher elevations—are pretty good. The afternoon thundershowers that are common throughout the Southwest normally come during July and August. Flagstaff, for example, gets 2.28 and 2.84 inches of rain respectively during these months, with about 11 days each month with measurable rain. Prescott, just to the south, gets 2.29 and 2.99 inches in July and August. Even arid Phoenix gets over an inch of rain in August, and records 5 rainy days. Tucson, in the southeast, gets 2.06 and 2.88 inches during July and August.

The rest of the summer months—and the winter—are normally dry in much of the state. Rainfall in May and June is about half an inch on the average in Flagstaff, and almost nil in Phoenix. Tucson also has very little rain during late spring and early summer.

Winter riding. The payoff comes in the winter climate. Phoenix has average daily highs in the mid-60s to low 70s during the winter months, very little rain, and light winds. Tucson is nearly as ideal, with average highs in the low to mid-60s in December, January, and February, and daily highs of 70 or more from March onward. Winds are light or moderate all winter long. Yuma has average daily highs in the high 60s in December and January, then moderate temperatures up until early May, when it starts getting hot—average high for May is 93 degrees. October and November are mild again in Yuma.

Visitors from snowy climates find this climate close to paradise for winter riding. Nights can get cool, dropping into the high 30s near Tucson, although a bit warmer elsewhere. But other than this minor limitation, and the rather short days during winter, southern Arizona is among the best—if it's not *the* best—winter riding areas in the West.

ROAD NETWORKS AND BICYCLE ROUTE GUIDES

With a sparse population spread over a wide area—much of it desert —Arizona lacks an extensive road network. Paved main roads are evenly spaced throughout the state, but there are definitely few connecting roads. Compounding this problem for the bicyclist is the rapid growth of the Phoenix area, where most roads seem to lead. This places an undue burden on the existing road network, particularly those routes leading to other cities or to popular resorts.

It helps that, with some exceptions, bicyclists are allowed to use shoulders of the Interstates for riding, as long as there is no frontage road or other nearby alternative. In some areas, there's no choice. We covered a good stretch of the southwestern desert by using Interstate 8 between Gila Bend and Yuma, quite a pleasant ride when we took it (in the autumn)—except for "rumble strips" laid across the shoulder to warn motorists when they are drifting off the road. We rode this section sticking a bit out into the traffic lane, dodging in when necessary. Traffic was light enough and visibility good enough that it was no problem. Other cyclists we met highly recommended Interstate 17 between Flagstaff and Phoenix, although for this stretch we preferred a backroad route via Mormon Lake, Happy Jack, and Payson.

In many parts of the state you must be prepared for long stretches with no services, not even water. This is true of much of southern and western Arizona, and it applies to parts of Indian reservations, of which Arizona has more proportionately than any other state. A rule of thumb for most reservation areas, in other Western states as well as Arizona, is that road surfaces deteriorate and supply sources become scarce. Before crossing any of these regions, particularly on state highways and secondary roads, you should inquire about what lies ahead; we've always found it useful to doublecheck the information. Remember that your best source of information is a provider in one place of the service you want later on—each is usually aware of the competition down the road.

In addition to our Tour 23 to the Grand Canyon area, there are two good sources of bicycle route information for Arizona. One is the *Southwest America Bicycle Trail* developed by the YMCA in Amarillo, Texas (available from Bikecentennial; see Appendix 2 for address). The Arizona portion of this route enters the state at Yuma, swings north to Flagstaff, makes a loop to the south rim of the Grand Canyon (which duplicates our route) then cuts through the Navajo and Hopi Reservations on Arizona 264 to Gallup, just over the New

Mexico line. There is one 52-mile stretch of this route east of Tuba City where there is no water or other services available. There are also long stretches through the eastern deserts where this is also true. Details of this route are given in Tour Summary 16.

Bike Tours in Southern Arizona (see Bibliography) is a good source of day trips near Tucson, a number of which can easily be put together to form a longer tour.

Phoenix, Flagstaff, and Tucson have active bicycling communities, and we found that bicycle shops in these cities were good sources of information on both local and long-range rides in the state.

NEW MEXICO

The cultural heritage of New Mexico is among the oldest in the United States, dating back well over a thousand years. Other parts of the country may boast roots as ancient as New Mexico's, but only here do these antecedents so influence everyday life. Traditions from the tribes who settled the mesa tops and cliffs some 1,100 or 1,200 years ago still find expression in fields as diverse as architecture, dress, religion, art, and language.

Mixed nearly inextricably with these earliest cultures is the legacy of Spain, first brought by Coronado in 1540 and cemented in 1610 with the establishment of Santa Fe—now the oldest capital city in the country. Religion, language, architecture, even the physical features of the people and subtle concepts of patronage and loyalty, are traceable to Spanish influence.

In the nineteenth century, when American—or Anglo—frontier influences were added, what resulted was a culturally distinctive land. Visiting New Mexico today may come as close to traveling in a foreign land as we can get without leaving our own.

TERRAIN

New Mexico is high, averaging over 5,700 feet. A series of mountain ranges run from north to south; the highest is the Sangre de Cristo Mountains in the north, just east of Taos and Santa Fe. In the western part of the state, the Continental Divide snakes in a north-south line from Chama in the north to Silver City in the south. Although these mountains along the Divide form the Atlantic-Pacific watershed, and range from 9,000 to 11,000 feet, the Sangre de Cristos are higher, topped by 13,161-foot Wheeler Peak just behind Taos.

The effect of these north-south chains is to fill the western two-thirds of New Mexico with either mountains or high basins. To the east of the Sangre de Cristos, the land is part of the eastern plains, and it slopes downward into Oklahoma and Texas.

The mountains of New Mexico are higher in the north than in the south. You'll ride at about 7,000 feet or higher near Taos or Santa Fe, drop to 5,000 feet at Albuquerque, and approach 3,000 feet in the south near Las Cruces.

Mountain riding in New Mexico is generally not as rigorous as in Colorado. Not only are the elevations lower, but also the general north-south orientation of the mountains creates numerous valleys or highland corridors that allow usable road systems. The longest of these corridors is formed by the Rio Grande, which just divides the state roughly in half.

In its north, the Rio Grande forms a large, rolling valley that has served mankind since prehistoric days. When the Anasazi (a Pueblo word meaning "ancient ones") abandoned their cramped cliff dwellings at Mesa Verde and similar spots, it was to the Santa Fe Valley that many migrated. In the ensuing centuries the permanent settlements became pueblos, many of which still house the descendants of the ancient cliff dwellers. These pueblos liberally dot the Rio Grande Valley, particularly in the area between Taos and Santa Fe. When the Spanish invaders came in the sixteenth and seventeenth centuries, they too settled in the uplands of the Rio Grande, often on the sites of the original pueblos or nearby. The most important of these towns, of course, is Santa Fe.

The low-lying valleys or basins of New Mexico generally have scattered tree cover, usually of juniper and piñon pine. The southern deserts boast an impressive variety of cacti and other low plants. The uplands and mountain slopes are usually covered with ponderosa, aspen, and fir.

Eastern New Mexico shares many characteristics with the plains states. The land is dry, composed primarily of sagebrush or short buffalo grass. A number of rivers drain east and south, the most important being the Canadian, which gathers waters from the eastern slopes of the Sangre de Cristo Mountains and flows eastward into Texas. The Pecos, which rises only a few miles east of Santa Fe, flows southward across desolate land, then past Roswell, Artesia, and Carlsbad.

The combination of the upland forests and the reddish soil and rock gives New Mexico—particularly in the north—an exceptionally warm effect visually. This, in combination with a generally sparse population, a very distinctive culture, and riding that is a bit easier than in some other Western states, make the state a haven for the bicyclist. The fact that these merits are relatively undiscovered adds zest to the equation.

CLIMATE

New Mexico's climate reflects its latitude, altitude, and distance from both Pacific and Gulf of Mexico storm systems. During the summer, most of the moisture comes from warm air currents carried up from the Gulf. In July and August particularly, they are lifted rapidly upward and result in brief, but often intense, thundershowers. The amount of rain that falls varies with the elevation and the exposure of the land to the incoming air. Santa Fe averages 2.19 inches of rain in July and 2.27 inches in August. Portales, in east-central New Mexico, gets 2.91 and 2.66 inches. Even relatively dry Albuquerque, at 5,000 feet, gets 1.20 and 1.33 inches during July and August, and has nine days each month with measurable precipitation. Clayton, in the northeast, is something of a thunderstorm capital, with an average of seventy such storms recorded each year—the second highest rate in the entire country.

Although these thunderstorms do not by any means make New Mexico a "wet" state, they do provide enough moisture to support abundant tree cover on the upper slopes, and they also serve to cut average daytime temperatures during what would otherwise be the hottest months of the year. In Albuquerque, for instance, August is even a bit cooler than June—a pattern common to many parts of the state.

The farther south you go in New Mexico, the warmer and drier it becomes, due to both lower elevations and lower latitudes. Stations such as Carlsbad Caverns report summer daytime highs well into the 90s. Deming, in the southwest, is even warmer.

But overall, the high elevations of New Mexico prevent it from being an oven like the lower Arizona desert or the arid valleys of southern California. Even in the south, average daytime highs stay below 100. In the north, typical highs will be in the 80s and low 90s, with nights cooling off enough for comfortable sleeping, usually to the mid 50s or low 60s.

ROAD NETWORKS AND BICYCLE ROUTE GUIDES

Because New Mexico's population is sparse and there are no big cities nearby, the road network is not extensive, and paving is often mediocre.

About 30 percent of the state's population lives in Albuquerque, and the most highly developed road network fans out northward in a V shape from here. Many of these routes are very old, some easily predating the Spanish period. Of the many roads cut up into the Sangre de Cristo Mountains, some were developed by early Spanish settlers colonizing the small, green mountain valleys, and others were built to carry the gold, silver, and coal from later mines. Almost all of these roads provide quiet although sometimes challenging cycling.

In eastern and southern New Mexico, roads and towns are generally rarer; the cyclist venturing into these regions must ask ahead about services and water sources.

One disturbing factor about many of New Mexico's roads is the incredible amount of litter and glass lying on the shoulders or nearby —broken beer bottles approach epidemic proportions. People we talked to blamed the problem variously on youthful enthusiasm, cultural traits, and visiting Texans. Whatever the case, you must constantly be on the lookout for glass litter; it transcends annoyance to become a hazard on many of New Mexico's roads.

Relatively few route guides for New Mexico have so far been developed. Active cycling groups in both Santa Fe and Albuquerque can give you a wealth of detail on possible backroad routes, and a well-known "century" (100-mile) ride that winds around Wheeler Peak north of Taos each year. Details of this ride are given in the American Bike Atlas and Touring Guide (see Bibliography). The Southwest America Bicycle Route (see Tour Summary 16) cuts across northern New Mexico, entering the state near Gallup, following old U.S. 66 to Albuquerque, then swinging north to Santa Fe, and from there going easterly through Las Vegas and Tucumcari into Texas.

Our own New Mexico tours are concentrated in the north, the one coming down from Denver to Santa Fe (Tour 20), the other leaving Santa Fe and working northwestward across the Colorado border south of Pagosa Springs to Mesa Verde (Tour 21).

SOUTHERN UTAH

The area of Utah lying south of Interstate 70 and U.S. 50 is one of the most astounding concentrations of incredible vistas found in the West. Within a 200-mile radius are found five great national parks, three national monuments, two primitive areas, a vast national recreation area, and a dozen or more state parks, historic sites, and scenic areas. No other part of the country can boast such a collection in such a limited space.

In spite of the tremendous scenic richness and the considerable popularity of two of the national parks—Zion and Bryce Canyon— southern Utah remains relatively little visited and unknown.

For the cyclist, it may present the opportunity of a lifetime. Although there are challenges to cycling here—summer heat and distance between supply points being the two greatest—the rewards are great. Most roads are quiet. And although road choice is limited, the network that does exist will take you to or through the best scenery. Southern Utah isn't green (although there are some sizable forest areas), but it yields nearly every other color you could imagine, from plain sandstone bluffs near Blanding to the rich pastel-and-blood-red layer cake of Bryce Canyon.

To explore it, you need to fasten another water bottle or two to your bicycle, make sure you know where the next grocery store is, then start out on an intensely concentrated display of color.

TERRAIN

The southern half of Utah can be divided into three roughly equal parts. In the west, the Great Basin continues over from Nevada. It is a flat land, extremely arid, with a few roads and no towns of any size. Occasionally breaking the surface of the basin are dusk-brown mountain ranges, for the most part devoid of vegetation.

East of this desert area, running northeasterly from near Saint George and Cedar City, are a series of mountain ranges, low hills, and high plateaus. Zion and Bryce parks are in the southern end of this massif. North of these parks are some high peaks, some above 12,000 feet. Throughout most of this massif, the upper slopes are covered with trees and the valleys carry year-round streams. In most places, irrigated farms or grazing lands dot the landscape.

To the east of these ranges, lying in their rain shadow, is a wide swath of low plateaus and ridges, the former often deeply cut by occasional streams or year-round rivers. The most important of these are the Green and Colorado Rivers, which join in this area and run southwest toward the Grand Canyon. The Colorado has been dammed just below the Utah-Arizona line, and the resulting Lake Powell spreads a number of long fingers northward. Much of the land surrounding the lake is part of Glen Canyon National Recreation Area. While these rivers and lakes do not provide lush greenery, they do break the rather constant display of rock and offer excellent recreational opportunities.

Given the orientation of the streams and mountain ranges, the cyclist crossing southern Utah on an east-west axis will do a lot of climbing. Roads tend to dip down into canyons or washes, then climb the other side. Roads cutting through the central mountainous region culminate in passes as high as 9,000 feet. But cycling is not as difficult here as the description may at first indicate. Most climbs are short, and even the long ones in the mountains tend to roll upward rather than climb sharply.

For a cyclist heading south or north, riding is generally easier, as roads often follow valleys or plateaus. Many of the roads follow washes where the water has gradually cut through ten or twelve geological ages. It is often on these roads, largely unknown, that the rider is exposed to the greatest treats of color and shape. Our tour from Mesa Verde National Park to Zion National Park (Tour 22) makes use of some of these routes, and we describe the landscape in more detail in the tour guide.

CLIMATE

Except for some of the highest mountain ranges, all of southern Utah is arid or semi-arid. Zion National Park, in the southwest, receives less than an inch of rain in June and July (0.58 and 0.86); during the thunderstorm season in August and September, averages climb to just over an inch per month. St. George, at the very southwestern corner, is lower and drier; August, its rainiest summer month, averages 0.67 inches of rain. Blanding, in the southeast, gets 1.24 inches and 1.47 inches in August and September, but less than an inch during the other summer months. Loa, in south-central Utah at about 7,000 feet, gets only 1.15 and 1.33 inches of rain in July and August, and about half of an inch during the other summer months.

Temperatures vary with elevation. Saint George, just under 3,000 feet, has average highs in July and August in the mid-90s. Loa, at

7,000 feet, has averages in the mid-80s. Because of the low humidity, nights cool off considerably, particularly in the higher areas. We experienced hard freezes when camping just above Loa in mid-September.

Except in early spring, winds are not high in southern Utah. Wind direction is primarily westerly, but this varies greatly, depending upon local topography.

ROAD NETWORKS AND BICYCLE ROUTE GUIDES

Except in the range of mountains running from near Saint George, the road network in southern Utah is not extensive. U.S. 89 makes its way southward through the mountains by using the Sevier River valley. There is a good shoulder on much of this road, but traffic is heavy, particularly in summer. A number of state and county roads parallel U.S. 89, and these offer better riding conditions.

In the eastern portion of southern Utah, there is only one through road that crosses the Colorado, and that is Utah 95. It is an excellent road, although services are sparse. In the arid westernmost portions of the state, there are only a few roads, and these too have few services available.

The only published route guide for southern Utah is the one found in this book (Tour 22), which takes you from Mesa Verde in southwestern Colorado to Natural Bridges National Monument, crosses Lake Powell to Capitol Reef National Park, then brings the rider southward to Bryce Canyon and Zion National Parks ending in Saint George. If you prefer, you can connect at Zion National Park with our Grand Canyon tour (Tour 23), which takes you out of Utah, loops around to the south rim of the canyon, then ends in Flagstaff.

ROUTE GUIDES

TOUR #21: SANTA FE—RIO CHAMA—
MESA VERDE NATIONAL PARK

Distance: 256 miles.
Terrain: Moderate climbs in New Mexico, hard climbs in Colorado.
Roads and Traffic: Light traffic through most of New Mexico, moderate traffic in Colorado.

Season: May to mid-October.

Weather: Generally dry, although chances of afternoon thundershowers in July and August. Moderate temperatures and winds.

Special Features: Considerable variety in color and terrain as one passes from the red earth and gorges of New Mexico to the green wooded slopes of the southern Rockies. Along the way, the rider is continually exposed to the three disparate cultural strains that make up the Southwest—Indian, Spanish, and Anglo.

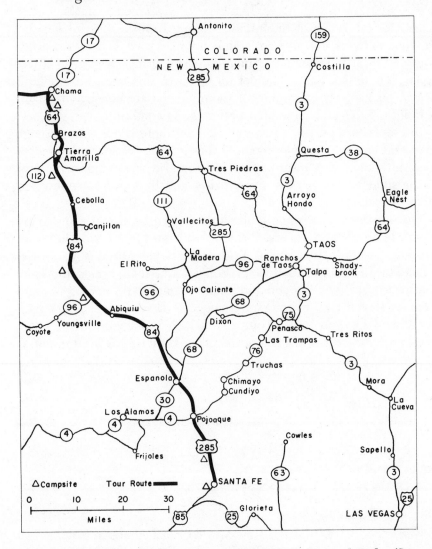

Tour #21 Santa Fe—Rio Chama—Mesa Verde National Park (Section one: Santa Fe to Chama, New Mexico)

Connecting Transportation:
        Santa Fe: Amtrak, Greyhound, Trailways.
        Cortez (near Mesa Verde): Trailways, air service.

The tour from Santa Fe to Mesa Verde is in many ways a voyage back through time. Santa Fe, a modern, thriving city, is also the oldest capital in the United States. It is a visually and culturally pleasing place, with an easy mixture of Indian, Spanish, and Anglo cultures. Of the three, the Spanish predominates, and you will no doubt want to visit the San Miguel Mission, the Loretto Chapel, the Saint Francis Cathedral, the shaded plaza, and the Palace of the Governors—all of which give a strong representation of the Spanish period that began in Santa Fe in the early seventeenth century.

Traveling north, you move even further back in time. Some of New Mexico's most important pueblos are on or near the tour route—the Nambe, Santa Clara, and San Juan to name just a few. It was places such as these that lured the first Spanish invaders, who came looking for gold and found a highly developed indigenous culture instead.

As you pass into Colorado, time takes a jog, as you pass through the nineteenth-century mining and smelter town of Durango, part of the frontier past but today a thriving, modern city which has carefully preserved some of the better remnants of the nineteenth century's architecture and ambiance.

The tour terminates among the oldest habitations found in the Southwest, the ingeniously constructed cliff dwellings at Mesa Verde. Stacked carefully inside the yawning mouths of shallow caves are the houses of a people who built, maintained, then mysteriously abandoned their carefully crafted homesites. The park takes easily a day to explore, and much more time than this could be spent on the mesa top so rich in remnants of a vanished culture. From Mesa Verde it is a short 10-mile ride to the end of the tour at Cortez, where all modern services are available, and from which connections may be made for other tours through the Southwest or the Rockies.

Santa Fe (grocery, restaurants, motels, camping, bicycle shops). Leave town north via U.S. 285, a busy four-lane highway with a wide shoulder. (Alternative route: Cyclists wishing a quieter although more rigorous beginning to the tour may reverse the latter stages of our Tour 20: Denver to Santa Fe. This takes you up into the Sangre de Cristo Mountains to Taos, then across the Rio Grande Valley to Tres Piedras. From here leave the tour route via U.S. 64 to Tierra Amarilla, where you intersect the present tour.) Riders leaving Santa Fe via U.S. 285 will note the Santa Fe Opera on your left, just at the city limits. From here you begin a long downgrade to the Rio Grande basin, then continue on a gently rolling ride to

Española (25 miles; grocery, motel, restaurants), an old town whose roots go back to Spanish times. Nearby is the San Juan Pueblo. You leave Española via U.S. 84, which follows the Rio Chama, a tributary of the Rio Grande, northward. Local farmers grow chili peppers in the valley and sell them at numerous road-side stalls in late summer and early fall. U.S. 84 has a wide shoulder for about 14 miles beyond Española. After that the shoulder is narrow or nonexistent, and caution is needed for the next 15 miles. When you pass Abiquiu Dam, you regain the shoulder and traffic thins out considerably. The road up the Rio Chama is a gentle, easy ride to

Abiquiu (22 miles; grocery). At the site of an abandoned pueblo, Abiquiu was resettled by the Spanish, who made it a haven for hostages rescued from Comanche and Apache tribes. In 1830 it became a stop on the Spanish Trail. From Abiquiu you begin a climb out of the valley to a hillcrest at Milepost 289, where you overlook the Abiquiu Dam. You have a nice down-hill run for about a mile through beautiful red-rock formations, then cross a broad valley, after which you begin another gentle climb through even more colorful rock formations, hues rang-ing from russets to deep, chocolate browns. Water is available at the Ghost Ranch Visitors' Center and at Echo Amphitheater National Forest campground. If you stop at the latter, walk back on guided trails to the amphitheater, a natural rock for-mation that will bounce even the most subtle noise back at you. Beyond the campground the climb steepens a bit, finally cresting at MP 309. From here you have excellent views of typical New Mexico mesas, and farther off to the north you can see the Colorado Rockies. Continue on a rolling ride to

Cebolla (31 miles; grocery). From here the road continues to roll, although climbs are not difficult. Just above Tierra Amarilla you begin a steep descent. To get to the town, take New Mex-ico 162, which branches off to the right about halfway down the hill. Follow 162 into

Tierra Amarilla (13 miles; grocery, café, motel). At one point this entire valley was covered in dense ponderosa pine forests. These were systematically cut down, much of the lumber go-ing to Denver for use in house construction. Tierra Amarilla bears the signs of a place that has seen more prosperous days. The valley is now used mainly for grazing. Leave via N. Mex. 162 for a mile or so until you rejoin U.S. 84, which has been joined by U.S. 64. Ride north through a pretty valley cut by the Rio Chama to

Chama (13 miles; grocery, restaurants, motels, camping). This is a popular fishing resort and a gateway into the mountains separating New Mexico and Colorado. It is also the terminus for the Cumbres and Toltec Scenic Railway, on which you may take day excursions if you wish. At Chama you turn west (left) on U.S. 84 and 64. You begin a gradual, rolling ride that takes you upward to an easy crossing of the Continental Divide (unmarked), about 7 miles from town. Tree cover, which has been sparse up to this point in the tour, increases in density, although it's still limited to the upper slopes away from the road. Continue west on to

Junction, U.S. 84 and 64 (13 miles; café). Turn north (right) on U.S. 84 toward Chromo, Colorado. You begin a rolling climb to-

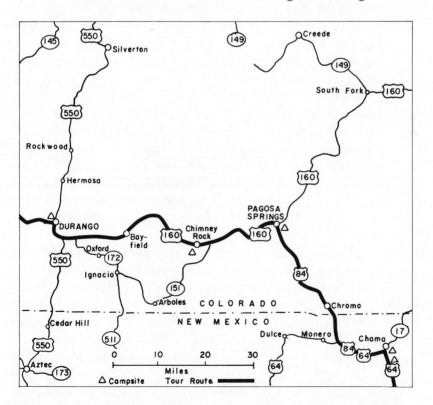

Tour #21   (Section two: Chama, New Mexico, to Durango, Colorado)

ward the Colorado state line. The farther north you go, the more the topography and the plant life change. You leave behind the mesas that characterize New Mexico terrain and move toward the tree-covered slopes and mountains of the Rockies. Continue over the state line, where you pick up a good riding shoulder, and begin a 4-mile downhill run that ends in

Chromo (11 miles; grocery, café, motel). As you leave town you begin a 4-mile climb that crests at MP 8. The ride from the hillcrest into Pagosa Springs rolls, but there are two short, steep climbs, each less than a mile in length. You are primarily in ponderosa forest, but with some blue spruce seen on the upper slopes. Ahead of you lie the Rockies. About 7 miles from Pagosa Springs you open up onto a nice horse-ranching meadow, with a panoramic view of the Rockies. A long downgrade carries you to

Pagosa Springs (24 miles; grocery, restaurants, camping, motels), an active little town with a hot springs. Turn west (left) on U.S. 160 toward Durango. As you leave town you have a hard 2-mile climb. The road is crowded for the first several miles, much of the traffic related to the development boom taking place to the west of town. About 5 miles from Pagosa Springs a good shoulder develops, and the road has been recently repaved. Services are scarce for the next 41 miles. You'll find a restaurant, minimal grocery store, and camping at Chimney Rock, and a fairly well-stocked grocery at the unmarked town of Piedra (near MP 121). Beyond that, there are only a few private campgrounds. The road crosses a series of small streams flowing down from the Rockies, and you have some climbing in and out of the resulting valleys. One of these climbs is 7 miles long, and begins as you leave Piedra. You crest at MP 114, then descend through nicely timbered country to

Bayfield (41 miles; grocery, café). The ride from here into Durango is a pleasant one, with sagebrush-covered valleys interspersed with ponderosa forests. Traffic picks up the closer you get to

Durango (17 miles; grocery, restaurants, motels, camping, bicycle shops). A lovely old mining town, currently enjoying a commercial and touristic revival. Leave west on U.S. 160. Just outside of town you begin a long climb up out of the Animas River valley. This climb is 10 miles long, the last 3.5 of which are very hard. The climb crests at MP 73.5, and has all the earmarks of a mountain pass, although it is not marked as such.

Continue on a rolling road with one additional hard 1.5-mile climb to MP 61.5. From here you descend through scrub-oak forests down into the valley town of

Mancos (28 miles; grocery, café, motels, camping). From here you get a good view of Mesa Verde, ahead of you and just off to the left. The cliff dwellings are on the far side. Begin a gradual climb toward the mesa and the entrance to

Mesa Verde National Park (8 miles; grocery, motel, restaurant, camping). To visit the cliff dwellings you must turn off the main road and begin a long, hard climb. The top of the mesa rests some 1,600 feet above the valley floor. Morefield Campground (grocery) is the only approved camping site within the park, although there are a number of private campgrounds near the entrance. If you are camping, you will probably want to stay either at the private sites or at Morefield, as the combination

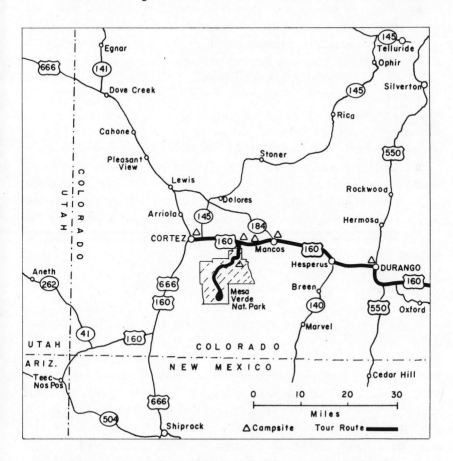

Tour #21   (Section three: Durango, Colorado, to Cortez, Colorado)

of stiff climbs and things to see will easily occupy a day. Cyclists not wishing to make the climb may go via bus out of Cortez. To get there, retrace your route to U.S. 160 then continue west (left) on a long downhill run into

Cortez (10 miles; grocery, restaurants, motels, camping). This is a pleasant town in an agricultural region. It draws much of its support from visitors to Mesa Verde, one of the most popular national parks in the country.

TOUR #22: FOUR NATIONAL PARKS: MESA VERDE, CAPITOL REEF, BRYCE CANYON, AND ZION

Distance: 543 miles.

Terrain: Most of the tour route is only moderately difficult, but there are steep climbs in or around nearly all the national parks and monuments. Stores and other facilities are also spaced out, and often offer only minimal supplies. Because of this we recommend this tour only for experienced cycle tourists or persons traveling with experienced riders.

Roads and Traffic: Light for most of the tour, some heavy traffic in the popular parks.

Season: May to October.

Weather: Mostly dry. Windy in spring. Hot weather and some thundershowers in July and August. Excellent autumn weather.

Special Features: The cyclist has the opportunity to visit four of the most colorful national parks, one national recreation area, and one national monument. Rewards of color outweigh long distances and scarce facilities.

Connecting Transportation:
Cortez: Trailways, air service.
Saint George: Greyhound, Trailways, air service.

In many ways the land traversed by this tour is among the least known in the West—which is something of an anomaly, as some of our most spectacular national parks are located here. The tour begins in Cortez, Colorado, just outside Mesa Verde National Park. After visiting Mesa Verde, you take a long swing across southern Utah, crossing almost the entire southern end of that state. Although you are often isolated, nearly every day you will cross through or visit some park, monument, or scenic area. All of these have a particularly Southwestern character, with the emphasis on color. Certainly the highlights in this respect are Bryce Canyon and Zion National Parks, where you come into intimate contact with what may represent the essence of Southwest geology—225 million years of rock formation laid bare by erosion. To the visitor from greener climes, the effect is unforgettable.

This is the longest tour in this volume. Although its physical demands are not as great as those of some other tours—such as those in the high Rockies, for instance—it does demand that you be independent-minded and willing to improvise. There are enough way stations along the route so that water and other necessities are available, but careful planning is needed to avoid getting stuck. If you're new to the Southwest, review Chapters 4 and 5 on conditions and

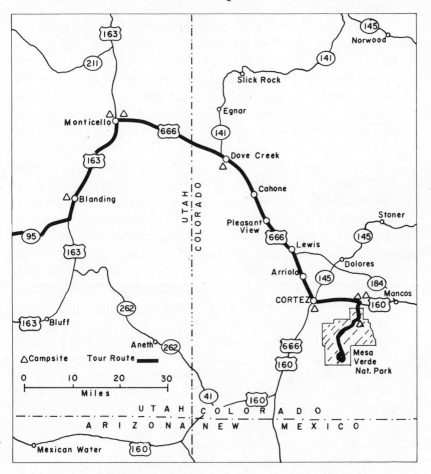

Tour #22   Four National Parks: Mesa Verde, Capitol Reef, Bryce Canyon, Zion (Section one: Cortez, Colorado, to Blanding, Utah)

equipment—particularly on the need for carrying reserves of food and water. Although in reality help is never far away if you really need it, most riders will find part of the enjoyment of the trip is in demonstrating their ability to manage—and sometimes nurse—the supplies and equipment they have on board.

Cortez, Colorado (grocery, restaurants, motels, camping) is an agricultural town, but also important as the gateway to Mesa Verde. To visit the park, leave Cortez east on U.S. 160 to

Mesa Verde National Park (10 miles; grocery, restaurant, motel, camping). The mesa top is nearly 1,600 feet above you, and the climb is hard. (For details on visiting the park see Tour 21.) Most cyclists will prefer to stay in or near the park, as it is a day's effort to explore it. Return via U.S. 160 to

Cortez (10 miles; grocery, restaurants, motels, camping). Leave town toward Monticello, Utah, on U.S. 666, a wide two-lane highway with a good riding shoulder. The first part of this stretch takes you through rolling dry farm country, which bills itself as the pinto-bean capital of the world. There may be merit in this claim, as the beans plants can be seen far and wide, as well as a scattering of beans along the road that have escaped from hauling wagons. There are two small agricultural settlements along the first part of the route where supplies may be purchased, Arriola (grocery) and Dove Creek (grocery, camping). Continue across the Utah state line and along rolling country interspersed with stands of juniper to

Monticello (60 miles; grocery, restaurants, motels, camping). There is a town park where you may picnic. At Monticello you turn south on U.S. 163. As you head toward Blanding, the terrain changes. While there is some farming and ranching around Monticello, the land soon gives way to the dry arroyos and crude rock bluffs most typical of southern Utah. These arroyos and canyons must be crossed, and some of the descents and ascents are steep, as you will discover in the next few days. The first of these occurs about 7 miles before Blanding, when after a gentle downgrade, you have a steep 2-mile descent into the basin cut by Johnson Creek. There is then a short run into

Blanding (21 miles; grocery, restaurants, motels, camping). There is a small state historical museum here. Blanding is an important supply center, as there are only two small grocery stores (Fry Canyon and Hite Marina) in the next 80 miles, and only three places to get water (Natural Bridges National Monument, Fry, and Hite). Only the store at Hite Marina on Lake Powell has a substantial supply of groceries. Leave Blanding south on U.S. 163 to

Junction, Utah 95 and U.S. 163 (4 miles). Turn west (right) on Utah 95. Here you begin one of the lovelier parts of the tour, going down first through deeply cut gorges, then past smooth-walled sandstone bluffs, utterly devoid of plant life. Off in the distance are contrasting russet mesas. Ten miles after the turnoff onto Utah 95, you descend into the Comb River Canyon, where you pass a few groves of cottonwood trees whose roots drink eagerly from the water flowing intermittently past. You

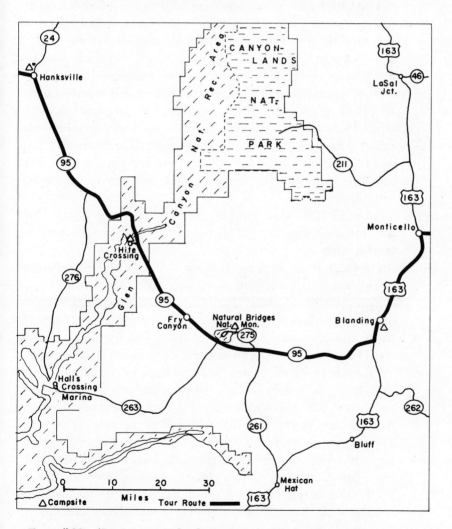

Tour #22 (Section two: Blanding, Utah, to Hanksville, Utah)

then have a hard 9.5-mile climb out of the canyon, the first 4.5 miles of which are the most difficult. The crest is at Milepost 97. From this point you have spectacular views of the country around you, including formations representative of everything you will find in the Southwest—high mesas, mountains, deep-cut valleys, and an astounding array of color. Off to the left of the road are some balancing rocks—as if to complete the picture. From this highpoint you have a gradual downhill run that lasts—with a few exceptions—until you reach Lake Powell. Two miles beyond the junction of Utah 261 you reach

Natural Bridges National Monument (33 miles; camping, water). The campground and monument headquarters are 5 miles off the tour route on Utah 275. Within a relatively small space are clustered three of the West's most spectacular natural bridges. They vary in height from 106 to 220 feet, and span distances of up to 268 feet. There are also some Anasazi cliff dwellings within the monument boundaries. The paved road follows a 13-mile loop. After visiting the monument continue west on Utah 95 down White Canyon, where you will see some interesting rock formations off to your right. The most prominent of these is the Cheesebox—a rectangular monolith. Beyond that are high mountains with peaks well above timberline. Continue to

Fry Canyon Store (20 miles; grocery, motel). You can get water here and minimal supplies. Continue down White Canyon to a turnoff for

Hite Marina (22 miles; camping, grocery, cabins). The grocery store is well supplied, including meat, fresh milk, and bread. Round trip to the store is about 3 miles. If you do not need supplies, continue northwest on Utah 95 to a crossing of the Colorado River, slowed nearly to a stop at this point by the Glen Canyon Dam. You then skirt another arm of the lake, this formed by the Dirty Devil River, pass under some disconcertingly close rock cliffs, then begin a 1-mile climb up out of the canyon (crest MP 41). From here the climb is a gradual one up North Wash. A small rivulet runs off to the side of the road. The gradual erosion of the rock, which took the small stream some 100 million years to accomplish, has revealed nine separate geological ages. As you clear the upper reaches of North Wash, the deep reddish sandstone gives way to a lighter-colored rock. Beyond the intersection with Utah 276 the ter-

rain rolls, and colors are much less striking. Continue on Utah
95 to
Hanksville (49 miles; grocery, restaurant, motel). This is another important supply point for you, although the next stretch is not
nearly as long as the one you have just traversed. You leave
Hanksville west on Utah 24 along the Fremont River, past
farms where, with considerable effort, the land is being con-
verted to pasture and some crops are being raised. Other than
these few farms, the first 20 miles outside Hanksville are
through nearly moonlike landscape, harshly eroded, and bereft

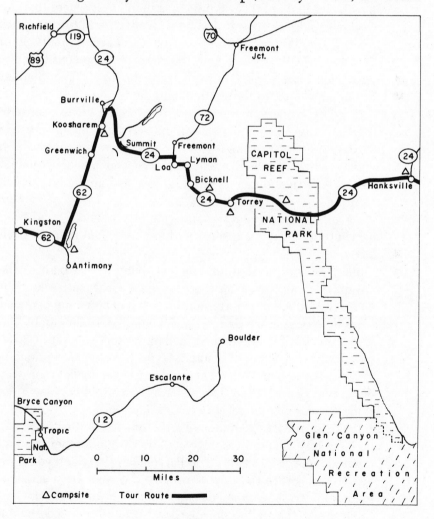

Tour #22   (Section three: Hanksville, Utah, to Kingston, Utah)

of plant life. You also have a number of short climbs as you leave, then return to, the Fremont River valley. The severity of the landscape changes as you draw close to

Capitol Reef National Park (28 miles; camping near the Visitors' Center). One of the newest national parks, it draws its name from the domed formations capped with white sandstone that resemble man-made structures. But there is considerable variety beyond this, including fantastic spires, sheer fluted cliffs, and intricate sculptured rock formations that resemble gargoyles on ancient cathedrals. The 15-mile ride through the park is mostly gradual uphill. You pass by a number of places that are easy to explore on foot, including a lovely natural bridge. After passing the Visitors' Center, you have a hard 1.5-mile climb (crest at MP 77.5). From here the vistas open up considerably, with mesas set back far away from the road. The Boulder Mountains lie off to the south. Continue to

Torrey (23 miles; grocery, motel), a pretty Mormon town located in a green valley. The houses are of cut red stone taken from the surrounding area. From Torrey the ride is gradual across high valleys where, through much diligence and use of mountain waters for irrigation, grass crops, grains, and alfalfa are grown. Continue to

Bicknell (8 miles; grocery, restaurant, motel), a fairly good-sized agricultural town lying on a wide valley. Continue on Utah 24 to

Loa (7 miles; grocery, restaurants, motel), lying at the base of the Awapa Plateau. Loa boasts an excellent local cheese factory, and natural-food stores from around the country import meat from here. Leave on Utah 24 and begin a 13-mile climb (the first 4 miles are hard, the rest moderate) to a summit at 8,385 feet (MP 41). From the summit you have an exceptionally steep descent over 8-percent grades as you make your way down into Grass Valley. There is a rest area midway down the slope where you can get water. Continue to

Junction, Utah 62 and 24 (23 miles). Turn south (left) toward Kanab on Utah 62. You are in a pretty valley, with a number of small towns on its western flank. The Parker Range (which you have just crossed) is to the east of you. To the west are a series of mountains, with Monroe Peak, at 11,226 feet, the highest. Continue down the valley on an easy turn through Koosharem (grocery, café, motel, camping) and Greenwich (no services), and past Otter Creek Reservoir (camping). There the road takes a sharp right turn and heads down the East Fork of the Sevier River past Kingston to

Junction, U.S. 89 and Utah 62 (44 miles). Head south (left) on U.S. 89—a busy highway, but one with a good riding shoulder for this stretch. Continue to

Circleville (4 miles; grocery, restaurant, motel). Butch Cassidy, who must have had nine lives in order to appear in so many parts

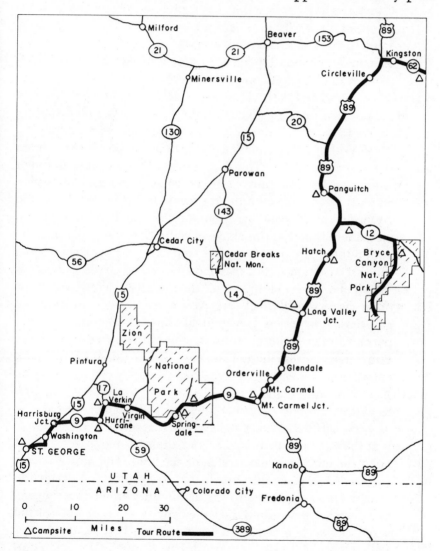

Tour #22   (Section four: Kingston, Utah, to St. George, Utah)

of the West, grew up here. Continue south, using a wide shoulder on U.S. 89. You make your way up along the Sevier River through a narrowing canyon to

Panguitch (29 miles; grocery, restaurants, motels, camping). This is a thriving town on the route to Bryce Canyon National Park. Follow U.S. 89 south out of town on an easy uphill ride to

Junction, Utah 12 and U.S. 89 (8 miles). Turn east (left) toward Bryce Canyon. You begin a very pretty ride up through Red Canyon, which is something of a prelude to the unparalleled colors of Bryce itself. There are a number of campgrounds, small stores, cafés, and motels on the way to the park entrance. The initial climb is 9 miles in length (crest MP 9), from which point you roll over an open plateau to

Bryce Canyon National Park (17 miles; motel, camping). While every national park has its advocates, there is probably no disputing the supremacy of Bryce Canyon in terms of color and shape. Most written descriptions cannot hint at the park's effect upon the first-time visitor. The first surprise may be that although it appears to be a canyon, Bryce is really a series of twelve amphitheaters carved into the pink limestone edge of the Paunsaugunt Plateau by tributaries of the Paria River; you view them from the rim above. The brilliancy of color and the variety of shape in the eroded stone is nearly surreal. While the first Mormon settler may have described Bryce Canyon as "a hell of a place to lose a cow," the bicyclist—along with most other visitors—will likely regard it as an overwhelming visual and sensual experience. A gradual climb of 18 miles from the park's entrance brings you to the end of the paved road at the Promontory. From here you must double back to the park entrance and then back down Utah 12 to

Junction, U.S. 89 and Utah 12 (17 miles). Turn south (left) on U.S. 89 and go through the small towns of Hatch (camping, motel, grocery, café) and Long Valley Junction (grocery). The latter is at the intersection of U.S. 89 and Utah 14, and is also a highpoint for this particular stretch of the road. The next 23 miles is a pleasant downhill stretch that lasts until you reach the turnoff for Zion National Park at Mount Carmel Junction. As you descend deeper into the valley cut by the East Fork of the Virgin River, the terrain is greener than that of the Sevier Valley that you followed upward. Pass through Glendale (grocery, motel) and continue on down the valley to

Orderville (39 miles; grocery, restaurants, motels), formed by Mormon settlers as a communal farming operation. It is a good point to buy groceries or make other supply stops, as the towns between here and Zion are small. Continue through Mount Carmel (motel) to

Mount Carmel Junction (5 miles; grocery, café, motel). Here you turn west on Utah 9 and begin an 8.5-mile climb up to a high-point above Zion National Park. The first 2 miles of this climb are hard, then it becomes more gradual, although it is continuously uphill to a crest at MP 47.5. About 2 miles beyond that crest you get your first views of the russet and gray stone of

Zion National Park (24 miles; grocery, café, camping; motels are at or near Springdale). This is one of the most exciting bicycle rides in the West, and is most likely the only national park that can be seen without turning a pedal—assuming you follow the tour route as given here. You plunge into rock canyons scoured by erosion. Colors vary, depending upon which tint the sandstone assumed. The road, reflecting the red hues of the rock, winds down near the riverbed of the East Fork of the Virgin River. Although the run through Zion is exhilarating, you should pause to view some of the formations in more detail and to read the instructive plaques placed along the roadside.

The only hitch to seeing Zion is a very long tunnel that you must go through with a park ranger driving behind you. To make arrangements, stop at the ranger station as you enter the park. On our crossing, which was in September, we were unable to locate a ranger and hailed a friendly motorist who rode behind us. Stay away from the right edge of the roadway, as there is glass and other debris that could give you a flat— about the last thing on earth you'd want here. (Cyclists going west to east are advised not to try bicycling through the tunnel, as there is a continual uphill grade that will make progress slow. Usually rides can be hitched with campers or other vehicles through this section.) Beyond the tunnel are a series of heartcatching switchbacks that you are advised to take slowly. A short distance behind the last of these you arrive at the Visitors' Center (camping nearby, and groceries just beyond the park boundary). Tram rides available at the Visitors' Center allow you to explore other areas of the park. Leave the Visitors' Center area and continue to the park's southern boundary and

Springdale (grocery, café, camping, motels), a small town serving visitors to the park. You follow Utah 9 westward along the Virgin River. This section of the route is narrow, has no shoulder, and is not well paved. Try to cover it early in the morning before tourist traffic picks up. Pass through Virgin (grocery, café), then climb and descend over dry, treeless washes. As elevation here is considerably lower than other parts of the tour, temperatures will increase accordingly. At the junction of Utah 17 and 9 turn south (left, still on Utah 9), and pass through La Verkin (grocery, café, camping), then up a short hill to

Hurricane (22 miles; grocery, restaurants, motels, camping). Lying on the banks of the Virgin River, Hurricane has a commercial hot springs and good grocery stores. (Riders wishing to continue their exploration of the Southwest will leave the tour route at Hurricane and proceed south on Utah 59. Details of that tour, which takes the cyclist to the south rim of the Grand Canyon, are found in Tour 23.) Riders ending their tour should leave Hurricane via Utah 9 to Harrisburg Junction, then proceed either via Interstate 15 or a secondary road to Washington. From there you must take Utah 212 to

Saint George (16 miles; grocery, restaurants, motels, camping), once the winter home of Brigham Young. Bus and air transportation are available from here.

TOUR #23: SAINT GEORGE, UTAH—GRAND CANYON— FLAGSTAFF, ARIZONA

Distance: 364 miles.

Terrain: There are a number of long climbs on the tour, ranging from 5 to 20 miles in length. The rest of the terrain is moderate. Lower elevations can get hot in summer.

Roads and Traffic: Mostly moderate, although traffic is heavy around Grand Canyon.

Season: May to mid-October.

Weather: Mostly dry, although subject to afternoon thundershowers in July and August.

Special Features: A spectacular 25-mile ride along the south rim of the Grand Canyon, some wonderful forest scenery near Jacob Lake, the Navajo Indian Reservation, colorful rock formations on some tour stretches, such as the Vermilion Cliffs of northern Arizona.

Connecting Transportation:

Saint George: Greyhound, Trailways, air service.
Flagstaff: Greyhound, Trailways, Amtrak, air service.

The Grand Canyon needs no amplification here. What is unusual is seeing it on a bicycle. Short of hiking along the rim or down into the canyon, there is no more intimate way of experiencing its many faces. From the time you enter the park, you are never far from the influence of the canyon, whether it be in passing through the dwarf forests near the rim (stunted by hot air rising from the canyon floor) or in observing from distances of a mile the lowest rock strata

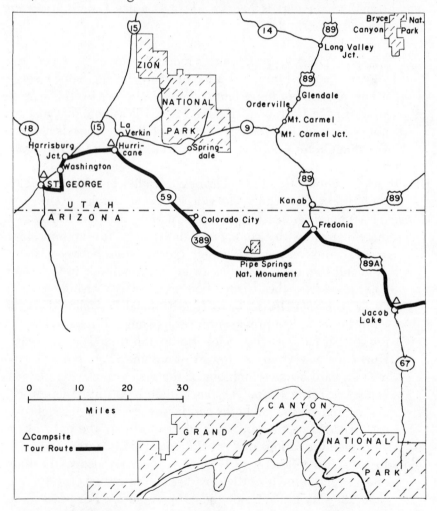

Tour #23   Saint George, Utah—Grand Canyon—Flagstaff, Arizona
(Section one: Saint George, Utah, to Jacob Lake, Arizona)

exposed by the Colorado, believed to be the oldest to be found in the United States.

But for the lover of desert country, there is much more. Always near at hand is something to remind the rider of time's passage. A simple rock face may reveal twelve previous eras. Also marking time in another way is the steadfast culture of the Navajos, whose angular hogans reflect centuries of accommodation to desert vastness.

The tour ends in Flagstaff, a modern town with strong roots in our own country's history.

Cyclists starting the tour at Saint George may wish to visit Zion National Park. To do so you need only leave the tour route at Hurricane. From there the park is an easy ride of 22 miles. Details are given in the preceding tour.

Saint George (grocery, restaurants, motels, camping). Once the winter home of Mormon leader Brigham Young, Saint George is now a small but important commercial center for this part of Utah. Leave Utah on Utah 212 toward Washington (you are not permitted to cover this stretch of I-15 on a bicycle). From Washington turn northeast on a road paralleling the Interstate to

Harrisburg Junction (10 miles). Turn east (right) on Utah 9 toward the town of Hurricane. The ride is through open country.

Hurricane (9 miles; grocery, restaurants, motels, camping). This is a bustling town with a commercial hot springs. It is an important supply point for you, as the only grocery store between Hurricane and Fredonia (58 miles away) is a small one in Colorado City, just across the Arizona border. (Cyclists wishing to take a side trip from Hurricane to Zion National Park should go via Utah Route 9. See previous tour for details) Riders not wishing to visit Zion or who are continuing on from Tour 22, leave Hurricane via Utah 59 toward Fredonia. You immediately begin a hard 5-mile climb out of the valley to a wide plateau known as Little Plain. The hard climb crests at Milepost 17, and from there the land rolls gently upward through sagebrush and irrigated pasturelands. Off to the north are the red Navajo sandstone formations of Zion National Park. Continue to

Colorado City (26 miles; general store). You must leave the tour route to get to town. Settled by dissident Mormons from Utah, Colorado City is just inside the Arizona border. For years there were only primitive lines of communication from the Arizona capital at Phoenix. With its unique location—outside the influence of both Utah and Arizona authorities—Colorado City was one of the last bastions of polygamy in the country. The small but prosperous town still retains habits of dress and custom that hearken back to former times. If you do not need supplies or water (the latter available from some of the small fabricating plants at the first turnoff into town), continue southeast on Arizona 389 to

Pipe Springs National Monument (19 miles; camping), just off the road. This was once a Mormon fort, and has some interesting rock formations. The campground is part of the Kaibab Indian Reservation. Continue on an easy ride to

Fredonia (13 miles; grocery, café, motel, camping). The two grocery stores in town, although not large, are nonetheless the most complete you will find until you arrive in Cameron, 152 miles distant. Most of the stores along the way are Navajo trading posts, and carry only a few groceries. Leave Fredonia south via Alternate U.S. 89. Traffic is moderate, and tends to dissipate away from town. Ahead of you lies the Kaibab National Forest and the uplift known as the Kaibab Plateau. About 15 miles from Fredonia you begin a steep climb of 14 miles. The first 6 miles are steady and hard (to MP 588). From there you climb at a more moderate pace with some short level stretches until you reach Jacob Lake. The lower slopes are covered with juniper, which soon gives way to dense groves of fragrant piñon pine. In autumn, Navajo families may be seen gathering the piñon nuts yielded by the pine cones. As you near the small resort town of Jacob Lake, you pass into ponderosa forests, which tower high above you and spread a rich blanket of needles on the forest floor.

Jacob Lake (29 miles; grocery, café, motel, camping). Grocery supplies are rather limited. (You may wish to take a 90-mile round trip from Jacob Lake to the north rim of the Grand Canyon. The route sweeps up gently for much of the first 25 miles, often through alpine meadows, then comes some more mountainous riding, but with spectacular views. You must go and return on the same road, Utah 67.) As you leave Jacob Lake heading east, still on Alternate U.S. 89, you begin a long downhill run that ends with a flourish of steep switchbacks. You reverse the sequence of tree covers, and end up in level, sagebrush plains. To the north of you lie the Vermilion Cliffs, which are com-

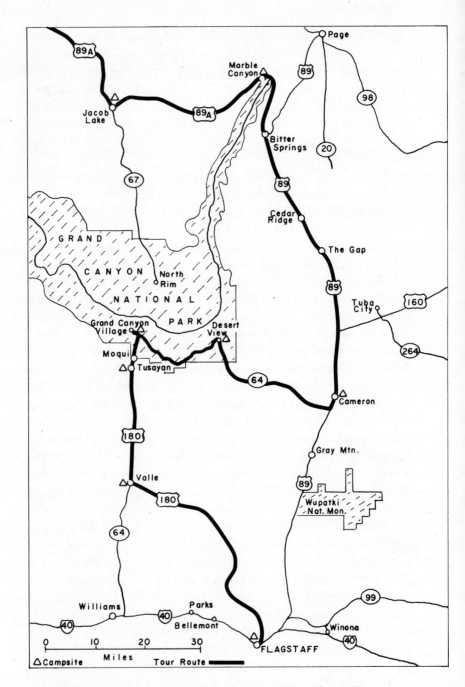

Tour #23   (Section two: Jacob Lake, Arizona, to Flagstaff)

posed of stone from four different geological ages. You follow a gradually sloping canyon floor which eventually brings you to the Colorado River at

Marble Canyon (36 miles; grocery, café, motel). Just beyond the settlement, you cross Marble Canyon on a high bridge, 467 feet above the Colorado, and enter the Navajo Indian Reservation. You will find some excellent examples of local jewelry in the small stands alongside the road. Although there are trading posts and service stations as you pass through the reservation, supplies are limited. Leaving the Colorado you begin a long, steady climb, up Tanner Wash, with the Echo Cliffs on your left. On either side of the road you see Navajo hogans, of both ancient and modern vintage. Continue to

Bitter Springs (14 miles; grocery). You continue south on U.S. 89 (no longer Alternate) toward Cameron. Although the Navajos are known primarily as sheep herders, you will see some examples of cornfields, which depend on the afternoon thundershowers of summer. Continue climbing gradually to

The Gap (28 miles; general store). Just before reaching the trading post you cross a highpoint and then begin a gradual downhill along the Hamblin Wash. The rock formations are more rugged, a bit less attractive than the Echo Cliffs. Continue on the gentle downgrade, crossing the Little Colorado, to

Cameron (32 miles; grocery, café, camping, motel). This is a Navajo town catering to tourists heading toward the Grand Canyon. The grocery store has a good supply of food. At the edge of town turn west (right) on Ariz. 64 toward Grand Canyon Village. The first 12 miles of this road are narrow and the road has no shoulder, so use caution. Soon after leaving Cameron you begin the climb toward the south rim, even though the river alongside you is flowing downward. Geologists have worked since the last century to solve the puzzle of how the Colorado could cut through a hill. There is still no answer that satisfies everyone. Various theories are depicted and explained at the Yavapai Point Museum near Grand Canyon Village. As you climb you pass into juniper and piñon forests. You reach a crest inside the park at

Desert View (32 miles; grocery, café, camping). This is a good stopping point to eat and study the map you are given when you enter the park. From Desert View you follow the Rim Drive. There are a number of picnic areas and viewpoints for looking at the canyon. The road itself winds through ponderosa forests,

with numerous rolls and hills. None of them are particularly
difficult or long, most less than half a mile. Continue to

Grand Canyon Village (25 miles; grocery, restaurants, camping,
hotels). This is the hub of the south rim, and you may wish
to leave your bicycle and take the free tram that serves most
points of interest in this area. If you are visiting Grand Canyon
in summer, remember that it is an exceptionally popular park,
with over three million visitors a year. Campgrounds sometimes fill by 8:00 A.M., and all sites are on a first-come basis.
Normally you can cycle through a camping area and find
someone willing to share a site with you. There is also a special
area set aside at Mather Campground for hikers and cyclists.
Site fees for the latter are minimal. As with any popular area,
keep valuables with you, and lock your bicycle securely. There
is an excellent range of guided tours, evening programs, films,
and visual displays to help explain canyon geology and history.
Leave Grand Canyon Village south on U.S. 180—but stock up
first. Between Grand Canyon Village and Flagstaff, which is
82 miles away, there is only one grocery store, at Tusayan. The
store at Grand Canyon Village is much better stocked. From

Tusayan (9 miles; grocery, restaurant, camping, motel) you continue
south on U.S. 180, descending very gradually out of the forests
and onto sagebrush plains. Traffic is heavy, but there is a good
riding shoulder.

Valle (22 miles; camping, motel). Turn southeast (left) on U.S. 180
toward Flagstaff. Much of the traffic will disappear at this
point. For some miles on your left you will notice that the
sagebrush plateau has been divided up into streets and lots,
although there is not a house to be seen for miles. The com-
pletion of this development may have to wait some centuries
until water surfaces nearby. As of now, there is none available.
The road runs gradually uphill, taking you from the plain into
ponderosa forests. Some 30 miles beyond the turnoff at Valle,
you have a steep 2-mile climb that crests at MP 244. You then
have a rolling uphill climb through pretty glades of ponderosa
and aspen trees, and past nice, open, alpine meadows. Finally
at MP 228 you go over a final rise where you are just above
8,000 feet elevation. From here you start a downhill run
toward Flagstaff. This downhill continues almost to town,
where you reach a broad meadow. Off to the north is one of
Arizona's most important ski slopes, the Arizona Snow Bowl.

Continue for another 8 miles through increasingly urban areas to

Flagstaff (60 miles; grocery, restaurants, motels, youth hostel, camping, bicycle shops). Situated just below 7,000 feet elevation, Flagstaff is an attractive town, somewhat marred by very rapid growth at its south end. There is a large city park where you can lounge around. A university adds a certain leavening to the town.

Cyclists wishing to go south to Phoenix may opt for the route via Mormon Lake, Happy Jack, and Paysan. Avoid the stretch between Paysan and Phoenix on weekends, when frantic city residents stream into the mountains.

SUMMARIES OF OTHER ROUTE GUIDES

Although there are some publications dealing with cycling day trips or urban cycling, the only full-fledged route guide (other than those presented in this book) for the Southwest is the Southwest America Bicycle Trail, developed by a number of YMCAs with the intention of developing an all-weather route connecting the Trans America Trail in Kansas to the Pacific coast above San Diego.

An earlier portion of that route was detailed in Tour Summary 2, found in Chapter 6. The remaining portions of that route through the larger region covered by our book are detailed below.

TOUR SUMMARY #16

Title: Southwest America Bicycle Trail.
Area covered: Yuma, Arizona, to Texas border outside Grady, New Mexico. (Guide continues route to Larned, Kansas).
Source: Southwest America Bicycle Trail, YMCA Affiliate Program, 816 Van Buren, Amarillo, Tex. 79101
Cost: None indicated. Available from Bikecentennial (see Appendix 2 for address) for $2.75 members; $3.25 nonmembers.

The route detailed below winds mostly through low desert areas of Arizona and New Mexico, but does rise into the mountains and plateaus of central Arizona, passing through Prescott and Flagstaff.

SUMMARY: Leave Yuma, Arizona, north on U.S. 95 to Quartzsite. Out of Quartzsite follow frontage route on south side of I-10, then shoulder of I-10 to U.S. 60. Follow that through Vicksburg, Salome, Wenden, and Aguila. Outside Aguila take Ariz. 71 over Merritt Pass to Congress. Take U.S. 89 north to Prescott, then U.S. 89A through Cottonwood and Sedona, and into Flagstaff. Take U.S. 180 north to Valle (for details of portion to Cameron see our own Tour 23). From Valle take U.S. 180 to Grand Canyon, then Ariz. 64 to Cameron. From Cameron go north on U.S. 89 to U.S. 160. Turn east on U.S. 160 through Tuba City. Take Ariz. 264 southeast through Ganado, Saint Michaels, Window Rock, and across New Mexico state line. Follow N. Mex. 264 east to U.S. 666. Turn south on U.S. 666 to Gallup. From Gallup follow old Highway 66 and frontage roads of I-40 via Grants. Take I-40 from Grants to San Fidel, then old Highway 66 and frontage roads, then I-40 to Albuquerque. Leave Albuquerque via U.S. 85 north via Alameda and Bernalillo, then frontage roads to Santa Fe. Leave Santa Fe via U.S. 84/85 to Las Vegas. From Las Vegas go east via N. Mex. 65 to Tucumcari. Leave south via N. Mex. 18 to N. Mex. 93 east, then N. Mex. 241 east to Texas state line. For continuation see original guide.

Route guides, maps, and books

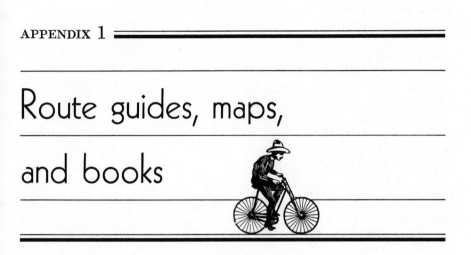

Here, listed state by state, are all the published route guides, specific maps, and books that you can use to develop a tour in the Western United States. Nevada and Utah are missing from the list; as far as we have been able to learn no guides have been published for those states. Two basic books are useful for all states; in some cases they're the only books that have information on a state:

Browder, Sue. *The American Biking Atlas and Touring Guide*
American Youth Hostels. *North American Bicycle Atlas*

Complete listings for these, and all books mentioned below, are given in the Bibliography.

ARIZONA

ROUTE GUIDE
Southwest America Bicycle Trail (summary in Chapter 8)
  A YMCA Affiliate Program
  816 Van Buren
  Amarillo, Tex. 79102

BOOK
Stiles, Ed, and Mort Solot. *Bike Tours in Southern Arizona*

CITY MAPS AND GUIDES
Phoenix Recreation Bicycle Loops
  City of Phoenix Parks, Recreation, and Library Department
  125 E. Washington
  Phoenix, Ariz. 85004

Phoenix and Vicinity Bicycle Map, Anita Notdurft Hopkins, developer
  Available from Bikecentennial (address in Appendix 2)

CALIFORNIA

ROUTE GUIDES
Central Valley Bicycle Touring Guide
Berkeley to Lake Tahoe Bicycle Touring Guide
Lake Tahoe Area Bicycle Touring Guide
California Aqueduct Bikeway (Southern Section)
American River Bicycle Trail
Sacramento County Bikeways
   Division of Highways
   P.O. Box 1499
   Sacramento, Calif. 95814

Southwest America Bicycle Trail (summary in Chapter 6)
   A YMCA Affiliate Program
   816 Van Buren
   Amarillo, Tex. 79101

Caltrans no longer has specific officers in charge of programs for bicyclists, and a spokesperson says it no longer produces bike maps, but it is probably still the best source for general maps and information.

   Caltrans
   6002 Folsom Blvd.
   Sacramento, Calif. 95819

Northwest: Del Norte, Humboldt, Mendocino, and Lake counties:

   Caltrans District 1
   P.O. Box 3700
   Eureka, Calif. 95501
   (707) 442-5761

Northeast: Siskiyou, Modoc, Trinity, Shasta, Lassen, Tehama, and Plumas counties:

   Caltrans District 2
   P.O. Box 2107
   Redding, Calif. 96099
   (916) 246-6482

Sacramento–Lake Tahoe Area: Glenn, Colusa, Yolo, Yuba, Sacramento, Sutter Butte, Sierra, Nevada, Placer, and El Dorado counties:

   Caltrans District 3
   P.O. Box 911
   Marysville, Calif. 95901
   (916) 674-4337

San Francisco Bay Area: Sonoma, Marin, San Francisco, San Mateo, Santa Cruz, Napa, Contra Costa, Alameda, and Santa Clara counties:

   Caltrans District 4
   P.O. Box 3366 Rincon Annex
   San Francisco, Calif. 94119
   (415) 557-0130

Central Coast: Monterey, San Benito, San Luis Obispo, and Santa Barbara counties:

   Caltrans District 5
   P.O. Box L
   San Luis Obispo, Calif. 93406
   (805) 549-3225

South Central: Fresno, Western Kern, Kings, Madera, and Tulare counties:

   Caltrans District 6
   P.O. Box 12616
   Fresno, Calif. 93778
   (209) 488-4124

Los Angeles: Los Angeles, Orange, and Ventura counties:

Caltrans District 7
120 S. Spring St.
Los Angeles, Calif. 90012
(213) 620-3090

San Bernardino Area east to Nevada state line and southwest to Riverside county:

Caltrans District 8
P.O. Box 231
San Bernardino, Calif. 92403
(714) 383-4671

East Central: Eastern Kern, Inyo, and Mono counties:
Caltrans District 9
P.O. Box 847
Bishop, Calif. 93514
(714) 873-8411

Central—Includes Stockton: Alpine, Calaveras, San Joaquin, Solano, Stanislaus, and Merced counties:

Caltrans District 10
P.O. Box 2048
Stockton, Calif. 95201
(209) 948-7666

Southern: Western Riverside, San Diego, and Imperial counties:

Caltrans District 11
P.O. Box 81406
San Diego, Calif. 92138
(714) 294-5262

BOOKS

Caltrans. *Bicycling through the Mother Lode*
Emmery, Lena, and Sally Taylor. *The Grape Escape*
Jackson, Joan. *50 Biking Holidays*
Johnston, Joanne. *JJ's Best Bike Trips*
Kolsburn, Ken, and Bob Burgess. *Discovering Santa Barbara . . . Without a Car*
Murphy, Tom A. *50 Northern California Bicycle Trips*
Olmstead, Camille. *A Cyclist's Guide to Oakland History*
Paul, Bill. *Bicycling California's Spine: A 750-Mile Tour of the Sierras From Mt. Lassen to Kern County*
Ross, Carol, and Thomas E. Ross. *Great Bike Rides in Northern California*
Schad, Jerry, and Don Krupp. *50 Southern California Bicycle Trips*
Standing, Tom. *Bay Area Bikeways*
Stimson, Judy. *Bicycle Tour the Border-to-Border Pacific Coast Route*
Weltman, Gershon, and Elisha Dubin. *Bicycle Touring in Los Angeles*
Yeardon, David. *Backroad Journeys of the West Coast States*

CITY MAPS AND GUIDES
Bay Area Bicycle Route Guide
Bike Routes in San Francisco and Marin County
Caltrans District Coordinator, District 4 (address given above)

Map of Bicycle Routes and Campgrounds in Orange County
Rue de Gravelles
225 Carnation Ave.
Corona Del Mar, Calif. 92626
(714) 675-7196

COLORADO

ROUTE GUIDES

Front Range Route—New Mexico to Wyoming
Across-the-Plains Route—Denver to Vail
South Platte Route—Denver to Kansas
Rockies Route—Denver to Nebraska
Primary Bicycle Routing on the Colorado State Highway System
   Colorado Department of Highways, Bicycle Program
   4201 E. Arkansas
   Denver, Colo. 80222

Great Parks Bicycle Route: Southern Section (summary in Chapter 7)
Trans America Trail: Rocky Mountains (summary in Chapter 7)
Bikecentennial (address in Appendix 2)
Summit County Trail System (connecting route for Trans America Trail and the
   Across-the-Rockies Route)
   Summit County Parks and Recreation Department
   Box 70
   Frisco, Colo. 80443

BOOKS

Bicycle Touring in the Boulder, Colorado, Area
Wolfe, Fredrick. *Bicycle Denver—107 Bicycle Tours*

CITY MAPS AND GUIDES

Colorado Springs Area Bicycle Access Map
   City Planning Dept.
   Colorado Springs, Colo. 80901
Cross-Country Bicycling in Pueblo, Colorado
   Urban Transportation Planning Division
   210 S. Mechanic St.
   Pueblo, Colo. 81003
Denver Bikeway Map
   Denver Planning Office
   1445 Cleveland Place, Room 400
   Denver, Colo. 80202

IDAHO

ROUTE GUIDES

Suggested Bike Routes in Idaho
   Idaho State Parks and Recreation (address in Appendix 4)
Trans America Trail: Coast–Cascades
Central and Southern Idaho
Southern Idaho
   Bikecentennial (address in Appendix 2)

MONTANA

ROUTE GUIDES
Trans America Bicycle Trail (summary in Chapter 7)
Great Parks: Northern Section (summary in Chapter 7)
Alaska to Canada to Montana
Missoula, Montana, to Seattle, Washington
   Bikecentennial (address in Appendix 2)

NEW MEXICO

ROUTE GUIDE
Southwest America Bicycle Trail (summary in Chapter 8)
   A YMCA Affiliate Program
   816 Van Buren
   Amarillo, Tex. 79102

OREGON

ROUTE GUIDES
Oregon Bike Routes (summary in Chapter 6)
   Oregon Department of Transportation (address in Appendix 4)
Oregon Loop Bicycle Trail (summary in Chapter 6)
Trans America Trail: Coast–Cascades (summary in Chapter 6)
   Bikecentennial (address in Appendix 2)

BOOKS
Stimson, Judy. *Bicycle Tour the Border-to-Border Pacific Coast Route*
Yeardon, David. *Backroad Journeys of the West Coast States*

CITY MAPS AND GUIDES
Eugene Area Bikeways
   Commuter Map
   City Hall, 858 Pearl
   Eugene, Oreg. 97401
Portland Bicycle Map
   Bicycle and Pedestrian Program
   400 S.W. Sixth Ave.
   Portland, Oreg. 97204

WASHINGTON

ROUTE GUIDES
Burke Gilman Trail, Interurban Trail and Sammamish River Trail
   King County Department of Planning and Community Development
   Parks Division
   W 226 King County Courthouse
   516 Third Ave.
   Seattle, Wash. 98104

Missoula, Montana, to Seattle, Washington: A Bikecentennial Route Exchange Guide

For address see Appendix 2

Bicycling Touring the Evergreen State: Strip Maps for the entire state. Order by number from the Washington State Department of Transportation. See Appendix 4 for address. Donation is $1.50 for each packet making up a tour. The donation is requested when the packets are mailed to you.

Bicycle Map Code	Route
1.	Maryhill to Yakima
2.	Yakima—Junction SR 2
3.	Junction SR 2—Pateros
4.	Pateros to Omak
5.	Omak—Oroville—Canada
6.	Vancouver—Maryhill
7.	Maryhill—Pasco
8.	Anacortes to SR 537
9.	SR 537 to Sedro Woolley
10.	Sedro Woolley to Twisp
11.	Twisp to Omak
12.	Pateros to Twisp
13.	Spokane to Idaho State Line
14.	North Division Y (SR 2—SR 395) to Colville
15.	Colville to Junction of SR 20 & SR 395 (Kettle Falls)
16.	Junction SR 20 and SR 395 (Kettle Falls) to Canada
17.	Tonasket to Junction 395
18.	Colville—Newport
19.	Federal Way—Woodinville
20.	Woodinville—Monroe
21.	Woodinville—Snohomish
22.	Spokane to North Division Y (SR 2—SR 395)
23.	(None)
24.	Megler to Kelso
25.	Megler to Olympia
26.	Pasco—Wallula—Dodge
27.	Dodge—Clarkston
28.	East Wenatchee—Othello
29.	Pasco—Hatton Coulee
30.	Hatton Coulee—Spokane
31.	Vancouver—Yale—Woodland
32.	Olympia—Tenino
33.	Centralia—Tenino
34.	Tenino—Milton
35.	Issaquah to Fall City
36.	Snohomish to Sedro Woolley
37.	Sedro Woolley—Sumas
38.	(None)
39.	Junction SR 537—Sumas
40.	Federal Way—South Seattle
41.	Mukilteo—Anacortes—Whidbey Island

Bicycle Map Code	Route
42.	South Seattle to University of Washington
43.	Dodge—Dusty
44.	Colfax—Pullman, Idaho
45.	North Division Y (SR 2—SR 395) to Newport
46.	Vancouver—Woodland
47.	Woodland—Kelso
48.	Kelso—SR 12 Vicinity
49.	SR 12 Vicinity—Centralia
50.	Olympia—Centralia
51.	University of Washington to Lake Forest Park
52.	Lake Forest Park—Mountlake Terrace
53.	Mountlake Terrace to Mukilteo
54.	Lake Forest Park to Woodinville
55.	Mountlake Terrace to Edmonds Ferry
56.	Interstate 5—Yakima Via SR 12
57.	Yakima—Othello
58.	Othello—Hatton Coulee
59.	Hatton Coulee—Dusty
60.	Dusty—Spokane
61.	Mukilteo—Spokane
62.	SR 103 Seaview to Ocean Park
63.	SR 6 Raymond to Chehalis
64.	SR 12 & 8 Aberdeen to Mud Bay
65.	SR 108 McCleary to Kamilche
66.	SR 3 Shelton to Port Gamble
67.	Junction SR 101 to Junction SR 3
68.	SR 16 Tacoma to Gorst
69.	SR 160 Junction SR 16 to Southworth
70.	SR 305 Winslow to Junction SR 3
71.	SR 104 SR 101 to Kingston
72.	SR 20 Discovery Bay to Port Townsend
73.	SR 410 Tacoma to Naches Junction
74.	(None)
75.	SR 125 Ohanepecosh to Cayuse
76.	SR 162, 165 Puyallupto Ohanepecosh
77.	SR 164 Auburn to Enumclaw
78.	SR 169 Enumclaw to Renton
79.	SR 202 Redmond to North Bend
80.	SR 203 Fall City to Monroe
81.	SR 12 Elma to Rochester
82.	SR 542 Bellingham to Lawrence
83.	SR 12 SR 22 to Kennewick
84.	SR 17, 174 Junction SR 97 to Wilbur
85.	SR 155 Junction SR 2 to Omak
86.	SR 25 Davenport to Kettle Falls
87.	SR 95, 195 Idaho Line to Pullman
88.	SR 125 Oregon Line to Walla Walla
89.	SR 546 to Canada

BOOKS

Browder, Sue. *The American Bike Atlas and Touring Guide*
North American Bicycle Atlas—American Youth Hostel
Wilson, Janet. *Exploring by Bicycle in Southwest British Columbia and Northwest Washington*
Steward, Chuck. *Bicycling around Seattle*
Vale, Patrick. *Whatcom County Bike Book*
Washington State Bike Book. Washington Department of Transportation
Woods, Erin, and Bill Woods. *Bicycling the Backroads of Northwest Washington*
Woods, Erin, and Bill Woods. *Bicycling the Backroads of Southwest Washington*
Yeardon, David. *Backroad Journeys of the West Coast States*
    See Bibliography for complete listing.

CITY MAPS AND GUIDES

Seattle Bicycle Guide Map
    Seattle Engineering Department
    9th Floor Information Counter
    Municipal Building
    600 Fourth Ave.
    Seattle, Wash. 98104
Seeing Southeast Seattle
    Seattle Department of Community Development
    400 Yesler
    Seattle Building
    Seattle, Wash. 98104
    Bicycle Hotline—Bicycle information for Seattle—(206) 522-BIKE

WYOMING

ROUTE GUIDES

Trans America Trail—Rocky Mountains. A Bikecentennial Publication
    For Summary see Chapter 7
    For Address see Appendix 2

BOOKS

Browder, Sue. *The American Bike Atlas and Touring Guide*
North American Bicycle Atlas—American Youth Hostels
    See Bibliography for complete listing.

Established touring

organizations

This appendix covers the established touring organizations that can offer information, touring advice and possibly tours. Bicycle clubs with no touring interests are not included.

American Youth Hostels, Inc. (AYH)
National Campus
Deleplane, Va. 22025
(703) 592-3271
AYH publishes the North American Bicycling Atlas; offers tours, coordinates tours with their local groups and promotes and develops the hostel program throughout the United States. Services available to members of AYH.

Bikecentennial
P.O. Box 8308
Missoula, Mont. 59807
(406) 721-1776
Bikecentennial offers complete routing services and tour exchange program; a totally comprehensive library of touring books; coordinates individualized touring service and lists all of the tours available from other organizations. They also offer mail-order service for some bicycle safety equipment. Services are open to members and non-members alike.

International Bicycle Touring Society
   (IBTS)
2115 Paseo Dorado
La Jolla, Calif. 92037
(714) 454-6428
IBTS offers its members a number of different tours in the United States and abroad. Leadership of tours is on a volunteer basis and the direction of the tour is suggested by the membership.

League of American Wheelmen
   (LAW)
10 East Read St.
P.O. Box 988
Baltimore, Md. 21203
(301) 727-2022
LAW is the oldest touring association still in existence in the U.S. They offer tours as well as promote bicycling and bicycling legislation. They have clubs on local levels, throughout the U. S. Write to the above address for local information.

Mountain Bicyclists' Association, Inc.
1290 Williams St.
Denver, Colo. 80218
The association is very politically active and promotes bicycling development and education. The members receive a monthly publication. They do not offer tours but will help plan and coordinate tours in their area.

The Mountaineers
Seattle Bicycle Section
719 Pike St.
Seattle, Wash. 98101
The membership of this organization is very actively promoting bicycling within their state as witnessed by the large number of services available there. They also have tours, weekend trips, classes and services available to their members.

Sponsors of guided

bicycle tours

This appendix offers a current listing of organizations within the United States that offer tours in the West. These organizations offer different tours each year and should be contacted well in advance of the desired departure time for information and reservations.

American Youth Hostels (AYH)
National Campus
Deleplane, Va. 22025
(800) 336-6019/Va. 592-3271
AYH offers a variety of tours throughout the U.S. each year. Minimum age is 13 and all ability levels accepted. Adult leaders accompany each tour. Accommodations: campgrounds or hostels. Tour length: may vary in length from 3-6 weeks.

AYH
Boston Council
251 Harvard St.
Brookline, Mass. 02146
(617) 731-5430
Council offers cross-country tours and tours within California. No age limit, all ability levels accepted. Adult leadership provided. Accommodations: Campgrounds and hostels. Tour length 10 days-1 month.

AYH
Metropolitan Detroit Council
3024 Coolidge
Berkeley, Mich. 48072
(312) 345-0511
Trips throughout the U.S. including the Rocky Mountains. No age limit, all ability levels. Adult leadership provided, sag wagon included. Accommodations: Campgrounds and hostels.

AYH
Metro New York Council
132 Spring St.
New York, N.Y. 10012
(212) 431-7100
Coast to coast and regional tours offered. Age limit: 13 years with different tours offered for different age groups. Trained adult leaders accompany each tour. Accommodations: Campgrounds, inns and hostels.

AYH
Washington State Council
1431 Minor St.
Seattle, Wash. 98101
(206) 382-4180
Local tours of the state. No age or ability limitation. Trained leaders accompany the tours. Accommodations: local hostels. Tour length 2 days to 1 week.

Backroads Bicycle Touring
P.O. Box 5534
Berkeley, Calif. 94705
(415) 652-0786
Short tours offered throughout the western states—including National Parks. No age limit with all ability levels welcome. All tours are accompanied by 2 adult leaders and a sag wagon. Accommodations: motels with some camping.

Bikecentennial, Inc.
P.O. Box 8308
Missoula, Mont. 59807
(406) 721-1776
Offer transcontinental tours and shorter tours within the West. Average age is 24. Tours are led by a trained leader but chores are shared. Accommodations: Campgrounds and hostels. Average distance 45-55 miles per day.

Biking Expedition, Inc.
Box 547
Hall Ave.
Henniker, N.H. 03242
(603) 428-7500
Tours of the Pacific Northwest for people 13-18 years of age. Led by 2 adult leaders. Difficulty varies with tours ranging between 25-45 miles per day.

Freewheelin' Fantasy
230½ N. Champlain St.
Burlington, Vt. 05401
(802) 862-9548
Cross-country bicycle tours that average 60 miles per day. Two leaders for every fourteen people help arrange camping and cooking.

Gerhard's Bicycle Odysseys
1137B S.W. Yamhill St.
Portland, Oreg. 97205
(503) 223-5190
One-week guided tours of the Oregon coast. Minimum age is 18, and all ability levels are welcome. Tours are led by 2 adults, accompanied by a sag wagon and a mechanic.

International Bicycle Touring Society
2115 Paseo Dorado
La Jolla, Calif. 92037
(714) 454-6428
Year-round tours that average 50 miles per day. Volunteer leaders accompany with a sag wagon. Age span 24-80.

Keep Listening Wilderness Trips for
    Women
Box 446
Sandy, Oreg. 97055
(503) 239-6896
Short tours of the Pacific Northwest for women. Emphasis is on appreciation of the outdoors, but no previous experience is required. Minimum age: 16 years. Accommodations: Campgrounds.

Kokopeli Adventures in Learning, Inc.
P.O. Box 1557
Flagstaff, Ariz. 86002
(602) 774-0510 or 774-3778
Short tours of the Southwest, including the Grand Canyon and the Rocky Mountains. The focus is on environmental awareness. Minimum age is 14; all ability levels are welcome. Leader and sag wagon are provided. Accommodations: Campgrounds.

Ninety-second Street YM-YWHA
1395 Lexington Ave.
New York, N.Y. 10028
(212) 427-6000 ext. 140
Summer tours of California for people 13-18 years old. All ability levels invited. Tour is led by adult. Accommodations: camping.

Northwest Bicycle Touring Society
3411 77th Pl. S.E.
Mercer Island, Wash. 98040
(206) 323-7311
Short tours of the Pacific Northwest.
All age and ability levels welcome.
Services include leader, sag wagon,
meals, and accommodations. Distance
50 to 60 miles per day.

Oregon Trek Bicycle Tours
1435 N.E. Mason St.
Portland, Oreg. 97211
(503) 284-7799
Tours of the Pacific Northwest that
are open to families with a minimum
age of 14. Accommodations: Motels
and campgrounds. Trips are "facili-
tated" by an adult leader.

Out-Spokin' Bicycling Organization
Box 370
Elkhart, Ind. 46515
(219) 294-7523
Long and short tours within the United
States, with emphasis on spiritual
growth. All age levels are welcome.
Leadership and maintenance crews
are provided. Accommodations: Camp-
grounds.

Pacific Adventures
Box 5041
Riverside, Calif. 94517
(714) 684-1227
Weekend tours and longer coastal
tours of the West Coast and British
Columbia and the Rocky Mountains.

Minimum age: 14. All ability levels
welcome. Trained leaders and mechanics accompany the tour. Accommodations: Campgrounds.

Sierra Club Outing Program
530 Bush St.
San Francisco, Calif. 94108
(415) 981-8634
One-week and two-week tours are
offered between May and October.
Age limit of 18 unless accompanied
by parent. Difficulty varies but is
usually moderate. Accommodations:
campgrounds.

Touring Exchange
1320 N. Fir Villa Rd.
Dallas, Oreg. 97338
(503) 623-6352
One- and three-week tours in the
wilderness areas of the West. All tours
are limited to eight people. Leadership and camping equipment are provided. People under 21 must be accompanied by a sponsor. Individual
tour plans are also available.

Western Wheels
6678 South Arapahoe Dr.
Littleton, Colo. 80120
(303) 794-9518
Tours in Colorado, Montana, and
Wyoming. Minimum age is 13; participants should be able to ride 30 to
90 miles per day. Leaders, bicycle
rental, food, and camping are provided, as well as a sag wagon.

State government sources

for information on roads,

tourism, and parks

This state-by-state listing covers agencies that provide information on roads, parks, and recreation.

ARIZONA _____

For state highway maps:
Arizona Highways Magazine
2039 W. Lewis
Phoenix, Ariz. 85009
(602) 258-6641

For state and county maps:
Arizona Department of
Transportation
206 S. 17th Ave., Rm. 134A
Phoenix, Ariz. 85007
(602) 261-7325

For state recreation information:
Arizona State Office of Tourism
1700 W. Washington Ave., Rm. 501
Phoenix, Ariz. 85007

CALIFORNIA _____

For state highway maps:
Office of Tourism
1120 N St.
Sacramento, Calif. 95815
(916) 445-4616

For state and county maps:
See Appendix 1 for Caltrans District
listings

For state recreation information:
California Department of Parks
and Recreation
P.O. Box 2390
Sacramento, Calif. 95811

For reservations in state parks:
Los Angeles area (213) 670-2311
San Diego area (714) 565-9947
San Francisco area (415) 788-2828
Sacramento area (916) 445-8828

COLORADO _____

For state highway maps:
Department of Highways
Public Relations Officer
4201 E. Arkansas
Denver, Colo. 80222

For state bicycle routes:
See Appendix 1 for route listings

For state recreation information:
Colorado Division of Parks and
   Outdoor Recreation
Centennial Bldg., Rm. 604
1313 Sherman St.
Denver, Colo. 80203

IDAHO ―――――――――――――――

For state highway maps (state,
county, and traffic-flow maps
available):
   Idaho Transportation Department
   P.O. Box 7129
   Boise, Idaho 83707

For state recreation information:
Tourist and Industrial Information
Idaho Division of Tourism and
   Industrial Development
Capitol Bldg., Rm. 108
Boise, Idaho 83720
(800) 635-7820

MONTANA ――――――――――――――

For state highway maps:
Montana Travel Promotion Unit
Montana State Department of
   Highways
Helena, Mont. 59601
(406) 449-2654 in state
(800) 548-3390 out of state

For county road maps:
Montana Department of Highways
Planning and Research Building
2701 Prospect
Helena, Mont. 59601

For state recreation information:
Montana Travel Promotion Unit
   (address above)

NEVADA ―――――――――――――――

For state highway maps (state, county,
and traffic-flow maps available):
Nevada Department of
   Transportation
Map Section, Rm. 206
1263 S. Stewart St.
Carson City, Nev. 89712

For state recreation information:
Nevada Division of State Parks
1923 N. Carson St.
Capitol Complex
Carson City, Nev. 89710

NEW MEXICO ――――――――――――

For state highway maps:
New Mexico State Highway
   Department
1120 Cerrillos Rd.
P.O. Box 1149
Santa Fe, N. Mex. 87503

For state recreation information:
New Mexico Travel Division
Commerce and Industry
   Department
Bataan Memorial Bldg.
Santa Fe, N. Mex. 87503
(800) 827-5571 in state
(800) 545-2040 out of state

OREGON ―――――――――――――――

For state highway maps:
Oregon Department of
   Transportation
Travel Information Section
101 Transportation Bldg.
Salem, Oreg. 97310

*For Oregon county road maps and
traffic-flow maps:*
Oregon Department of
   Transportation
101 Transportation Bldg., Rm. 17
Salem, Oreg. 97310

For recreation information:
Recreation Trail Coordinator
Department of Transportation
525 Trade St., S.E.
Salem, Oreg. 97310

For reservations in state parks:
Oregon State Parks
Campsite Information Center
(503) 238-7488 from Portland or
   out of state
(800) 452-5687 from Oregon

UTAH ————————————————

For state highway maps:
UDOT Transportation Planning
Division
First Security Bank Bldg., Suite 800
Salt Lake City, Utah 84111

For state recreation information:
Utah Travel Council
Council Hall, Capitol Hill
Salt Lake City, Utah 84114

WASHINGTON ————————————

For state highway maps (state and
county maps available):
Washington State Department of
Transportation
Transportation Admin. Bldg.
Olympia, Wash. 98504

For state bicycle routing information:
Complete listing in Appendix 1

For state recreation information:
Washington Department of
Commerce and Economic
Development
Travel Development Division
General Admin. Bldg.
Olympia, Wash. 98504

For state ferry system information:
Office is open between 6:30 A.M.
and 10:00 P.M.
464-6400 from Seattle
(800) 542-0810 from all other
locations

WYOMING ————————————————

For state highway maps (county maps
also available):
Assistant Chief Engineer
Planning and Administration
Wyoming Highway Department
P.O. Box 1708
Cheyenne, Wyo. 82001

For state recreation information:
Wyoming Travel Commission
I-25 at Etchepare Circle
Cheyenne, Wyo. 82002
(307) 777-7777

Mail-order sources for bicycling accessories, camping equipment, books, and maps

This appendix covers mail-order sources for bicycle equipment and accessories, camping equipment, and books and maps not covered in the bibliography or other appendix listing. It does not include any equipment source that does not offer mail-order service.

BICYCLING EQUIPMENT AND ACCESSORIES

Bikecology Bike Shops
1515 Wilshire Blvd.
Santa Monica, Calif. 90406
(213) 829-7681 inside California
(800) 421-7153 outside California
  number is toll free
Catalogue $2

Bike Warehouse
215 Main
Middletown, Ohio 44442
(800) 321-2474
Catalogue 50¢

Hartley Alley's Touring Cyclist Shop
P.O. Box 4009 Y
2639 Spruce St.
Boulder, Colo. 80306
(303) 449-4067
Catalogue free

International Pro Bike Shop Inc.
3733 Wilmington Pike
Kettering, Ohio 45429
(513) 293-2126
Catalogue $2

Lickton's Cycle City
310 Lake St.
Oak Park, Ill. 60302
(312) 383-2130
Catalogue $1

Palo Alto Bicycles
P.O. Box 1276
Palo Alto, Calif. 94302
(415) 328-0128
Catalogue free

Pedal Pushers, Inc.—Wheels 'n' Things
1130 Rogero Rd.
Jacksonville, Fla. 32211
(904) 725-2211

Redwood Cycling Apparel
1593 G St.
Arcata, Calif. 95521
Catalogue 25¢

CAMPING EQUIPMENT

Frostline Kits
Frostline Circle
Denver, Colo. 80241
Catalogue free

L. L. Bean
997 Main St.
Freeport, Maine 04033
(207) 865-3111
Catalogue free

Recreational Equipment, Inc.
P.O. Box C 88125
Seattle, Wash. 98188
(800) 426-4840
Catalogue free to members

BOOKS

Bikecentennial
P.O. Box 8308
Missoula, Mont. 59807

Books about Bikes
William Allan Bookseller
P.O. Box 315
Englewood, Colo. 80151

Mother's Bookshelf
P.O. Box 70
Hendersonville, N.C. 28739

TOPOGRAPHICAL MAPS

Distribution Section, U.S. Geological
  Survey
Federal Center
Denver, Colo. 80225
    Topographical maps for areas west
    of the Mississippi.

International Backpackers Association,
  Inc.
P.O. Box 85
Lincoln Center, Maine 94458
    Even nonmembers can get maps
    covering the entire country.

Average temperature,

rainfall, and wind

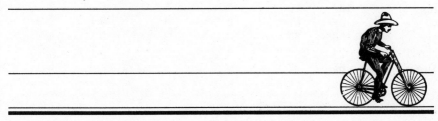

In areas where year-round riding is possible, weather data are given for all twelve months. Elsewhere, data are given for the riding season, usually April through October. The "days" listing under "Precipitation" refers to the average number of days each month on which measurable precipitation falls.

ARIZONA

FLAGSTAFF

Month	Temperature		Precipitation		Wind	
	high (F)	low	total (in.)	days	speed	direc.
Apr.	59	28	1.18	5	8.8	SSE
May	68	34	0.51	3	8.1	SSW
June	77	42	0.69	3	8.0	SSW
July	81	50	2.28	11	6.1	SSW
Aug.	79	49	2.84	11	5.5	S
Sept.	75	42	1.58	6	6.5	S
Oct.	63	31	1.52	5	6.6	N
Nov.	74	42	0.49	2	5.1	E

PHOENIX

Month	Temperature		Precipitation		Wind	
	high (F)	low	total (in.)	days	speed	direc.
Jan.	64	35	0.73	4	4.9	E
Feb.	68	39	0.85	4	5.6	E
Mar.	75	43	0.66	4	6.3	E
Apr.	84	51	0.32	2	6.6	E
May	93	57	0.13	1	6.7	E
June	102	66	0.09	1	6.6	E
July	105	75	0.77	4	6.9	W
Aug.	102	73	1.12	5	6.4	E
Sept.	98	67	0.73	3	6.1	E
Oct.	86	55	0.46	3	5.5	E
Nov.	74	42	0.49	2	5.1	E
Dec.	66	37	0.85	4	4.9	E

TUCSON

Month	Temperature		Precipitation		Wind	
	high (F)	low	total (in.)	days	speed	direc.
Jan.	63	37	0.82	4	7.8	SE
Feb.	66	40	0.84	3	8.1	SE
Mar.	72	44	0.53	4	8.5	SE
Apr.	81	51	0.27	2	8.8	SE
May	89	57	0.13	1	8.6	SE
June	98	67	0.29	2	8.5	SSE
July	99	74	2.06	10	8.2	SE
Aug.	95	72	2.88	9	7.6	SE
Sept.	93	67	1.0	4	8.1	SE
Oct.	83	57	0.64	3	8.4	SE
Nov.	72	44	0.62	3	8.0	SE
Dec.	65	39	0.92	4	7.8	SE

YUMA

Month	Temperature high (F)	low	Precipitation total (in.)	days	Wind speed	direc.
Jan.	67	43	0.38	2	7.3	N
Feb.	73	46	0.27	1	7.4	N
Mar.	78	50	0.21	2	7.8	WNW
Apr.	86	57	0.11	1	8.3	W
May	93	71	0.03	0	8.3	WNW
June	101	71	0.00	0	8.4	SSE
July	106	81	0.18	1	9.4	SSE
Aug.	104	81	0.44	2	8.9	SSE
Sept.	100	74	0.22	1	8.9	SSE
Oct.	90	62	0.27	1	6.5	N
Nov.	77	51	0.22	1	6.7	N
Dec.	68	44	0.34	2	7.2	N

WINSLOW

Month	Temperature high (F)	low	Precipitation total (in.)	days	Wind speed	direc.
Apr.	70	37	0.36	3	11.3	SW
May	80	46	0.28	3	10.9	SW
June	90	54	0.28	2	8.9	WSW
July	94	63	1.18	7	8.2	SW
Aug.	91	62	1.50	9	8.1	SW
Sept.	85	54	0.85	5	7.6	SE
Oct.	73	41	0.69	4	7.2	SE

CALIFORNIA

EUREKA

Month	Temperature high (F)	low	Precipitation total (in.)	days	Wind speed	direc.
Jan.	54	41	7.42	17	6.9	SE
Apr.	55	44	2.95	12	8.0	N
May	57	48	2.11	8	7.9	N
June	60	51	0.66	5	7.4	N
July	60	52	0.14	2	6.8	N
Aug.	61	53	0.27	2	5.8	NW
Sept.	62	51	0.65	4	5.5	N
Oct.	60	48	2.23	9	5.6	N

RED BLUFF

Month	Temperature		Precipitation		Wind	
	high (F)	low	total (in.)	days	speed	direc.
Apr.	72	47	1.79	6	9.6	SSE
May	81	54	0.98	4	9.2	SSE
June	89	62	0.47	3	9.3	SSE
July	98	67	0.04	1	8.0	SSE
Aug.	96	64	0.18	1	7.6	SSE
Sept.	91	61	0.31	2	8.0	SSE
Oct.	78	52	1.17	5	8.4	NW

MOUNT SHASTA

Month	Temperature		Precipitation		Wind	
	high (F)	low	total (in.)	days	speed	direc.
Apr.	58	34	3.05	8	NA	NA
May	67	40	1.87	8		
June	74	46	1.08	5		
July	85	51	0.32	2		
Aug.	83	49	0.31	2		
Sept.	78	45	0.69	3		
Oct.	65	38	2.54	6		

SACRAMENTO

Month	Temperature		Precipitation		Wind	
	high (F)	low	total (in.)	days	speed	direc.
Apr.	71	45	1.54	6	9.0	SE
May	79	50	0.51	3	9.4	SW
June	86	55	0.10	1	10.0	SW
July	93	58	0.01	0	9.2	SSE
Aug.	91	57	0.05	0	8.7	SW
Sept.	88	55	0.19	1	7.9	SW
Oct.	77	50	0.99	3	6.9	SW

SAN FRANCISCO

Month	Temperature		Precipitation		Wind	
	high (F)	low	total (in.)	days	speed	direc.
Apr.	64	47	1.59	6	12.0	WNW
May	67	50	0.41	3	13.2	W
June	70	53	0.13	1	13.9	W
July	71	54	0.01	0	13.6	NW
Aug.	72	54	0.03	0	12.8	NW
Sept.	74	55	0.16	1	11.0	NW
Oct.	70	52	0.98	4	9.2	NNW

FRESNO

Month	Temperature high (F)	low	Precipitation total (in.)	days	Wind speed	direc.
Apr.	74	46	1.24	5	7.2	NW
May	83	51	0.32	2	8.0	NW
June	90	58	0.06	1	8.1	NW
July	98	63	0.00	0	7.1	NW
Aug.	96	61	0.02	0	6.6	NW
Sept.	91	57	0.07	1	5.9	NW
Oct.	80	49	0.42	2	5.3	NW

LONG BEACH

Month	Temperature high (F)	low	Precipitation total (in.)	days	Wind speed	direc.
Jan.	65	43	2.26	5	5.7	WNW
Feb.	66	45	2.16	4	6.2	W
Mar.	67	47	1.50	4	6.8	W
Apr.	70	51	0.89	3	7.4	W
May	74	54	0.07	1	7.3	S
June	77	58	0.04	1	6.9	S
July	83	62	0.00	0	6.7	WNW
Aug.	84	63	0.02	0	6.5	WNW
Sept.	83	61	0.09	1	6.2	WNW
Oct.	78	56	0.19	2	5.9	WNW
Nov.	73	48	1.38	4	5.7	WNW
Dec.	69	44	1.65	5	5.3	WNW

LOS ANGELES

Month	Temperature high (F)	low	Precipitation total (in.)	days	Wind speed	direc.
Jan.	64	45	2.52	6	6.7	W
Feb.	64	47	2.32	6	7.3	W
Mar.	64	48	1.71	5	8.0	W
Apr.	66	52	1.10	3	8.4	WSW
May	68	55	0.08	1	8.2	WSW
June	70	62	0.03	1	7.9	WSW
July	75	62	0.01	1	7.6	WSW
Aug.	76	63	0.02	0	7.5	WSW
Sept.	76	62	0.07	1	7.1	WSW
Oct.	73	58	0.22	2	6.8	W
Nov.	70	51	1.76	4	6.6	W
Dec.	67	47	2.39	6	6.6	W

SAN DIEGO

Month	Temperature high (F)	low	Precipitation total (in.)	days	Wind speed	direc.
Jan.	65	46	1.88	7	5.6	NE
Feb.	66	48	1.48	6	6.3	WNW
Mar.	66	50	1.55	7	7.2	WNW
Apr.	57	54	0.81	5	7.6	WNW
May	70	57	0.15	2	7.6	WNW
June	71	60	0.05	1	7.5	SSW
July	75	64	0.01	0	7.1	WNW
Aug.	77	65	0.07	0	6.9	WNW
Sept.	77	63	0.13	1	6.7	NW
Oct.	74	58	0.34	2	6.3	WNW
Nov.	70	52	1.25	5	5.6	NE
Dec.	66	48	1.73	6	5.5	NE

COLORADO

ALAMOSA

Month	Temperature high (F)	low	Precipitation total (in.)	days	Wind speed	direc.
Apr.	59	25	0.69	5	11.9	NA
May	68	34	0.62	6	12.1	
June	78	42	0.52	5	10.2	
July	82	48	1.17	10	8.6	
Aug.	80	46	1.15	11	8.1	
Sept.	74	36	0.71	6	8.2	
Oct.	63	25	0.69	5	7.7	

COLORADO SPRINGS

Month	Temperature high (F)	low	Precipitation total (in.)	days	Wind speed	direc.
Apr.	59	33	1.45	7	12.2	NNW
May	68	42	2.12	10	11.7	NNW
June	79	51	2.31	9	11.0	SSE
July	84	57	3.10	14	9.7	NNW
Aug.	83	56	2.58	11	9.3	N
Sept.	76	47	1.11	7	9.7	SSE
Oct.	65	37	0.92	5	9.8	NNE

DENVER

Month	Temperature		Precipitation		Wind	
	high (F)	low	total (in.)	days	speed	direc.
Apr.	61	34	1.93	9	10.4	S
May	70	44	2.64	10	9.4	S
June	80	52	1.93	9	9.0	S
July	87	59	1.78	9	8.5	S
Aug.	85	57	1.29	8	8.2	S
Sept.	77	48	1.13	6	8.2	S
Oct.	69	37	1.13	5	8.2	S

GRAND JUNCTION

Month	Temperature		Precipitation		Wind	
	high (F)	low	total (in.)	days	speed	direc.
Apr.	65	39	0.79	6	9.8	ESE
May	76	49	0.63	6	9.8	ESE
June	86	57	0.55	4	10.0	ESE
July	93	64	0.46	5	9.4	ESE
Aug.	89	62	1.05	7	9.1	ESE
Sept.	81	53	0.84	5	9.2	ESE
Oct.	67	42	0.83	6	8.1	ESE

PUEBLO

Month	Temperature		Precipitation		Wind	
	high (F)	low	total (in.)	days	speed	direc.
Apr.	66	37	1.29	6	10.4	WNW
May	76	47	1.65	8	9.7	SE
June	86	56	1.36	7	9.4	SE
July	91	62	1.87	10	8.7	SE
Aug.	89	60	1.96	9	7.9	W
Sept.	82	51	0.79	5	7.9	SE
Oct.	71	38	0.42	4	7.4	W

IDAHO

BOISE

Month	Temperature		Precipitation		Wind	
	high (F)	low	total (in.)	days	speed	direc.
Apr.	61	37	1.14	9	10.3	SE
May	71	44	1.32	8	9.5	NW
June	78	51	1.06	7	9.2	NW
July	91	59	0.15	2	8.5	NW
Aug.	88	57	0.30	2	8.3	NW
Sept.	78	49	0.41	4	8.3	SE
Oct.	65	39	0.80	7	8.6	SE

LEWISTON

Month	Temperature		Precipitation		Wind	
	high (F)	low	total (in.)	days	speed	direc.
Apr.	62	39	1.58	9	NA	NA
May	71	45	1.55	9		
June	78	52	1.73	8		
July	90	58	0.43	4		
Aug.	88	56	0.43	4		
Sept.	78	49	0.90	5		
Oct.	64	40	1.21	8		

POCATELLO

Month	Temperature		Precipitation		Wind	
	high (F)	low	total (in.)	days	speed	direc.
Apr.	60	33	1.06	8	11.8	SW
May	69	45	1.29	9	10.6	SW
June	78	48	1.28	7	10.2	SW
July	90	58	0.36	4	9.2	SW
Aug.	88	56	0.62	4	8.6	SW
Sept.	78	49	0.61	4	9.2	SW
Oct.	64	40	0.75	5	9.3	SW

MONTANA

BILLINGS

Month	Temperature		Precipitation		Wind	
	high (F)	low	total (in.)	days	speed	direc.
Apr.	57	35	1.31	9	11.8	SW
May	68	45	1.88	11	11.0	NE
June	76	54	2.55	12	10.4	SE
July	89	61	0.90	7	9.8	SE
Aug.	85	58	0.90	6	9.6	SE
Sept.	74	47	1.19	7	10.4	SE
Oct.	62	37	1.09	6	11.2	SE

GREAT FALLS

Month	Temperature		Precipitation		Wind	
	high (F)	low	total (in.)	days	speed	direc.
Apr.	55	32	1.18	9	13.2	SW
May	65	42	2.37	11	11.5	SW
June	72	50	3.11	12	11.4	SW
July	84	55	1.27	7	10.3	SW
Aug.	82	53	1.09	7	10.5	SW
Sept.	70	45	1.17	7	11.7	SW
Oct.	59	37	0.68	6	13.7	SW

HELENA

Month	Temperature		Precipitation		Wind	
	high (F)	low	total (in.)	days	speed	direc.
Apr.	56	31	0.83	8	9.4	W
May	69	40	1.56	11	9.0	W
June	72	47	2.23	13	8.6	W
July	84	52	1.03	7	7.9	W
Aug.	82	50	0.89	7	7.6	W
Sept.	71	41	0.95	7	7.6	W
Oct.	59	32	0.66	6	7.4	W

KALISPELL

Month	Temperature		Precipitation		Wind	
	high (F)	low	total (in.)	days	speed	direc.
Apr.	54	30	1.01	9	8.6	NA
May	64	38	1.80	11	7.8	
June	70	44	2.56	12	7.5	
July	81	48	1.03	6	6.8	
Aug.	79	46	1.30	8	6.7	
Sept.	68	39	1.13	8	6.8	
Oct.	54	31	1.21	10	5.7	

MISSOULA

Month	Temperature		Precipitation		Wind	
	high (F)	low	total (in.)	days	speed	direc.
Apr.	57	31	0.97	10	7.4	NW
May	67	39	1.87	12	7.2	NW
June	73	44	1.91	12	6.8	NW
July	85	49	0.85	6	6.6	NW
Aug.	83	47	0.72	7	6.6	NW
Sept.	72	39	1.02	8	5.9	NW
Oct.	58	31	0.99	9	5.0	NW

NEVADA

ELKO

Month	Temperature		Precipitation		Wind	
	high (F)	low	total (in.)	days	speed	direc.
Apr.	59	28	0.82	7	7.2	SW
May	69	35	1.03	8	6.9	SW
June	78	42	1.01	6	6.7	SW
July	90	49	0.41	3	6.2	SW
Aug.	88	46	0.61	3	6.0	SW
Sept.	79	36	0.34	3	5.5	SW
Oct.	66	28	0.66	5	5.2	SW

RENO

Month	Temperature		Precipitation		Wind	
	high (F)	low	total (in.)	days	speed	direc.
Apr.	64	30	0.47	4	8.0	WNW
May	72	37	0.66	5	7.6	WNW
June	80	43	0.40	3	7.2	WNW
July	91	47	0.26	3	6.5	WNW
Aug.	89	45	0.22	2	6.2	WNW
Sept.	87	39	0.23	2	5.5	WNW
Oct.	70	31	0.42	3	5.3	WNW

LAS VEGAS

Month	Temperature		Precipitation		Wind	
	high (F)	low	total (in.)	days	speed	direc.
Jan.	56	33	0.45	3	7.1	W
Feb.	61	37	0.30	2	8.2	SW
Mar.	68	42	0.35	2	9.6	SW
Apr.	78	51	0.23	2	10.7	SW
May	88	60	0.08	1	10.9	SW
June	97	69	0.04	1	10.6	SW
July	104	76	0.50	3	9.9	SW
Aug.	101	73	0.48	3	9.2	SW
Sept.	99	66	0.34	1	8.7	SW
Oct.	80	53	0.20	2	7.7	SW
Nov.	65	40	0.31	2	6.8	W
Dec.	56	34	0.40	2	6.9	W

NEW MEXICO

ALBUQUERQUE

Month	Temperature		Precipitation		Wind	
	high (F)	low	total (in.)	days	speed	direc.
Jan.	46	24	0.41	3	7.8	E
Feb.	52	28	0.38	4	8.8	NW
Mar.	59	33	0.48	4	10.0	NW
Apr.	69	42	0.47	3	10.9	S
May	78	52	0.75	4	10.4	W
June	89	61	0.57	4	9.9	SE
July	91	66	1.20	9	9.0	E
Aug.	88	64	1.33	9	8.1	SE
Sept.	82	58	0.95	6	8.5	SE
Oct.	71	45	0.75	5	8.2	N
Nov.	56	31	0.38	3	7.7	NW
Dec.	48	26	0.46	4	7.5	SE

CLAYTON

Month	Temperature		Precipitation		Wind	
	high (F) low		total (in.)	days	speed	direc.
Jan.	46	20	0.35	3	NA	NA
Feb.	49	23	0.37	4		
Mar.	55	27	0.63	5		
Apr.	65	38	1.19	5		
May	73	46	2.74	8		
June	84	56	1.48	8		
July	88	61	2.33	11		
Aug.	87	60	2.09	9		
Sept.	80	53	1.65	5		
Oct.	69	41	1.00	4		
Nov.	55	28	0.33	3		
Dec.	49	23	0.35	3		

OREGON

ASTORIA

Month	Temperature		Precipitation		Wind	
	high (F) low		total (in.)	days	speed	direc.
Apr.	56	40	4.61	18	8.6	WNW
May	60	44	2.72	15	8.4	NW
June	64	49	2.45	13	8.2	NW
July	68	52	0.96	7	8.4	NW
Aug.	68	52	1.46	8	7.8	NW
Sept.	67	49	2.83	11	7.3	SE
Oct.	61	45	6.80	17	7.4	SE

BURNS

Month	Temperature		Precipitation		Wind	
	high (F) low		total (in.)	days	speed	direc.
Apr.	58	30	0.70	7	8.7	NA
May	67	38	1.03	7	8.6	
June	74	44	0.97	6	7.9	
July	86	51	0.32	3	7.7	
Aug.	83	49	0.44	3	7.1	
Sept.	75	41	0.46	3	7.0	
Oct.	63	32	0.89	6	6.4	

MEDFORD

Month	Temperature high (F)	low	Precipitation total (in.)	days	Wind speed	direc.
Apr.	64	37	1.00	9	5.8	WNW
May	72	43	1.44	9	5.7	WNW
June	79	49	0.89	5	5.9	WNW
July	90	54	0.25	1	5.7	WNW
Aug.	88	53	0.33	2	5.3	WNW
Sept.	82	47	0.56	4	4.5	WNW
Oct.	67	39	2.05	8	3.7	S

PORTLAND

Month	Temperature high (F)	low	Precipitation total (in.)	days	Wind speed	direc.
Apr.	62	42	2.09	14	7.1	NW
May	68	48	1.99	12	6.8	NW
June	72	52	1.67	10	6.7	NW
July	79	56	0.41	3	7.3	NW
Aug.	78	55	0.65	5	6.9	NW
Sept.	74	51	1.63	8	6.2	NW
Oct.	63	45	3.61	13	6.4	NW

SEXTON SUMMIT

Month	Temperature high (F)	low	Precipitation total (in.)	days	Wind speed	direc.
Apr.	52	34	2.06	11	10.6	S
May	58	39	2.22	10	10.2	S
June	66	45	1.26	6	11.1	N
July	76	51	0.33	2	11.8	N
Aug.	75	51	0.44	2	10.9	N
Sept.	70	49	1.03	5	11.1	N
Oct.	58	43	3.63	10	12.0	S

UTAH

MILFORD

Month	Temperature high (F)	low	Precipitation total (in.)	days	Wind speed	direc.
Apr.	64	32	0.76	4	10.0	SSW
May	74	40	0.74	6	9.6	N
June	84	48	0.45	2	9.8	N
July	93	56	0.77	5	9.0	S
Aug.	89	54	0.81	4	8.9	S
Sept.	81	44	0.40	2	8.6	SSW
Oct.	67	33	0.88	4	5.2	SSW

ROSWELL

Month	Temperature		Precipitation		Wind	
	high (F)	low	total (in.)	days	speed	direc.
Apr.	79	39	0.73	2	11.8	W
May	87	49	1.28	4	11.4	N
June	96	59	1.05	5	10.8	W
July	95	62	1.77	8	9.4	SW
Aug.	93	60	1.62	7	8.4	W
Sept.	87	52	1.82	5	8.3	NW
Oct.	77	41	1.07	4	8.2	W

SALT LAKE

Month	Temperature		Precipitation		Wind	
	high (F)	low	total (in.)	days	speed	direc.
Apr.	63	37	2.12	10	9.4	SE
May	73	45	1.49	8	9.4	SE
June	82	52	1.30	6	9.4	SE
July	92	61	0.70	4	9.6	SE
Aug.	90	59	0.93	5	9.7	SE
Sept.	79	49	0.68	5	9.0	SE
Oct.	67	39	1.16	6	8.6	SE

WENDOVER

Month	Temperature		Precipitation		Wind	
	high (F)	low	total (in.)	days	speed	direc.
Apr.	62	40	0.44	5	NA	NA
May	72	50	0.68	5		
June	81	58	0.73	5		
July	92	67	0.22	3		
Aug.	89	64	0.36	3		
Sept.	79	53	0.27	2		
Oct.	64	42	0.45	4		

WASHINGTON

SEATTLE

Month	Temperature		Precipitation		Wind	
	high (F)	low	total (in.)	days	speed	direc.
Apr.	57	40	2.46	14	9.9	SW
May	64	46	1.70	10	9.2	SW
June	69	51	1.53	10	9.0	SW
July	75	54	0.71	5	8.5	SW
Aug.	74	54	1.08	6	8.1	SW
Sept.	69	50	1.99	9	8.3	N
Oct.	59	45	3.91	14	8.9	S

SPOKANE

Month	Temperature high (F)	low	Precipitation total (in.)	days	Wind speed	direc.
Apr.	57	35	1.12	9	9.8	SW
May	67	43	1.46	9	8.8	SSW
June	74	49	1.36	8	8.7	SSW
July	84	55	0.40	4	8.2	SW
Aug.	82	54	0.58	5	8.0	SW
Sept.	73	47	0.83	6	8.1	NE
Oct.	58	38	1.42	8	8.1	SSW

WALLA WALLA

Month	Temperature high (F)	low	Precipitation total (in.)	days	Wind speed	direc.
Apr.	63	43	1.43	9	6.1	S
May	71	50	1.58	8	5.7	S
June	79	56	1.18	7	5.5	S
July	89	62	0.33	3	5.4	S
Aug.	86	61	0.45	3	5.1	S
Sept.	77	54	0.85	5	4.7	S
Oct.	64	45	1.49	9	4.5	S

YAKIMA

Month	Temperature high (F)	low	Precipitation total (in.)	days	Wind speed	direc.
Apr.	64	35	0.51	6	8.0	W
May	73	43	0.55	4	8.7	WNW
June	80	49	0.73	5	8.4	WNW
July	88	53	0.16	5	8.2	NW
Aug.	86	51	0.25	2	7.7	WNW
Sept.	78	44	0.31	3	7.4	WNW
Oct.	65	35	0.58	3	7.4	WNW

WYOMING

CASPER

Month	Temperature high (F)	low	Precipitation total (in.)	days	Wind speed	direc.
Apr.	56	31	1.69	10	12.9	WSE
May	66	40	2.03	10	11.8	WSE
June	77	49	1.25	9	11.1	WSE
July	87	56	1.00	7	9.9	WSE
Aug.	85	55	0.72	5	10.4	SW
Sept.	74	45	0.90	6	11.2	WSW
Oct.	61	36	0.84	6	12.4	SW

CHEYENNE

Month	Temperature		Precipitation		Wind	
	high (F)	low	total (in.)	days	speed	direc.
Apr.	55	30	1.57	10	15.0	WNW
May	65	40	2.52	12	13.1	WNW
June	74	48	2.41	11	11.7	WNW
July	83	55	1.82	11	10.6	WNW
Aug.	82	53	1.45	9	10.9	W
Sept.	73	49	1.03	7	11.5	W
Oct.	62	34	0.95	5	12.6	W

LANDER

Month	Temperature		Precipitation		Wind	
	high (F)	low	total (in.)	days	speed	direc.
Apr.	55	30	2.36	9	8.0	SW
May	66	40	2.59	9	8.0	SW
June	75	47	1.93	7	7.8	SW
July	86	55	0.61	6	7.7	SW
Aug.	84	54	0.42	4	7.6	SW
Sept.	73	44	1.05	5	7.1	SW
Oct.	60	33	1.24	5	6.2	SW

SHERIDAN

Month	Temperature		Precipitation		Wind	
	high (F)	low	total (in.)	days	speed	direc.
Apr.	56	31	2.12	11	9.9	NW
May	66	40	2.45	12	9.0	NW
June	74	48	2.99	11	8.1	NW
July	86	55	1.07	7	7.2	NW
Aug.	85	53	0.95	6	7.3	NW
Sept.	73	43	1.28	7	7.5	NW
Oct.	63	33	1.02	7	7.5	NW

Bibliography

We've included here books specifically about bicycling and bicycle touring as well as general books on camping, physical conditioning, travel, cooking, and food. Books that contain only route guides aren't listed here but can be found in Appendix 1. Mail-order sources for books, where available, are listed in Appendix 5. You'll find the periodicals on bicycling currently available listed at the end of this section.

BOOKS

Adams, Ray. *Serious Cycling for the Beginner*. Mountain View, Calif.: Anderson World, Inc., 1977. A detailed guide to enjoyable bicycling.

Adshead, Robin. *Bikepacking for Beginners*. Oxford, England: Oxford Illustrated Press, 1978. Guide to selecting bicycles, equipment, and camping gear; techniques for riding and camping.

Alaska-to-Montana Bicycle Route. Bikecentennial Publications. Route guide from Missoula to Alaska; tips on food and handling the terrain.

Anderson, Bob. *Stretching*. Mountain View, Calif.: Shelter Publications, 1980. A well-illustrated guide to physical fitness for everyone, with programs for specific needs or sports.

Barish, Jane, and Mort Barish. *Mort's Guide to Low-Cost Vacations and Lodgings on College Campuses, U.S. and Canada*. Princeton: CMG Publishing Co., 1978. A guide to lodging in college dormitories across the United States.

Basic Riding Techniques. Emmaus, Pa.: Rodale Press, 1979. Covers all aspects of riding, from body position in wind to climbing mountain passes.

Beinhorn, George. *Food for Fitness*. Mountain View, Calif.: World Publications, 1975. Foods that enhance and inhibit fitness are covered and discussed in relation to the athlete.

Bennett, Margaret. *Biking for Grown-ups*. New York: Dodd, Mead and Co., 1976. An introduction to bicycling for the adult.

Bevan, James, M.D. *The Pocket Medical Encyclopedia and First Aid Guide*. New York: Simon and Schuster, 1979. Survival techniques, first aid, and safety tips are all covered in this small book.

Bicycle Touring in the Boulder, Colorado, Area. Boulder, Colo.: The Spoke, Ltd., 1977. A series of easy-to-follow bicycle tours of the area.

Bicycle Tourist's Cookbook. Missoula, Mont.: Bikecentennial Publications, 1977. Planning, buying, and cooking meals on the road. Especially designed for group cooking.

Bicycling and Photography. Emmaus, Pa.: Rodale Press, 1979. Tips on the selection and use of equipment and photography techniques, by the editors of *Bicycling* magazine.

Bicycling through the Mother Lode. Sacramento, Calif.: California Dept. of State Parks and Recreation, 1975. Tour of the Gold Rush area of the Sierra foothills. Tours from 6 to 36 miles long.

Bridge, Raymond. *High Peaks and Clear Roads.* Harrisburg, Pa.: Stackpole Books, 1978. A practical guide to outdoor skills and survival, though not specific to bicycling.

Bridge, Raymond. *Freewheeling: The Bicycle Camping Book.* Harrisburg, Pa.: Stackpole Books, 1974. A useful book covering techniques and equipment for the camping bicyclist.

Bridge, Raymond. *Bike Touring: The Sierra Club Guide to Outings on Wheels.* San Francisco: Sierra Club, 1979. A complete guide to bicycle touring— buying a bicycle, equipment, camping, and safety.

Browder, Sue. *American Biking Atlas and Touring Guide.* New York: Workman Publishing Co., 1974. Contains 150 bicycle tours in the 50 states. Includes information on shopping and bicycle shops. Maps are removable for touring.

Burke, Ed., et al. *Inside the Cyclist: Physiology for the Two-Wheeled Athlete.* Brattleboro, Vt.: Velo News, 1980. Collection of articles on nutrition, training, and the scientific aspects of bicycling.

Campground and Trailer Park Guide, Western Edition. Chicago, Ill.: Rand McNally and Co., 1981. Covers regional campgrounds for our eleven Western states plus Alaska, Arkansas, Hawaii, Kansas, North Dakota, South Dakota, Texas, and Canadian provinces. Updated yearly.

Climates of the States. 2 vols. Detroit: Gale Research, 1972. The most authoritative guide to weather. Details on rain, wind, and amount of sunshine.

Cohen, Marjorie A. *Where to Stay, U.S.A.* San Francisco, Calif.: Council on International Educational Exchange, 1980–81. A nationwide guide to low-cost accommodations, listing hostels, farms, dormitories, and campsites, all under $20 a night.

Complete Guide to America's National Parks. Washington, D.C.: Office of Public Information, 1979. A detailed guide to the services, accommodations, activities, and fees in our national parks. Separate brochures for the individual parks are available from the same address.

Country Inns and Historic Hotels, 1980–81. New York: Burt Franklin and Co., 1980. A series of regional guides for the U.S. Gives cultural information as well as places to stay.

Crain, Jim, and Terry Milne. *Camping around California.* Westminster, Md., 1980. Covers private and public campgrounds.

Cuthbertson, Tom. *Anybody's Bike Book.* Berkeley, Calif.: Ten Speed Press, 1971. A step-by-step guide to survival with your bicycle. Well illustrated and clear.

Cuthbertson, Tom. *Bike Tripping*. Berkeley, Calif.: Ten Speed Press, 1972. A low-key guide to planning and having a happy tour.

Cyclist's Yellow Pages. Missoula, Mont.: Bikecentennial Publications, 1981. The most complete sourcebook for bicycling information, equipment, tours, and personal contacts. Covers touring in U.S. and abroad.

Delong, Fred. *Delong's Guide to Bicycles and Bicycling*. Radnor, Pa.: Chilton Book Co., 1978. Comprehensive guide to buying, riding, and touring on a bicycle. Excellent technical information.

Emmery, Lena, and Sally Taylor. *The Grape Escape*. San Francisco: Sally Taylor and Friends, 1980. Tours of the Napa Valley, designed for the wine-tasting cyclist.

Faria, Irvine E. *Cycling Physiology for the Serious Cyclist*. Englewood, Colo.: Charles C. Thomas, 1978. A detailed book on cycling energetics.

Faria, Irvine E. *The Physiology and Biomechanics of Cycling*. Englewood, Colo.: Charles C. Thomas, 1980. A systematic and scientific approach to bicycling and improvement of performance.

Get Fit with Bicycling. Emmaus, Pa.: Rodale Press, 1979. By the editors of *Bicycling* magazine. Gives exercise programs and information on nutrition and equipment for fitness.

Getting in Shape for Bicycle Touring. Missoula, Mont.: Bikecentennial Publications, 1979. Covers the steps in a conditioning program, including diet, the effects of weather, and measuring your pulse rate.

Great Parks Bicycle Route: Northern Section. Missoula, Mont.: Bikecentennial Publications, 1980. Covers a route through National Parks in the U.S. and Canada. This volume details a route from Missoula, Montana, to Jasper, Alberta, through Glacier-Waterton, Banff, and Jasper Parks.

Great Parks Bicycle Route: Southern Section. Missoula, Mont.: Bikecentennial Publications, 1980. Details a route and services from Steamboat Springs to Durango, Colorado, passing through Rocky Mountain and Mesa Verde National Parks.

Hawthorn, Margaret, Elizabeth Hawthorn, and James Mafchir. *The American Youth Hostels' Bike Hike Book*. Harrisburg, Pa.: Stackpole Books, 1978.

Hemstad, Rachael. *The Hungry Pedaler's Cookbook*. Hemstad Publications, 1974. Dietary tips for the tourist and a collection of recipes.

Heilman, Gail. *Complete Outfitting and Sourcebook for Bicycle Touring*. Marshall, Calif.: Great Outdoors Trading Co., 1980. A catalogue and resource guide covering equipment for touring, information on touring in various states, and suggested routes.

Hosteling USA. Charlotte, N.C.: Fast & McMillan, 1979. Complete listing of Youth Hostel facilities. Essential for the user of hostels.

Immler, Robert. *Bicycling in Hawaii*. Berkeley, Calif.: Wilderness Press, 1978. Tips and tours on bicycling the big island.

Jackson, Joan. *50 Biking Holidays*. Fresno, Calif.: Valley Publishers, 1977. Route guide and maps for short tours in the area between San Francisco and Monterey.

Johnston, Joanne. *JJ's Best Bike Trips: Northern California Bay Area*. Berkeley, Calif.: Ten Speed Press, 1972. Day trips in and around the Bay Area. Maps and narratives.

KOA Camper's Atlas. Billings, Mont.: Kampgrounds of America, 1980. A guide to KOA campgrounds in the U.S. Updated yearly.

Kolsburn, Ken, and Bob Burgess. *Discovering Santa Barbara . . . Without a Car.* Santa Barbara, Calif.: Friends for Bikecology, 1974. An informative guide to the area, with maps, and discussion of points of interest and transportation support.

Krolin, Michael, and Denise de la Rosa. *The Custom Bicycle.* Emmaus, Pa.: Rodale Press, 1979. A complete guide to the selection of frames and components for the ultimate, personalized bicycle.

Krolin, Michael, and Denise de la Rosa. *Understanding, Maintaining and Riding the Ten Speed Bicycle.* Emmaus, Pa.: Rodale Press, 1979. The building and maintenance of a touring bicycle as well as tips on clothing and accessories for the tourist.

Most Frequently Asked Questions about Bicycling. Emmaus, Pa.: Rodale Press, 1980. An informative and informal guide to all aspects of the sport of bicycling, compiled by the editors of *Bicycling* magazine.

Murphy, Tom A. *Fifty Northern California Bicycle Trips.* Beaverton, Oreg.: Touchstone Press, 1972. Fifty short day trips; includes narratives and maps.

Mohn, Peter. *NOL's Cookery.* National Outdoor Leadership School, 1974. A nutritional guide to eating on the move. Includes recipes and equipment lists.

Norback, Peter, and Craig Norback. *Travel Guide to the United States.* New York: Newsweek Books, 1979. Covers state and national parks, weather, bicycle trails, camping, and other essential planning information.

Notdurft-Hopkins, Anita. *How to Ride a Bicycle Safely, Efficiently, and Painlessly.* Paradise Valley, Ariz.: Phoenix Books, 1980. A discussion of effective riding techniques for the tourist and commuter.

North American Bicycle Atlas. Delaplane, Va.: American Youth Hostels, 1981. A collection of routes based upon Youth Hostel tours. Covers U.S. and Canada.

Olmstead, Camille. *A Cyclist's Guide to Oakland History.* Oakland, Calif.: Publications Committee, Oakland Museum, 1976. A historical guide for the cyclist to this Bay Area city.

Olney, Ross R. *Simple Bicycle Repair and Maintenance.* New York: Doubleday and Co., 1973. A small, compact fix-it guide for the cyclist.

Pacific Coast Bicentennial Route. Sacramento, Calif.: Caltrans, 1981. A detailed route guide covering 1,000 miles from Oregon to Mexico. Developed by the California Transportation Department.

Paul, Bill. *Bicycling California's Spine: A 750-Mile Tour of the Sierras from Mt. Lassen to Kern County.* San Francisco: Alchemist/Light Publishing, 1980. Maps and narrative of a tour from Redding to Kernville through the mountains.

Perrin, Tim, and Janet Wilson. *Exploring by Bicycle in Southwestern British Columbia and the San Juan Islands.* Vancouver, B.C.: Douglas and McIntyre, Ltd., 1980. Complete tours, maps, and ferry schedules for forty-one tours in the upper Puget Sound area.

Planning Your Own Bicycle Trip. Missoula, Mont.: Bikecentennial Publications, 1979. Route planning, packing, bicycle safety, and suppliers of bicycle equipment are covered.

Powers, Edward, and James Witt. *Traveling Weatherwise in the U.S.A.* New York: Dodd, Mead and Co., 1972. An excellent, detailed guide to weather patterns in the U.S. Includes data on rainfall and sunshine.

Rakowski, John. *Cooking on the Road.* Mountain View, Calif.: Anderson World, Inc., 1980. All you'll need to know about one-burner cooking. Covers stoves and techniques.

Rathbur, Linda M. *Bicycler's Guide to Hawaii.* Hilo, Hawaii: Petroglyph Press, 1976. Tour guide with maps.

Reconditioning the Bicycle. Emmaus, Pa.: Rodale Press, 1979. Basic adjustments, repairs, painting, and total disassembly and reassembly of the bicycle. By the editors of *Bicycling* magazine.

Ritchie, Andrew. *The King of the Road.* Berkeley, Calif.: Ten Speed Press, 1975. The illustrated history of bicycling.

Ross, Carol, and Thomas E. Ross. *Great Bike Rides in Northern California.* Pasadena, Calif.: Ward Ritchie Press, 1973. Long and short routes through northern California.

Ruffner, James A., and Frank E. Bair, eds. *The Weather Almanac.* Second Edition. Detroit: Gale Research Co., 1977. A general guide to weather and weather patterns in the United States.

Schad, Jerry, and Don Krupp. *50 Southern California Bicycle Trips.* Beaverton, Oreg.: Touchstone Press, 1976. Tours include maps and narratives.

Schultz, Barbara, and Mark Schultz. *Bicycles and Bicycling: A Guide to Information Resources.* Detroit: Gale Research Co., 1979. A complete bibliography of bicycling that includes print and nonprint materials.

Scott, David, and Kay Woelfel Scott. *Traveling and Camping in the National Park Areas.* Chester, Conn., 1978. The guide covers all national parks, including those of the western United States.

Sherman, Steve. *Bike Hiking.* Garden City: Doubleday and Co., 1974. A guide for the camping bicyclist.

Sloan, Eugene A. *The New Complete Book of Bicycling.* New York: Simon and Schuster, 1974. The history, mechanics, and techniques of bicycling.

Standing, Tom. *Bay Area Bikeways.* Berkeley, Calif.: Ten Speed Press. Twenty 1-day trips in the San Francisco Bay area. Cultural notes, maps, and historical narratives.

Steward, Chuck. *Bicycling around Seattle.* Seattle: Recreation Consultants, 1980. A route guide to the area, including maps and descriptions.

Stimson, Judy. *Bicycle Tour the Border-to-Border Pacific Coast Route.* Photocopy available from the author, 2102 Vienna Woods Dr., Cincinnati, Ohio 45211. A personalized route guide of a trip along the Pacific Coast from Canada to Mexico.

Sunset Guide to Western Campsites. Sunset Publications, 1981. The best camping guide to the West. Gives elevations of camps, distances to nearest services. Includes private and public campgrounds. Updated yearly.

Tobey, Peter, and Tarvex Tucker, eds. *Two-Wheel Travel: Bicycle Camping and Touring.* New Canaan, Conn.: Tobey Publishers, 1974. A guide to touring, techniques, and camping along the road.

Touring Cyclists' Hospitality Directory. Compiled by John Mosley, 13623 Sylvan, Van Nuys, Calif. 91401. This directory is available to anyone willing to offer hospitality to other cyclists and have their name listed.

Trans America Trail Guidebook and *Trans America Trail Map*. Missoula, Mont.: Bikecentennial Publications, 1976. Matching sets of maps and guidebooks for the Trans America Bicycle Trail. A Trail Directory is included for each set, giving names, addresses and locations of services.

The following sets cover the western United States:

Coast–Cascades. Astoria, Oregon, to Missoula, Montana.

Rocky Mountains. Missoula, Montana, to Pueblo, Colorado.

Plains–Ozarks. Pueblo, Colorado, to St. Genevieve, Missouri.

Vale, Patrick. *Whatcom County Bike Book*. Lynnwood, Wash.: Signpost Press, 1977. Tour maps and information for sixteen tours in this northwestern Washington county.

Washington State Bike Book. Olympia, Wash. Gives list of strip maps available from the Washington State Department of Transportation. Details in Appendix 1.

Weltman, Gershon, and Elisha Dubin. *Bicycle Touring in Los Angeles*. Pasadena, Calif.: Ward Ritchie Press, 1972. Information and maps.

Wilhelm, Tim, and Glenda Wilhelm. *The Bicycle Touring Book*. Emmaus, Pa.: Rodale Press, 1980. A complete guide by veteran bicycle tourists on all subjects relating to the activity. Excellent advice for the touring cyclist and technical discussions on equipment.

Wilson, Janet. *Exploring by Bicycle: Southwest British Columbia, Northwest Washington*. Vancouver, B.C.: Gundy's and Bernie's Guide Books, 1973. Offers a variety of tours of Canada and northern Washington, ranging up to 100 miles.

Wolfe, Frederick L. *Bicycle Denver: 107 Bicycle Tours*. Denver, Colo.: Graphic Impressions, 1976. A guide to the area.

Woodall's Campground Directory, Western Edition. Highland Park, Ill.: Woodall Publishing Co., 1981. Covers their approved campgrounds in the region. Updated yearly.

Woods, Erin, and Bill Woods. *Bicycling the Backroads of Northwest Washington*. Seattle: The Mountaineers, 1976. Excellently detailed route guides and maps. The short day tours may be connected to make longer trips. Index gives connecting points.

Woods, Erin, and Bill Woods. *Bicycling the Backroads of Southwest Washington*. Seattle: The Mountaineers, 1980. Mate to the above.

Wright, Robert. *Building Bicycle Wheels*. Mountain View, Calif.: Anderson World, Inc., 1980. How to build and true your own bicycle wheels.

Yeardon, David. *Backroad Journeys of the West Coast States*. New York: Harper and Row, 1979. Travel descriptions of lightly traveled roads in Washington, Oregon, and California. Meant for the car tourist, but an excellent bicycle guide as well.

PERIODICALS

American Wheelmen. 10 E. Read St., P.O. Box 988, Baltimore, Md. 21203. The monthly magazine of the League of American Wheelmen.

The Bicycle Paper. Recreation Consultants, P.O. Box 842, Seattle, Wash. 98111. Deals with bicycling in the Pacific Northwest.

Bicycling. 33 E. Minor St., Emmaus, Pa. 18409. A monthly publication covering all aspects of bicycling.

Bikereport. Bikecentennial, Inc. P.O. Box 8308, Missoula, Mont. 59807. A bi-monthly news journal for members of Bikecentennial. Gives lists of tours, books, touring aids, articles of general interest.

ABOUT THE AUTHORS

Karen and Gary Hawkins live in Sacramento,
California. Together with their young son, Benjamin,
they have bicycled extensively [...] country
and Europe, covering on t [...] most recent trip over
four thousand miles from London to the Portuguese
coast and back.